Advanced Batch File Programming

3rd Edition

Advanced Batch File Programming

3rd Edition

Dan Gookin

Windcrest®/McGraw-Hill

THIRD EDITION
SECOND PRINTING

Library of Congress Cataloging-in-Publication Data

Gookin, Dan.
    Advanced batch file programming / by Dan Gookin.—3rd ed.
      p.   cm.
    Rev. ed. of: Advanced MS-DOS batch file programming. 1991.
    Includes index.
    ISBN 0-8306-2532-1
    1. MS-DOS.   2. Microcomputers—Programming.   3. File organization
(Computer science)   4. Electronic data processing—Batch processing.
I. Gookin, Dan. Advanced MS-DOS batch file programming.   II. Title.
QA76.76.O63G664 1991
005.26—dc20   91-19794
                                       CIP

TAB Books offers software for sale. For information and a catalog, please contact
TAB Software Department, Blue Ridge Summit, PA 17294-0850.

Acquisitions Editor: Ron Powers
2nd Edition Technical Editor: David M. Harter
3rd Edition Technical Editor: David M. McCandless
Production: Katherine G. Brown
Book Design: Jaclyn J. Boone
Cover: Sandra Blair Design, Harrisburg, PA   WP1

Contents

_____PART ONE_____

BASICS

BATCH FILE PROGRAMMING

BEYOND BATCH FILES

_____PART FOUR_____

MACROS AND CONTROL LANGUAGES

_____PART FIVE_____

HARD DISK STRATEGIES

_____PART SIX_____

BATCH FILE COOKBOOK

APPENDICES

Acknowledgments

I had a lot of fun writing the first edition of this book, and even more fun writing the second. For making the first one so good (and keeping all my humor and snide comments intact), I'd like to thank David Harter. Also from TAB Books, thanks go to Ron Powers and Stephen Moore.

The winner of my "not through the proper channels but pulled through anyway" award goes to Katherine Hinch of Microsoft. Thanks also goes to Paul Heim, a true batch file zany, and to his friend Larry Spiwak, who would really like $10 from anyone who uses his DPATH utility. And to all my competitors who try to write better batch file books: Thanks for showing me what not to do.

What this book is about

Batch file programming is more than writing short routines to save key-strokes, run a program, or get you from one place to another. Batch files can offer your computer system more than an AUTOEXEC file to "get you up in the morning." Learning about batch files, and how to program them, teaches you more about DOS. Once you know more about DOS, you know more about your computer. And the more you know about your computer, the more effectively you can use it to make yourself more productive.

Don't let the title fool you. This isn't an advanced, technical book, full of cryptic programmer's talk. Nor is this an all-assuming text on the virtues of keeping a clean system, thumping DOS commands into your head, or warning you of the perils of not frequently backing up your hard disk. Instead, this book was written for people who enjoy DOS and want to make it more useful for them. This book offers instruction in the finer aspects of learning to use DOS, and ultimately your computer. This is done through batch file programming.

The funny thing about DOS (if you ever wondered, indeed there are funny things about DOS) is that it's really not that hard to learn. The problem is that DOS is powerful and versatile; and like anything powerful and versatile, it takes time to learn. So rather than sit down and type each command in the DOS manual, which can lead to frustration and immediate greying of the hair, why not learn about batch file programming?

Batch file programming is a way of communicating with your computer. Fundamentally, "programming" is just a word for human-to-computer communications. There are many ways to program a computer, and many programming languages as well. Fortunately, the batch file "language" consists of DOS commands—most of which you already know.

Batch files allow you to type one command—a command you make up yourself—to do many things that would otherwise require a lot of typing. Batch files are really quite simple to do, and, as this book will demonstrate, they can be quite elegant and powerful. Nothing too rough for any DOS dummy to tame.

The underlying theme throughout this book is, "Learn batch file programming and you'll learn DOS; learn DOS and you'll know more about your computer; know more about your computer and you'll be able to use it more productively." If you're using your computer at work, mastering the batch file is the quickest path to computer "guru-hood." And we all know how the boss likes to smile on a PC guru.

A "PC guru" is someone who knows the MODE command.

Who this book is for

. . . for you, of course; or, just about anyone who's dabbled with batch files, found them interesting, and then wanted more information but could never find it.

Actually, this book is about more than writing nifty batch files. It's about understanding DOS; learning how DOS controls your programs; hard disk organization; using your computer more efficiently; and so on. It's not that this book deliberately teaches you all that (and besides, it would be a pain to put all that on the cover), but by learning about batch files, you learn more about DOS and how to control your computer.

This can be compared to learning how to drive. You can take a class and they'll teach you operation of the car, some basic repairs ("remember class, this is a 'lug nut' "), and the rules of the road. Yet, that information is just enough to get you started. If you want to be a better driver—or better yet, a race car driver—you'll need to know more. This book teaches you more about DOS by instructing you in the finer aspects of batch file programming.

This book is for anyone who owns an MS-DOS computer, IBM PC/XT, AT, PS/2, IBM-compatible or "clone" computer. You don't need to know anything about batch file programming, though some programming knowledge will help; but don't let that frighten you away from learning more about your computer system.

You should also be familiar with your computer's operating system, or DOS. This means you should have played with your computer a while, formatted some disks, copied files from hither and thither, renamed files, created new ones, used some software—all the stuff anyone does who owns an MS-DOS computer.

Conventions, assumptions and stuff

IBM, clone, or compatible?

Hello, IBM and gang! A few years ago, a great deal of emphasis was placed upon computers that were "IBM compatible." That is, computers that could run the same software as the original IBM PC. If those computers carried a national brand name, such as AST, Compaq, Dell, Epson, Leading Edge, Tandy, Zenith, and so on, they were called IBM "compatibles." If Larry made the computer in the back of his store and sold it as "Larry's PC"—and it too was IBM compatible—the computer was known as a "clone." There's no official designation for a compatible or clone beyond what's mentioned in this paragraph, though it seems to be an accepted convention. Chances are, if your computer uses MS-DOS (or PC-DOS), you're okay.

In this book, the task of mentioning IBM PC/XT/AT, PS/2, compatible or clone is served by using the abbreviation "PC" or just "computer." Whenever you see "PC" or read about "your computer," it refers to any popular computer capable of running MS-DOS machines (the old Tandy 2000 and HP 150). If you're a user of one of those systems, the routines demonstrated here might not work with your equipment. Sell it.

Hard drive anyone?

This book makes the assumption that you have a hard disk. Everyone should have a hard disk. They're just too inexpensive and there's no reason not to have one. Although all the batch file programs and routines will work on floppy systems, only by using them on a hard drive will you realize their full potential.

In case you do have a floppy-only system, mentally change all references of "drive C" to "drive A." (Drive C is the hard drive.) You might also want to format a system disk (FORMAT /S) and a blank data disk for use with this book.

ENTER or Return

Many books and manuals have trouble telling these two keys apart. The ENTER or Return key is the key you press to complete a line of text—the same key you'd press on an electric typewriter keyboard to move the carriage from one side of the machine to the other. Some keyboards list the carriage return key as ENTER, like the common calculator. Others call the key Return, like the common typewriter. Still others, to be novel, seem to have it both ways.

It's been supposed that because IBM couldn't decide if their computer was a calculator or a typewriter that they opted to put a cryptic back arrow symbol on their keyboard (see FIG. 1). What is that key?

1 The funky IBM Return key.

In this book, ENTER is used to represent the carriage return (or Return) key. (Currently, IBM is using ENTER in all their documentation.) If your keyboard has a Return key or some other symbol, press that key when this book tells you to "press ENTER."

DOS

Throughout this book references are made to "DOS." The program being referred to is MS-DOS, also known as the Microsoft Disk Operating System, or PC-DOS, IBM's own version of the same. This book primarily concentrates on DOS 3.3—the most popular version ever. DOS 4 is covered where applicable. But because of its announcement and release, DOS 5 is mentioned here as well. Note that all the material here applies to all IBM and compatible systems running any version of DOS. Variations, when they occur, are noted.

Which version number?

In the old days, I used to tell everyone that you should always have the latest version of DOS. Yes, that's expensive. Personally, I always buy the latest DOS (at about $200 a pop) just to see what it does. However, I've settled on DOS Version 3.3 (for now) as my favorite release of the operating system. DOS 4 was announced years ago, but it was a semi-flop. Dos 5 is now out and shows a lot of promise. Because I already have many of the utilities that DOS 5 offers, there's no pressing need here. That won't, however, solve your problem about which version to use.

If you work in an office where all the PCs have been upgraded to DOS 5 (the latest version,) then you should upgrade your home system to DOS 5. Why? Compatibility. Also, if you're buying a new machine, and won't be interfacing with other machines that already use a specific DOS version, you can choose the latest version of DOS. For example, if you like DOS 5 features (and a few of them really are quite interesting) then buy DOS 5.

On the question of upgrading, you should definitely upgrade to DOS 3.3 if you have anything less. If a newer version of DOS comes out with features you like, then upgrade to it—eventually. Give yourself about a year for the industry pundits to weigh out the new DOS, for its bugs to be identified and destroyed, software to become compatible, and to see if any of your PC friends are making the upgrade. Gauge their reactions before you make the move.

In this book, the batch file programs were written under DOS 3.3 or 4. They all work under DOS 5 as well. If the DOS version is important to some aspect of the batch file, then it will be noted in the text. Otherwise, if you have DOS 3.3, 4, or 5, you should have no problems with anything listed here.

All set?

This book contains material on system management. That implies that you already have a computer and have installed several programs that you use regularly. Granted, DOS all by itself can only be entertaining for a few moments. Without programs to run or things to do, DOS is terribly boring.

Your computer system should be all set up and ready to go. If not, please refer to your DOS manual for setting things up. The setup procedure varies with each version of DOS, so make sure you have the right manual.

Your expertise

As far as prior knowledge about batch files go, you really don't need any. If you consider yourself a more-than-typical DOS user, or you know a programming language, such as BASIC, or you're just enthusiastic, then you have enough knowledge to make the techniques shown in this book work for you.

As was stated earlier, a knowledge of programming could come in handy. You'll probably also want to look into some of the software, including some of the public domain and shareware goodies, discussed in this book. The best stuff has been made available on a companion floppy disk that you can order from TAB Books. More information about this disk is provided at the end of this introduction, in chapter 11, and in appendix K.

Organization of this book

This book is divided into six parts: the basics; batch file programming; beyond batch files; macros and control languages; hard disk strategies; and a batch file "cookbook" reference.

Part One introduces you to batch files, along with some interesting information about DOS. For some, this might be review material. But, even if you consider yourself an "old hand," you should look it over. There's some information hidden in there that might surprise a few self-proclaimed computer gurus.

Part Two covers batch file programming—how to get things done. Everything is covered from the fundamentals of any programming language: looping, variables, and so forth, on through structure, batch file communications, and troubleshooting.

Part Three goes beyond batch files. DOS merely gives you the basics. "Beyond batch files" discusses third-party software that will enhance your batch file programs' performance. Additionally, you'll read about using BASIC and DEBUG to assist your batch files, as well as third-party batch file enhancement programs.

Part Four is about macros and control languages. True, this isn't batch files. Macros and control languages are specific to certain powerful and popular applications. Yet, it's a concept similar to batch file programming, and it goes right along with the idea of making your computer easier to use. Covered here are macros in general, *WordPerfect* and Lotus *1-2-3* macros, and using macros in the popular *DESQview* and *Windows* environments.

Part Five mulls over the basics of hard disk strategy. There are quite a few interesting things batch files can do to make an unruly hard drive behave more efficiently. Also, this section introduces a batch file menu manager and other "shell program" techniques that you can incorporate into your own system.

Part Six is the batch file cookbook. This is a virtual encyclopedia of all batch file commands, along with format, description, examples, demonstration programs, and a cross-reference.

Finally, there are over ten appendices full of handy information about DOS to help you go on to write better batch files.

OS/2—where art thou?

While writing round one of this book, OS/2 was in its infancy. In fact, I bought OS/2 just to write the first edition of this book. Since that time, no OS/2 user has bothered to write in and thank me. The reason? There are no OS/2 users (at least none who will admit to it). However, in the case that there is some secret, hidden hoard of OS/2 users out there, this book still has some limited information on OS/2's neglected batch file functions. The OS/2-only stuff is listed in chapter 6. Otherwise, everything else here applies in the OS/2 "real" mode, "DOS box," or whatever they're currently calling the DOS compatibility mode.

Given the graphical interface future of OS/2, the few OS/2-only batch file commands documented here probably won't grow, either in number or in glory. Therefore, only one chapter needs to be devoted to the subject. But you'll probably find it interesting reading, whether you are an OS/2 dandy or not.

For further reading

This book does get into two, possibly even three other topics that might catch your interest. Of primary concern would be additional books on DOS. The best book on DOS is your DOS manual. Another handy reference would be *The MS-DOS Encyclopedia*—a gargantuan, technical, hefty and expensive book, yet it's worth every ounce and every cent. Alone this book replaces half a dozen others on my shelf.

For good information on batch file programming and hard disk management, three books come to mind: *Hard Disk Management with DOS* written by yours truly; *MS-DOS Batch File Programming* by Ronny Richardson—an excellent introduction and reference manual for any batch file nut; and a more technical, programmer's level books, *Enhanced Batch File Programming* also by me.

For BASIC programming, two books I've had the privilege of working on are *Learning IBM PC BASIC* and *The IBM BASIC Handbook*. While geared toward the IBM PC, information in these books generally applies to GW BASIC, a widely available version of PC BASIC.

For assembly language programming, the following three books are recommended: *Assembly Language Primer for the IBM PC & XT*, Ray Duncan's *Advanced MS-DOS, The 8086 Book*, and the documentation for Microsoft's Macro Assembler. This information is a little advanced and only the seriously daring should venture into an area as scary as assembly language programming.

Macros in *WordPerfect* and *1-2-3* have been written about at length. (In order to be an ordained computer book publisher you must have at least two books each on the subject.) Because it's not covered here in detail, you might want to consider looking up more information on programming macros. Two books that come to mind are Windcrest's *Working with Lotus Macros* by Tymes and Prael, and *WordPerfect 5.1 Macros* by Mosich, Bixby, and Adams-Regan.

Duncan, Ray, *Advanced MS-DOS*, Washington: Microsoft Press, 1989.

Duncan, Ray et al, *The MS-DOS Encyclopedia*, Washington: Microsoft Press, 1988.

Gookin, Dan, *Hard Disk Management with MS-DOS and PC-DOS*, Pennsylvania: TAB Books, 1990.

Gookin, Dan, *Mastering Batch File Programming*, Pennsylvania: TAB Books, 1990.

Lafore, Robert, *Assembly Language Primer for the IBM PC & XT*, Virginia: Plume/Waite, 1984.

Lien, David, *Learning IBM BASIC*, California: CompuSoft, Inc., 1984.

Lien, David, *The IBM BASIC Handbook*, California: CompuSoft, Inc., 1986.

Mosich, Donna et al, *WordPerfect 5.1 Macros*, Pennsylvania: TAB Books, 1990.

Rector/Alexy, *The 8086 Book*, California: Osborne/McGraw-Hill, 1980.

Richardson, Ronny, *MS-DOS Batch File Programming . . . Including OS/2*, Pennsylvania: TAB Books, 1989.

Tymes, Elna and Prael, Charles, *Working With Lotus Macros*, Pennsylvania: TAB Books, 1990.

Supplemental diskette offer

In conjunction with this book, TAB Books is offering a diskette. On this diskette are all of the major batch files discussed in this book, several batch file enhancement programs written specifically for this book (that you can't find anywhere else), plus all the public domain batch file utilities and other goodies that would fit on a 360K diskette.

To get this diskette, you should complete and mail in the order form at the end of this book. If you get into batch files (and why not?), you'll really enjoy some of the programs on the diskette. For a sneak preview, read appendix K.

Part One

Basics

Welcome to advanced batch file programming.

In Part One, I'll get you up to speed on batch files and on some aspects of DOS with which you're probably not familiar. The purpose of this section is twofold: The first is to acquaint the new DOS gurus with some of the more interesting aspects of DOS. The second is to check the knowledge of the older DOS gurus with what they'll need to do some real, advanced batch file programming. Whatever your situation, the end result will be the same: you'll know more about your computer and be able to use it more effectively.

1
Batch files

Learning about anything new means you must build upon what you already know. It's assumed, largely because of this book's title, that you already know a little bit about DOS and batch files. Or, you could be an experienced DOS user and think you don't have the time to mess with an "intro" book. In either case, some background information is in order.

This chapter contains information on batch files, both general and specific. It's assumed you have some knowledge of batch files, so most of this should be review. Yet, to go beyond that normal knowledge a review is in order.

Most of the information here is also gone over in detail later in the book. In fact, there were so many parenthetical clauses that read "(this is covered in Chapter 900)" that I randomly went through here and deleted a few of them. So, if a few concepts seem fuzzy, keep reading and they'll be detailed later in this book.

Then, to whet your appetite before things get off and running, there are several quick-and-dirty batch file examples at the end of this chapter. While some of them might seem confusing at this stage, type them in and give 'em a try. You're bound to find at least a couple of them useful.

Introduction

Learning about batch files must be one of the last things people get around to when they learn DOS. It's sad because, by learning about batch files, all the other commands will come naturally. In fact, some of the more bizarre commands actually start to make sense after you take a stab at learning batch file programming.

Normal DOS users, and even a few pros, tend to get stuck in a rut.

After a while, they resort to using just a few well known and trusted favorites: FORMAT, DISKCOPY (sometimes), COPY, REN, DEL (or ERASE), and few others. By knowing those commands you can use your computer—and use it quite effectively. There's nothing wrong with this, except that you're cutting yourself short on the power of your system.

What's missing are batch files. Not just the simple, easy batch files that everyone learns to write, but extremely elegant and powerful batch files. Nothing too complex—just some extraordinary and interesting DOS commands, plus a few hidden secrets that most people (including some professed "power users") ignore.

Remember, what you have sitting in front of you (or near you if you're reading this on the couch) is a computer. Computers can do many things, and many boring and repetitious things over and over again without complaining. Typing several DOS commands will get the job done. Yet it's possible to cut down on your typing time by taking advantage of batch files.

> A batch file program is simply several DOS commands executing one after the other.

Batch files give you the capability to issue several DOS commands over and over using DOS's "batch processor." The batch processor was added to DOS on the insistence of IBM. The IBM people wanted to be able to run "scripts" of several commands one after another to test different parts of their new microcomputer. Microsoft, developers of DOS, complied by building a batch file interpreter into DOS.

So, DOS's ability to run IBM's "scripts" blossomed into what we know today as batch files. Over the years, and with each updated version of DOS, the capability of batch files has grown. Now, you can write batch files that can issue multiple DOS commands, make decisions, and extend the power of your system—all by typing the name of a batch file.

Of course, there's more to it than that.

Batch file programming

Some people jump up and go screaming when they hear "programming language." The odd thing is that most of them program every day without even knowing it. Washing your hair is following a simple program:

1. Lather
2. Rinse
3. Repeat

(Of course, the computer program would need to know exactly what

"Repeat" meant and how many times to repeat before it smothered your head with shampoo.)

If those three verbs were DOS commands, "SHAMPOO" would be the basics of a batch file (without the line numbers).

Cooks and chefs—even of the macaroni and cheese variety—follow programs when they make a meal. Even building the office spreadsheet is considered programming. So many people create interesting spreadsheets, yet they'd cry out in pain if you ordered them to "learn programming."

It's all the same thing: telling the computer what you want it to do. Programming puts the power of the computer into your hands. You control what's going on. And to be in control, you only need to know a handful of words, or programming commands.

The BASIC programming language has about 100 commands; the typical spreadsheet user can choose from about 150 commands and functions; the C programming language has only about 25 routines (hard-core, C nerds will argue over that one); and batch files may use 10 commands, plus the standard DOS commands. Compare this to the 50,000 words the average speaker of English uses. Programming isn't all that hard.

Of course, programming isn't for everyone either. It's assumed that because this book is titled *Advanced Batch File Programming* that you have some inclination toward programming. A little experience helps, but isn't necessary. A strong knowledge of DOS and how your computer works is also recommended. But again, everything you need to know is covered here.

So what is a batch file?

In a nutshell: batch files are simply a list of DOS commands. For example, consider the following two commands. Most people type these two commands to start their word processor:

```
CD\WP
WP
```

CD\WP changes to the WP subdirectory. This is followed by the command to run the word processing program, WP.

Now, suppose both those commands were contained in a batch file. This isn't hard because batch files are simply commands you'd type at DOS. For reference sake, call the batch file WP.BAT.

All batch files have the filename extension .BAT

To execute the above commands, or to "run" the WP.BAT files, you type WP at the command prompt and press ENTER:

```
C> WP ENTER
```

This is the level at which most people are familiar with batch files. Even knowing that you could write such a batch file—just to save a single step over typing the two commands separately—doesn't convince the average person to learn about batch files.

The batch file most people are familiar with is AUTOEXEC.BAT. It's one of the first programs DOS looks for and runs when the computer starts. These same people don't necessarily write their own AUTOEXEC file. No, most people rely on "the store" to set one up for them. Or they use the talents of a DOS-literate friend (that's you) or consultant to build them an AUTOEXEC.BAT file.

This is sad. A lot of important things can take place inside an AUTO EXEC.BAT file. A well-written AUTOEXEC.BAT can save a computer user a lot of time and pain. (Of course, this would put some consultants out of business, so then again . . .)

Recently, many applications have these new "INSTALL" programs that automatically alter an AUTOEXEC.BAT file. Personally, I *hate* them. Running two or three of these INSTALL.EXE programs can mess up a computer system faster than a novice can press CTRL–ALT–DELETE. Because of this, it's important to know what can be done in a batch file. It's even more important to know what's inside the AUTOEXEC.BAT file.

This book devotes an entire chapter (more or less) to the functions of AUTOEXEC.BAT. Even with all the importance placed on it, AUTOEXEC .BAT is still one of the only batch files many users will ever have. Because of this, I refer to it as a low-level batch file.

Mid-level

Besides simply executing a group of commands, or a script, as IBM wanted it, batch files can do more. While not really a pure programming language, there are certain things a batch file is capable of that can commonly be found in "real" programming languages. (This book will even introduce you to some extraordinary programs that take the concept of the batch file programming language far, far beyond what DOS has to offer.)

Because Microsoft wrote MS-DOS, many of the batch file commands are similar to those found in their popular BASIC interpreter:

```
FOR
GOTO
IF
REM
```

Other batch file commands have a unique flavor:

```
ECHO
PAUSE
SHIFT
```

These commands could be blended with DOS commands, I/O redirection, and take advantage of system "variables" to make batch file programming quite capable. Batch file programs could create files, evaluate conditions, make decisions, execute specific code, and even execute other batch files. This takes the power of batch file programming beyond the simple WP .BAT programming. But still, there's more.

Take a user who's very familiar with DOS. Because this user has boned up on all the DOS commands, and is familiar with his system, his version of the WP.BAT file might look something like FIG. 1-1.

1-1 What the WP.BAT might look like is shown here.

```
C:
MODE COM1:12,n,8,1,n
MODE LPT#2=COM1
SUBST W: C:\WP
SUBST M: C:\WORK\PROJECTS\MGM\SCNPLAY\ACT01
ECHO Drives substituted:
SUBST
PATH=W:;C:\DOS;C:\UTILITY
M:
W:\WP
SUBST M: /D
SUBST W: /D
PATH=C:\DOS;C:\UTILITY
C:
CD \
```

Granted, this program is an extreme example. The difference between this and the previous WP.BAT program is that this one takes advantage of pure DOS power. The user who wrote this knows a lot about DOS. The only real way to do that (without typing yourself to death) is to use batch files.

A few things missing in this batch file are the flow-control and decision making batch file commands: IF and GOTO. Also, the user might have added a few REM, or remark, statements to clue us into what exactly the batch file is accomplishing. (You'd be surprised how many people will gander at their old batch files and not have the slightest idea what some of the commands are trying to accomplish. That is, until the same thing happens to you. And it will.)

This level of sophistication over simple, two-liner, batch files is what I call a "mid-level" batch file. This book covers this type of batch file extensively. But more importantly, there's a third, almost secret layer to batch file programming—advanced batch file programming.

Advanced batch file programming

Beyond simple and mid-level batch files are (can you guess?) advanced batch files.

What is it that makes an advanced batch file? Several things: DOS tricks; ANSI.SYS; the PROMPT command; the PATH command; Environmental variables; and batch file extensions through DEBUG, BASIC, and third-party software.

DOS tricks are things that DOS can do that no one will ever tell you. Only the intrepid DOS freak will discover them. I've tried to gather most of them from myself and other DOS gurus, and put them here in this book. As a preview: there are ways to get DOS to do things faster than is normally possible with batch files. For example, using TYPE to list a number of text statements instead of multiple ECHO commands; using I/O redirection instead of the pipe (filter) command; and so on. (All this is covered in detail later.)

Another example is the ANSI.SYS screen driver. Most people have a line in their CONFIG.SYS file that goes:

```
DEVICE = C: \ ANSI.SYS
```

Yet, no one takes advantage of the things ANSI.SYS has to offer. For example, using ANSI.SYS and the TYPE example mentioned above, you can create a complete menu system, rivaling those of commercial companies—all using DOS. ANSI.SYS can reassign your function keys for speeding up certain activities. And third-party ANSI.SYS replacements can speed up your overall screen output.

The PROMPT command is usually only used once (if at all) in a user's AUTOEXEC.BAT file. But you don't have to keep it that way. Each program can have its own customized PROMPT by using batch files. The same holds true with the PATH command. If you're tired of living with a limited search PATH, then you haven't really read the DOS manual on PATH. (Don't worry, it's covered here.)

Environment variables are another thing most users—and programmers—ignore. It's probably because it's a big, complex word "environment." Or maybe it's because there are too many warnings in the DOS manual about it (or that the examples there are the lamest I've ever seen). A lot can be done with environmental variables to make using your system easier.

Batch files can also be extended beyond what comes with DOS. After all, there are a lot of batch file nuts out there. They scratch their heads and ask themselves questions like "Wouldn't it be neat to have a batch file respond to a yes/no question?" Then they write a utility whose sole purpose is to be included in a batch file. You'll learn how to do this later when the ASK.COM and READKEY.COM programs are introduced.

There are three ways to obtain these batch file extenders. The first two involve creating the program using raw data, assembled via either the DEBUG programming utility or the BASIC programming language—both of which, thank Bill Gates, come with DOS. The third way is to buy a commercial package of batch file helpers, such as EBL, the Extended Batch

Language, Beyond.Bat, the amazing Builder, or the nifty programming utilities that come with Peter Norton's Norton Utilities. All of these methods allow you to use custom programs that DOS's batch file interpreter doesn't offer.

This book goes into detail about all the goodies you'll need to become an advanced batch file programmer, including what the previously mentioned commands do and how they can help you.

Creating batch files

A batch file consists of DOS commands, and special batch file directives. However, the batch file itself is merely a text file on disk. The only thing making a batch file "runnable" by DOS is its filename extension: BAT. Whenever you type the name of a file with the .BAT extension at the command prompt, DOS executes that file as a batch file.

Theoretically, if you renamed any text file with a .BAT extension, DOS would interpret it as a batch file. However, if the text file is a letter to Mom, you'll see a lot of "Bad Command or Filename" error messages pop up. In order for the batch file to work, it must contain batch file commands.

Text or ASCII?

There are two common types of files under DOS: text files and program or data files. Text files contain characters you can read, usually sentences, figures, quotes, memos—common English text. Program or data files contain information only digestible by the computer. Even though you can look at and examine the contents of program or data files, only the computer understands the instructions or information.

A batch file must be a text file containing commands—just as you'd type at the command prompt. ASCII is also used to refer to text files because ASCII codes define all the text characters, letters, numbers, and symbols used in a text file. (*See* appendix A.)

The object of creating a batch file is to get the batch file commands into a text file and give that file a .BAT extension. There are three methods to do this:

1. Using DOS
2. Using a text editor
3. Using a word processor

All three of these methods get the job done; they're all capable of creating a text file on disk with the .BAT extension. The differences between them are in power and convenience.

The following are brief examples of creating batch files using DOS, a text editor, and a word processor. More details on these methods, including some tips and recommendations, are provided in chapter 7.

From DOS

Creating a batch file from DOS is the quick-and-dirty method. In fact, most two- or three-line batch files are made this way. Because DOS is device-oriented (which is discussed in detail later), you can directly copy input from your keyboard to a file. The COPY command does the work:

```
COPY CON TEST.BAT
```

This is the famous "COPY-CON" function. It copies all input from the CON, or CONsole device, to the file TEST.BAT. Incidentally, TEST.BAT is created by the COPY function (just as any other file is created by the COPY function). COPY will not tell you if the file created already exists—the new file will overwrite anything on disk with the same name. (This is a typical oversight on Microsoft's part.)

What the COPY command does is to take the contents of one device and copy them to another. CON, for CONsole, is a fancy term for your keyboard and screen. TEST.BAT is a batch file you hope to create. After typing the above command, each line you type at the keyboard will be copied into the file TEST.BAT:

```
CD \ WP
WP
```

Before you press ENTER, you can backspace, use the DOS editing keys, all the normal commands—but nothing fancy. When the line looks good, press ENTER. There's no using the up arrow to correct a previous line. Once ENTER is pressed, that line is locked into memory.

After typing the last line, you'll need to tell DOS that you're done creating your batch file. Normally, when you're using COPY to copy one file to another, DOS will detect the end of the file by checking the file's size in the directory, or by looking for the Control–Z character. Because your CONsole doesn't have a file size, you need to type the Control–Z yourself. Hold down Control and press Z:

```
^Z
```

Or, you can press the F6 key, which is the same thing:

```
^Z
```

DOS finishes the action by creating TEST.BAT and putting your commands into it. You'll see:

```
1 File(s) copied.
```

The batch file is created.

This is called the quick-and-dirty method because there's no editing on the file you create. You can't "fix" the file using COPY CON. Instead, you'll have to use a text editor or word processor to make corrections to the batch file.

This method is most convenient—especially when you're working on a strange computer or one that might not have your favorite text editor or word processor handy. Then, the COPY-CON function really comes in handy.

Using a text editor

A text editor is a program that lets you edit text (surprisingly enough). It's very similar to a word processor, but it lacks all the printing functions, fancy text formatting, and document management. For example, you can enter text, edit, search and replace, move blocks, delete, cut and paste—but you can't underline, boldface, change type style, have footnotes, check your spelling, or print.

Text editors are usually a little more powerful than word processors. They allow a lot of text manipulations that word processor developers probably find too trivial. Because text editors are primarily used by programmers to write code, these tricks come in very handy.

A reason for using a text editor to write batch files is convenience and power. It's convenient because text editors are fast. Several text editors are sold on their loading and saving speeds alone (programmers don't want to waste time). Text editors lack all the printing and "pretty text" commands that word processors do, so there's nothing to slow you down.

Your reasons for using the text editor would be to compose or fix a batch file, then save it back to disk. (Yes, you could print it, but don't expect a Pulitzer for it.)

There are many text editors on the market. In fact, the one I personally use costs only $50. Other text editors typically cost less than $100. It might sound like a great expense, but if you're doing a lot of work with batch files (and other programming as well) you'll need it.

Because the various text editors differ in the way they do things, a complete example can't be given here. You just create the text, save it as a .BAT file, then return to DOS to "run" the batch file. Because batch files are interpreted by DOS, you don't need to compile or link them as you would with other programming languages. Also, because the text editor deals strictly with text, there's no special saving techniques or options as you would have with a word processor.

Using a word processor

Yes, you can use a word processor to write your batch files. It's a lot like using a 747 to help your kid cross the street, but it is possible.

The drawback to using a word processor is that you have a big, clunky program doing a small job. The biggest problem is that most word processors save their files in a special document file mode—not a straight text file. Even if you put the .BAT extension on the filename, DOS will not understand the word processor's formatting code. Instead, you must direct the word processor to save your batch file in the text-only, or ASCII, mode. This is an extra step that might not seem worth it—especially when composing small batch files.

Also, unlike a text editor, you'll need to be careful about word-wrapping your batch file commands. Batch files can accept a line of commands up to 128 characters long. Most word processors will wrap text at about character position 70. Even if the word processor saves the program in the text mode, it might insert a carriage return in the middle of a long command, breaking the command in two and messing up your batch file.

If you wind up using a word processor to write batch files, remember to save your work in the text mode. If that seems like too much work, use a text editor. There's one that came free with DOS called EDLIN. Though EDLIN is perhaps the worst text editor you'll ever use, everyone who has DOS also has EDLIN.

No matter which method is chosen, the end result is a text file, with a .BAT extension, consisting of batch file commands. Typing the name of this file (with or without the .BAT extension) executes the commands held within the file.

How batch files work

To understand how batch files work you'll need to know how DOS runs other types of program files. Quite frankly, DOS is really kind of lame when it comes to running programs. This is due primarily to its history; DOS was written to quickly bring the IBM PC into business computing. Back in 1981, all the decent business software was running under the CP/M operating system. Because of this, DOS has its roots in CP/M and uses some of CP/M's conventions to run its programs.

OS/2, the "future" operating system for IBM computers, tried to change the way programs were run, but it still has its roots in the CP/M operating system. Eventually, OS/2 will offer a little more flexibility. But for now, everything relies on the name of the file, not its contents. (Or, as they used to say: never judge a book by its cover, but judge a DOS filename by its extension.)

COM, EXE, and BAT files

There are three types of files you can "run" using DOS. Unlike other operating systems, the only way DOS knows which files it can run is determined by the file's extension. More sophisticated operating systems use information contained inside the file to determine if it's "runnable." But in DOS, everything relies on a filename's extension.

The three "runnable" file extensions are:

    COM
    EXE
    BAT

COM is short for COMmand file and it's the oldest of the file formats. The COM file contains microprocessor instructions and data in the exact format that is loaded into memory. This is considered an older-style format, and behaves exactly like the type of programs that ran under the old CP/M operating system.

Most small programs are written using the COM format because it loads quickly. However, COM files can be no more than 64K in size. This limitation is why most larger files use the more flexible EXE program format.

EXE is short for EXEcutable file. The EXE format saves programs into separate modules, one for the program's code, another for data, and a third for the "stack." A special 512-byte file header contains information about how the three modules are loaded into memory. Because of this independent loading scheme, EXE files are slower to load than COM files, but they can be much larger (terribly huge, in fact).

BAT is short for BATch file. It signals to DOS that the program is actually a batch file, or a series of DOS commands stored in a text file. When you run a batch file, DOS reads in each line from the text file and executes each line as if it was typed in at the command prompt. Additionally, each line is run through a "batch file interpreter" that performs certain manipulations on certain items in the batch file.

Whenever a file has an extension of COM or EXE, DOS *assumes* it's a program file and will attempt to load and run it. BAT files are interpreted by DOS, and are not loaded in the same manner as COM and EXE files.

DOS "assumes" a program is runnable because, as I've said before, DOS really doesn't know what's in a file and only knows a program by its file extension. So you can rename any file on disk to a COM file. DOS will try to execute that file as a program. But don't expect it to work.

For all three types of runnable files, no matter what the file extension, you only need to type the first part of the filename to run the program. For example, to run the program "MAILLIST.COM" you only need to type "MAILLIST". To run "BACK-UP.BAT" just type "BACK-UP".

Incidentally, if you have three files on disk:

HELLO.COM
HELLO.EXE
HELLO.BAT

and if you typed HELLO at the command prompt, the file named HELLO .COM would run. Because of the way DOS works, you will never be able to run HELLO.EXE or HELLO.BAT—even if you typed in their full names. If the COM file didn't exist, HELLO.EXE would run. The HELLO.BAT batch file ranks last. The priority scheme with filenames is: COM, EXE, then BAT.

Batch file execution

Each type of program file, COM, EXE, and BAT, are treated differently by DOS. COM files are loaded into memory ("dumped," actually) directly from disk. EXE files are loaded according to their modules. But how are batch files executed?

The secret lies in COMMAND.COM, the command interpreter. COMMAND.COM interprets a batch file one line at a time. When a BAT file is run, COMMAND.COM reads in one line from the file (all the characters up to the carriage return) and executes that line as if it were typed at the keyboard. Additionally, it expands any environmental variables and keeps track of batch file labels for the GOTO statement. COMMAND.COM also scans the keyboard to see if Control–C or CTRL–BREAK was pressed. If so, the user is asked if they want to stop the batch file and is given a chance to type a "Y" or an "N".

Because batch files are interpreted one line at a time, they tend to be slow. While running some long batch files you might have noticed that DOS is constantly accessing the disk. This is because each line is read from the batch file one at a time. There are ways to avoid this, the first of which is to write better batch files (which, by the way, is what this book is about). The second method is to use a disk caching program. Disk caching isn't directly related to batch file programming, however it does speed things up a bit.

Batch files are really quite simple then: It's COMMAND.COM that makes them work.

A potential problem when running batch files—especially when you get fancy with them—is that the original file will become "lost." Because DOS fetches one line from the batch file at a time, if you change your system's path or, worse, your batch file erases itself, you'll get an error and the batch file will stop. Normally this shouldn't happen. (But how often do things go normally?)

Another interesting question that usually crops up is "Because a batch file can contain any command you'd normally type at the DOS command prompt, can you have one batch file 'run' another?"

Oh, you mean something like the following (the line numbers have been added for reference):

```
1: @ECHO OFF
2: CLS
3: ECHO About to run another batch file
4: SECOND.BAT
5: ECHO How was that?
6: END
```

In line 4, "SECOND.BAT" is the name of another batch file. And to answer the question: yes the first batch file will run the second. However, the remaining lines (5 and 6) in the first batch file will not be executed. Once control is passed to another batch file it takes over. The first batch file stops executing. You can have one batch file execute another, but only by using special tricks covered in the book can you have execution return to the first batch file. Stay tuned.

So, to summarize, batch files are run, or interpreted, one line at a time by COMMAND.COM. A lot of extra translation work is performed by COMMAND.COM, expanding environmental variables, remembering labels, and so on. But ultimately, batch files are the simplest type of program run by DOS.

Examples

Knowing what you know so far about batch files, you can type in and test the following. These were designed as quick-and-dirty methods for accomplishing things you'd normally have to sort out by hand (or eyeball), or buy an expensive utility program to get the job done.

You can use COPY CON to create these, unless you're intimately familiar with a text editor or word processor. Remember to save these files in the text mode if you're using a word processor.

Note: These batch files are written using DOS 3.3. If you have DOS 3.2 or less, do not precede the initial ECHO OFF command with an @ (at) sign.

Directory sort by name

All line numbers in the sample batch files are used for reference purposes only; you should not type them in when entering your batch files.

Name: DSN.BAT

```
1: @ECHO OFF
2: REM Sort directory by name
3: DIR | SORT > ZIGNORE.ME
4: MORE < ZIGNORE.ME
5: DEL ZIGNORE.ME
```

(The "ZIGNORE.ME" file is not displayed in the sorted list of filenames.)

Directory sort by size

Name: DSS.BAT

```
1: @ECHO OFF
2: REM Sort directory by file size
3: DIR | SORT/+14 > ZIGNORE.ME
4: MORE < ZIGNORE.ME
5: DEL ZIGNORE.ME
```

Directory sort by date created

Name: DSD.BAT

```
1: @ECHO OFF
2: REM Sort directory by date
3: DIR | SORT/ + 10 > ZIGNORE.ME
4: MORE < ZIGNORE.ME
5: DEL ZIGNORE.ME
```

Directory sort by file extension

Name: DSE.BAT

```
1: @ECHO OFF
2: REM Sort directory by file extension
3: DIR | SORT/ + 10 > ZIGNORE.ME
4: MORE < ZIGNORE.ME
5: DEL ZIGNORE.ME
```

Directory sort by time created

Name: DST.BAT

```
1: @ECHO OFF
2: REM Sort directory by time
3: DIR | SORT/ + 35 > ZIGNORE.ME
4: MORE < ZIGNORE.ME
5: DEL ZIGNORE.ME
```

Notes on directory sorting

These batch files take advantage of DOS's SORT filter. More information on SORT is provided in the following chapter. If these batch files produce a "Bad Command or Filename" error, it means you might not have the SORT command available. Information on fixing this (by putting SORT on the "path") is provided in chapter 4. Also, these batch files make use of I/O redirection and the MORE filter. (That information is also provided in chapter 2.)

The reason sorting a directory works is that DOS displays the directory in a consistent format. No matter how long the filename, all filenames start at column 1. The extension always starts at column position 10. The size starts at column 14 (though it may not always display out that far), and so on (see FIG. 1-2).

This makes sorting by column an easy way to present a directory. For example, to sort on column 14 (where the file size starts), simply include SORT's column switch, / +, followed by the column number:

```
SORT / + 14
```

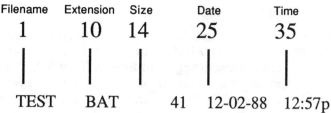

Filename	Extension	Size	Date	Time
1	10	14	25	35
TEST	BAT	41	12-02-88	12:57p

1-2 Column positions in a directory listing are illustrated here.

Note that sometimes you'll see some "garbage files" in with the rest of the files and programs. These are special, temporary files used by DOS and are erased after the SORT is done. Also, when sorting on some columns, you'll see other information interspliced with the rest of the directory listing (see FIG. 1-3).

This is a by-product of the SORT command. Because SORT is actually sorting the directory listing as a *file*, it sorts all the directory information as well as the filenames.

1-3 A file directory, sorted by file size, is shown here.

```
DSN        BAT      70    6-08-88   10:25p
DSS        BAT      74    6-08-88   10:24p
DST        BAT      74    6-08-88   10:25p
DSD        BAT      74    6-08-88   10:26p
DSE        BAT      74    6-08-88   10:26p
DISKETTE           129    5-30-88    2:08p
 Directory of   C:\BATCH\DISK
.             <DIR>        6-08-88   10:24p
..            <DIR>        6-08-88   10:24p
        8 File(s)  10389504 bytes free
 Volume in drive C is VERY HARD
 Volume Serial Number is 001C-3246
```

ZIGNORE.ME?

The ZIGNORE.ME file is used in each of the above examples as a temporary file on disk. The name itself, ZIGNORE.ME, is probably one you don't have anywhere in your system. (The initial Z was added because you might have an IGNORE.ME file for some reason.) ZIGNORE stores the directory output and it's then used as input for the MORE filter, which pages the output one screen at a time. This is much quicker than the following, which also does the same thing:

    DIR | SORT | MORE

Also, using ZIGNORE with I/O redirection is easier to follow if you're fresh to the concept. (We'll dig this up again in the following chapter, so just nod and smile if you don't understand it right away.)

Reversing the sort

The SORT filter normally sorts in ascending order. That is, from low numbers and letters (1 and "A") to higher numbers and letters (9 and "Z"). SORT can also sort in reverse order by adding an /R switch. Any of the preceding batch file examples can be modified to sort in reverse order by inserting an "/R" after the SORT command and before the /+ column indicator.

Printing the sort

To print any of the sorted directory listings, change the line with the "MORE" command in each batch file to:

    COPY ZIGNORE.ME PRN

This copies the sorted directory file (ZIGNORE.ME) to the printer device, PRN. There will be more sophisticated printing examples presented later in this book.

DOS 5 and directory sorting

All of this directory sorting is a bit old-fashioned to DOS 5. The DIR command's /O switch can be used to specify a sort order according to name, extension, size, date and time, and whether or not the entry is a directory or file. The /O switch has five options that control the sort:

N   Sort by filename
E   Sort by extension
S   Sort by size
D   Sort by date and time
G   Group directories first, files second

The order of the sort can be reversed by putting a minus in front of an option.

The following single-line DOS commands perform the same functions as the above batch file examples in DOS 5:

Directory sort by name:

DIR /O:N

Directory sort by filename extension:

DIR /O:E

Directory sort by file size:

DIR /O:S

Directory sort by date and time:

DIR /O:D

Note that both the date and time are factored into the sort. You still need to use a separate SORT filter to get at the time specifically, as discussed under "Directory sort by time created" on page 16.

Directory sort by group:

DIR /O:G

With all of these, you can specify the DIR command's /P switch to have output pause after each screenful of text.

Gang copy

You'll find this batch file program extremely useful. It copies a group of files from one place to another. OS/2's COPY command provides this feature. But when you use DOS, you must rely on batch files like the one in FIG. 1-4.

1-4 This batch file copies a group of files from one place to another.

Name: COPY2.BAT

```
 1: @ECHO OFF
 2: REM A 'Gang Copy' batch file example
 3: IF %1NOTHING==NOTHING GOTO HELP
 4: SET DISK=%1
 5: ECHO Copy a group of files to drive %DISK%
 6: :LOOP
 7: SHIFT
 8: IF %1NOTHING==NOTHING GOTO END
 9: COPY %1 %DISK% >NUL
10: ECHO %1 copied to %DISK%
11: GOTO LOOP
12: :HELP
13: ECHO COPY2 Command format:
14: ECHO copy2 [drive:[\path]] [file1] [file2] .... [fileN]
15: :END
16: SET DISK=
```

This file takes input such as:

C> COPY2 A: FILE1 FILE2 FILE3.TXT FILE4 FILE5 FILE6

It copies to drive A: all the files listed—any number of files up to 128 characters of input (the maximum number of characters you can type at the DOS prompt). If you're copying the files to a disk drive, remember to include the letter and colon. Wildcards are allowed, so the input could just as well have been:

C> COPY2 A: C:\SOURCE*.ASM C:\SOURCE*.C

How this relatively "simple" (I wrote it in less than four minutes) batch file works is covered later in this book.

Mega copy

Another problem DOS's COPY command has is that it won't tell you if you're copying one file over another. Suppose you have two files, one is named SECRET and the other CRUCIAL. If you want to make a copy of CRUCIAL and rename it SECRET, you use the following command:

COPY CRUCIAL SECRET

DOS will copy the file CRUCIAL to a file named SECRET. Both of them will have the same contents. However, your original file SECRET will be overwritten. DOS doesn't let you know that. Instead, it happily prints the message "1 file(s) copied" and you're left to suffer the consequences alone later.

The batch file in FIG. 1-5, CP.BAT, uses the same format as DOS's COPY, but it will let you know when a duplicate filename exists.

1-5 This batch file checks to see if duplicate filenames exist before copying over them.
Name: CP.BAT

```
 1: @ECHO OFF
 2: :REM COPY FILES FROM %1 TO %2
 3: REM Test parameters
 4: IF %1NOTHING==NOTHING GOTO WARNING
 5: IF %2NOTHING==NOTHING GOTO WARNING
 6: REM Test for existence of duplicate files
 7: IF NOT EXIST %2 GOTO CP01
 8: ECHO %2 already exists!
 9: GOTO END
10: :CP01
11: REM Test for subdirectory\file(s)
12: IF NOT EXIST %2\%1 GOTO CP02
13: ECHO %2\%1 already exists!
14: GOTO END
15: :CP02
16: ECHO Copying File(s)...
17: COPY %1 %2 >NUL
18: ECHO Files copied
19: GOTO END
20: :WARNING
21: ECHO You must specify a source and destination filename with
22: :END
```

Again, CP uses the same format as DOS's COPY command. However, if you attempt to copy CRUCIAL to SECRET with CP, you'll see the following:

SECRET already exists!

The CP (copy) command will then stop, and you'll be given a second chance to copy your file, or rename the original SECRET to something else. (DOS should have had this feature all along.)

Dial the phone

As a last batch file example, consider those phone dialing programs that sprouted up a few years ago. Using a modem attached to your computer, you could dial a phone number automatically—no more phone books or misdialing numbers. Of course, remember to pick up the phone after the number is dialed; no human wants to talk with your modem.

The batch file in FIG. 1-6 dials the phone for any Hayes-compatible modem hooked up to COM1, your first communications port, on your PC. Just enter the phone number after DIAL on the command line, wait for it to ring, then you're in business. (Aren't you glad you own a computer?)

1-6 This batch file dials a phone number.

Name: DIAL.BAT

```
 1: @ECHO OFF
 2: IF $%1==$ GOTO OOPS
 3: ECHO This program will dial a phone number. Make sure your modem
 4: ECHO is on-line and ready to go.
 5: PAUSE
 6: ECHO Dialing %1
 7: ECHO ATDT%1 > COM1
 8: ECHO Wait for the phone to ring, then
 9: PAUSE
10: ECHO AT > COM1
11: GOTO END
12: :OOPS
13: ECHO Please specify a phone number after dial, and try again.
14: :END
```

Again, I/O redirection is used in this batch file, this time to send characters out to your modem. You follow DIAL with the phone number you want to dial on the command line. For example:

DIAL 555-1212

The batch file sends that string out to your modem in line 7, using the common Hayes command set. (This might not work on all PCs or with all modems.) You then listen for the ring, pick up your own phone's handset, and press ENTER.

And to think that some people paid over $50 for similar programs. Tsk, tsk.

Summary

Batch files are one of three types of program files that DOS can run. The differences between batch files and other program files are that batch files are easy to create—they're text files; batch files are interpreted one line at a time, just like commands typed at the system prompt; and anyone can use batch files to make their system run more efficiently.

Normally, batch files are considered rather humdrum. But as this book will go on to show, batch files can become quite sophisticated, lending even more power to your computer system.

2

DOS

This chapter is about DOS. But it's not your typical "This is the on-off switch" chapter. Instead, this is powerful stuff; information every DOS guru should know. Even if you already think you know all the finer aspects of DOS, the information here might surprise you.

First of all, it's assumed that because this is an advanced book, you already know some of the finer points of using DOS. In fact, you can get by here only knowing how to use the COPY function. But I encourage you to learn more about your system. If you're just starting out, you might want to order a copy of *Hard Disk Management with DOS*, written by me and available through TAB Books.

System operation

You've probably had the opportunity to turn on an MS-DOS or PC-DOS computer and watch it start. Even a novice user has seen this happen maybe one hundred times at the least. When the computer starts, you hear its fan whir, and if there's a hard drive, you hear its gears rev up to 3,600 RPMs. Some clone systems might immediately display a copyright message, or they might show you a visual rendering of their RAM check. Older IBM computers, for some reason (perhaps because They Were First), just display a blinking cursor on the screen.

Then, suddenly, the floppy disk drive crunches to life. The speaker beeps once. The floppy drive crunches again. Your system tries to load DOS. Eventually, it will get there—if not from the floppy drive, then from that rapidly spinning hard disk. You might not have a clue as to what's really happening inside your computer at that time, but a lot of activity is taking place before you get your command prompt.

That activity, the loading, or "booting," of a DOS disk, is the subject of this section. This is truly trivial information. No one really needs to know this to use a computer, and you only need to have a passing knowledge of it to program batch files.

Why then am I describing it? Because this is a book on Advanced Batch File Programming. This information is important if you expect to know a lot about your system. It's what separates a typical user from an advanced user. The men from the boys, the women from the girls, etc. The more you know about your machine, the better you'll understand it. And the information does become useful later on.

Batch files do come into play here, but only toward the end. In the meantime, the following information describes the composition of your system, microprocessor, BIOS and DOS, and how those three items work together to give your computer a personality all its own.

Startup

There are three key players that compose the personality of your computer system: your microprocessor (or CPU), BIOS, and DOS (see FIG. 2-1).

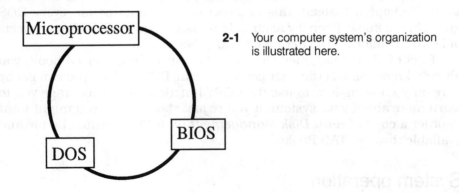

2-1 Your computer system's organization is illustrated here.

The microprocessor is your computer's brain. However, the brain really doesn't do any thinking on its own. Instead, the microprocessor must be told what to do. It must be given instructions. The first instructions it gets are from the BIOS, or ROM, inside your computer.

How does this work?

According to the documentation for the Intel 8088 microprocessor (Part No. 999-999-845), the chip will innately start executing instructions at memory location FFFF:0000 (hexadecimal) when it's first turned on. This memory location typically contains "jump" instruction directing the microprocessor to the computer's BIOS (which is another memory location containing microprocessor instructions).

The original IBM PC's BIOS began at memory location F000:0000. The instructions located at that address would systematically warm-up all the various parts of the computer; initialize low-level interrupt vectors; check for port assignment conflicts; determine which type of video display adapter was attached; and perform two memory checks. It also scanned the system for other BIOSs, such as an EGA BIOS, and executed them if found. Then, after a time, it attempted to check for a diskette in the first floppy disk drive.

If nothing was found in the first floppy drive, the original PC would load a ROM version of Microsoft BASIC. (The first PC had a cassette port for loading and saving programs, though none ever came out on cassette. This allowed some insane users to use the computer without disk drives. I seriously doubt if anyone ever used their IBM PC as a cassette tape-only computer.)

If a disk was found in the first drive, the BIOS would read in the first 512 bytes of that diskette. Then, once that information was in memory, BIOS checks to see if it was program code, or just garbage (meaning an unreadable disk).

If the first 512 bytes of the disk contained program code, plus special identification bytes, the BIOS would "jump" right into the code and keep on going. If the disk contained DOS, an initialization procedure would begin whereby the first 512 bytes would load information from another part of the disk, and eventually, somewhere down the line, code would be executed to look for and load DOS from disk.

Since the addition of hard drives, the BIOS was modified to check to see if a hard disk is installed. If a diskette isn't found in the first floppy drive, the BIOS will attempt to load information from the hard disk. If DOS is on the hard drive, it will be loaded and executed similar to a floppy disk—only much faster.

This is all a simplified explanation of a very complex process. A lot of work is involved to get DOS up in the morning. By the way, this entire process is called "bootstrapping," and is illustrated in FIG. 2-2.

If all goes well, DOS takes over and begins loading itself into memory. Of course, it's really not as easy as that (as you'll discover in the next section). If DOS can't be loaded, an error message is displayed and, typically, your heart goes pitter-patter.

Since then

The above description was written based on the operations of an original IBM PC modified with hard disk ROMs. They also apply to your typical PC/XT. Since then many more IBM computers, as well as a whole slew of clones and compatibles, have come to market. They generally follow the same scheme as above, though a few of the more eccentric computers may deviate here and there. Basically the premise is the same as detailed in FIG. 2-2.

Power on, jump to memory location FFFF:0000, which passes control to the BIOS

 Does power-on self-text (POST) routines, checks memory, then attempts to load information from disk.

 Information is loaded from disk into memory by the BIOS. The information loaded is then executed. If the disk is a DOS disk, the code will attempt to load DOS.

 If a floppy disk isn't in Drive A, the BIOS will check for a hard disk.

 As with the floppy disk, information from the hard disk is loaded into memory by the BIOS. If the disk is a DOS disk, DOS will be loaded.

"Bootstrapping"

2-2 The bootstrapping sequence is illustrated here.

Along with the new computer systems came upgrades to the BIOS and to the microprocessor itself. No matter what configuration is being used, the procedures are still the same (see TABLE 2-1).

Table 2-1

Computer	Microprocessor	Speed
IBM PC	8088	Average
IBM PC/XT	8088	Average
IBM PC-AT	80286	Faster
IBM PS/2	80386	Much Faster

Loading DOS

DOS is a general term that refers to the entire MS-DOS, or PC-DOS, operating system. Actually, there are many programs and files that make up DOS. DOS 3.3 comes on two 360K 5¹/₄-inch floppy disks, or one 720K 3¹/₂-inch disk. DOS 4 comes on five 360K 5¹/₄-inch floppy disks, or two 720K 3¹/₂-inch disks. There are over 50 files (programs, filters, "sys" files, and overlays) that come with either version of DOS. Future versions will doubtless come with more files.

At the core of DOS are three programs. Their names differ depending on whether you have PC-DOS or MS-DOS (see TABLE 2-2).

Table 2-2

PC-DOS	MS-DOS	Function
IBMBIO.COM	IO.SYS	DOS BIOS
IBMDOS.COM	MSDOS.SYS	DOS "kernel"
COMMAND.COM	COMMAND.COM	User interface, or "shell"

These files are your DOS—your Disk Operating System. Their responsibilities vary from integrating DOS with a computer's individual components to interfacing with a human being.

All three of these files will make the minimum DOS system disk. IBM BIO.COM and IBMDOS.COM are the first two files on disk. (It's done that way so that the bootstrap loader can easily find the files.) Both files are hidden, meaning they aren't listed by the DIR command. With DOS versions prior to 3.3, IBMBIO.COM and IBMDOS.COM had to be the first two files on a system disk and both files had to be contiguous or the bootstrap loader wouldn't consider the disk a DOS disk (even if they were elsewhere on disk).

COMMAND.COM is the third required file to create a minimum system disk. Unlike IBMBIO.COM and IBMDOS.COM, COMMAND.COM is a visible file and doesn't need to be one of the first files on disk. Individually, the functions of these files are as follows:

IBMBIO.COM is the first system file loaded into memory by the bootstrapping routines. This program serves two functions: It contains all the low-level DOS-to-hardware code, and it performs other DOS loading functions that come under the term SYSINIT.

The DOS-to-hardware code is referred to as the MS-DOS BIOS. It's customized by each computer manufacturer (or OEM for Original Equipment Manufacturer) to personalize DOS with the computer's hardware. These BIOS routines and low-level device drivers interface DOS directly to a computer's hardware. Once in place, the SYSINIT routines take over and continue loading DOS.

IBMDOS.COM is loaded by the SYSINIT routines of IBMBIO.COM. This file is considered to be the MS-DOS kernel, containing all the meat of the operating system: file management, memory management, device and character input/output, time and date support, the system environment and configuration. Additionally, the routines in IBMDOS.COM set up the low-level interrupt services that are used by other programs to access DOS functions.

The next thing SYSINIT does (after loading IBMDOS.COM) is to check for a CONFIG.SYS file. If the file exists, SYSINIT reads it and sets any parameters specified as well as loads any user device drivers, such as a screen driver (ANSI.SYS) or a mouse driver if the computer has a mouse. (CONFIG.SYS is covered in detail in chapter 5.)

The final act of loading DOS is to run the COMMAND.COM program. COMMAND.COM is the user "shell," or a program that allows a human being access to DOS and all the DOS routines. (The shell insulates the user from the kernel. What a nutty idea.)

Because MS-DOS can have other shells besides COMMAND.COM, SYSINIT checks for a "SHELL" command in the CONFIG.SYS file. If another shell is listed, SYSINIT loads it instead of COMMAND.COM. Otherwise, SYSINIT looks for the good ol' COMMAND.COM that came with DOS (see FIG. 2-3).

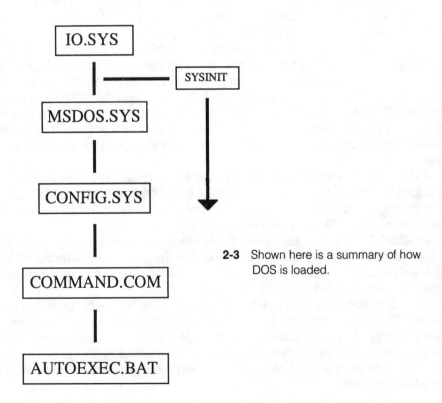

2-3 Shown here is a summary of how DOS is loaded.

Anyone can write their own COMMAND.COM program to be used as a user shell. For example, JP Software's popular 4DOS shell is a commonly found replacement for COMMAND.COM. The only stipulation is that a replacement shell be named COMMAND.COM, or specified in the CONFIG.SYS file using the SHELL command (see the 4DOS manual). As far as the scope of this book is concerned, the COMMAND.COM Microsoft supplies must be used because it contains the batch file interpreter.

COMMAND.COM has three parts, or modules: Initialization, Resident, and Transient. The first duty of COMMAND.COM is to fire up the initialization module. This module copies the transient part of COMMAND.COM to high memory. The transient module is the part of COMMAND.COM that displays the command prompt and accepts commands. The resident module stays in memory all the time. It's the resident module that accepts control from a program after the program runs. It then checks to see if the transient portion of DOS is still up there in high memory. If everything's intact, the command prompt again appears. Otherwise, if the transient portion of COMMAND.COM is not present or was overwritten by a program, the resident portion reloads COMMAND.COM from disk. (This is when, on some floppy disk systems, you'll see the message: "Insert disk with COMMAND.COM in drive A and strike any key when ready." Or worse, if COMMAND.COM cannot be found on a hard disk system, you see the error "Cannot load COMMAND, system halted." What a heart stopper!)

Why split the command processor into two parts? Primarily to give you more memory to run your programs. In the early days of computing, memory size was restricted. The original PC came with only 64K of RAM, so any memory that could be released to a running program was important. Even with today's memory-hog programs, every byte of RAM is important.

DOS 5 will semi-solve the problem for you. You can load all of DOS's modules—including COMMAND.COM—into what are called UMBs, upper memory blocks. (Those are secret memory locations above the 640K RAM barrier.) When you do this, it gives you more free memory, plus it lessens the chance of a "Cannot load COMMAND, system halted" type of error message.

Batch files

Batch files are part of the user shell, COMMAND.COM—the one supplied by Microsoft. COMMAND.COM is called a CLI, or Command Line Interface. It accepts commands typed in from the keyboard (as opposed to a pull-down menu interface or graphic environment interface). These commands are then translated by a command interpreter and the instructions passed to the DOS kernel.

At the time DOS was developed, this was the way most computers operated. Since then, and because computing power has increased and memory prices have dropped, other types of interfaces have been developed. But for using batch files, the command line interface is the only way to get the job done.

Batch files were originally a scripting language. The first implementation of batch files under DOS Version 1.0 was quite limited. In fact, the first version of DOS had only these two batch file commands:

PAUSE
REM

Other batch file commands were simply DOS commands or program names. (There wasn't even an ECHO command to suppress the listing of a batch file as it was executing.) This all stems from the original script-like nature of batch files per IBM's request.

When DOS Version 2.x came out, several commands were added to the batch file repertoire:

ECHO
FOR
GOTO
IF
SHIFT

And with DOS Version 3.3, a final and very useful batch file command was added:

CALL

Additionally, all the DOS commands can be used in batch files, as well as interesting third-party software, some of which is custom designed to integrate with batch files.

Anatomy of an operating system

Most of this book's readers probably claim to know DOS quite well. Personally, I'll never make a mistake and admit to something like that. Because, just as soon as I think I have DOS mastered, along comes a friend or foe who shows me some simple trick I would have never guessed. "It's in the manual," they usually say. This is a good argument for reading the manual. Again.

The material covered here is not introductory, nor is there any hand holding or DOS tutorial. Instead, this is mid-level to advanced material dealing with the finer aspects of DOS. The purpose of this section is two-fold: First it will reacquaint you with some things about DOS you may already know—or already think you may know. Second, it will introduce you into some things about DOS you may not know.

The items covered in this section include some trivia about the history of DOS (facts to amaze your friends), details about DOS's organization, the way it handles files and devices (more facts), and information on some of the less-practiced aspects of DOS, filters, pipes, I/O redirection, and shelling (even more facts).

History

This first version of PC-DOS came on one 160K, single-sided floppy diskette. Three programs came with DOS (EDLIN, FORMAT, and DEBUG) and it needed only 8K of RAM to run. The latest version of DOS comes on five 360K diskettes, consists of dozens of files and needs a minimum of 256K to run.

PC-DOS was written by Microsoft for IBM's first personal computer. At the time, the CP/M was the most popular microcomputer operating system. CP/M ran on the 8-bit 8080, or Z80, microprocessor. It had the lure of the largest base of business software, which meant that most businessmen interested in personal computers were buying CP/M machines. IBM wanted a piece of that action.

Under encouragement from Bill Gates, president of Microsoft, IBM planned their new machine around the 8086 microprocessor. The 8086 was a 16-bit chip and far more powerful and capable than the 8080. (For cost reasons, the 8088, a similar chip, was used instead on the first PC.)

Because the 8086 had no operating system and could not run CP/M programs, Microsoft promised IBM it would write one—and make that operating system similar to CP/M. This would make it easy for software developers to rewrite, or port, their software over to the IBM machine.

The initial release of DOS, Version 1.0, looked a lot like CP/M. Even the filenames and structure were similar. Microsoft wanted to pave the way for CP/M business applications to move up to DOS, so everything was done accordingly. There were even translation programs built that would take Z80 or 8080 CP/M code and re-output it as 8086 MS-DOS code.

Programs started to appear for the IBM PC and PC-DOS almost overnight. This made the PC a magnificent success. Because Microsoft owned the rights to DOS (they merely licensed it to IBM), they soon released their own version called MS-DOS. This version could be sold to clone and compatible manufacturers and customized for each machine. It also ensured the popularity of what is now generically called "DOS" in the microcomputer world.

With the release of DOS 2.0, DOS began to move away from CP/M. Bill Gates was quoted as saying the second release of DOS was the version they wanted to do in the first place. Many new features were added to DOS 2.0, which coincided with the release of IBM's PC/XT.

The most attractive addition of DOS 2.0 was the hierarchical file structure, similar to the one used by Microsoft Xenix, a clone of AT&T's UNIX operating system. This file system made storing and organizing files and programs on a large volume disk, such as the ten megabyte hard drive on the PC/XT, much easier.

DOS 2.0 also offered support for different types of floppy drives. Besides the single-sided 160K and 180K diskette formats, DOS 2.0 could support double-sided drives. This brought floppy disk storage (which was still the most popular form of storage) up to 320K. Incidentally, since Version 2.0, almost every new release of DOS has centered around some new, funky disk drive format.

DOS 3.0 was designed to deal with the needs of the IBM PC/AT. The AT had a new format of floppy disk drive (see?) and a new microprocessor: the 80286. Still, you didn't need to have a funky 1.2 megabyte drive to use DOS 3.0. It was compatible with all machines and all serious DOS users upgraded to it immediately. (Since then, the question of upgrading DOS has become confusing; see the Introduction.)

One of the best additions to DOS with Version 3.0 was the ability to run programs from any subdirectory. For example, suppose dBASE is in your \DB subdirectory. You happen to be in the \WP directory. To run dBASE under DOS 2.x, you'd have to type two commands:

```
CD \DB
DBASE
```

Under DOS 3.x, you can type:

```
\DB\DBASE
```

Normally, this would result in a "Bad Command or filename" error message. But DOS 3 is smart enough to recognize a full pathname and execute the file. (There's more on subdirectories later in this chapter.)

DOS 3.1 quickly followed DOS 3.0, primarily to fix bugs in Version 3.0 and to add some networking capabilities. DOS 3.2 was introduced with the IBM laptop computer, and yet another diskette drive format: the 3½-inch disk. (This gets worse and worse.)

DOS 3.2 was a dog in the opinions of most consultants. It was little improvement over DOS 3.1 and offered few new features. Most people waited for DOS 3.3 and then immediately upgraded.

DOS 3.3 was a vast improvement over previous versions of DOS, with one remarkable feature: It's almost entirely rewritten by IBM.

As far as batch files are concerned, DOS 3.3 added a nice new command: @. This command (usable only in batch files) suppresses the echoing of batch file commands to the screen. This eliminated the almost mandatory "ECHO OFF" command at the head of each batch file. They also added a new CALL command that made running second batch files easier (more on that later).

DOS 3.3 additionally provided (probably thanks to IBM) a better and smarter BACKUP command, an improved method of upgrading DOS versions, and support for yet another funky type of disk drive: the 3½-inch 1.44 megabyte drive on the PS/2 series of computers. (Time to throw in the towel on different disk size formats. In fact, the optional switches for the FORMAT program are so complex only the truly insane bother to memorize them.)

Strangely enough, the next version of DOS, 4.0, wasn't coupled with the announcement of a new disk drive format. Also strange is that this version is, once again, written entirely by IBM and not Microsoft.

Version 4.0 of DOS offered three things that DOS users have wanted for a long time: The first was support for very large capacity hard drives. DOS 4.0 can handle really large hard drives, way beyond the imposed 32 megabyte limit of earlier versions of DOS.

Second, DOS 4.0 incorporated support for expanded memory, that is memory beyond the 640K "boundary." Certain DOS commands could now take advantage of that extra memory, leaving more room in main memory to run your applications. (Though rumor has it the expanded memory commands under DOS 4 don't work as well as some third-party utilities.)

Finally, DOS 4.0 came with a mouse-driven shell program. This program is really nice, similar to those offered by other software developers— but free with DOS. The shell can be customized somewhat, making DOS painless for the first-time user.

Then, in 1991, Microsoft announced DOS 5. It seems no matter how hard they tried to push OS/2, DOS just wouldn't die. So soon we will have DOS 5—which is a heck of a lot better than DOS 4. (Rumor has it that DOS 5 is Microsoft's attempt to undo the damage IBM did when they developed DOS 4 independently.)

DOS 5's main benefit is that it can move itself up into the HMA (High Memory Area) on 286 and 386 systems, giving you almost a full 640K free RAM in which to run your applications. It also offers improved compatibility commands and some much needed features. Indeed, it's a major upgrade to DOS. (Appendix M covers DOS 5 in detail.)

Because of the dominance of OS/2 (discussed heavily in chapter 6), many people made predictions that DOS 5 will be the last version of DOS ever written for PCs. But because Microsoft let the cat out of the bag on DOS 6, we know this isn't true. (Will OS/2 die and DOS 6 be nirvana? Will DOS 5 be everything we need? Will Jim and Donna get back together again? Hmmm. The world of DOS at times resembles a soap opera.)

The purpose of this section was purely review—and trivia. About the most important thing to be gained from all this is to make sure that your system is running a current version of DOS. That is, DOS 3.3 at the minimum or DOS 5. (DOS 4 users: upgrade to DOS 5 quickly—end the madness!) To see if this is true, you can use the trivial VER command, which displays the version of DOS your computer is using:

```
C> VER
MS-DOS Version 3.30
```

DOS operation

Because this is an advanced book, it's assumed you know how to operate DOS. This includes the following:

- Being able to copy a file from one place to another
- Being able to rename a file
- Being able to delete a file
- Being able to format disks
- Being able to copy a group of files from one place to another
- Being able to run a program and quit properly

As long as you can do those simple operations, continue reading. (Really, that's all it takes to be an intermediate DOS user. If you're rusty on any of those items, take a moment to read over your DOS manual, or read the self-promotional plug in the next paragraph.)

Again, the best book for boning up on DOS just has to be *Hard Disk Management with MS-DOS and PC-DOS*. It's available from TAB Books. Even though it says "hard disk" on the cover, the first several chapters offer an excellent DOS tutorial. (I promise this will be the last self-promotion in this book—maybe.)

Device-oriented

DOS is "device oriented." This means that everything in the system is considered a "device." The disk drives are devices, your keyboard is a device, the screen is a device, everything's a device. So what is a device?

A device is something DOS can deal with. It's typically a source for input or output. A device can receive information or produce information (or both). DOS controls your computer by processing information through various devices.

The simplest device (concept-wise) is the disk drive. It's an I/O device, capable of input and output. DOS can both write information to disk, as well as read it back. With some operating systems, this is the extent of the devices that they can handle. However, with DOS, the disk drive isn't the only device.

Another example of device is the printer. The printer isn't an I/O device like the disk drive. Instead, it's just an "O" device (only capable of output; you don't "read" characters from the printer). DOS treats the printer as a device just like the disk drive. Other operating systems may only deal with the printer at a low level, or not at all.

The advantage to having the printer as a device means that DOS is able to deal with it just as it would a disk drive. So, for example, instead of putting information into a file on disk, DOS could just as easily send the information to the printer. (Both are devices.)

Because, according to DOS, everything is a device, DOS can easily deal with various parts of your computer. Later in this chapter, you'll see how input and output can be redirected from one device to another. A non-device-oriented DOS wouldn't be capable of this. But MS-DOS/PC-DOS is capable, and much more versatile because of it.

A list of the devices that DOS recognizes is shown in TABLE 2-3.

Table 2-3

Device	Device name	Input	Output
First floppy drive	A	X	X
First serial port	AUX	X	X
Second floppy drive	B	X	X
Hard drive	C	X	X
Cassette (PC only)	CAS	X	X
System Clock	CLOCK$	X	X
First serial port	COM1	X	X
Second serial port	COM2	X	X
Third serial port	COM3	X	X
Fourth serial port	COM4	X	X
Console	CON	X	X
First printer	LPT1	X	
Second printer	LPT2	X	
Third printer	LPT3	X	
Null device	NUL	X	X
First printer	PRN		X

DOS knows each of these devices by their Device Name. For example, the first serial port is AUX, or COM1. The first floppy drive is "A" (though floppy drives are not normally included in a device list; still, they are devices).

Listed in the chart is whether a device is capable of Input or Output or both. Only the printers are output-only devices. Other devices can accept input or produce output. A variation on this is the CON, or console, device. CON is actually a combination of the keyboard and screen. When CON is selected for input, the device monitored is the keyboard. When CON is selected for output, the information is displayed on the screen.

Device tricks

Because DOS treats everything in the system as a device, you can take advantage of some file manipulation commands for use with devices. The best trick is to use the printer device, LPT1 or PRN, as a file. For example, say you want a hard copy of your favorite batch file. Try:

```
C> COPY FAVORITE.BAT PRN
```

This copies the file FAVORITE.BAT (a text file) to the printer device, PRN. The net effect is that your batch file is now printed.

A better example of this type of trick is to get hard copy from within a text editor. Remember, text editors lack any decent printing capability. Some text editors even lack a printing function. However, the text editor will let you save a file to disk. So . . . to get a hard copy from within your text editor, choose the "Save" command and for the filename type "PRN". Voila, you have instant hard copy.

Another device trick involves listing files on the screen. Normally, to see the contents of a text file, you'd use the TYPE command. If you wanted to look at your FAVORITE.BAT file, you'd type:

```
C> TYPE FAVORITE.BAT
```

Your batch file would be displayed on the screen in all its glory. Because the screen is also a device, the following command does the same thing:

```
C> COPY FAVORITE.BAT CON
```

You get the same result. The file is just "copied" to the screen, just as it was earlier copied to the printer.

Using COPY instead of TYPE has one distinct advantage. During your travels, you might have come across some files that won't display to the screen with the TYPE command. This is because TYPE (and COPY, for that matter) looks for the end of file marker, CTRL–Z, to determine where a file ends. Some clever (?) programmers will stick a CTRL–Z at the start of their programs to prevent you from TYPEing them on the screen. There's a way to get around this using the COPY command.

Normally, COPY will look for the CTRL–Z character, just like the TYPE command does. So, if a file starts with a CTRL–Z, COPY will have the same effect as TYPE: you won't see the file. However, COPY has a special switch, /B, that allows the file to be copied in the *binary* mode. This mode relies upon the file's size to determine the end of file position, not the CTRL–Z.

```
C> COPY FILENAME/B CON
```

This command will "TYPE" any file on disk to your screen. But beware: many of these files contain programming code that you won't be able to read. Worse, if the files contain the CTRL–G character, your computer will beep at you each time a CTRL–G is "displayed." To stop the COPY display, press CTRL–BREAK.

Null for something different

An odd little device is the null device. NUL comes from the UNIX "null" device. It's an input/output device that's basically treated the same as other devices, except NUL is non-existent. When output is sent to NUL the output goes nowhere and is not saved. However, because NUL is a device, DOS treats writing to the NUL device just as writing to any other device. In fact, when copying a file to NUL, DOS responds accordingly:

```
C> copy TEST.BAT NUL
1 File(s) Copied
```

Because NUL is a device, DOS really did do something. But don't expect to find an extra copy of TEST.BAT anywhere.

NUL is also an input device, however don't count on it for too much input. When the NUL device is read by DOS, an immediate end-of-file character is produced. So copying from the NUL device to a file produces a very short file:

```
C> copy NUL TEMP
0 File(s) Copied
```

Actually, no file was created. But you can still use NUL for input. Later in this chapter, when I/O redirection is covered, you'll see how the NUL device can be used to create an empty file. Those are the scary directory entries with a byte size of zero (that usually indicate something is dreadfully wrong with your system—but not in this case).

As is shown by the above examples, devices can be used like filenames when manipulating information. This is the key to understanding devices and what they can do. The ability to manipulate these devices through the DOS commands covered in this book is a cornerstone to writing good batch files.

DOS commands

DOS is famous for its cryptic commands. Using these puzzling commands is how you communicate with your computer. And once you learn them, they don't seem so cryptic anymore. Still, they seem to baffle the neophyte.

DOS's commands deal with files, their storage and organization. Because files are stored on devices, DOS commands also deal with devices and they allow the devices to interact with each other.

There are other maintenance and utility commands, as well as setup commands and, of course, batch file commands. But primarily DOS is there to help you manipulate files and devices—and to keep the computer novices from messing with your system.

DOS commands come in two flavors: Internal and External. The internal commands are in that transient portion of COMMAND.COM you read about earlier. The external commands are actually stand-alone support files that came on the disk with DOS.

Table 2-4 shows all the DOS commands, internal and external, that came with DOS Version 4.0. Also shown is if the command is a filter (covered later), if that command has an abbreviation and if the command is considered network compatible.

Table 2-4

Command	I/E Filter	Abbreviation	Network?
APPEND	I/E		
ASSIGN	E		
ATTRIB	E		
BACKUP	E		
BREAK	I		
CHCP	I		
CHDIR	I	CD	
CHKDSK	E		No
CLS	I		
COMMAND	E		
COMP	E		
COPY	I		
CTTY	I		
DATE	I		
DEL	I		
DIR	I		
DISKCOMP	E		No
DISKCOPY	E		No
DOSSHELL	E		
ERASE	I		
FASTOPEN	E		
FDISK	E		
FIND	E	X	
FORMAT	E		No
GRAFTABL	E		
GRAPHICS	E		
JOIN	E		No
KEYB	E		
LABEL	E		
MEM	E		
MKDIR	I	MD	
MODE	E		
MORE	E	X	
NLSFUNC	E		
PATH	I		
PRINT	E		
PROMPT	I		
RECOVER	E		No
RENAME	I	REN	
REPLACE	E		
RESTORE	E		
RMDIR	I	RD	
SELECT	E		
SET	I		
SHARE	E		
SORT	E	X	

Table 2-4 Continued.

Command	I/E Filter	Abbreviation	Network?
SUBST	E		No
SYS	E		No
TIME	I		
TREE	E		
TYPE	I		
VER	I		
VERIFY	I		
VOL	I		
XCOPY	E		

Note: TABLE 2-4 is limited to DOS commands and doesn't contain other programs that come with DOS, including BASIC, the BASIC demonstration programs (PC-DOS), DEBUG, EDLIN, or any system drivers.

In TABLE 2-4, I and E are used to designate a command internal or external. Internal commands are part of COMMAND.COM. In some cases, you don't even need to have a disk in the drive to use these commands. External commands are typically .COM or .EXE files on disk.

APPEND is an internal/external command. Strange. It's actually what's known as a memory-resident program (covered at the end of this chapter). APPEND starts out on disk as APPEND.EXE. Once you type APPEND, it loads itself into memory and there it stays until you reset or turn off your computer. Therefore, it's an internal/external command.

A "filter" is a special type of program. There are three that come with DOS: FIND, MORE, and SORT. These filters can be used to control or manipulate the flow of input and output between various devices. They're covered later in this chapter.

Five DOS commands have shorthand versions. CHDIR, LOADHIGH, MKDIR, RENAME, and RMDIR can be abbreviated CD, LH, MD, REN, and RD respectively. Most people use the shorthand versions rather than the longer versions. Don't ask me why there are two versions (possible compatibility with Xenix/UNIX). Some intrepid DOS programmers have even taken to "patching" out the longer versions of the command names and replacing them with programs of their own.

Finally, the "Network?" category indicates those commands that are not network compatible. They can, however, be used on a single-user system, normally to allow disk and file control that would really foul up a network.

Beyond those simple categories of DOS commands, I've divided them up further in TABLE 2-5. For better and complete descriptions, refer to your DOS manual.

Table 2-5

Device and File commands

COMP	Compares two files
COPY	Copies between devices
DEL	Deletes files
DIR	Displays files
ERASE	Deletes files
FC	Compares two files in more detail than COMP
RENAME	Renames files
TYPE	Displays contents of a file
XCOPY	A faster version of COPY

System maintenance commands

ATTRIB	Sets or resets file attributes
BACKUP	Archives files
CHDIR	Changes the current directory
CHKDSK	Checks files and disks
FORMAT	Formats/erases disks
LABEL	Adds or changes a disk's label
MEM	Displays information about memory usage
MKDIR	Creates a new subdirectory
REPLACE	Updates old files and adds new ones
RESTORE	Restores BACKUP archives
RMDIR	Removes subdirectories
SYS	Installs/updates DOS onto a properly formatted disk

Utility commands

APPEND	Modifies the search path
ASSIGN	Reroutes I/O from one drive to another
CHCP	Changes the Code Page
CTTY	Changes the console device
DATE	Changes the system date
DISKCOMP	Compares two diskettes
DISKCOPY	Copies two diskettes
DOSKEY	The keyboard enhancer
EDLIN	The old line editor
EXPAND	Decompresses files shipped with DOS 5.0
FASTOPEN	Buffers the last few disk reads (makes opening files faster)
FDISK	Partitions a hard drive
FIND	Locates string filter
GRAFTABL	Loads extended ASCII character set for graphics
GRAPHICS	Allows graphics characters to be printed
JOIN	Deceives DOS into thinking a disk drive is a subdirectory
KEYB	Loads keyboard information for non-U.S. users
LOADFIX	Allows programs to handle low memory locations
MIRROR	Preventive file and disk utility
MODE	Controls the serial ports, screen and printers.
MORE	A display paging filter

Table 2-5 Continued.

MSHERC	Allows QBASIC programs to use Hercules graphics
NLSFUNC	Used with CHCP for foreign users
PATH	Sets the search path
PROMPT	Sets the system prompt
QBASIC	Microsoft's QuickBASIC interpreter
RECOVER	Attempts to restore damaged files
SET	Establishes system variables
SETVER	Program version table trickery
SHARE	Used with file sharing
SORT	A filter used to sort information
SUBST	Deceives DOS into thinking subdirectories are disk drives
TIME	Changes the system time
TREE	Graphically displays the hierarchical file system
UNDELETE	Undeletes files
UNFORMAT	Unformats disks

Miscellaneous commands

BREAK	Monitors CTRL–BREAK for halting programs
CLS	Clears the screen
COMMAND	Runs the command interpreter
DOSSHELL	Starts up a user-friendly DOS interface program
EMM386	Expanded memory control
EXE2BIN	Programmer's conversion utility
EXIT	Quits the command interpreter
HELP	Help!
LOADHIGH	Loads memory resident programs into upper memory
PRINT	Starts a background print spooler
VER	Displays the DOS version number
VERIFY	Sets the diskette verify-write function on
VOL	Displays the disk's volume name (set with LABEL)

Hierarchical file system

With Version 2.x, DOS incorporated a hierarchical file system. This was DOS's first step away from CP/M and a giant leap toward Xenix, Microsoft's version of the popular UNIX operating system.

A hierarchical file system employs subdirectories, or directories within directories, to store files. A disk is no longer one large set of files. Instead, you can create a number of subdirectories and organize your files into them. Furthermore, you can create subdirectories within subdirectories for more organization. This is also commonly referred to as a "tree structured" directory (although the tree in this case is upside down). The main, or top, directory is called the "root." Branching off from it are subdirectories much like the (upside-down) branches of a tree (see FIG. 2-4).

The reason for the hierarchical file system is to allow DOS to make the best use of a large volume drive, or hard disk. Face it, a ten megabyte drive

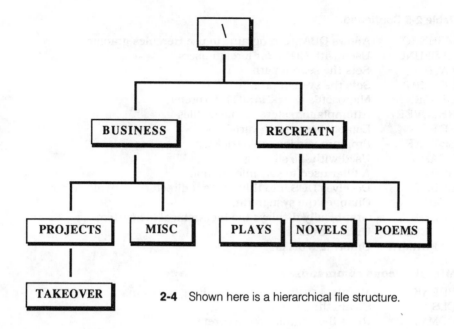

2-4 Shown here is a hierarchical file structure.

with one thousand files all in one directory would be a total mess. And besides, the programmers at Microsoft originally wanted DOS to have the hierarchical file structure, but time constraints forced them to make it a later addition.

With the introduction of the hierarchical file system came three new DOS commands, which have similar counterparts in UNIX, as shown in TABLE 2-6. (CHDIR has two counterparts in UNIX):

Table 2-6

Command	Abbreviation	UNIX	Function
MKDIR	MD	mkdir	Create (make) a directory
CHDIR	CD	cd	Change (sub)Directory, go "home"
CHDIR	CD	pwd	Print working directory
RMDIR	RD	rmdir	Remove a directory

MKDIR, or MD, is used to make a new subdirectory. All disks start out with one directory, the root. This is signified under DOS by a single back-slash character, \. To create a subdirectory you type MKDIR followed by the name of the subdirectory. Subdirectories are named just like files, though they usually don't have a file extension. (Filenames are covered in the next section.)

C> MKDIR DB3

This command creates the subdirectory DB3. If you're in the root directory, you've just created \DB3. If you're in another directory, you've just created a subdirectory of that directory. So, if you're in the DATABASE subdirectory, you've just created:

    \DATABASE\DB3

CHDIR, or better, CD, is the most common of the directory commands. Under DOS, CD changes to the directory specified. For example:

    C> CD \SYSTEM\UTIL\MACE

This command changes from the current directory to the \SYSTEM\ UTIL\MACE subdirectory. \SYSTEM\UTIL\MACE is now the current directory. The same command would work under UNIX—except UNIX wouldn't understand the long-hand version (CHDIR) and UNIX uses forward slashes and lowercase directory names, usually.

The reason why DOS doesn't use forward slashes is primarily to annoy UNIX people. Actually, in DOS 1.x, the forward slash was used as a "switch" to specify options for certain commands. To be consistent, Microsoft decided to use the backslash, \, to separate directory names. A painful, regrettable decision, but one we have to live with. (There are third-party programs that will patch DOS to accept both the forward and reverse slashes to separate directory names. However, because most computers don't use these patches, this book remains consistent with DOS as is.)

Another difference between DOS and UNIX is that typing CD by itself under DOS displays the current working directory. If after the above command you typed CD, you would see:

    C> CD
    C:\SYSTEM\UTIL\MACE

Also, typing CD followed by a drive letter displays the current working directory for that drive:

    C> CD A:
    A:\

Under UNIX, the pwd command is used to print the "working" (currently logged) directory. Typing CD by itself in UNIX changes you back to your "home" directory.

RMDIR, or RD, is one of the least-used directory commands. Very rarely does anyone remove an entire subdirectory. The only limitation to RD is that the directory must be empty before you can remove it. All files must be deleted first, or you'll get an "Invalid path, not directory, or directory not empty" error message. This can be annoying at times because some DOS programs deposit these hideous invisible files that DEL *.*, or ERASE *.*, do not remove.

To summarize, the hierarchical system gives your hard disk better organization than could be possible otherwise. (You can still use subdirectories on floppy diskettes, though it's not as necessary.)

Keeping a clean root

There is no limit to the number of ways you can organize your system using subdirectories, though a common philosophy seems to be "keep the root directory clean." This means keep as few files in the root directory as possible (otherwise it gets junked up).

For trivial purposes (again), TABLE 2-7 shows a few of the files that *must* be in the root directory.

Table 2-7

File	Comments
IBMBIO.COM	Hidden, first file on disk
IBMDOS.COM	Hidden, second file on disk
CONFIG.SYS	Must be in the root directory
COMMAND.COM	Could be elsewhere (see previous section)
AUTOEXEC.BAT	Must be in the root directory

Some other programs might require files in the root directory, but it's not common. Other than the above files (two of which are invisible), most root directories have only subdirectory names. The number of subdirectories you have off your root directory is up to you. Several suggestions for keeping the number small are offered in Part Three of this book.

Why keep the number small? First, because a crowded root directory is usually the sign of an inexperienced DOS user. Second, because the root directory can only hold so many files. Once that number of files have been allocated, DOS will tell you the disk is full—even if you have several megabytes of free space on the drive (see TABLE 2-8).

Table 2-8

Disk format	Maximum files in the root directory
160K	64
180K	64
360K	112
720K	112
1.2MB	224
1.44MB	224
Hard Disk	512

A directory utility that comes with DOS is the TREE command.

TREE *drive* /F /A

TREE is used to display a graphic rendition of your hierarchical file system. Optionally, it will also display all the files on your hard drive and where they're located. (But, alas, it will not locate specific files. You need a third-party utility like FINDFILE or WHEREIS for that.)

drive is the name of the disk drive that you want to examine. If *drive* is omitted, the current drive is used.

/F is an optional switch that displays all the files in the subdirectories encountered.

/A is an optional switch that uses ASCII character graphics to display the tree, as opposed to the Extended ASCII characters (which won't copy correctly to some non-IBM printers).

What TREE does is to start with the current directory and work its way alphabetically down the hierarchical directory structure, displaying each directory as it's encountered. If you specify another drive or directory, TREE will display a graphic picture of that drive's hierarchical file structure.

DOS 4.0 offers the most elegant version of TREE—one that displays your directory structure using character graphics rather than simply listing directory names. (For older versions of DOS, try VTREE by Charles Petzold.)

Figure 2-5 is an example of the TREE program's output when the /A switch is specified.

File organization and manipulation

Most of the DOS commands deal with files.

A file is a collection of stuff on disk.

Generally speaking, files contain either data or instructions. Data files can be documents for a word processor, text files, spreadsheet data—anything that doesn't "run" as a program. Instruction files contain programming instructions, which include binary overlays, system drivers, utilities, and applications programs. Blandly speaking, this is all there is to a file system: storing files on disk, using some files as data and using other files as programs (instructions for the microprocessor).

No matter what's in the file, all files share a similar name format. The format of a filename is as follows:

drive path filename.ext

```
Directory PATH listing for Volume 20 MEGGER
Volume Serial Number is 001C-3246
C:\
+---AEPRO
¦    \---DATA
+---ASM
¦    +---BATCH
¦    +---CFONT
¦    +---COM
¦    +---EDITOR
¦    +---MAKETAB
¦    \---TELECOM
+---BASIC
+---BOOKS
¦    +---BATCH
¦    ¦    +---RYAN
¦    ¦    +---DISK
¦    ¦    \---OTHER
¦    +---GROWING
¦    +---SK
¦    \---PAN
+---PLAN
+---SYSTEM
¦    +---BORLAND
¦    ¦    \---DATA
¦    +---DOS
¦    +---HERCULES
¦    +---NORTON
¦    +---TOOLS
¦    +---UTIL
¦    \---MOUSE
¦         \---PAINT
+---TEMP
+---TURBOC
¦    +---BGI
¦    +---INCLUDE
¦    ¦    \---SYS
¦    +---LEARN
¦    \---LIB
\---WORDP
     +---BB
     ¦    +---CFNSC
     ¦    +---COLUMN
     ¦    \---MAJOR
     +---DATA
     \---MJ
```

2-5 Shown here is an example of the TREE program's output.

drive is optional. It specifies the disk drive where the file is located. If the file in question is not on the current disk drive, *drive* must be specified. *drive* is followed by a colon:

A:*filename*

path is the full pathname (all the subdirectories) indicating where the file is on the drive. If the file is in the subdirectory GAMES, then the path is:

    \GAMES

A second backslash must follow games to indicate the complete path:

    \GAMES*filename*

For files in the root directory, only a single backslash is specified:

    filename

or:

    C:*filename*

If the file is in the current directory, the *path* can be omitted.

filename is the important part of a filename. It's a one-to-eight character string (no spaces) identifying the file. Any ASCII or Extended ASCII character can be used to identify a file, save for the following riffraff:

    . " / \ [ ] : * | < > + = ; , ?

Also, the space characters and control characters (ASCII 0 through 31) are not allowed in the filename. A period can be used, but only once and then to define the start of the filename extension.

ext is an optional one-to-three character extension. The power of this extension is one of the most overlooked aspects of DOS file management. Even so-called "experienced" users fail to see the convenience of naming files in a similar category with the same extension. I will now rant on this considerably.

DOS uses only three file extensions to define a program file:

    COM   "Old style" program file
    EXE   Executable program file
    BAT   Batch file

Additionally, these extensions are used by DOS:

    BAK   EDLIN (and other program's) backup file
    BAS   BASIC program file
    CPI   Code page information file
    MOS   Mouse driver
    SYS   Device driver

Aside from these there can be over 9,129,329 possible filename extensions. (That's 256 ASCII characters, minus 32 control characters, space, and 14 reserved characters, cubed.) Granted, not everyone uses the 128 extended ASCII characters in a filename, but it is possible. In fact, using those 128 extended ASCII characters is a clever way to provide system security. (Without the extended ASCII characters, you still have 531,441 variations. Golly.)

Table 2-9 is one of the lists you've probably come across at one time or another in your PC travels. Due to space considerations, of course, this is only a small sample of the over eight dozen "common" extensions I found.

What's the point? The point to all this is that file organization is easier when you have similar file extensions. In some cases, organizing by file extensions is easier than splitting small items off into subdirectories. For example, when I write a book there are several types of files in my working directory. Each of them is marked by a special file extension to make dealing with them easier:

(none)	Working WordPerfect document
WP	Completed WordPerfect document
TXT	Text document
BAT	Batch file
LST	Program listing
TBL	Table
FIG	Figure
SCR	HotShot Graphics figure
PZP	Pizazz Plus figure
@	Document has been proofread, paginated, and is ready to print

These extensions only mean something to myself. Yet they make transferring and copying files much easier. When the finished manuscript needs to go to the publisher, it's a simple DOS command:

```
COPY *.@A:
```

This copies all the finished work to the diskette in drive A without my having manually to search through a directory for the proper files—or scanning several subdirectories for lost files.

Anyone can do this with any files. For example, if a number of people use the same program on one computer, it's a good habit to have each of them use their initials as a file extension. If you have a subdirectory into which you place miscellaneous word processing documents, use the filename extension to provide a little organization. Use LTR for letters, MM for mail merge documents, LST for lists, and so on. (This is all provided that your software allows you to supply your own filename extension. That's not always the case.)

Table 2-9

Extension	(Usually) Defines
ARC	Archive file (multiple files, data compression)
ASM	Assembler source code (text file)
BIN	Binary image file
BK!	Backup file
BMP	Windows bitmap graphics format
C	C language source code (text)
CAL	SuperCalc spreadsheet data file
CBL	COBOL source code (also COB)
CFG	Configuration file
DAT	Data file
DBF	dBASE database file
DEF	Definition file
DIF	Data Interchange Format spreadsheet file
DOC	Text file containing documentation, or Microsoft Word document
DRV	Driver file
FON	Font file
FOR	Fortran source code (text)
FNT	Font file
GIF	Graphic Interchange Format file
H	C language include file
INC	Pascal include file
INI	Windows init or information file
LIB	Library file
MNU	Microsoft Mouse menu file
NDX	An index file in dBASE format
OBJ	Linker or compiler object code
OVL	Overlay file
OVR	Overlay file
PAS	Pascal source code (text)
PCX	PC Paintbrush graphics file
PIC	Lotus 1-2-3 graphic file
PIF	Program Information File for Windows
PRG	dBASE program file
RBS	R:BASE database file
SCR	HotShot Graphics screen file
SLK	SYLK formatted spreadsheet file (also SYL)
TFF	TIFF formatted graphics file
TXT	Text file
TMP	Temporary file
WKS	Lotus 1-2-3 spreadsheet (also WK1)
XLC	Excel spreadsheet (also XLM, XLS, XLW)
ZIP	Archive/file compression formatted file

Using wildcards

Don't be confused about the use of wildcard characters. There are only two of them: * and ?.

? is the single character wildcard. ? matches only one character in the filename. For example:

    D?N

This matches any filename with D as the first letter and N as the third. You can use more than one character ? to match for more than one character. However, the character ? still matches only a single character:

    FILE?.D??

This matches all five-letter filenames, the first four letters of which are FILE. The machine files must also have an extension starting with "D" but followed by any other two characters.

A special note: Even though the character ? can replace one character, it also replaces none. If a file named "FILE.D" were on disk, it will also match the above wildcard.

The character * matches a group of characters. However, the * character isn't as smart as most people assume:

    C> DIR *.*

displays a directory of all files in the current directory.

    C> DIR T*.*

displays a directory of all files in the current directory that start with T and have any file extension.

    C> DIR T*

does the same thing as DIR T*.*

    C> DIR T*.

displays all the files in the current directory starting with the letter T that have no file extension.

    C> DIR T*ING.*

displays all files in the current directory that start with T. The "ING" is ignored because the character * wildcard is not as logical as you may assume. In fact, internally, DOS replaces the character * wildcard with a series of question mark wildcards. So the following:

    T*.*

Becomes:

    T???????.???

The following two commands both display all filenames in the current directory starting with T:

```
C> DIR T*.*
C> DIR T???????.???
```

The most common wildcard is **.**, for the "whole shebang," or every file in the currently logged directory. It's not common knowledge that this wildcard has an abbreviation. It's "." The period is used in the hierarchical file structure to indicate the current directory. (Two periods mean the "parent" directory.) So:

```
C> DIR *.*
```

and

```
C> DIR .
```

Both display a directory of the current directory. Additionally:

```
C> DEL .
```

attempts to delete every file in the current directory. Be careful with that one.

XCOPY

Besides the DIR command, a popular command for using wildcards is the COPY command. However, COPY is slow. It reads and copies one file at a time—even when you specify a group of files using wildcards.

The way the COPY command works internally is to take the file to be copied, read it from disk into memory, then copy it to the destination. If you use a wildcard, DOS translates it (see pages 49-50), then searches for each match one at a time. As each match is found, that file is read into memory, then copied to the destination. This is tedious to say the least.

Rather than fix the COPY command, Microsoft introduced the XCOPY command with DOS 3.2. XCOPY does everything the COPY command does and more. The best improvement is that XCOPY reads all the files to be copied into memory all at once—then it copies them to the destination.

The format for COPY and XCOPY is the same, so you can use XCOPY any time you'd normally use COPY. However, XCOPY has a few new switches—options that come in handy for moving complete subdirectory structures around your hard disk. (This is referred to as "pruning," and it's always best to rearrange your subdirectory structure on Arbor day.)

XCOPY's pruning switches are /S and /E. When specified, the /S switch causes XCOPY to copy all the files matching the wildcard in the current directory—plus all subdirectories under the current directory. The /E switch does the same thing, but it also copies empty subdirectories. This is a great way to move "branches" of your tree structure around without losing anything.

XCOPY has about half a dozen other switches, each of which allows you to copy a specific group of files. Some of the switches make XCOPY behave almost like a mini-BACKUP command. But be warned: XCOPY will not ask you to "insert another diskette" when a floppy gets full (as BACKUP will). The manual reads like XCOPY is capable of copying files across several diskettes. But that's just not the case.

Orientation

DOS keeps track of every drive in your system, as well as which directory is currently logged for that drive. All DOS computers have an A drive, the first floppy disk drive. Some computers have a second internal floppy drive, B, and nearly all computers now have hard drives, C.

If your computer only has one internal floppy drive, it's A. However, a second "logical drive," B also exists. To prove it, type B: on your single drive system:

```
Insert diskette for drive B: and strike
any key when ready
```

The physical drive A has just become the logical drive B. Microsoft did this to make copying disks (and using a single drive system—which is crazy) possible. DOS keeps track of whether the physical drive A is presently logical drive B or logical drive A, and it will instruct you to change disks if needed.

Besides all these logical assumptions, DOS keeps track of the currently logged directory for each (logical) drive in the system. To see how this works, you can use the CD command to display the currently logged directory of a specific drive. Just type the drive letter and colon after CD (see FIG. 2-6).

2-6 You can use the CD command to display the currently logged directory of a specific drive.

```
C> CD A:
A:\

C> CD B:
B:\EBL

C> CD C:
C:\WP\BOOKS\BATCH
```

It's important to know that DOS remembers the currently logged directory when dealing with multiple file systems. In fact, quite a few gurus will make a so-called bozo mistake by typing the following:

```
C> COPY *.* A:
```

Most would assume that this means copy all the files in the current directory to the root directory on drive A. In fact, many people assume that if you're not logged to a particular disk drive, then all references to that drive are to the root directory. Wrong. Wrong. Wrong. If, for the above example, drive A is logged to the subdirectory BACKUPS, then all the files will be copied to that subdirectory. This could possibly cause some devastating effects, including mental anguish.

Because of this, it's important to know about DOS's orientation, or "where everything is." Never assume anything to be where you "think" it is. This gets very important later when you'll use the JOIN and SUBST commands to create a multitude of pseudo disk drives and subdirectories on your system.

DOS orientation refers to its ability to keep track of where everything is. Orientation allows you to type COPY A:*.* and have DOS know that you want all the files from drive A to be copied to your current directory. DOS knows the orientation, so this is possible.

As an example of orientation, consider the following. A group of files are in the \GAMES\KIDS directory on drive C. You want to copy them to the subdirectory \DAVID on drive A. The absolute safest way to do this is:

```
C> COPY C:\GAMES\KIDS\*.* A:\DAVID
```

This makes no assumptions. Yet, it's a lot of typing for one command. Three other (separate) commands could do the same thing, as follows:

```
C> A:
A> CD \DAVID
A> COPY C:\GAMES\KIDS\*.*
```

In the last command, DOS assumes the target directory (where all the files are to be copied to) is the currently logged directory on drive A. The full pathname for all the files could have been omitted if the following command were used first:

```
C> CD \GAMES\KIDS
```

This initially logs drive C to the KIDS subdirectory. Now the final command could be:

```
A> COPY C:*.*
```

It's very easy to mess up a complex system by making assumptions. It's even easier when you use batch files (and it's harder, in that case, to detect and trap the errors). So be aware of DOS's orientation when writing batch file copying routines.

Filters, pipes, and I/O redirection

Besides being able to bandy about the various devices using DOS's file copying functions, you can also take advantage of devices using filters, pipes and I/O redirection. This is one of the best aspects of DOS and one of the least understood.

You know DOS deals with the input and output of each of the various devices. However, there are ways of using DOS that allow you to intercept the input or output of a device, modify it, change it, or send it to someplace else. For example, you can send output that normally goes to the screen to the printer, or to a file, or to any other device. Or, you can modify the input or output of a device by use of a filter program. All this is possible because DOS is device-oriented.

Before getting into this, you should know that only programs using the standard input and output DOS calls can take advantage of filters, pipes and I/O redirection. These include all of the DOS functions, plus a few utilities. Rarely will sophisticated applications programs, such as spreadsheets, databases, and word processors, use DOS's input and output functions.

I/O redirection

Normally, unless told otherwise, DOS uses so-called standard devices for input and output. The standard input device is the keyboard. The standard output device is the screen. An example of using standard output is the DIR command. Normally, DIR sends its output to the CONsole device. Standard input is done by the keyboard, also the CONsole device. When a DOS program, such as EDLIN or DEBUG, asks for input, the input is provided by the keyboard. However, DOS allows you to perform input/output redirection, meaning that the standard input and output devices don't necessarily have to be the CONsole (keyboard and screen).

To redirect standard input or output, the less-than and greater-than symbols are used. (This is why they are reserved characters and cannot be part of a filename.)

    <   Redirect standard input
    >   Redirect standard output

Either symbol is followed by the name of a device that will either provide input or output, replacing the standard devices. When DOS evaluates a command you've typed at the system prompt, it looks for either < or >. If either one or both is encountered, DOS makes the appropriate adjustments and redirects input or output to the indicated device(s).

For example, the output of the DIR command normally goes to the standard output device, the CONsole. You can redirect the output to the printer device, PRN, to get a hard copy of your directory listing:

    C> DIR > PRN

Or, just as easily, you could direct the output of the DIR command to a file. This would allow you to look at and edit the directory listing using a word processor or text editor:

    C> DIR > DIRFILE.TXT

An interesting use of redirected output is a small DOS command I use to eject a page from the printer. ECHO is a batch file command used to "echo" a string of text to the CONsole. However, using I/O redirection, I can echo my string to the printer:

```
C> ECHO ^L > PRN
```

This sends the character CTRL – L to the printer, forcing a new page. If you use batch files to print lists of information, you might want to include the above command at the end of the file to eject a page for the user.

You can also use redirected output to make a copy of a text file. Suppose you have a text file DOCS. To make a copy of it, try:

```
C> TYPE DOCS > DOCSCOPY
```

Normally, TYPE sends its output to the standard output device. However, > redirects the output to the file DOCSCOPY. Remember the NUL device? I mentioned that using I/O redirection and the NUL device, you can create blank files. Here's how:

```
C> TYPE NUL > TEMP
```

The output of the NUL device is sent to a file TEMP. Because NUL contains nothing, the file TEMP will as well (see FIG. 2-7).

One drawback to redirecting output to a file is, like so many other DOS commands, that if the file already exists, it will be overwritten. With the example in FIG. 2-7, if TEMP is already on disk, the redirected output from the NUL device will overwrite the old TEMP file, effectively erasing it. DOS will give you no warning when this happens. But there is a half-way solution.

2-7 TEMP is a file generated by output from the NUL device.
```
C> DIR TEMP

 Volume in drive D is DIRTY
 Volume Serial Number is 00CC-1701
 Directory of  D:\EXAMPLES

TEMP                 0   6-14-88   10:55p
         1 File(s)     165920 bytes free
```

A variation on output redirection is the double greater-than sign, > >, or redirect standard output with append.

> > Redirect standard output/append

The > > characters work just like output redirection with a single greater-than sign, except when the output is directed to a file, it's *appended* to that file. (This is yet another trick borrowed from UNIX/Xenix.) For example:

```
C> DIR > DIRFILE
```

The output of the DIR command is sent to the file DIRFILE. If DIRFILE already exists, it's overwritten, otherwise DIRFILE is created. If you type a second command:

C> DIR > > DIRFILE

The output of the DIR command is now appended to whatever is already inside DIRFILE. Again, if DIRFILE doesn't exist, it's created. (Later you'll see how > > can be used to create an on-going log of who uses the computer at what time.)

Redirected input using the less-than sign, <, is a little trickier than redirected output. Because all input is provided from a device other than the keyboard, that device (usually a file) must have *all* the proper keystrokes stored in it. (This isn't as difficult as it seems, just tricky.)

The following commands are used with EDLIN to create a brief text file:

```
I
This is a brief text file.
^C
E
```

Each line is followed by a carriage return, just as you'd press ENTER when typing those commands in EDLIN. Note that ^C is a CTRL–C.

Normally, all those keystrokes would be used to create a very short text file in EDLIN. However, consider that the keystrokes are saved in a text file called INPUT. INPUT can be used with < to provide the input for EDLIN. When typed at the system prompt, you'll see what's displayed in FIG. 2-8.

2-8   The file INPUT can be used to provide the input for EDLIN.

```
C> EDLIN BRIEF.TXT < INPUT
New file
*I
        1:*This is a brief text file.
        2:*^C

*
*E

C>
```

This all happens quickly—you never touch the keyboard. DOS reads the input from the file INPUT to create BRIEF.TXT. Later in this book, you'll see how complex programs are created using redirected input and the DEBUG program.

First, a word of warning: When providing input to a file using <, *all* of the program's input must be in the file. If for some reason the file supplies the wrong input, your computer might freeze. Your keyboard control might be lost with some programs because, after all, you've told DOS to get input from a file or some other device. In this case, the only recourse is to whack the reset button.

Normally, as long as you're careful about your keystrokes and know the program you're redirecting the input to very well, you should have no problems.

Filters and pipes

Filters and pipes also deal with I/O redirection, but in a different way. The filter intercepts the input, or more commonly the output of a program and modifies it. The pipe is a device that allows the output of one program to be used as the input for another. Pipes and filters are not two separate items. Instead, they work together to modify the input or output of DOS and other programs that use standard input and output.

DOS comes with three filter programs:

FIND   Locates a string in a text file
MORE   Pauses the display after a screen full of text
SORT   Sorts text files

Note that even though "text files" are mentioned, the filter programs actually rely upon standard input. In fact, I've found that quite a few neophyte DOS users will often type the following at their command prompt to test the SORT filter:

C> SORT

They press ENTER and DOS just sits there. No, nothing is wrong. It's just that SORT is waiting for something to sort, in this case, standard input from the keyboard. If you type:

APPLES
ORANGES
GRAPES

And then press CTRL – Z, SORT displays:

APPLES
GRAPES
ORANGES

SORT has just sorted standard input and displayed the results as standard output. Normally, SORT doesn't use standard input and output in this way. Instead, as with the other two filters (and any additional filters other programmers may write), SORT relies on a text file or other DOS command to replace standard input.

For example, to sort a text file containing a list of items, I/O redirection is used:

C> SORT < FRUIT

Suppose FRUIT is a file containing an alphabetical list of fruits. The SORT filter will read input from that file (provided by DOS's I/O redirection) and display the sorted list to the CONsole. If you want the sorted list in another file, use I/O redirection to create the file:

```
C> SORT < FRUIT > FRUITSRT
```

The MORE filter is used to pause long displays of text. MORE displays the message "Press any key to continue" after every 23 lines of text have scrolled up the screen. This avoids the necessity of pressing CTRL–S every so often to pause a long display.

To use MORE as a filter for displaying a long text file, use I/O redirection as follows:

```
C> MORE < LONGTEXT
```

There will be more examples of these and other filters later in the book. Just remember that they rely upon standard input and most often that input is provided from a file (or DOS command) using I/O redirection.

Using these filters on DOS commands is different than using them on plain text files. After all, if you type:

```
C> DIR > MORE
```

You create a text file called "MORE" that contains the current directory. And you can't type:

```
C> MORE < DIR
```

unless you have a text file on disk named "DIR".

The way around this is to use the pipe. The pipe uses the output of one command as the input for another. Because DIR uses standard output, you can use the pipe to make that output the standard input of a filter.

The pipe character is the vertical bar, |. Some displays show that character with a space in the middle, so it looks like a tall lowercase I. To use the pipe, position it between the command providing the output and the command requiring the input:

```
C> DIR | SORT
```

This reads: take the output of the DIR command and use it as the input for the SORT command. What you'll see on the screen is a sorted directory listing. (This example was used at the end of chapter 1 for a sorted directory batch file.) Note that you must define the %TEMP% environmental variable to use the pipe—refer to chapter 4.

If you want the sorted directory saved to a file, you can add I/O redirection:

```
C> DIR | SORT > ZIGNORE
```

To summarize, use I/O redirection to channel output or input of a program from the standard output or input device to another device. Use a filter to modify the output or input of a device. And use the pipe to cause the output of one command to be used as the input of another.

One final note:

> You cannot use piping or I/O redirection on the same command line with a batch file

The symbols |, <, and > are not allowed after the name of a batch file on the command line. However, if you do want to redirect all the output of a batch file or use the pipe, the COMMAND /C command can be used. For example,

```
COMMAND /C filename.BAT
```

Filename is the name of your batch file. After it, you either can place whatever I/O symbols you want to redirect or pipe the output elsewhere. This only works with the COMMAND command, however.

Multiple programs at once

A final interesting thing about DOS is its ability to run more than one program at once. This isn't the classic sense of multitasking, where more than one thing is going on at a time. Instead, DOS has the ability to load and execute more than one program. It's like stacking several books inside a box: you can have a number of books in the box, but you're only allowed to read from or use one of them at a time.

There are two ways DOS runs more than one program at a time. The first is by making the program *memory-resident*. The second method is where DOS leaves one program to run a second program, which is called *shelling*. Both of these methods involve different programming and they lead to different results.

Memory-resident

Memory-resident programs are just like other programs in every respect except for the way they quit. When a program quits, it calls one of the many DOS quit functions (there are five of them). These quit functions, shown in TABLE 2-10, are low-level machine language vectors to internal DOS routines.

To quit and return to the DOS command prompt, a programmer will choose one of the functions in TABLE 2-10. The normal way programs quit is through Interrupt 20h and Interrupt 21h, functions zero and 4Ch. These three functions simply return control to COMMAND.COM and release the memory taken by the program, freeing it up for other functions. Interrupt 21h function 4Ch is considered the most preferable

Table 2-10

Interrupt	Function	Description
20h	none	Return to COMMAND.COM
21h	0	Terminate program (same as above)
21h	31h	Terminate and stay resident (TSR)
21h	4Ch	Terminate with return code (best)
27h	none	Terminate and stay resident (semi-dangerous)

method because it allows the program to generate a "return code." This return code can be evaluated by batch files as an ERRORLEVEL, which you'll discover later in this book. The other two functions will also quit to DOS, but without a return code.

Memory-resident programs use Interrupt 21h function 31h or Interrupt 27h to quit. These are known as the Terminate but Stay Resident routines, which is why some call memory-resident programs "TSRs."

Unlike a normal program, a TSR exit quits the program but does not release the memory used by the program. DOS keeps the program in memory and then loads a new resident copy of COMMAND.COM "on top" of the memory-resident program. The user can go on using DOS without knowing the program he just ran is still lurking in memory.

The tricky part about memory-resident programs is that they hook into low-level routines inside the computer. For example, they may steal the keyboard routines to check for certain keystrokes. Most likely, they steal a low-level interrupt used by the PC's timer chip. This chip "ticks" 18.5 times a second. A programmer will modify the interrupt used by the timer chip so that his code will be executed every time the chip ticks. When this happens, the dormant code in memory becomes active and the program runs, suspending whatever else is going on. Needless to say, writing these programs is tricky and only a few can peacefully exist in many computer systems.

The reason memory-resident programs were written was so they'd always be available, or to allow them to modify some part of your system. A simple type of memory-resident program is a clock that may display the current time in the upper right corner of your screen. The memory-resident clock program may monitor the system's time and display it on the screen—even though you may be using some other program.

The most popular type of memory-resident program is the "pop-up" application. These are usually (though not limited to) mini-programs that serve some handy function, such as an appointment calendar or calculator. These programs monitor keyboard input for certain key combinations. For example, a calculator program may wait for you to press ALT – C. Once pressed, the memory-resident program suspends all other computer operations and, zip!, you have a calculator on your screen.

Some users love these programs. They just can't live without their memory-resident software. Personally, I must profess that I find these programs annoying. They take up too much memory and often are incompatible with other software.

Another drawback to memory-resident software is that once it's in memory it's usually there to stay. Only a few memory-resident programs allow themselves to be removed. Even then, they must be removed in the exact order they were placed in memory. Otherwise, your system will go down in a blaze of glory.

Starting with DOS.5, you can load memory resident programs into high memory, into locations called Upper Memory Blocks (UMBs). This is done only on 80386 or later PCs with special DOS memory commands. Other systems and non-DOS 5 users can take advantage of third-party programs that do the same things. This is all covered in chapter 5.

Shelling

The second method of running more than one program at a time is technically referred to as the MS-DOS EXEC function. Commonly, it's known as "shelling" out of a program. The primary difference between leaving a program memory-resident and shelling is that shelling provides a quick way to get back to the original program.

Shelling operates similarly to the terminate-but-stay-resident situation. The difference is that the program you leave in memory just waits there, unlike a memory-resident program that could "pop up" at any given time. What shelling allows you to do is leave one program in memory, return to DOS and run another program. You can also, optionally, avoid DOS and just run the second program directly.

A good example of shelling is in the writing of this book. If I need to write a quick demonstration batch file, I can "shell out" of this word processor and return to DOS. My word processor, complete with my text, is still in memory—sitting there, waiting. While in DOS, I can write batch files, even run other programs (though there's not much memory left over). Then, once I'm done, I return to the word processor by using the EXIT command. Shelling lets me do this and save a few steps.

Why shell? The reasons for shelling will differ depending on who uses it. Most people don't understand what's going on, so they never bother. What it boils down to is that shelling is handy. When a program allows you to shell, it gives you the freedom to immediately return to DOS to perform some other activity. The original program, the "parent," is still in memory, intact. To return to it, type EXIT and you're back where you started. This avoids having to save your information, quit the program, then return to DOS, do what you want done, re-load the program, and start over. It's handy.

An example

When you shell you have two choices. The MS-DOS EXEC function allows a program name to be specified as a "child." So, you can shell to a second child program, or you can shell to DOS by specifying COMMAND.COM as the child program. (Most applications do this automatically.)

In fact, you can shell to a new copy of COMMAND.COM at any time by typing \COMMAND at your system prompt. This runs the COMMAND.COM program in your root directory. You see something like:

```
C> \COMMAND
Microsoft(R) MS-DOS(R) Version 3.30
    (C)Copyright Microsoft Corp 1981-1988
```

You are now in a shell program, in this case you're running a second copy of COMMAND.COM. The original copy is still there in memory, just as an applications program would be had you shelled from it.

To prove that you're running COMMAND.COM you could check your system's memory size and notice a decrease of several thousand bytes. Or, better yet, change your command prompt. Type:

```
C> PROMPT I'm in a shell$g
```

This changes your command prompt to:

```
I'm in a shell>
```

When the second copy of COMMAND.COM was loaded, it copied what is known as the system environment over from the old, original copy of COMMAND.COM. One of the items contained in the environment is your system prompt. In the new copy of COMMAND.COM, you've just changed that prompt. When EXIT is typed, the new COMMAND.COM will be removed from memory, and you'll be returned to the original COMMAND.COM with your original system prompt. Type EXIT to get out of the shell:

```
I'm in a shell> EXIT
C>
```

You're now back at the original command prompt. The second copy of COMMAND.COM, with its modified environment and prompt is gone. If you had shelled from a word processor or other application, you'd now be back in that program. (The PROMPT command and the environment are covered in chapter 4.)

Shelling is another way that DOS can run more than one program at a time. Running a second copy of COMMAND.COM may seem a little redundant now, but later you'll learn that sometimes it's necessary to create a larger environment, or when you want to modify your system without messing with the original COMMAND.COM.

Summary

There is more to DOS than many users think. The fact that this is the fattest chapter in this book proves that. Yet, this chapter has only begun to scratch the surface. The important points covered were:

- DOS is based on older operating systems and this explains why some things are done some ways (such as filenames and the way programs are loaded).
- DOS is device-oriented. This means that DOS isn't limited to manipulation of files on disk. Different devices can interact via DOS, which makes it a more flexible operating system and allows such things as I/O redirection and the use of filters and pipes.
- DOS uses a hierarchical file system, similar to UNIX and Xenix. This allows files to be organized into subdirectories. DOS's method of naming files can also be used for further file organization.
- DOS remembers the currently logged directory for each drive in your system. This should be taken into consideration when copying files.
- Using I/O redirection, filters and pipes, the input and output of DOS commands can be manipulated.
- DOS allows more than one program to be in memory at a time. Memory-resident programs are loaded and then stay in memory. Shelling also allows a program to stay in memory, but provides a way to return to the original program.

3
Extra control with ANSI.SYS

One of the most misunderstood, yet most often used, goodies that comes with DOS is the ANSI.SYS driver. ANSI.SYS not only provides codes that enhance the way information is displayed on the screen, but it can redefine your keyboard, give you the ability to create more interesting system prompts, and really spice up some boring batch files.

Very few users bother to tread on the grounds of ANSI.SYS. Mostly, their reasons are that the ANSI commands aren't well documented. Another reason may be that there aren't enough interesting or useful examples to build upon. This chapter provides both of those: all the ANSI .SYS commands documented, as well as interesting examples for everything.

Also, as an added bonus, several ANSI.SYS replacements are covered, including FANSI-CONSOLE, NANSI.SYS and ZANSI.SYS. These alternative screen-drivers offer more ANSI compatibility and versatility than the ANSI.SYS driver provided with DOS. And that means you can do more tricks with them.

All of these ANSI tricks can be incorporated into your batch files later, giving you more control over your computer system.

ANSI.SYS is a device driver that controls your screen and keyboard—the CONsole device. A device driver is a low-level routine loaded when DOS is booted (specified in the CONFIG.SYS file). The purpose of a device driver is to modify the input and output of a device. Because DOS is device-oriented, it's easy to control the way devices behave by using a device driver.

DOS comes with several device drivers, as shown in TABLE 3-1.

Table 3-1

Driver name	Device	Controls
ANSI.SYS	Console	Character display and can be used to modify keyboard input
DISPLAY.SYS	Screen	Used with the Enhanced Graphics Adapter (EGA), laptops, and foreign computers to allow "code page switching."
DRIVER.SYS	Disk	Sets the capacity of external drives; indirectly allows PCs and XTs to support a 720K $3\frac{1}{2}$ inch floppy drive.
PRINTER.SYS	Printer	Used with IBM's Proprinter and QuietWriter III printers to allow code page switching, similar to the DISPLAY.SYS driver.
VDISK.SYS	none	Simulates a disk drive using Random Access Memory (RAM).

Two other SYS commands also come with DOS. These are not device drivers, and should never be used that way in a CONFIG.SYS file:

COUNTRY.SYS   Contains time, date, capitalization and other information for using DOS in various countries besides the USA.

KEYBOARD.SYS   Used by the KEYB command to allow non-American keyboards to be used with DOS.

There are also third-party device drivers, for example, MOUSE.SYS, which controls the Microsoft mouse. Three public domain/shareware ANSI.SYS replacements, FANSI-CONSOLE (actually called FCONSOLE.DEV), NAN SI.SYS and ZANSI.SYS, are covered at the end of this section.

ANSI.SYS installation

Device drivers are installed into your system's CONFIG.SYS file and loaded when you boot your machine. (If you change CONFIG.SYS, you must reboot for the change to take effect.) They are used by the CON FIG.SYS directive DEVICE, followed by an equal sign (=), followed by the full pathname of the device driver (including a drive letter if it's not on drive C and a path if it's not in the root directory).

For example, a CONFIG.SYS file with ANSI.SYS in it could look like this:

```
BUFFERS = 32
FILES = 20
DEVICE = C:\SYSTEM\DOS\DRIVER.SYS /D:1 /T:80 /S:9 /H:2 /F:2
DEVICE = C:\SYSTEM\DOS\ANSI.SYS
DEVICE = C:\SYSTEM\MOUSE\MOUSE.SYS
```

(More information about CONFIG.SYS is provided in chapter 5.)

For years I was putting the ANSI.SYS device driver into my own CON FIG.SYS file and never knew what it did. Oh, I knew that it controlled the screen display. In fact, on one clone I've worked with you had to have the ANSI.SYS driver installed or your screen wouldn't clear when you typed CLS at the command prompt. But ANSI.SYS goes beyond controlling the screen.

Without jumping ahead to material already covered in chapter 5, to install the ANSI.SYS driver in your system you simply need to add the line:

```
DEVICE = ANSI.SYS
```

to your CONFIG.SYS file. If ANSI.SYS is not in your root directory, include its full pathname.

Once the above line (or something similar) is in CONFIG.SYS, reboot your machine and you'll be able to access the ANSI device driver. Now the fun begins.

ANSI.SYS has three optional switches: /X, /L, and /K. These switches give the ANSI.SYS driver more control over your system.

/X is used for reassigning extended keyboard keys, most notably F11 and F12 along with the arrows and other additional keys that didn't appear on earlier keyboards. Older versions of ANSI.SYS, to be compatible, ignore these keys.

/L is used by ANSI.SYS to retain the number of rows on the screen. Using ANSI.SYS, the MODE command, and a high resolution graphics adapter, you can change the number of rows displayed on your monitor. Some applications programs may change that value back to the default of 25. When the /L switch is specified, ANSI.SYS will attempt to keep the number or rows you want, regardless of whether or not an applications program changes it. It also helps when using the Clear Screen ANSI command to have your entire screen cleared, not just the traditional 80×25 patch of characters.

/K suppresses the detection of extended keyboard functions. This switch can be used with older programs that may not understand, or detect, extended keyboard functions.

ANSI

ANSI stands for the American National Standards Institute. The institute defines a number of standards for use with computers. For example, there's the ANSI standard BASIC programming language. The funny thing about that one is that no one uses it; Microsoft GW BASIC is by far more popular than the ANSI standard. (Which makes you wonder who pays those ANSI people.)

ANSI has also defined a method for screen and keyboard control, and this is the standard that's employed by DOS's ANSI.SYS driver. These screen controlling commands use "escape sequences" to control output to the screen, as well as to redefine the keyboard. An escape sequence is a series of codes sent to the screen, with the first code being the ESCape character, ASCII 27.

The ANSI.SYS driver included with DOS actually uses a subset, or only a few of the commands defined by ANSI. Other screen drivers, such as FANSI-CONSOLE, NANSI.SYS and ZANSI.SYS, use most or all of the ANSI defined escape sequences. (The drawback is that not all DOS machines use those two alternative drivers.)

There are good and bad things about the ANSI.SYS driver. The good thing is that, assuming all DOS machines have it installed, programs which take advantage of the ANSI escape sequences to control the screen are compatible with all DOS machines.

The bad thing about the ANSI.SYS driver is that it's slow. Because of this, most programs write to the computer's screen hardware directly, circumventing DOS and the ANSI.SYS driver. But from DOS, and in the case of batch files, ANSI.SYS is a blessing.

ANSI escape sequences

All ANSI commands start with the ESCape character (ASCII 27). This is immediately followed by a left bracket, [(ASCII 91). Following those two characters are the codes that tell ANSI how to control your console. These codes are somewhat similar to Digital Equipment Corp.'s VT100 terminal control codes, though far more limited.

The problem with the ANSI control sequences starting the ESCape is that you can't readily enter the ESCape character from your keyboard. From DOS, pressing ESCape cancels the current line. In most word processors, ESCape changes mode or performs some other command. Even using the ALT-keypad trick (see appendix A) won't work properly. However, there is one common way around this: EDLIN.

Though everyone who uses DOS hates EDLIN, it's one of the few text editors around that lets you enter the ESCape character safely and sanely from the keyboard.

No, you can't press ESCape in EDLIN—that cancels the current line just as with DOS (both EDLIN and DOS use the same keyboard input routines). Instead, you type a CTRL – V and then follow that with the uppercase ASCII character corresponding to any control key.

EDLIN Trick: Press CTRL – V and follow it with an uppercase letter to insert a control character.

Table 3-2 shows which control characters are associated with other ASCII characters (also refer to appendix A).

Table 3-2

Control	Char.	Decimal	Hex	ASCII Char.
^@	NUL	0	00h	@
^A	SOH	1	01h	A
^B	STX	2	02h	B
^C	ETX	3	03h	C
^D	EOT	4	04h	D
^E	ENQ	5	05h	E
^F	ACK	6	06h	F
^G	BEL	7	07h	G
^H	BS	8	08h	H
^I	HT	9	09h	I
^J	LF	10	0Ah	J
^K	VT	11	0Bh	K
^L	FF	12	0Ch	L
^M	CR	13	0Dh	M
^N	SO	14	0Eh	N
^O	SI	15	0Fh	O
^P	DLE	16	10h	P
^Q	DC1	17	11h	Q
^R	DC2	18	12h	R
^S	DC3	19	13h	S
^T	DC4	20	14h	T
^U	NAK	21	15h	U
^V	SYN	22	16h	V
^W	ETB	23	17h	W
^X	CAN	24	18h	X
^Y	EM	25	19h	Y
^Z	SUB	26	1Ah	Z
^[	ESC	27	1Bh	[
^\	FS	28	1Ch	\
^]	GS	29	1Dh	]
^^	RS	30	1Eh	^
^_	US	31	1Fh	_

To include an ESCape in an EDLIN file, first type CTRL–V, then a left bracket. EDLIN displays this as "^V[". However, when you edit the file a second time, you'll see "^[" listed for the ESCape character. Note that you must type the exact corresponding ASCII character as case is sensitive. Typing CTRL–V followed by a lowercase "a" does not insert a ^A into your text. It must be an uppercase "A", just as in the chart on page 67.

Of course, if you have a word processor that allows embedded control characters, you can use them. For example, most WordStar-like editors, including the MS-DOS editor and my favorite—QEdit, use the CTRL – P prefix. Pressing CTRL – P opens up the keyboard. It's like saying, "Whatever you type next, I'll literally accept it." Any key from ENTER to ESCape is then inserted into your text file—but only if you type a CTRL – P first.

The purpose here is to get the ESCape character into a file to control the ANSI.SYS driver. Once this is done, you can write batch files that take advantage of the ANSI commands. (As an aside, ESCape is the only ASCII control character used by the ANSI driver; all other code values are entered using the ASCII characters "0" through "9.")

Once you get ESCape into a file, you'll want to output it to the screen via DOS. ANSI codes only work when they're interpreted by DOS. Spitting the same codes out to the BIOS or directly to the screen (two common and faster display methods than using piddly old DOS) won't be interpreted by the ANSI driver. So to use ANSI you can either TYPE the file or redirect its output to the screen—or use any command that sends its output directly to the CONsole device.

ANSI commands

There are two categories of ANSI commands: Screen formatting control and keyboard control. Screen formatting commands are further divided into cursor movement commands and character display commands (see TABLE 3-3).

Each of the above commands is associated with an ANSI escape sequence. The escape sequence for each ANSI command is prefixed by two characters: ESC and the left bracket, [. Any other characters appearing in the command string are case sensitive. All capitals must remain capitals and lowercase letters must be used in lowercase for the ANSI commands to work.

Various examples of the commands are placed through the rest of this chapter. A complete list of ANSI commands is provided in appendix B.

Screen manipulating examples

Table 3-4 is a list of ANSI commands that will do strange things to your display. "ESC" is used here to represent the ESCape character. Because ESC is always followed by a [(left bracket) in the ANSI scheme of things, don't let ESC[confuse you:

Erase Display clears your screen the same as typing CLS. In fact, to prove that, try the following:

    C> CLS > TEMPFILE

Table 3-3

ANSI commands	Cursor movement
Locate Cursor	Move cursor to row/column coordinate
Position Cursor	Same as above
Move Cursor Up	Move cursor up one row
Move Cursor Down	Move cursor down one row
Move Cursor Right	Move cursor right one column
Move Cursor Left	Move cursor left one column
Save Cursor Position	Stores cursor's current position
Restore Cursor Position	Restores position saved with above command

Character display	
Erase Display	Clears the screen (same as CLS)
Erase Line	Erases from the cursor's position to the end of the line
Set Graphics Rendition	Changes color/attributes of displayed text
Set/Reset Mode	Changes screen mode
Character Wrap On/Off	Turns character wrap on/off

Keyboard control	
Key Reassignment	Replaces one character with another
String Reassignment	Replaces one character with a string

Table 3-4

ANSI command	ESC sequence	What it does
Erase Display	ESC[2J	Clear screen, home cursor
Set Graphics Rendition	ESC[34m	Change text color to blue
Position Cursor	ESC[12;1H	Move to row 12, column 1

This redirects the output of CLS (which is redirectable, by the way) to the file TEMPFILE. If you have a file-peeker program, you can examine the contents of TEMPFILE to see that it contains the ANSI escape sequence for Erase Display (in hex: 1B 5B 32 4A). Also, if you have the ANSI.SYS driver installed (and you should), you can type TYPE TEMPFILE at your command prompt and it will clear your screen. Nifty.

Set Graphics Rendition is one of the more popular ANSI commands—on a color display. It changes the text color, foreground and background, as well as other display attributes. (If you try changing color on a monochrome monitor it usually changes display attributes to underline, flashing, bold, or a combination of each—including the dreaded invisible text.)

If you've studied the way color text graphics are programmed on the PC, you'll notice that there's little logic to the way ANSI programs its screen colors (see below). Normally, the PC uses bit positions to determine text foreground and background color, so a logical pattern is created among the various text color commands. But ANSI's text color commands are different. (It's probably because ANSI is a standard across many computers, not just the PC.)

The ANSI command to Set Graphics Rendition, or change the color, is:

ESC[n;nm

n is replaced by an ASCII number sequence (rather than a numeric value) to change the color of the text display. There can be any number of n's listed in this command, each of which is separated by a semicolon.

The code values to change the color are in TABLE 3-5.

Table 3-5

ANSI code	Text color	Monochrome
0	Normal	Normal (white on black)
1	High-intensity	High-intensity
2	Normal-intensity	Normal-intensity
4	Blue	Underline
5	Blinking	Blinking
7	Inverse video	Inverse video
8	Invisible text	Invisible text
30	Black foreground	
31	Red foreground	
32	Green foreground	
33	Yellow foreground	
34	Blue foreground	Underline
35	Magenta foreground	
36	Cyan foreground	
37	White foreground	
40	Black background	
41	Red background	
42	Green background	
43	Yellow background	
44	Blue background	
45	Magenta background	
46	Cyan background	
47	White background	

Finally, the *Position cursor* sequence does what it says, it moves the cursor to any row or column on the screen. If you've programmed a PC compatible before, and used the BIOS cursor positioning routines, note that ANSI starts numbering rows and columns with one, not zero.

The format for Position Cursor is:

ESC[*row;column*H

A second, though unpopular, version of the same command is:

ESC[*row;column*f

The values for *row* are from 1 (the top row) through 25 (the bottom row). For *column*, the values range from 1 (left side) through 80 (right side). If either *row* or *column* is omitted, 1 is used. (If you leave out *row*, remember the semicolon.)

An ANSI example

The following batch file uses the commands in TABLE 3-4 to clear the screen, display text in blue (or underline), and then move the cursor to line 12. It uses the ECHO command to send the ANSI sequences to the screen.

Just to show you how EDLIN can be used, the following describes a step-by-step outline for entering the batch file. First, type the name of the batch file, EXAMPLE.BAT, after EDLIN at the command prompt:

```
C>EDLIN EXAMPLE.BAT
New file
*
```

EDLIN displays its * prompt character. To insert the lines of this batch file, press I, then type:

```
1:*@ECHO OFF
2:*ECHO ^V[[2J
3:*ECHO ^V[[34m
4:*ECHO Feeling Blue?
5:*ECHO ^V[[0m
6:*ECHO ^V[[12;1H
7:*^C
```

CTRL–C is typed to stop input. Remember to press CTRL–V to get ^V to display. Typing a caret followed by a "V" does not activate the control character entering ability of EDLIN. (You need to get those ESC characters in there.) Also, if you're using a DOS version prior to Version 3.3, don't precede the ECHO command in line one with the @, "at" sign.

After CTRL–C is pressed, you're returned to the * prompt. Type 1P to "print" from the first line to the last, displaying your input:

*1P

```
     1:@ECHO OFF
     2: ECHO ^[[2J
     3: ECHO ^[[34m
     4: ECHO Feeling Blue?
     5: ECHO ^[[0m
     6:*ECHO ^[[12;1H
```

Finally, type E to save the file EXAMPLE.BAT to disk.

When you run EXAMPLE.BAT, it will clear your screen, display "Feeling Blue?" in the color blue (or underline on monochrome screens), then move the cursor to line 12.

Before moving on, I should point out what's wrong with this batch file. First, there are no REM statements commenting the code. This is bad because it makes modifying the code difficult. For example, what does line 5 do? (It returns the text back to normal, otherwise everything displayed after this batch file is run will be blue.)

Second, this whole batch file could be written in one line. If you can do it, go ahead and use EDLIN to create the new batch file. Otherwise, take a peek at this example:

```
@ECHO ^[[2J^[[34mFeeling Blue?^[[0m^[[12;1H
```

The only reason the first example wasn't all one line was to make it easier to read. You may elect to move all your ANSI commands on one line when doing your own batch files. It has the advantage of being much faster than the above example (because DOS doesn't have to keep reading the batch file from disk for each new screen formatting command).

Also, you should intersplice them with some comments to make future referencing easier (see FIG. 3-1).

3-1 Intersplice batch files with comments to make future reference easier.

```
 1: @ECHO OFF
 2: REM ANSI display example
 3: REM First, clear the screen
 4: ECHO ^[[2J
 5: REM Turn on Blue foreground color, underline monochrome
 6: ECHO ^[[34m
 7: REM Display our message
 8: ECHO Feeling Blue?
 9: REM Reset color back to normal
10: ECHO ^[[0m
11: REM Move cursor to row 12, column 1
12: ECHO ^[[12;1H
```

Determining ANSI's status

One of the drawbacks to ANSI.SYS is that you can't readily tell if ANSI .SYS is active or not. Nothing looks uglier than spewing out a slew of ANSI codes to dazzle your user, only to find out they don't have ANSI.SYS installed. The resulting display is about as gross as your windshield after a long car trip.

The sad part is DOS offers no real solution to figure out if ANSI.SYS is active or not. However, a utility available on the supplemental programs diskette will help. It uses some ANSI screen positioning commands to move the cursor about. Then it uses DOS's internal controls to monitor the cursor's position. If they match, ANSI is controlling the screen and the program returns a value to your batch file. If they don't match, then ANSI .SYS isn't installed and your batch file can act upon that information, avoiding any ANSI codes that may look messy on the screen.

The name of the program is ISANSI. It returns a value to your batch file as an ERRORLEVEL code. (ERRORLEVELs will be covered in chapter 10.) The batch file ANSITEST (below) determines whether or not ANSI is present and displays a message based on what it finds.

Name: ANSITEST.BAT

```
1: @ECHO OFF
2: ISANSI
3: IF ERRORLEVEL 1 GOTO IS-ON
4: ECHO ANSI driver not present
5: GOTO END
6: :IS-ON
7: ECHO ANSI driver present
8: :END
```

As you get into batch file programming, and using ANSI, you can incorporate the above program into your own programs to determine the status of ANSI.SYS. (And, again, more information on how this program works, GOTOs and ERRORLEVELs, is covered later in this book.)

More examples

The following batch file examples demonstrate some ANSI.SYS tricks you can incorporate into your batch files. Use EDLIN to create them if you feel up to it.

Change of colors   The ANSI batch file in FIG. 3-2 draws an American Flag (more or less) on a color display.

> Note: There are 25 spaces used in the first group of ECHO statements, and 38 spaces used in the second group. The equal

signs (=) are used as a positioning guide for entering the spaces—they do not need to be part of the final batch file.

Only the *Set Graphics Rendition* command is used in this example (I could have used ESC[2J to clear the screen, but CLS is easier to type). The only thing odd about this use of color is the display of the red and white stripes on the flag; they're actually space characters with the background color set to either white or red. Don't forget the final ANSI command to set the screen mode back to normal.

3-2 This ANSI batch file draws an American flag on a color display.
Name: FLAG.BAT

```
 1: @ECHO OFF
 2: REM American Flag ANSI display program
 3: CLS
 4: ECHO ^[[37;44m * * * * * *  ^[[41m          =
 5: ECHO ^[[37;44m  * * * * *   ^[[47m          =
 6: ECHO ^[[37;44m * * * * * *  ^[[41m          =
 7: ECHO ^[[37;44m  * * * * *   ^[[47m          =
 8: ECHO ^[[37;44m * * * * * *  ^[[41m          =
 9: ECHO ^[[47m                         =
10: ECHO ^[[41m                         =
11: ECHO ^[[47m                         =
12: ECHO ^[[41m                         =
13: ECHO ^[[0m
```

Want more color? ANSIDRAW or TheDRAW are public domain/shareware programs. What they do is allow you to create "graphics" on a text screen using the IBM graphics characters (the extended ASCII line drawing characters). You can change colors, draw patterns, cut and paste, and move graphics around one screen. Then, the program allows you to save the graphics screen as an ANSI text file on disk.

For example, you could create the American Flag (above) using ANSI DRAW, then save it to disk as FLAG.DAT. To see the final result, simply type at the command prompt:

C> TYPE FLAT.DAT

ANSIDRAW and TheDRAW are available from public domain houses like PC-SIG, national on-line computer networks, or local user groups or computer clubs.

Graphics/screen mode The ANSI batch file example in FIG. 3-3 displays a menu on color displays in the 40-column mode. Note how screen positioning is used. Unfortunately, this batch file only displays the menu. After the display, you're returned to the command prompt where, sadly, you can't enter options three or four. However, in Part Five of this book, you'll learn

3-3 This ANSI batch file displays a menu in the 40-column mode.

Name: MENUEX.BAT

```
 1: @ECHO OFF
 2: REM ANSI batch file to create a 40-column menu
 3: CLS
 4: REM Set 40 column screen mode (color):
 5: ECHO ^[[=1h
 6: ECHO ^[[5;15HM A I N   M E N U
 7: ECHO ^[[8;10H1. Break into company computer
 8: ECHO ^[[10;10H2. Look at payroll files
 9: ECHO ^[[12;10H3. Give me raise
10: ECHO ^[[14;10H4. Give Jamison demotion
11: ECHO ^[[16;10H5. Stealthily log off
12: ECHO ^[[20;15HEnter choice:
```

how to coordinate your PROMPT command with a menu like the one in FIG. 3-3.

The LOCATE batch file   The ANSI batch file example in FIG. 3-4 will come in really handy. Basically, it uses the ANSI screen positioning commands to move the cursor to a specific spot on the screen.

3-4 This ANSI batch file moves the cursor to a specific spot on the screen.

Name: LOCATE.BAT

```
 1: @ECHO OFF
 2: REM LOCATE batch file, positions cursor on the screen
 3: REM input is %1=row, %2=column, %3 through %9=message
 4: REM if insufficient input, cursor is unchanged
 5: REM First, save the cursor position:
 6: ECHO ^[[s
 7: IF !%1==! GOTO OOPS
 8: IF !%2==! GOTO OOPS
 9: ECHO ^[[%1;%2H%3 %4 %5 %6 %7 %8 %9
10: GOTO END
11: :OOPS
12: REM Error condition, restore cursor position
13: ECHO ^[[u
14: :END
```

LOCATE.BAT accepts three input parameters: the row, column, and a string to display. Because of the way batch files accept information from the command line, all parameters, %3 through %9 must be specified for the string to be displayed. For example:

C> LOCATE 12 40 Hello

Displays "Hello" near the center of the screen.

C> LOCATE 12 40 Hello there

Displays "Hello there" near the center of the screen. "Hello" and "there" are actually two command line parameters. This is why LOCATE specifies parameters %3 through %9—just in case a long string needs to be displayed.

Because LOCATE.BAT needs both a row and column coordinate, those two parameters must be tested for. If either one is missing, LOCATE does nothing. (Actually, because the initial cursor position was saved, the error condition, OOPS above, restores the cursor's position.)

More information is provided later in this book about replaceable parameters, as well as information on testing for missing parameters.

Character wrap demo Character wrap is a rather strange addition to the ANSI.SYS driver. Character wrap controls how characters are displayed after the 80th column on the screen. Normally, with character wrap on, any character displayed after column 80 is displayed in column one on the next row down. However, with character wrap turned off, all characters after column 80 in the current row are displayed in column 80.

Turning character wrap off seems kind of dumb, yet I assume there's a reason for it. To see how character wrap works you can write two batch files:

Name: WRAP-ON.BAT

```
1: @ECHO OFF
2: ECHO ^[ = 7h
3: ECHO Character wrap is on
```

Name: WRAP-OFF.BAT

```
1: @ECHO OFF
2: ECHO ^[ = 7l
3: ECHO Character wrap is off
```

Note: The command to turn character wrap off ends in a lowercase L, not a number "1."

To demo character wrap off, run the WRAP-OFF batch file, then type on the command line until you reach column 80. Once the cursor is at column 80 it will stay there. Each character you type will be echoed in that one spot until you press ENTER or hit the ESCape key. (You can type 128 characters at the command prompt.)

To turn the wrap back on (face it, it's annoying to have it off), just run the WRAP-ON batch file.

Keyboard key reassignment

ANSI has the ability to replace any key you press on the keyboard with another key. Actually, what goes on is that you press one key and a character not necessarily associated with that key will be displayed. For example, you could assign the "N" key to display a "G".

On the surface, keyboard key reassignment sounds fun. My old boss thought it would be neat if the "5" key on the numeric keypad could double as the down-arrow key. This would give him a keen "inverted-T" cursor pattern, like he was used to on an older computer. Unfortunately, ANSI keyboard key reassignment wouldn't work with the "5" key on the keypad. (It's considered a "dead key" by DOS.) Also, the program he was using ignored the DOS keyboard input routines and read the keyboard directly. *C'est la glabre glace* [sic].

The ANSI format for keyboard key reassignment is:

ESC[*n1*;*n2*p

n1 and *n2* are usually ASCII values. *n1* is the value of the key you're replacing, and *n2* is the character to replace it with. The only time this command gets complex is when you're replacing various CTRL and ALT key combinations. In those instances, you're not using ASCII character codes, but rather keyboard scan codes—an entirely different thing. But for most substitutions, ASCII characters are all you'll ever use. (There is a list of keyboard scan codes in appendix C.)

There are two exceptions to this format. The first is when zero prefixes the first code, *n1*. Typically, these are with ALT-key values. For example:

ESC[0;104;65p

This command reassigns the ALT – F1 key combination (0104) with a capital A (ASCII 65).

Also, though it's not written down in any manuals (until now), you can place two ASCII values next to each other in quotes. For example, to reassign "A" to "G" you can use either of the following commands:

ESC[65;71p

or

ESC["AG"p

Examples So what can you do with keyboard key reassignment? An interesting application comes from the "*glabre glace* [sic]" sentence in a previous paragraph: Foreign text characters.

Say you write a lot of Spanish, yet you don't want to reconfigure your computer under DOS to a Spanish configuration (covered in chapter 5). About the only character you need to type is n, an "n" with an accent grave or tilde over the top. This character is crucial to the pronunciation and meaning of dozens of Spanish words.

The following batch file can be written to use ANSI to assign the key combination ALT – N and CTRL – N to the n and N characters respectively.

The ALT – N character code is 0;49. The character n has an extended ASCII code value of 164. CTRL – N has a character code of 14. And the character N has an extended ASCII code value of 165.

Name: EN-AY.BAT

```
1: @ECHO OFF
2: REM change Alt-N to n
3: ECHO ^[[0;49;164p
4: REM change Control-N to N
5: ECHO ^[[14;165p
```

Some users might find it easier to assign an unpopular key to a foreign language character, rather than messing with ALT-this and CTRL-that. The following batch file program reassigns the accent grave and tilde key to produce an e and an E when shifted.

The accent grave, character, has a character code of 96. The character e has an extended ASCII code value of 130. The tilde, ~ character, has a character code of 126. And the character E has an extended ASCII code value of 144.

Name: ACCENT-E.BAT

```
1: @ECHO OFF
2: REM change  to e
3: ECHO ^[[96;130p
4: REM change ~ to E
5: ECHO ^[[126;144p
```

Keep in mind when you do this that the key reassignment only works from DOS and programs that use the DOS keyboard scanning routines. This rules out most common applications such as word processors and databases (where this kind of stuff would really come in handy).

Dvorak keyboard layout Another example of switching keys around would be a batch file program to make your keyboard respond as a Dvorak-style keyboard. The Dvorak keyboard layout was designed with the most often used keys logically placed on the "home row," making typing faster and easier than the stupid old QWERTY keyboard English-speaking people are used to.

To cause DOS to interpret your keystrokes as if you're typing on a Dvorak keyboard, you could write an ANSI batch file to change all the necessary QWERTY keys to Dvorak keys. Some keys, A and M for example, don't change. Others change according to FIG. 3-5.

The translation simply involves replacing the differing uppercase, lowercase, and control characters on the standard keyboard with those found on a Dvorak keyboard. Some things won't work properly, for example, translating CTRL–H (backspace) on a standard keyboard to a CTRL–D on a Dvorak keyboard means that your backspace key (interpreted by DOS as CTRL–H) is translated as CTRL–D. Also, there's no way to read CTRL–;, CTRL–', or CTRL–/ from the PC keyboard to translate them into CTRL–S, CTRL–_, or CTRL–Z for a Dvorak keyboard.

Standard Keyboard Layout

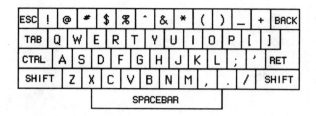

Dvorak Keyboard Layout

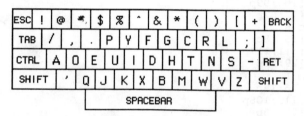

3-5 Dvorak and QWERTY keyboard layouts are shown here.

Therefore, an exercise in writing an ANSI batch file to create a Dvorak keyboard wouldn't really have any practical applications. But if you're curious, it would look something like FIG. 3-6.

3-6 This is a Dvorak keyboard layout batch file.

```
 1: @ECHO OFF
 2: REM Dvorak keyboard Layout:
 3: ECHO Installing Dvorak Keyboard Layout
 4: ECHO Press Control-Break to stop, or
 5: PAUSE
 6: REM - to [, _ to {
 7: ECHO ^[[31;27p
 8: ECHO ^[[45;91p
 9: ECHO ^[[95;123p
10: REM q to /, Q to ?
11: ECHO ^[[113;47p
12: ECHO ^[[81;63p
13: REM w to ,, W to less-than
14: ECHO ^[[119;44p
15: ECHO ^[[87;60p
16: REM e to ., E to greater-than
17: ECHO ^[[101;46p
18: ECHO ^[[69;62p
19: REM R to P
20: ECHO ^[[18;16p
21: ECHO ^[[114;112p
```

```
22: ECHO ^[[82;80p
23: REM T to Y
24: ECHO ^[[20;25p
25: ECHO ^[[116;121p
26: ECHO ^[[84;89p
27: REM Y to F
28: ECHO ^[[25;6p
29: ECHO ^[[121;102p
30: ECHO ^[[89;70p
31: REM U to G
32: ECHO ^[[21;7p
33: ECHO ^[[117;103p
34: ECHO ^[[85;71p
35: REM I to C
36: ECHO ^[[9;3p
37: ECHO ^[[105;99p
38: ECHO ^[[73;67p
39: REM O to R
40: ECHO ^[[15;18p
41: ECHO ^[[111;114p
42: ECHO ^[[79;82p
43: REM P to L
44: ECHO ^[[16;12p
45: ECHO ^[[112;108p
46: ECHO ^[[80;76p
47: REM [ to ;, { to :
48: ECHO ^[[91;59p
49: ECHO ^[[123;58p
50: REM S to O
51: ECHO ^[[19;15p
52: ECHO ^[[115;111p
53: ECHO ^[[83;79p
54: REM D to E
55: ECHO ^[[4;5p
56: ECHO ^[[100;101p
57: ECHO ^[[68;69p
58: REM F to U
59: ECHO ^[[6;21p
60: ECHO ^[[102;117p
61: ECHO ^[[70;85p
62: REM G to I
63: ECHO ^[[7;9p
64: ECHO ^[[103;105p
65: ECHO ^[[71;73p
66: REM H to D
67: ECHO ^[[8;4p
68: ECHO ^[[104;100p
69: ECHO ^[[72;68p
70: REM J to H
71: ECHO ^[[10;8p
72: ECHO ^[[106;104p
73: ECHO ^[[74;72p
74: REM K to T
75: ECHO ^[[11;20p
76: ECHO ^[[107;116p
77: ECHO ^[[75;84p
78: REM L to N
79: ECHO ^[[12;14p
80: ECHO ^[[108;110p
```

3-6 Continued.

```
 81: ECHO ^[[76;78p
 82: REM ; to S
 83: ECHO ^[[59;115p
 84: ECHO ^[[58;83p
 85: REM ' to -
 86: ECHO ^[[39;45p
 87: ECHO ^[[34;95p
 88: REM Z to '
 89: ECHO ^[[122;39p
 90: ECHO ^[[90;34p
 91: REM X to Q
 92: ECHO ^[[24;17p
 93: ECHO ^[[120;113p
 94: ECHO ^[[88;81p
 95: REM C to J
 96: ECHO ^[[3;10p
 97: ECHO ^[[99;106p
 98: ECHO ^[[67;74p
 99: REM V to K
100: ECHO ^[[22;11p
101: ECHO ^[[118;107p
102: ECHO ^[[86;75p
103: REM B to X
104: ECHO ^[[2;24p
105: ECHO ^[[98;120p
106: ECHO ^[[66;88p
107: REM N to B
108: ECHO ^[[14;2p
109: ECHO ^[[110;98p
110: ECHO ^[[78;66p
111: REM , to W
112: ECHO ^[[44;119p
113: ECHO ^[[60;87p
114: REM . to V
115: ECHO ^[[46;118p
116: ECHO ^[[62;86p
117: REM / to Z
118: ECHO ^[[47;122p
119: ECHO ^[[63;90p
```

Keyboard string reassignment   The second form of keyboard key reassignment replaces a single key with a string of characters. So, instead of getting "A" when you press the "A" key, you could get "Alexis."

The format for this ANSI command is the same as the single key reassignment program, except the *n2* value is a string enclosed in quotes:

ESC[*n*;"*string*"p

n is the ASCII code of the key to reassign. For example, to reassign A as "Alexis," you would use:

ESC[65;"Alexis"p

65 is the ASCII character code for capital A. Every time you press A in DOS, or when running an application that uses the DOS keyboard func-

tions, you'll see "Alexis" displayed. Nifty—if you know someone named Alexis.

Extended keyboard codes, such as ALT-key combinations and the various function keys, all start with zero. So their format includes the leading zero, followed by a semicolon. For example, the following code changes ALT-F1 to the string "Alt–F1":

ESC[0;104;"Alt–F1"p

Now, pressing ALT–F1 in DOS displays "Alt–F1." (Golly, won't that come in handy some day?)

Example   Here is a keyboard reassignment trick. This batch file assigns strings to your function keys. The unshifted function keys are needed for editing DOS commands and for EDLIN. However, ALT-function keys are rarely used. Therefore, this batch file assigns strings to the function keys ALT–F1 through ALT–F10 with various, useful DOS commands.

You could replace the strings in FIG. 3-7 with whichever DOS commands or application names you use most frequently. Notice how some of the strings are followed by "13"? That's the carriage return character. By tacking on a "13" before the "p" and after the string, the keyboard string reassignment function automatically adds a carriage return to the end of the command—just as if you'd typed ENTER at the keyboard.

A listing of popular ALT-key and function-key scan codes is provided in appendix C.

3-7   This batch file reassigns your ALT-Function keys to certain DOS command strings.

Name: NIFTY.BAT

```
 1: @ECHO off
 2: ECHO ^[[0;104;"DIR";13p
 3: ECHO ^[[0;105;"COPY "p
 4: ECHO ^[[0;106;"DEL "p
 5: ECHO ^[[0;107;"CD ";13p
 6: ECHO ^[[0;108;"CD ..";13p
 7: ECHO ^[[0;109;"CD \";13p
 8: ECHO ^[[0;110;"WP";13p
 9: ECHO ^[[0;111;"123";13p
10: ECHO ^[[0;112;"DBASE";13p
11: ECHO ^[[0;113;"PARK";13p
```

ANSI.SYS replacements

There's always someone out there who tries to do DOS one better. That's at least one reason to be thankful for having such a basically poor operating system: enterprising individuals have come up with better ways to do things. And improving upon ANSI.SYS is a popular activity.

Three public domain/shareware ANSI.SYS replacements are FANSI-CONSOLE, NANSI.SYS and ZANSI.SYS. These are ANSI.SYS replacements that implement more of the ANSI standard features, as well as added speed that ANSI.SYS doesn't provide.

If you buy the DESQview environment, you get another ANSI.SYS replacement, DVANSI.COM. It has the advantage of being a memory-resident program, as opposed to a device driver. This means you can load DVANSI using a batch file way after your computer has booted.

FANSI.SYS FANSI.SYS is a public domain ANSI.SYS replacement that's also known as FANSI-CONSOLE. FANSI-CONSOLE has many advantages over ANSI.SYS. For one it's faster; you have the option of writing directly to the screen hardware using FANSI-CONSOLE and bypassing all the relatively slow DOS routines.

FANSI-CONSOLE offers more ANSI compatibility, including more VT100 commands. Also, extended control for EGA monitors is available. The actual system driver file for FANSI-CONSOLE is called FCONSOLE .DEV. It's placed in your CONFIG.SYS file, just like ANSI.SYS:

```
DEVICE = FCONSOLE.DEV
```

There are optional switches that follow FCONSOLE.DEV, but, alas, I'm unable to locate any further documentation to tell you what they are and what they do.

There are several drawbacks to FANSI-CONSOLE. The first is that it's huge. The archive file I have is half a megabyte in size. Also, like other ANSI.SYS replacements, there's no guarantee that every system you come across will have it. Finally, FANSI-CONSOLE is a bear to find. One version is available from PC-SIG, but it only comes as part of some game. So if you find it, check it out. Otherwise you might have better luck with NANSI .SYS or ZANSI.SYS.

NANSI.SYS Like FANSI-CONSOLE, NANSI.SYS is a fast and more complete ANSI console device driver than plain old ANSI.SYS.

There are four NANSI device drivers you can use:

```
NANS88.SYS
NANS88B.SYS
NANS286.SYS
NANS286B.SYS
```

The NANS88 files are for older, PC and PC/XT compatible computers (using the 8088 microprocessor). The NANS286 files take advantage of the extended instruction set offered with the 80186 and 802818 and NEC V series chips. In other words, they're fast.

The "B" version of each NANSI driver allows the ANSI codes to be interpreted by the BIOS write character function in addition to the DOS write character functions. This means some applications programs that wouldn't accept the ANSI.SYS commands will accept NANSI's commands.

Also, better than FANSI-CONSOLE, NANSI.SYS comes with complete documentation and it's easy to find. It's listed in the PC-SIG catalog and is included with a game (NetHack) that proves how useful NANSI.SYS can be. (Ask for Disk 1000 if you'd like NetHack and NANSI.SYS. See appendix M for ordering information.) The copy of NANSI.SYS that comes with NetHack also includes documentation. So, if you order NetHack, you also get NANSI.SYS and its documentation for use in your own programs. I recommend it above FANSI-CONSOLE. If you enjoyed playing with the ANSI .SYS batch files in this chapter, you'll go nuts with NANSI.SYS.

ZANSI.SYS ZANSI.SYS seems to be a favorite of most DOS ANSI lovers. They claim it's much faster than FCONSOLE or NANSI.SYS (which are also both faster than ANSI.SYS). And when you read the documentation, you'll find that Zephyr ANSI is actually built upon NANSI.SYS.

The advantages of ZANSI is that it's smaller on disk and in memory than the original NANSI.SYS. Yet it's not as powerful, missing some of the completeness that NANSI offers. So if you want speed and small memory size, go with ZANSI. But if that isn't important to you, get NANSI. (And if you have the time, construct a limerick for tomorrow's class using all the ANSI driver names mentioned in this chapter.)

DVANSI.COM DESQview is Quarterdeck's multitasking solution for DOS. Using DESQview, you can run a number of DOS programs all at once on one single PC. Of course, having a 386 with buckets and buckets of RAM helps. But even on the meekest PC, DESQview really helps to boost the power of silly old DOS. (Having a few megabytes of EMS Expanded memory always helps.)

If you're going to bring up a "DOS window" under DESQview, you might want to have handy an ANSI.SYS driver. True, if you're using ANSI .SYS in your CONFIG.SYS file (or any of the other ANSI drivers covered here), you'll have access to your ANSI codes. But if you don't, you can simply specify DVANSI on the command line, and your DOS window will have access to the ANSI codes.

Why use DVANSI?

The purpose behind DESQview (and Quarterdeck's two memory management packages, QEMM and QRAM, as well), is to get more out of your system. The ANSI.SYS driver takes up only a measly 1.6K of resident-memory. Yet that's a potential 1.6K less RAM you'll lack in *all* of your DESQview windows.

To solve this problem, I recommend removing ANSI.SYS from your CONFIG.SYS file when you run your PC under DESQview. (Or you can install ANSI.SYS in high DOS memory using the LOADHI.SYS command; refer to the QEMM or QRAM manual.) Instead, start all of your DOS sessions under DESQview using the following batch file:

Name: RUNDOS.BAT

```
1: @ECHO OFF
2: C:\DV\DVANSI > NUL
3: C:\DOS\COMMAND /P /E:1024
```

On my system, the DOS session ("Big DOS") has RUNDOS.BAT listed as the program to run. When I start each DOS session, RUNDOS loads DV ANSI to give me ANSI access, then it runs COMMAND.COM with the /P option (to run AUTOEXEC.BAT) and the /E option (to give me a large environment, covered in the next chapter).

A second, side-effect of running a DOS session this way is that it prevents the DOS window from accidentally being closed via the EXIT command. However, for the purposes here, a RUNDOS batch file in DESQview gives your DOS session access to ANSI commands without the need for loading ANSI.SYS in your CONFIG.SYS file.

Summary

ANSI.SYS is a console device driver that can modify your keyboard and the way items are displayed on the screen. Although the power of the ANSI.SYS driver included with DOS is quite limited, it can be used to give your batch files more power, as well as make them more visually interesting.

If you're looking for more screen formatting power, you might try to locate FANSI-CONSOLE, NANSI.SYS, or ZANSI.SYS, ANSI.SYS replacements. For completeness use NANSI.SYS. For speed, try ZANSI.SYS. And if you use DESQview, consider the DVANSI driver instead of any ANSI driver in your CONFIG.SYS file.

For a complete list of the ANSI.SYS command, refer to appendix B.

4
The environment

DOS has many layers to it. The more you learn about DOS, the more there is to know. In fact, there are some very thick books on DOS (such as the MS-DOS Encyclopedia at 1,570-odd pages) that still don't tell everything there is to know about the operating system. One of those important items not mentioned in most books is the environment.

The environment is DOS's variable storage area—a scratch pad, if you will. The nice thing about this storage area is that DOS lets you modify it, and you can take advantage of the information stored there in batch files. In fact, there are some interesting and incredible things you can do, and all you need to know about is the environment.

This chapter covers the environment, the place where DOS keeps important information that your batch files can use. Remember, just because other books and manuals might overlook the environment doesn't mean that it's not important.

The environment

The environment is where DOS keeps important information, similar to a variable pool that would be used by a programming language such as BASIC. Because this information can be changed or modified by DOS, applications programs, or us users, the environment is kept in RAM (as opposed to disk).

There are two ways you can view the environment. The first is via the SET command. The second is by peeking into your computer's RAM using the DEBUG utility that comes with DOS. Most DOS aficionados would prefer that you use the first method. But because this is an advanced book and I happen to be in an exceptionally good mood today, I'm going to show you both.

SET

The SET command is one of those strange DOS commands that is "bimodal." That means it does two nearly different things depending on how you use it. Normally, SET is used to set, or create, an environment variable. However, when typed by itself, SET displays a copy of the current DOS environment on the screen:

```
C> SET
COMSPEC = C: \ COMMAND.COM
PROMPT =
PATH = C: \ SYSTEM \ DOS;C: \ SYSTEM \ BATCH;U:;..
TEMP = C: \ TEMP
```

If you type SET, doubtless what you see will be different. Each computer system will probably have a different environment set up, depending on how much the user knows (or doesn't know) about DOS.

Most of the above items are set by commands in an AUTOEXEC.BAT file. If a user doesn't have an AUTOEXEC.BAT, or they don't bother to set a PATH or PROMPT or any environment variables, the environment looks like this:

```
C> SET
COMSPEC = C: \ COMMAND.COM
PATH =
```

Boring. These items are the only two that DOS automatically assigns unless you change them. Actually, nothing has been assigned for the PATH. The COMSPEC is set by DOS when the system boots. It indicates the location of the COMMAND.COM program. COMMAND.COM will typically be in the root of the boot disk, or a floppy disk if you boot from it.

The second way of viewing the environment is via DEBUG. This is the dangerous way that most power users will tell you to avoid. By using DEBUG you can look directly at the environment as DOS stores it in memory. Scary.

DEBUG is a tool provided with DOS that can do many interesting things. With DEBUG, you can examine raw information on disk, "peek" at memory locations, disassemble program files (and change them), or create new programs. DEBUG is quite versatile, yet it's cryptic and backwards (or just "simple" if you don't want to be mean about things) so many people avoid using it.

In order to examine the environment using DEBUG we have to know where the DOS keeps a copy of its environment. This information is obtained by examining what's known as the Program Segment Prefix, or PSP.

Each time DOS runs a program it creates a PSP. The PSP is a 256-byte block of memory into which DOS places all kinds of interesting stuff. For example, there are important memory locations, vectors, information about any filenames typed on the command line, the command line itself (a copy of the command line you typed to run the program—which is how some programs know that information), and the various reserved buffers and storage places. As far as the environment is concerned, one of those storage places holds the address of your system's environment.

Because the environment location differs with each computer, observe the following directions carefully. The numbers you type will be different from the ones in the example.

First, enter DEBUG:

C> DEBUG

DEBUG's cryptic command prompt is the hyphen. To display the PSP (actually, this is a special PSP created by DEBUG—but it looks like the normal PSP), type D0 L100. This displays memory locations starting at address zero through address 100. The numbers are in hexadecimal, so 100 is really 256:

-D0 L100

You will see about 16 lines of information scroll up the screen, similar to what is shown in FIG. 4-1.

4-1 DEBUG displays your PSP.

```
159C:0000   CD 20 00 A0 00 9A EE FE-1D F0 F4 02 ED 11 2F 03   . ............/.
159C:0010   ED 11 BC 02 ED 11 6F 0F-03 04 01 00 02 FF FF FF   .......o........
159C:0020   FF FF FF FF FF FF FF FF-FF FF FF FF AD 11 4E 01   ..............N.
159C:0030   27 15 14 00 18 00 9C 15-FF FF FF FF 00 00 00 00   '...............
159C:0040   00 00 00 00 00 00 00 00-00 00 00 00 00 00 00 00   ................
159C:0050   CD 21 CB 00 00 00 00 00-00 00 00 00 00 20 20 20   .!...........
159C:0060   20 20 20 20 20 20 20 20-00 00 00 00 00 20 20 20        .....
159C:0070   20 20 20 20 20 20 20 20-00 00 00 00 6E 67 65 73       ....nges
159C:0080   00 0D 20 0D 6E 20 6B 69-6C 6C 0D 61 74 63 68 00   .. .n kill.atch.
159C:0090   0D 3A 5C 53 59 53 54 45-4D 5C 42 41 54 43 48 3B   .:\SYSTEM\BATCH;
159C:00A0   55 3A 3B 2E 2E 0D 70 6C-65 3A 0A 0A 43 3E 20 43   U:;...ple:..C> C
159C:00B0   44 20 5C 53 59 53 54 45-4D 5C 55 54 49 4C 5C 4D   D \SYSTEM\UTIL\M
159C:00C0   41 43 45 0A 0A 54 68 69-73 20 63 6F 6D 6D 61 6E   ACE..This comman
159C:00D0   64 20 63 68 61 6E 67 65-73 20 66 72 6F 6D 20 74   d changes from t
159C:00E0   68 65 20 63 75 72 72 65-6E 74 20 64 69 72 65 63   he current direc
159C:00F0   74 6F 72 79 20 74 68 65-20 74 6F 20 5C 53 59 53   tory the to \SYS
```

Each line starts with a segment address, followed by a memory offset (see FIG. 4-2). The segment address value varies the most from machine to machine. The more memory-resident programs you load in when you start your system, the higher this number will be. The offset value is the byte offset within the segment. For everyone, this will start with 0.

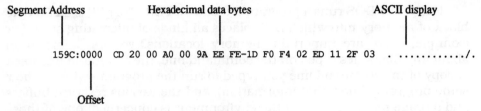

Segment Address · Hexadecimal data bytes · ASCII display

159C:0000   CD 20 00 A0 00 9A EE FE-1D F0 F4 02 ED 11 2F 03   . .../.

Offset

4-2 This display is broken down in this way.

The hexadecimal data bytes display shows the value of each byte at each memory location. The ASCII display shows the bytes as ASCII characters. Non-ASCII characters are displayed with a dot. You might see some readable characters around line 80. These are the remnants of any previous commands you've typed at the keyboard. The other information displayed is of trivial importance right now—except for the two bytes at offset 2C. To specifically see these two bytes, type:

-D2C L2

This displays the two bytes at offset 2C. What you'll see is something like what is shown in FIG. 4-3.

4-3 This shows the segment of your environment table.

-d2c 12

159C:0020   AD 11

Again, the numbers you see will probably be different. On my system I got the above, AD 11. This is the segment address value of my computer's environment. Note that it's a segment address and not an offset. The offset is really 0 (so it's not listed). To see your environment, you simply display the block of information at that segment address.

The two pairs of numbers displayed are in reverse order (because that's the way the 8088 stores them in memory and it's a long story). So, to display the information at that segment address, use DEBUG's "D" command followed by the segment address (in reverse order):

-D11AD:0

This command is different from the others because the segment address is included. The segment address should be followed by a colon and a zero. After pressing ENTER, your system's environment is displayed, as shown in FIG. 4-4. Items are in the exact order as they are displayed by the SET command. A few things to note:

- Each item in the environment is separated by a "null" character, zero.
- The last item in the environment is followed by two nulls.

4-4 Your RAM environment is shown here.

```
-d11ad:0

11AD:0000   43 4F 4D 53 50 45 43 3D-43 3A 5C 43 4F 4D 4D 41   COMSPEC=C:\COMMA
11AD:0010   4E 44 2E 43 4F 4D 00 50-52 4F 4D 50 54 3D 2E 20   ND.COM.PROMPT=.
11AD:0020   00 4D 41 53 4D 3D 2F 56-20 2F 5A 00 50 41 54 48   .MASM=/V /Z.PATH
11AD:0030   3D 43 3A 5C 53 59 53 54-45 4D 5C 44 4F 53 3B 43   =C:\SYSTEM\DOS;C
11AD:0040   3A 5C 53 59 53 54 45 4D-5C 42 41 54 43 48 3B 55   :\SYSTEM\BATCH;U
11AD:0050   3A 3B 2E 2E 00 00 01 00-43 3A 5C 53 59 53 54 45   :;......C:\SYSTE
11AD:0060   4D 5C 44 4F 53 5C 44 45-42 55 47 2E 43 4F 4D 00   M\DOS\DEBUG.COM.
11AD:0070   5A B5 11 4B 8E 00 00 00-00 00 00 00 00 00 00 00   Z..K...........
-q
```

There's really nothing else that can be done at this point. After all, you've seen the environment in memory—what an honor! Seriously, if you mess with anything at this point you could damage your system. Nothing severe, you just might need to reboot to right things again.

To exit DEBUG, type a Q:

-Q

C>

and you're back at DOS.

Important environment notes

Don't pollute. Recycle. Ask for paper bags at the A&P. Etc.

On a more electronic note, you should keep the following items in mind when dealing with the environment. Items are placed in the environment at boot time, or by the SET command. Beware of programs (besides SET) that change the environment. You will notice how items in the environment will move around as you use SET to assign and unassign items. The order is not important, so don't let it bother you.

Because more programs can be loaded on top of the environment, its size is limited. One of the most common errors you might see with your batch files is "Out of environment space." This means the environment is full and you can't stick anything else into it. (Later in this chapter and the next you'll read about expanding the environment.)

When you "shell" a program, or leave a memory-resident program in memory, DOS makes a new copy of the environment. A simple way to keep a safety copy of your environment is to use COMMAND to start a second command processor shell. You can then modify the environment and, when you're done, type EXIT to return to your original command processor and your original environment.

COMSPEC

Your system's environment will contain only two variables unless you tell it otherwise: COMSPEC and PATH. COMSPEC tells DOS where to find

COMMAND.COM should the transient portion need to be reloaded. Also, programs that take advantage of DOS's "shelling" capabilities (see chapter 2) will examine the environment to look for COMSPEC= in order to run a second copy of the command processor.

Normally, if you have a hard drive, COMSPEC will look like this:

COMSPEC = C: \ COMMAND.COM

or, if you boot from a floppy drive:

COMSPEC = A: \ COMMAND.COM

Apparently, DOS (possibly the SYSINIT function) simply figures out which drive you booted from, then assigns COMSPEC to COMMAND.COM in the root directory of that drive—whether it's actually there or not. For example, if you boot from drive A, then remove your boot disk, COMSPEC is still set to A: \ COMMAND.COM. This is why some programs request that you "Insert DOS diskette in drive A, and strike any key."

You can change the location of COMSPEC using the SET command. (SET used in this manner is covered in detail below.) SET simply assigns an environment variable a new value, or creates a new variable if one doesn't already exist.

C> SET COMSPEC = Z: \ COMMAND.COM

This command resets COMSPEC in your system's environment to the COMMAND.COM file in the root directory of drive Z. You can type SET alone on the command line to verify this:

C> SET
PATH =
COMSPEC = Z: \ COMMAND.COM

The only drawback to this is that if you need to reload the transient portion of COMMAND.COM, DOS will look for it on drive Z. It better be there.

So why change the COMSPEC?

Because COMMAND.COM doesn't need to be in your root directory. In fact, you can tuck COMMAND.COM away somewhere in your deepest, darkest subdirectory where no one will ever find it. You do so with CON FIG.SYS's SHELL command.

SHELL is a command used in your CONFIG.SYS file. If you recall from chapter 2, CONFIG.SYS is run before COMMAND.COM is loaded. If DOS is informed via the SHELL command that COMMAND.COM is in another directory, it will look for it there. This has one clear advantage: it keeps your root directory clean.

To move COMMAND.COM out of your root directory, add the SHELL command to your CONFIG.SYS file:

SHELL = C: \ DOS \ COMMAND.COM

This instructs DOS to look for and run the command interpreter (or shell)

"COMMAND.COM" in the \DOS subdirectory. (SHELL also allows you to run other command processors besides COMMAND.COM, simply by specifying their name.) If you add this command to CONFIG.SYS, you can go ahead and move COMMAND.COM to your \DOS subdirectory and delete the old COMMAND.COM from your root directory.

A drawback to using the SHELL statement this way is that your AUTOEXEC.BAT file won't run. To run AUTOEXEC.BAT, you need to specify COMMAND.COM's /P option:

```
SHELL = C:\DOS\COMMAND.COM /P
```

This instructs COMMAND.COM to look for AUTOEXEC.BAT in the root directory (you can't move AUTOEXEC.BAT—it must stay in the root) and execute it.

A second option, /E, is used to adjust the environment space. This option is covered later in this chapter.

If you boot your machine now, DOS will look for and run COMMAND.COM from your \DOS directory. Also, if /P is specified, AUTOEXEC.BAT will run from the root directory. One thing that doesn't change, however, is your COMSPEC. It will still read that COMMAND.COM is found in the root directory of whatever drive you booted from. (It appears that whatever command creates the initial COMSPEC entry in your environment isn't that smart.)

To fix this anomaly, you'll need to add the following line to your AUTO EXEC.BAT file:

```
SET COMSPEC = C:\DOS\COMMAND.COM
```

This patches up any possible future "Insert DOS diskette in drive C, and strike any key" messages. (You can't reinsert your hard disk—you must reboot if this happens.)

With DOS5, you can cure the problem forever by specifying COMMAND.COM's subdirectory in the SHELL command as follows:

```
SHELL = C:\DOS\COMMAND.COM C:\DOS /P
```

The second instance of "C:\DOS" above tells the part of SYSINIT (from Chapter 2) to specify that subdirectory with the COMSPEC variable. If you use the above format in DOS 5, there will be no need to set a corrective COMSPEC variable in AUTOEXEC.BAT.

So, if you move COMMAND.COM to a different subdirectory remember the following:

- Specify the full pathname of COMMAND.COM using SHELL in CONFIG.SYS.
- Specify /P if you want AUTOEXEC.BAT (in the root) to run.
- Add a SET COMSPEC = line in AUTOEXEC.BAT to tell DOS where to look for COMMAND.COM, unless you're using DOS 5.0.

Otherwise, you can avoid this by keeping COMMAND.COM in your root directory. This will keep the COMSPEC variable "normal" the entire time you use your computer.

The PATH

The second environment variable DOS automatically gives you is PATH. Unlike COMSPEC, which DOS apparently makes a wild guess with, PATH starts out set to nothing; a path to nowhere, like a plot hook in a Stephen King novel.

The reason the path is blank is simple. DOS doesn't know your directory structure, where your files are located, or how you use them. That's the key to the PATH command's power.

Down the beaten path

Aside from being one of the "must haves" in your AUTOEXEC.BAT file (along with PROMPT and the command to set the system clock—more on this in the next chapter), little is ever done with the PATH command. It's sad, because a bad PATH can cause a lot of grief.

The PATH command was implemented along with subdirectories in DOS Version 2.0. Before then, all your files were kept in one big directory; the disk you were using. But because of the way DOS handles subdirectories, there needed to be a way for you to access commands, utilities, and applications that weren't necessarily in the same subdirectory that you're in.

Unless told otherwise, DOS only looks for program files in the current directory. If you type HELLO, and HELLO.COM (or HELLO.EXE or HELLO.BAT) is not in the current directory, nothing will happen. (Well, you'll get an error message, but the program won't run.)

The answer is the *search path*, yet another trick borrowed from the UNIX operating system. The search path gives DOS a list of other subdirectories to search through to look for files. So, you no longer need to be in the same subdirectory as a program to run that program. If that program's subdirectory is on the path, it doesn't matter where you are when you type the program's name.

Setting the path

To set the path you simply type PATH, followed by the names of the subdirectories you want DOS to look through. Subdirectory pathnames are separated by semicolons, and it's a good idea to include a drive letter in case you happen to be on another drive when you type a command. Also, unlike other environment variables, there's no need to type SET to set the path. PATH alone does the job.

To see your current system path, type PATH at the command prompt:

```
C> PATH
PATH = C: \ SYSTEM \ DOS;C: \ SYSTEM \ BATCH
```

Two directories are specified above: C:\SYSTEM\DOS and C:\SYSTEM\BATCH. Theoretically, you could have as many directories as would fit on the command line (up to 128 characters). But the drawback to long search paths is that it takes time for DOS to hunt through those directories for your commands—especially when you mistype something. (For example, if you accidentally typed BLECH, DOS would look for BLECH.COM, BLECH.EXE, or BLECH.BAT in each of the subdirectories listed on your path—a potentially time-consuming process.)

When your system starts, the PATH is set to zero, or only the current directory. To reset your PATH to zero at any time, simply follow the PATH command with a single semicolon:

```
C> PATH ;
```

This resets the path to nothing.

To change the path, specify the new directories to search through:

```
C> PATH C:\SYSTEM\DOS;C:\WP
```

This sets the search path to your C:\SYSTEM\DOS subdirectory, followed by your C:\WP subdirectory. Now, in addition to looking through the current directory, DOS will search in those two subdirectories for the names of program files you want to run.

Rarely does the path need changing, beyond the initial setup down in AUTOEXEC.BAT. However, in Part Five of this book you'll see various examples that do change the path.

Nifty trick

Without going too deeply into hard disk organization, there's a nifty trick you can play on the PATH command that alleviates typing complex subdirectory names, or maintaining a complicated PATH.

Most hard disks are organized into subdirectories that contain program files. For example, if you use *dBASE*, *Microsoft Word*, and *SuperCalc* as your primary applications, you may have four subdirectories on your system's hard disk (see FIG. 4-5). Underneath these subdirectories, you'll typically have the data files that work with the applications, each in their appropriate subdirectories (see FIG. 4-6).

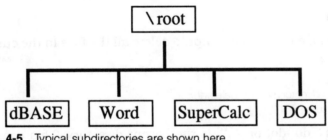

4-5 Typical subdirectories are shown here.

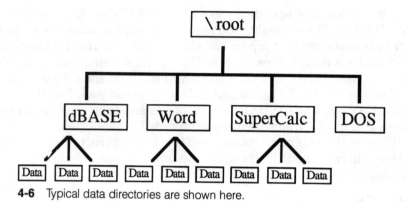

4-6 Typical data directories are shown here.

In this instance, you would probably want a path that looks something like the following:

C> PATH C:\DOS;C:\DBASE;C:\WORD;C:\SUPRCALC

This would ensure that wherever you were on your hard disk, you could access the appropriate applications file without necessarily having to be in that subdirectory. Right? Yes, but there's a better way.

The answer is ".."—that's double dot, and it's the way DOS abbreviates the parent directory. Every directory except for the root has a parent. You may have wondered what those two "dot" entries were in your directory listing, as shown in FIG. 4-7.

4-7 The double-dot abbreviates the parent directory.

```
Volume in drive C is LONELY
Volume Serial Number is 0000-0001
Directory of  C:\STUFF

.             <DIR>       2-17-88   8:56p
..            <DIR>       2-17-88   8:56p
    2 File(s)   9758720 bytes free
```

The single dot "." indicates the current directory.
Typing the following displays the current directory:

C> DIR .

Typing the following will attempt to delete all the files in the current directory:

C> DEL .
All files in directory will be deleted!
Are you sure (Y/N)?

Two periods, dot-dot or "..", is the parent directory. This command displays the directory of the parent directory:

    C> DIR ..

If you wish to change directories to the parent directory, type:

    C> CD ..

It's much easier than typing the full name. As far as the PATH command is concerned, the following path:

    C:\DOS;C:\DBASE;C:\WORD;C:\SUPRCALC

can be changed to:

    C:\DOS;..

This means DOS will first look for applications programs in the current directory (the default), then in the DOS subdirectory, then in the parent directory. If you're in one of the data subdirectories listed in FIG. 4-6, this would guarantee that you'd always have access to your applications program.

Of course, ".." isn't the solution to everything. If you were on drive A and needed to access *SuperCalc*, ".." wouldn't pass muster. So, for some important programs, especially those that you'll use often, it's best to keep their subdirectory on the path.

SUBST

The SUBST command was introduced with DOS Version 3.1. Because DOS Version 3.x is often cited for its "network support," many people assumed that SUBST was a network-only command. It's not. (In fact, it can't be used with a network drive at all.) Instead, SUBST can be used in a number of ways, one of which greatly boosts the performance of your search path.

Basically, SUBST lets you assign, or "alias," a disk drive letter to a pathname. For example:

    C> SUBST D: C:\DOS

This command SUBSTitutes the pathname C:\DOS with the drive letter D. If you typed D: to move to "drive D," DOS would *pretend* that you are on a drive D:

    C>D:
    D>

Although it looks like you've just logged on to drive D, in actuality, you're in the \DOS subdirectory on drive C. If you did a DIR command now, it would appear as though you were in the "root" directory of drive D. Any subdirectories under \DOS (which is really where you are) would appear as subdirectories on drive D.

Note that while you can SUBST drive letters for subdirectories, the subdirectories have not been removed from your system. In the above example, you can still go to the subdirectory \DOS on drive C. It's the same thing as going to drive D.

There are some limits to the SUBST command. The first of which is that DOS only lets you have five "logical" drives—no matter how many physical drives are in your system. If you have only one hard drive "C", then DOS allows you to use D: and E: with the SUBST command. Otherwise, you have to reset the number of available logical drives with the CONFIG.SYS command LASTDRIVE. (This is covered in chapter 5.)

The next limit is that quite a few commands will not work on a substituted drive: ASSIGN, BACKUP, DISKCOMP, DISKCOPY, FDISK, FORMAT, JOIN, LABEL, and RESTORE. Also, take care if you plan on using CHDIR, MKDIR, or RMDIR on a substituted drive. You're actually creating subdirectories from a subdirectory—not a disk drive.

To see which drives you've substituted, use the SUBST command alone:

```
C> SUBST
D:   = > C:\DOS
L:   = > C:\1-2-3
T:   = > C:\SYSTEM\TEMP
U:   = > C:\SYSTEM\UTILITY
W:   = > C:\WP
```

And finally, to remove a substitution, specify the /D (disable) switch after the substituted drive letter:

```
SUBST D: /D
```

This undoes the earlier example where drive D was substituted for C: \DOS. In the future you may come across some utility programs that won't recognize the substituted drives. When this is the case, simply use the full pathnames instead of the substituted drive letters.

Why SUBST?

There are more reasons to use SUBST than any other command introduced with DOS Version 3. The first thing many users found out was that SUBST allowed quick, abbreviated access to long subdirectory names. Typing "U:" was easier than typing "CD \SYSTEM\UTILITY." Also, a number of popular, well-frequented, directories could be abbreviated using SUBST, making writing and updating a PATH command much easier:

```
PATH = D:\;E:\;U:\;W:\;..
```

Some users only use SUBST with directories they want to put on their path. This way, SUBST allows them to place a number of directories on the path by using drive letters instead of full pathnames. (Remember, though this will let you put more directories on your search path, it still means DOS will slow down as it looks through the entire path to find a program.)

A second blessing SUBST offered was a way around certain older, CP/M-ish programs that didn't understand subdirectories. Yes, even in 1985, with millions of DOS users, *WordStar* didn't understand what a subdirectory was. SUBST allowed *WordStar* users to specify a drive letter instead of the subdirectory name that the program didn't understand. When word got out about this, thousands of users upgraded to DOS Version 3.1. (Today's "modern" version of *WordStar* doesn't have this problem.)

JOIN

The JOIN command is usually mentioned in conjunction with SUBST. JOIN is nearly the opposite of SUBST. Instead of assigning a drive letter to a subdirectory, JOIN lets you access another disk drive (particularly a floppy drive) as a subdirectory:

    JOIN A: C:\DEV\DRIVEA

This command allows you to reference all the files and directories in drive A as the subdirectory \DEV\DRIVEA on drive C. So:

    C> A:

is the same as typing:

    C> CD \DEV\DRIVEA

You'll end up in the same place.

This command also makes dealing with partitioned hard drives easier. In earlier versions of DOS, a hard disk could only be 32 megabytes in size. When your system had a 40-megabyte (or larger) hard drive, you had to partition it into divisions smaller than 32 megabytes. So the 40-megabyte drive would become two logical drives: a 32-megabyte drive C and a 10-megabyte drive D. When this happened, you could use JOIN to make drive D a subdirectory of drive C (and keep yourself sane in the process).

    C> JOIN D: C:\DRIVED

Now drive D is just a subdirectory of C, easily referenced without having to train yourself to type "D:" each time you want to access files there.

As with SUBST, to remove a JOIN substitution you specify the /D switch:

    C> JOIN D: /D

This removes the assignment. Also, to display a list of joined drives, type JOIN on a line by itself:

    C> JOIN
    D: = > C:\DRIVED

Also, the following commands will not work properly on a JOINed drive: ASSIGN, BACKUP, RESTORE, DISKCOMP, DISKCOPY, and FORMAT. And, for Pete's sake, don't mess around with JOINing and SUBSTituting the same drives and subdirectories over and over—unless you have a recent backup of your system.

APPEND: A swell addition

DOS 3.3 added a new PATH-like command to the search path repertoire: APPEND. It works a lot like PATH, in fact, many people confuse the two. What APPEND does is to create a search path for nonprogram files; any files on disk without a .COM .EXE or .BAT file extension.

There is some confusion about PATH and what it does and can't do. Any program filename you type in will be located by DOS as long as it's on the path. However, PATH doesn't allow DOS to search for data files. Nope. Not at all. To find your data files, you use APPEND.

APPEND works almost exactly like PATH. The exceptions are that APPEND doesn't normally store its information in the environment. Instead, APPEND is actually a memory-resident program. Once you type APPEND, it stays in memory and keeps track of its own search path. To start APPEND, type APPEND on the command line:

C> APPEND /X/E

The /X switch is used to accommodate the DOS functions "search first," "find first," and "exec." These functions are used by DOS commands, such as COMP, BACKUP, and RESTORE, to locate files. Additionally, your applications may use them to locate data or document files.

The /E switch is used to place APPEND's search path into the environment. This way, you can modify that search path using either APPEND or the SET command (discussed below). However, the manual recommends that you not use the environment and instead let APPEND keep track of its own search path (which is more efficient and uses less memory).

After typing APPEND, you can set a search path for nonprogram files, just like the PATH command. For example:

C> APPEND C:\1-2-3\JUNE\DATA;C:\DOS\MISCINFO

This command places two subdirectories, \1-2-3\DATA and \DOS\MISCINFO, on APPEND's search path. If the data file PHONE# was in the \DOS\MISCINFO subdirectory, and you were currently logged to the \DOS subdirectory, then the following command:

C> TYPE PHONE#

would display the PHONE# file. Normally, you'd get a "File Not Found" error message. But because APPEND is loaded and you've specified \DOS\MISCINFO on the search path, the PHONE# file was found and displayed, like magic.

Just like PATH, typing APPEND on the command line alone displays the current APPEND search path:

```
C> APPEND
APPEND = C: \ 1-2-3 \ JUNE \ DATA;C: \ DOS \ MISCINFO
```

Also, if the /E option was specified at startup, you'll see a copy of APPEND in the environment:

```
C> SET
COMSPEC = C: \ COMMAND.COM
PROMPT =
PATH = C: \ SYSTEM \ DOS;C: \ SYSTEM \ BATCH;U:;..
APPEND = C: \ 1-2-3 \ JUNE \ DATA;C: \ DOS \ MISCINFO
```

To reset the APPEND search path to nothing, type APPEND followed by a semicolon:

```
C> APPEND ;
```

To verify that nothing is there, type APPEND again:

```
C> APPEND
No Append
```

Or use the SET command to view it in the environment:

```
C> SET
COMSPEC = C: \ COMMAND.COM
PROMPT =
PATH = C: \ SYSTEM \ DOS;C: \ SYSTEM \ BATCH;U:;..
APPEND =
```

APPEND is a useful and sometimes necessary command. However, some problems may occur with other applications, especially when the /X option is specified. Also, because APPEND is memory-resident, once it's in there there's no way to get it out again.

The system PROMPT

The system prompt provides a place for input from the user. It's the first thing you become familiar with when you use DOS. Yet, it doesn't necessarily need to be so intimidating.

Normally the system prompt is set to the current drive letter, followed by a greater-than sign:

```
C>
```

The prompt can be changed, however, to just about anything you'd like using the PROMPT command. With the PROMPT command, you can use special *meta* commands to customize your prompt, and even incorporate ANSI commands. The only limitation is the 128 input length at the command prompt—no prompt command can be more than 128 characters long.

The format of the PROMPT command is:

PROMPT = *meta_commands*

The equal sign is optional. If you don't include any *meta_commands*, the prompt is reset to the default drive letter plus greater than sign. But more likely than not, you'll use some of the nifty PROMPT commands to create your own custom prompt.

Prompt commands

There are 13 prompt meta commands. Each of them is prefixed by a dollar sign. Any other character included in the PROMPT command becomes part of the prompt. Note that > | and < can be included in your system prompt only via the meta commands in TABLE 4-1. If you attempt to use them straight (as if you wanted to perform I/O redirection with them), you'll get an "Unable to create file" message.

Note that in TABLE 4-1, the alphabetic commands (P, G, B and so on) can be in either upper- or lowercase.

Table 4-1

Meta command	Displays
$$	$, dollar sign character.
$b	| character.
$d	the date (according to the system clock).
$e	the ESCape character.
$g	> character.
$h	backspace (erase previous character).
$l	< character
$n	the logged disk drive letter.
$p	the logged disk drive and subdirectory.
$q	= character.
$t	the current time (according to the system clock).
$v	DOS version.
$_	Carriage return/line feed (new line).

In addition to these commands, ANSI cursor and screen control can be introduced into the system prompt. The $e meta command provides the ESCape character, you simply supply the other information. The only drawback to this is that some prompts (see below) will look awfully confusing.

Popular system prompts

The most popular system prompt is:

```
PROMPT = $p$g
```

Some users will follow the $g with a space (which you can't see above). This makes the prompt read:

```
C:\SYSTEM\MOUSE> _
```

The cursor is one space after the > character. Some potentially claustrophobic users prefer this to the straight pg prompt, which puts the cursor right-butt-against the final > character:

```
C:\SYSTEM\MOUSE>_
```

There are so many things you can do with your prompt. But first, a confession: My personal system prompt, the one I use all the time, is merely a dot. That's right, a single dot—just like dBASE gives you. This is perhaps the most cryptic and unusual prompt I've ever seen. And it also keeps the neophytes from messing with my system. (I even wrote an assembly language program called QUIT that displays "This isn't dBASE!" This is in case the unsuspecting power user saunters along and tries to use my system without knowing what my personal dot prompt is!)

Most UNIX lovers change their system prompts to "$" or "#", depending on which flavor of UNIX they love the most. But before you choose your own favorite cryptic system prompt, make sure you've memorized your directory structure. The good ol' pg prompt is the best one for navigating a directory-laden hard drive. (Which makes you wonder why *Microsoft* didn't make it the default system prompt starting with DOS Version 2.0.)

Date and time

This system prompt is quite popular around the office at work. It displays the current date, time, and directory:

```
PROMPT = $d$_$t$_$p$g
```

The next effect of this prompt is something like:

```
Mon 11-30-1992
13:19:57.26
C:\SYSTEM\TEMP>
```

Quite a few people like this prompt because it gives them the current date and time by simply pressing ENTER at the DOS prompt. Others don't like the prompt because it takes up three lines on the display, sometimes scrolling important information "off the top."

Memory daze prompt

My first computer was a Radio Shack TRS-80. Its system prompt can be emulated under MS-DOS:

```
PROMPT = TRSDOS Ready$_$e[s.... (64 dots) ...$e[u
```

There are 64 dots between the ESC[s and ESC[u commands. Refer to appendix B if you're curious about the ANSI ESC[s and ESC[u commands.

UNIX-lovers prompts

UNIX is boring and cryptic, if you've ever thought the two could go together. Here are some popular UNIX-type prompts:

```
PROMPT = #
```

This is the "root" user's prompt, a number sign followed by a space.

Rarely will the UNIX nut use the lower-level user's prompt, the dollar sign. If they did, the PROMPT command to do so is:

```
PROMPT = $$
```

Because the dollar sign is the prefix meta character with the prompt command, two of them are issued to create a dollar sign system prompt. An interesting variation on this would be a system prompt you could write for your greedy, money-mad boss at the office. Try:

```
PROMPT = Think$$
```

Prompts that use backspace

The backspace prompt command, $h, can be used for a number of special prompt effects. Most often, however, it's used to erase the seconds and decimal portions of the time (and sometimes the date) display. For example:

```
PROMPT = $t$h$h$h$h$h$h$g
```

This prompt displays something like:

```
13:19>
```

The $t displays the time. But the time is displayed with seconds and hundredths of seconds as follows (in the U.S.—for other countries, see the following chapter):

```
13:19:57.26
```

To erase the six extra characters (:57.26), six backspace characters are added to the prompt command, hhhhhh. This is followed by the $g, and optionally followed by a space.

The backspace command, $h, is most often used with date and time strings to erase extra information. The only drawback is that the prompt appears to be displayed twice—the first time the entire time string is displayed, then you can see the backspacing, then the "`>`" character is displayed. Some users may find this annoying. It's also possible to use the ANSI backspace command, ESC[D or $e[D, to backspace without erasing.

Screen update

The screen update prompt displays the current directory, date and time at the top of the screen. The system prompt is then just a > character somewhere else on the screen. This system prompt makes heavy use of ANSI commands to move the cursor around the screen, save its position, change color, and whatnot.

```
PROMPT = $e[s$e[1;1H$e[7m$e[K$p$e[1;45H$d @ $t$e[0m$e[u$g
```

I'm going to break this down into several elements to make reading easier:

$e[s	Save the current cursor position
$e[1;1H	"Home" the cursor
$e[7m	Set inverse video on
$e[K	Erase that line
$p	Print the current directory and path
$e[1;45H	Move the cursor to just past the middle of the screen, still the top row.
$d	Display the date
@	Display a space, then the "at" character
$t	Display a space, then the current time
$e[0m	Change the color back to normal video
$e[u	Restore the cursor position
$g	Display a > character, followed by an optional space

All this makes sense—move the cursor around, displaying the date and time (the @ sign may confuse, but it separates the date and time strings well), and the rest. But the Erase Line command (ESC[K) may seem odd. Why erase the top line? Two reasons:

First, the screen might have scrolled over the old directory/date/time display. If so, the new directory/date/time display would look awkward printed over the old.

Second, if the line is not erased, only the directory, date and time will be displayed in inverse video. That would look rather tacky. Instead it's a better effect to have the entire line in inverse video. That's what erasing that line does (with the inverse video mode set on).

Making complex system prompts like this can be really fun. There's an example in chapter 19 that works with a batch file menu program. However, a major drawback to overworking the ANSI commands is that some users will do some unpredictable and stupid things that can ruin the effectiveness of your prompt.

Limited input prompt

This prompt is designed for the user who will only be typing in a few single letter commands:

```
PROMPT=Commands are:$_1 - Help$_2 - WP$_3 - 123$_4 - dBASE$_Choice
[ ]$e[D$e[D
```

This PROMPT displays as follows:

```
Commands are:
1 - Help
2 - WP
3 - 123
4 - dBASE
Choice [ ]
```

The cursor is positioned between the brackets by the two ESC[D commands. This way, the system prompt appears as a menu and to the unsuspecting user, it would look as though only one command is allowed. (Supposedly batch files would be named 1.BAT, 2.BAT and so on to carry out the commands.)

However, this is just a fancy display for the normal system prompt. A user could type DIR or COPY or any DOS command in the choice "box," and that information will ruin the menu effect. There's no way to limit input at the system prompt so the reasoning behind such prompts should be carefully taken into consideration.

The TEMP variable

DOS 5, in its efforts to clean up some DOS mess, has added a new variable you use in your environment: TEMP. That variable indicates to DOS a place where it can stow temporary files. (Quite a few other programs, such as Microsoft *Windows*, also make use of a TEMP variable for the same purpose.)

For example, suppose you have a JUNK, TRASH, or TEMP subdirectory on your system. That's where you stuff files that you don't want to delete but may need later, where you download files to when you dial up an on-line system, or a general type of dust bin for storing temporary files. To let DOS know about TEMP, put the following variable into your environment:

```
SET TEMP=C:\TEMP
```

C:\TEMP is the name of your temporary subdirectory. When DOS 5 now needs to create a temporary file, it will put it into that subdirectory. For example, when you use the SORT filter, DOS 5 will now locate its oddly-named sorting files into C:\TEMP. (They're deleted after the SORT is done.)

It's a good idea to place the above line in your system's AUTOEXEC

.BAT file, as you do with the other types of environment variables covered in this chapter. Also, if your system sports a RAM drive, consider making it your temporary files directory. For example, if the RAM drive is drive D, put the following in your AUTOEXEC.BAT file:

```
SET TEMP = D: \
```

Environment variables

Environment variables come into play in two areas: those few applications programs that take advantage of them, and with (are you ready?) batch files. In fact, because so few applications programs bother to take advantage of environment (or system) variables, only those who have bothered to learn batch file programming know about variables.

Environment variables can be created at any time, though it's best to create them early, such as in your AUTOEXEC.BAT file. The reason is that they take up space. Without knowing otherwise, the environment is limited to a size of 160 bytes (it varies with the version of DOS). This fills up rather quickly when you assign a lot of variables.

Normally your environment space won't overflow. When it does, or if you plan on using a lot of environment variables, you'll need to increase the size of your system's environment. This is covered below, as well as in the next chapter under the CONFIG.SYS file's SHELL command.

The SET command

Of all the environment commands, COMSPEC, PROMPT, and PATH, the most important one as far as batch files are concerned is SET.

Earlier in this chapter, you saw how SET is used to display the current contents of the environment. Also, at other points in this book (especially a few of the batch file examples), you may have seen SET used to create a variable. This is the primary function of the SET command: it places an environment variable into your system's environment.

SET is used to assign a value to an environment variable

SET is really simple to use. In fact, knowing *Microsoft*, it's a wonder why they didn't call it "LET" instead. After all, the BASIC language command to assign a variable is LET.

In BASIC:

```
LET A$ = "DATA
```

In DOS:

```
SET ASTRING = DATA
```

In both examples, the variable name comes first, followed by an equal sign, and finally the data the variable is assigned to. You must use the equal sign with SET to create the assignment or you'll get a "Syntax error." And, unlike some traditional programming language, all the variables SET deals with are strings—not values. So assigning the number 123 to a variable simply assigns the string "123" to that variable—not the value one hundred twenty-three.

```
SET myname = dan
```

This assigns the string "dan" to the environment variable MYNAME. To make sure of it, type SET to see your environment:

```
C > SET
COMSPEC = C: \ COMMAND.COM
PROMPT =
MYNAME = dan
```

Internally, DOS capitalizes the variable names—but it leaves your string data exactly as entered. The variable name, as well as the data you assign to it, can be as long as a DOS command line. (Well, 128 characters minus 3 for "SET" and 2 for the space after set and the equal sign, plus the length of your variable name, etc.)

```
SET long = this is a long string assigned to the variable long
```

This command places "this is a long string assigned to the variable long" into the environment.

```
SET unusualvariablename = hi
```

This command assigns "hi" to the variable name "UNUSUALVARI ABLENAME."

There might be a temptation to enclose strings in quotes. Don't do it unless you want the quotes to become part of the variable data. For example:

```
SET greetings = "Hello"
```

This command assigns the seven characters "Hello"—including the quotes—to the variable GREETINGS.

Also, SET pays attention to spaces:

```
SET TEST = HELLO
```

This sets the variable "TEST_" (note the space) to "_HELLO" (note the space). There's nothing wrong with those extra spaces, but they do take up room in the environment table and they could lead to confusion later on.

To remove a variable, simply assign it an empty string:

```
SET temp =
```

By pressing ENTER after the equal sign, the variable TEMP, as well as whatever string was assigned to it, is removed from the environment. This is good to remember. Because environment space can get tight, it's wise to remove unneeded variables after you've used them. Otherwise, they'll sit in the environment table taking up space that can be used by other variables.

Using variables

Obviously, it's nice that DOS allows you to create variables. They can be used in two circumstances:

1. with programs that recognize the environment
2. with batch files

Quite a few applications programs are taking advantage of the environment and use it for setting certain values. Where normally you would type something like the following:

    C> LM /A/P/T = C: \ TEMP

Programs are letting you SET an environment variable to pass along the same information:

    SET LM = /A /P/T = C: \ TEMP

Programs (that are smart enough) will examine the environment and use any data there to assist running the program. Typically, these SET statements will be issued in an AUTOEXEC.BAT file, though they could better be issued in a batch file to run the program—and then reassigned to nothing after the program is run, as in FIG. 4-8.

4-8 This is an example of using and then losing an environment variable.
```
1: @ECHO OFF
2: REM Batch file to run "LM" program
3: C:
4: CD \LM
5: SET LM=/A/P/T=C:\TEMP
6: LM
7: SET LM=
8: :END
```

This batch file will first move to the \LM subdirectory, set the environment, then run the LM program. After LM is through, the environment variable LM is cleared and the batch file is done.

The second example of using environment variables is to use the variable names in batch files. This is similar to using replaceable command line parameters, but don't confuse the two. (Replaceable command line parameters are covered in chapter 7.)

DOS's batch file interpreter uses the character %, percent sign, to translate environment variables. When surrounded by percent signs, the batch file interpreter expands the environment variable to its string assignment. This happens only in batch files—not on the command line.

For example, suppose the variable NAME is assigned to "Fred Flintstone" by an AUTOEXEC.BAT file:

    SET NAME = Fred Flintstone

The following batch file is used to extract that variable:

    1: @ECHO OFF
    2: ECHO Glad to meet you, %NAME%.

When you run the GREET.BAT file, you'll see the following:

    C > GREET
    Glad to meet you, Fred Flintstone

Because NAME is an environment variable, and it's surrounded by percent signs, the batch file interpreter expands it to whatever string is assigned in the environment table. If you change NAME to something else with the SET command, that new data will appear when you run GREET .BAT.

The secret is the expansion of the variable names by the batch file interpreter. This explains why the following happens when you try to use an environment variable on the command line:

    C > ECHO %NAME%
    %NAME%

The information on the command line does not pass through the batch file interpreter. DOS does exactly what you tell it to: "Echo '%NAME%' to the console."

To see how the expansion works, simply remove the @ECHO OFF command from the GREET.BAT file and watch your screen as the batch file works:

    C > GREET
    ECHO Glad to meet you, Fred Flintstone
    Glad to meet you, Fred Flintstone

    C >

The batch file interpreter is converting the names even as the lines are displayed. This just doesn't happen in the command line.

DOS5's environment variables

DOS 5 has two other variables you can use besides the TEMP variable: DIRCMD and DOSSHELL. DIRCMD helps you customize the output of the DIR command. DOSSHELL is used by the DOS Shell program to specify a location for the DOSSHELL.INI file.

DIRCMD can really come in handy. Because the DOS 5 DIR command has so many optional switches, you can use it to avoid the toil of having to always type in your favorites. Try the following:

SET DIRCMD = /O /L /P

The above assigns the DIRCMD variable to the following DIR command switches: /O, to display a sorted directory; /L to display the directory in lower case; and /P to pause between pages. Now every time you enter the DIR command, it will automatically assume those switches. Neat, eh?

If you want to override the switches specified by the DIRCMD variable, then put a minus in front of them on the command line. For example,

DIR /-L

This turns off the lowercase switch, as specified by the DIRCMD variable.

The DOSSHELL variable is recognized by DOS but severs a rather obscure function. Using the DOSSHELL variable, you can specify another location for the DOSSHELL.INI file (the system information file for DOS Shell). But reason me this: if DOSSHELL and its hoard of files are always in one directory anyway (and usually your DOS directory), why bother? Still, it's a recognized environment variable and a good example of how some applications use them.

Out of space

The only error you can get with the SET command, besides the above mentioned "Syntax error," is "Out of environment space." As you might discover, environment variables can use a lot of memory.

Unless told otherwise, DOS only gives you 160 bytes for the environment. (Some versions of DOS may have less.) That's only 160 bytes for everything: variable names, their assignments, the equal sign, and the final null, or zero, character. That space can go rather quickly when each character you type is one byte.

If you plan on using more than 160 bytes for storing environment variables, you'll need to increase your environment size. You can reassign some variables to nothing. That will clear some space, but it's not really the answer.

Creating an environment larger than 160 bytes is done with the SHELL command in CONFIG.SYS (discussed in the following chapter). SHELL is used to specify a command interpreter other than COMMAND .COM, or to specify a different location on disk for COMMAND.COM (discussed earlier), or to change the environment size. It's the /E: switch that does the trick:

SHELL = COMMAND.COM /E:n

The n is a number ranging from 160 through 32,768. It specifies the number of bytes DOS allocates to the environment. If the number is less than 160 or greater than 32,768, then those two values are used (respectively).

Incidentally, DOS will round the number you specify up to the nearest multiple of 16.

If you suppose that you'll be using 1K (1,024 bytes) of environment space, you can boost it up to that by adding the following line to your CON FIG.SYS file:

```
SHELL = C:\ COMMAND.COM /E:1024
```

This CONFIG.SYS command still uses COMMAND.COM in the root directory (just like normal), but sets aside 1K, or 1,024 bytes, of storage for the environment. Also, if you still want COMMAND.COM to run your AUTOEX EC.BAT file, remember to specify the /P switch:

```
SHELL = C:\ COMMAND.COM /P/E:1024
```

SHELL is a nifty way to increase the size of your environment. Unfortunately, it's only available with DOS Versions 3.2 or later. So what can you do if you're "stuck" with an older version of DOS and want a bigger environment size?

The answer always lies in those busy geniuses who write utility programs. One utility (not in the public domain) is called *SETENV*. It comes with the *Microsoft Macro Assembler* package and was specifically written to alter the environment size for users of DOS 2.0 through 3.1.

The drawback to SETENV is that you must pay $150 retail (often $99 discounted) for it and you get the macro assembler package that you may never ever use. The happy part is that there may be some public domain programs that do the same thing. Offhand I don't know of any, but if they do pop up, a public domain/shareware software warehouse like PC-SIG would know about it. See appendix L for information on contacting PC-SIG.

The environment and batch files

You can use any or all of the environment commands, SET, PATH, and PROMPT in any of your batch files. In fact, you probably already use PATH and PROMPT in your AUTOEXEC batch file. But the use of those commands, and of environment variables, need not be limited to AUTOEXEC .BAT.

Saving the old

One important use of batch files is to run other programs. This will be demonstrated in detail in Part Five of this book. But for now, consider some batch files that run other programs, like the LM.BAT program mentioned earlier in this chapter.

For each batch file that runs a program, you can modify the PATH and SET environment variables. For example, say you have a batch file that you use when writing programs in the C language. Because you only use the C compiler and all the other C goodies when you're programming, you don't need to have those subdirectories on your path all the time. So, you write a batch file called DO-C that sets up your computer's environment for writing C programs (see FIG. 4-9).

4-9 The DO-C batch file creates a C environment.
Name: DO-C.BAT

```
 1: @ECHO OFF
 2: REM Set up environment for C compiler
 3: C:
 4: CD \TURBOC
 5: PATH C:\DOS;C:\TURBOC;C:\UTILITY;..
 6: REM Set APPEND to look for include files and such
 7: APPEND C:\TURBOC\INCLUDE;C:\TURBOC\LIB
 8: REM Set TURBOC environment variable 87=N (no 8087)
 9: SET 87=N
10: ECHO Welcome to Turbo C, Phillipe thanks you.
```

A new path is set for the C program in line 5. In line 7, APPEND is used to set a search path for the include and library file directories. Line 9 sets the environment variable 87 to "N", meaning that this system lacks an 8087 numeric coprocessor.

The disadvantage to this type of batch file is that you will need to manually reset all the above items once you're done working in the C programming language environment. A second batch file, UNDO-C, can be written to do just that (see FIG. 4-10).

4-10 The UNDO-C batch file undoes the C environment.
Name: UNDO-C.BAT

```
1: @ECHO OFF
2: REM Reset computer back to normal
3: PATH C:\DOS;C:\UTILITY;..;C:\WORD
4: APPEND ;
5: SET 87=
6: ECHO System back to normal.
```

In this batch file, the PATH is reset to its previous value (supposedly), APPEND is disabled and the environment variable 87 is cleared. (You should always clear environment variables once you're done with them.)

While these two batch files will help you set your environment for programming in Turbo C (or any other program—simply change the directories and other variables), they lack a wee bit of elegance. For example, you can use an environment variable to temporarily store your old path rather than having to reenter it in UNDO-C.BAT. Try:

SET OLDPATH = %PATH%

The batch file interpreter will expand the variable %PATH% into your system's current path, making the variable OLDPATH equal to the path. Now, you can mess with your system's path and restore it back to what it was simply by using:

    PATH %OLDPATH%

In fact, quite a few intrepid users may already have an OLDPATH variable set by their AUTOEXEC.BAT file. Because OLDPATH always contains a copy of the original path, resetting it is as easy as typing the above command.

Status variables

Another interesting use of variables is to check the status of your batch file. On the supplemental programs diskette is an interesting batch file called HELP.BAT. HELP.BAT actually runs a "main menu" program, which in turn runs more batch file programs. When the secondary batch file programs are done, they rerun HELP.BAT. But before they do, they set a special environment variable called IN.

IN is used to determine which program is running the batch file HELP .BAT. If a secondary batch file is running HELP.BAT, then the value of IN is equal to YES. Otherwise, IN isn't equal to anything (in fact, it doesn't exist). This way, if IN is equal to YES, HELP.BAT will not display its initial screen and move right on the main menu. It uses the IF statement to determine if IN is equal to YES:

    IF "%IN%" = = "YES" GOTO MAIN

If IN has already been set to YES, the IF statement passes the test and batch file execution branches to the MAIN label. Otherwise, the startup screen is displayed.

At the end of the batch file, IN is reset to zero to conserve environment space. This is about the best use of environment variables in batch files. Sadly, batch files are not innately interactive (though chapter 9 offers some tricks to get around that). You can't assign the variables values as the batch file runs, at least not based upon a user's input. In a later chapter you'll see how a special batch file variable, ERRORLEVEL, can be used to get input from the user. But for now, environment variables are best used for saving useful information or keeping track of a specific status.

Summary

The environment is DOS's scratch pad, where it holds important information and where you can place environment variables for use by your batch files.

The SET command is crucial to the environment. It's used to assign variables, reset variables, and display the contents of the environment.

Other than the environment variables you create, the ones DOS offers are COMSPEC, to give the location of COMMAND.COM; PATH, to set a system search path; and PROMPT, for a system prompt.

Because the environment table is rather small, the SHELL command can be used to increase its size. This avoids those nasty "Out of environment space" error messages, but takes up more of your system's valuable RAM.

5
CONFIG.SYS, AUTOEXEC.BAT, and SHUTDOWN.BAT

This chapter deals with the most important files on your computer system—which also happen to be the only two system files you have direct control over: CONFIG.SYS and AUTOEXEC.BAT.

Because it's loaded first, CONFIG.SYS is covered first. CONFIG.SYS sets up your system by loading and running specific programs and device drivers. Although it's not a batch file, some of the items you place into CONFIG.SYS will greatly enhance the performance of your batch files.

AUTOEXEC.BAT is the first program you write that your computer runs (or vice versa). It's the primary batch file that controls how you want your computer to behave for the rest of the day. Sad to say, often AUTOEX EC.BAT is the only batch file anyone ever uses. But because this is an advanced book and you, of course, are a power user, you'll want to gather as much useful information on this batch file as possible. And there is a lot of ground to cover.

Finally, just to be goofy, I've thrown in a third program called SHUT DOWN.BAT. I don't know why Microsoft never saw fit to include this batch file, or something like it, in DOS. After reading about how useful a SHUT DOWN.BAT file can be, you may wonder yourself.

CONFIG.SYS

CONFIG.SYS is your system configuration file. It's used to customize your system. It's also the first one of your personal efforts that DOS pays heed to.

Because DOS lets you create your own CONFIG.SYS file, you can put into it whatever you want. Generally, it's a good idea to fill it up with just about anything you may think you'll need—even though you might not use it at the present.

DOS does let you modify CONFIG.SYS to remove or add commands at any time. The only stipulation is that you need to reset your computer to have the new configuration loaded into memory. (This isn't as bad as it sounds; you may only do it a few times—not the 200 or so I had to while researching this chapter.)

A well-written CONFIG.SYS file can make your system perform at top efficiency. Yet, there are only fifteen commands that CONFIG.SYS uses:

BREAK	DOS	LASTDRIVE
BUFFERS	DRIVPARM	REM
COUNTRY	FCBS	SHELL
DEVICE	FILES	STACKS
DEVICEHIGH	INSTALL	SWITCHES

These commands can be divided into two categories: Those that set your system's conditions, establish parameters, set limits, allocate buffers, etc., and those that load system device drivers or other files (see TABLE 5-1).

Table 5-1

Condition commands	Device control
BREAK	COUNTRY
BUFFERS	DEVICE
DOS	DEVICEHIGH
FCBS	DRIVPARM
FILES	INSTALL
LASTDRIVE	SHELL
REM	
STACKS	
SWITCHES	

The condition commands lay down the rules as far as DOS is concerned. Each one of the commands tells DOS how far to go, or how to handle a certain situation. Briefly, what the condition commands cover is shown in TABLE 5-2.

The device driver commands load a special type of memory-resident program that monitors, alters, or filters the I/O of a device. The most versatile, all-purpose command here is the DEVICE command (logically). The other two commands are more specific (see TABLE 5-3).

The only drawback to stuffing your CONFIG.SYS file with every conceivable command configuration is that several of the commands take up valuable memory. On a computer system with 640K (the "max"), this doesn't present a problem, and if you have DOS 5 it isn't an issue. But if

Table 5-2

Command	Does what?
BREAK	Monitors the pressing of CTRL–BREAK to cancel commands
BUFFERS	Allocates buffer space for file I/O
DOS	Allows for DOS, device drivers, and memory-resident programs to be loaded into reserved (high DOS) memory (DOS 5 only)
FCBS	Used with file sharing to control number of open files
FILES	Sets the maximum number of open files at a time
LASTDRIVE	Sets the maximum number of drive letters available
REM	Allows comments to be included in CONFIG.SYS
STACKS	Allows you to increase stack storage space
SWITCHES	Provides compatibility for programs that don't understand the extended keyboard functions; allows the WINA20.386 file to be moved to another directory

Table 5-3

Command	Does what?
COUNTRY	Set formatting instructions for date, time, etc.
DEVICE	Loads a device driver into low memory
DEVICEHIGH	Loads a device driver into high DOS memory (DOS 5)
DRIVPARM	Defines external disk drives
INSTALL	Loads a memory-resident program during system setup
SHELL	Specifies an alternate COMMAND.COM or location for COMMAND.COM

you have 512K or 256K, DOS 3.3, and your programs require a lot of memory (most of them do), saving a few bytes here and there will help.

For reference, TABLE 5-4 describes approximately how much memory is taken by each of the CONFIG.SYS commands. This isn't an absolute, "final authority" type of chart—just my own calculations based on a 640K PC with the latest version of DOS.

The DEVICE or INSTALL directives will take up the most memory, depending on the size of the driver or memory-resident program installed. For example, my Microsoft Mouse driver, MOUSE.SYS is about 31K in size, yet only uses about 13K of memory after it's loaded. RAMDRIVE, or the older VDISK, is an exception. Because RAMDRIVE creates an electronic, or "virtual," disk from your system's memory, it will use that much memory plus the size of the RAMDRIVE's device driver.

Figuring out the amount of memory LASTDRIVE uses is tricky. The amount of memory used per each drive letter after "E" varies. Yet, for calculation purposes, factor the drive letter (above "E") by 80 bytes and you'll get an approximate size.

Table 5-4

Command	Sucks up this much memory
BREAK	Nothing
BUFFERS	528 bytes per buffer
COUNTRY	Nothing
DEVICE	Approximate size of driver (.SYS) file, except for VDISK
DEVICEHIGH	Nothing (uses high DOS memory)
DOS	Nothing (actually adds memory!)
DRIVPARM	Depends on the size of the control blocks and number of drives defined
FCBS	Nothing
FILES	53 bytes for each value greater than 8
INSTALL	Approximate size of the memory-resident program
LASTDRIVE	80 bytes for each drive letter after "E"
REM	Nothing
SHELL	Depends on environment size
STACKS	Multiply the two values to get the amount of eaten memory
SWITCHES	Nothing

Again, the point to all this might be to save a few bytes here and there on systems that are memory-sparse. There's no use in being petty over bytes—especially for those huge database programs that require you to set FILES and BUFFERS to something ridiculous like 32 or 40. In that case, the one or two K you lose in system memory is made up for by the extra speed of the database. Trust me.

If you own DOS 5, and use some of the commands mentioned earlier, your total memory available will actually be less than with any other version of DOS—sometimes you can have up to 640K free! This is only possible under a few circumstances using what's called *high DOS memory*. (Refer to your DOS 5 manual for more information on the subject.)

CONFIG.SYS commands

There's no need to dwell on CONFIG.SYS in a batch file book. So the following are brief descriptions of the CONFIG.SYS commands, followed by some examples I've stolen from computers around the office and from various friends and not-friends. As far as batch files are concerned, and what's mentioned later on in this book, pay special attention to the DEVICE, LASTDRIVE, and SHELL commands.

BREAK

BREAK is set either on or off.

```
BREAK=ON
```

or

```
BREAK = OFF
```

BREAK's use is confusing to most users. Normally, you can press
CTRL – BREAK (or CTRL – C) to stop any action in DOS, or to return to DOS
from any program that uses the standard DOS keyboard and write-to-
screen functions. If a program doesn't use those functions, however, setting BREAK = ON in CONFIG.SYS allows some applications to be halted by
pressing CTRL – BREAK.

For example, if BREAK were set ON in CONFIG.SYS and a program
was adding a long list of numbers, or sorting, but not writing to the screen,
DOS would still monitor CTRL – BREAK. If pressed, the program would
immediately stop. Otherwise, with BREAK = OFF, DOS would wait until
the program wrote to the screen or made some other I/O call.

BUFFERS

BUFFERS sets the number of file buffers DOS uses:

```
BUFFERS = n.s
```

n can be any number, from 1 through 99, indicating how many disk
buffers your system will use. Each buffer uses 528 bytes of RAM.

s was introduced with DOS 4.0 and it specifies the number of sectors
DOS will read in advance—a sort of "buffering ahead" to speed up disk
access. If s is omitted, DOS won't bother with buffering ahead. Otherwise,
you can specify a value from 1 through 8 for s.

An optional /X switch is used only in DOS 4 to put the buffers into
expanded memory on systems that have expanded memory (of course).
DOS 5 dropped this convention.

The DOS manual babbles on and on about BUFFERS. Basically, the
more buffers you have, the better your system will be able to handle programs that read and write to disk a lot.

Unless told otherwise, the n value for BUFFERS is set internally as
shown in TABLE 5-5.

By not setting BUFFERS in your CONFIG.SYS file DOS "gives" you
the above amount. Note that by setting BUFFERS to something *less* than

Table 5-5

If your system has	BUFFERS =
Nothing specific	2
A 720K, 1.2M or 1.44M disk drive	3
More than 128K of RAM	5
More than 256K of RAM	10
More than 512K of RAM	15

what DOS would give you, you can save memory. But, never mind! Setting a large buffer size makes your system run faster. As a suggestion, set your BUFFERS to a value of 32 or greater. This is generally what some of the more disk-intensive database programs will request. So set BUFFERS to that value now and you won't have to do it later.

BUFFERS = 32

COUNTRY

COUNTRY is used to load country-specific information formatting routines:

COUNTRY = *phone code,code page,country file*

phone code is a three digit number that specifies a specific country. The code is based on the international telephone access code you use to dial foreign countries. The code must have been developed in the USA because that code is 001 (the one DOS automatically assumes if you don't specify COUNTRY in your CONFIG.SYS file).

code page is an optional three digit number used to specify a character set to be used for different countries. Basically, the ASCII characters stay the same, but the characters for codes 128 through 255 (the Extended ASCII set) can be altered. These alternative code pages will use some foreign characters that aren't available in the standard, "USA" code page. If *code page* is omitted, you must specify the second comma.

country file is the name of a country information file, usually COUN TRY.SYS that was supplied with DOS. If COUNTRY.SYS is not in your boot disk's root directory, you should specify a full pathname to it.

COUNTRY basically deals with the way DOS formats certain information, such as the date and time. For example, normally, or in the United States, the date has a specific format:

month, day, year

However, some European countries use other formats. In England (the United Kingdom), the following format is used for the date:

day, month, year

By using the COUNTRY command in CONFIG.SYS, you can tell DOS to format its date and time information, as well as the currency sign and decimal separator (which is a comma, not a period, in some countries) for a specific country. See TABLE 5-6 and TABLE 5-7 for a listing of *phone code* and *code page* values.

Note in TABLE 5-7 that a country can choose any of the code pages listed. Some may have more than one available, but only one code page can be specified at a time.

Table 5-6

Country/Region	Code
Arabic	785
Australia	061
Belgium	032
Canada	001
Canada (French)	002
China (PRC)	086
Denmark	045
English (Intl.)	061
Finland	358
France	033
Germany	049
Israel (Hebrew)	972
Italy	039
Japan	081
Korea	082
Latin America	003
Netherlands	031
Norway	047
Portugal	351
Simplified Chinese	086
Spain	034
Sweden	046
Switzerland	041
Tiawan	088
United Kingdom	044
United States	001

Table 5-7

Country/Region	Codes
Arabic	864, 850
Australia	437, 850
Belgium	437, 850
Canada	437, 850
Canada (French)	863, 850
China (PRC)	936, 850, 437
Denmark	865, 850
English (Intl.)	437, 850
Finland	850, 437
France	437, 850
Germany	437, 850
Israel (Hebrew)	437
Italy	437, 850
Japan	932, 850, 437
Korea	934, 850, 437
Latin America	437, 850
Netherlands	437, 850
Norway	865, 850
Portugal	860, 850
Simplified Chinese	936, 437
Spain	437, 850
Sweden	437, 850
Switzerland	437, 850
Tiawan	936, 850, 437
United Kingdom	437, 850
United States	437, 850

The following COUNTRY command sets up your system's formatting information for a computer in the United Kingdom:

```
COUNTRY = 044,437,C: \ DOS \ COUNTRY.SYS
```

The number 044 is the international phone code for the United Kingdom. The number 437 is the code page value (a good, general-purpose code page). And finally a full pathname to the default COUNTRY.SYS file is specified.

Changing keyboard definition

If you want to further define your system for a foreign country, use the KEYB command. KEYB reassigns the keyboard layout to match common typewriters for foreign countries. This allows users in non-English speaking countries to have access to their own, unique alphabetic characters.

To complete the transformation to a U.K. computer, you could add the following line to your AUTOEXEC.BAT file:

KEYB UK

This loads the standard keyboard layout that an ENGLISH typist would be used to. Various keys are replaced and reassigned on that keyboard, including the £ (English pound) key replacing the # (number-pound) sign.

To switch to the standard keyboard, press CTRL – ALT – F1. To switch back to the foreign keyboard, press CTRL – ALT – F2.

DEVICE

DEVICE is used to load a device driver:

DEVICE = *pathname*

pathname is the full pathname of the device. It's important to specify a full path because no PATH command has been set yet (it's done in AUTOEXEC) and no drive aliases have been assigned (using SUBST). The full pathname should include the drive letter and directories indicating the driver's location. In my own system, I put all the system drivers in my DOS directory and simply list the full path for each DEVICE I load (see below for an example).

There are ten drivers included with DOS 5:

ANSI.SYS
DISPLAY.SYS
DRIVER.SYS
EGA.SYS
EMM386.EXE (386 systems only)
HIMEM.SYS (286 and 386 systems only)
PRINTER.SYS
RAMDRIVE.SYS
SETVER.EXE
SMARTDRV.SYS

(The ninth driver, PARTDRV.SYS, has no documentation, though I'm guessing it has something to do with multiple hard drive partitions.)

EMM386 and SETVER are still device drivers, even though they end with EXE. These programs are bi-modal. You can load them, as device drivers, but then they can also be run from the command prompt. Note that the following device drivers should not be loaded on a non-80386 or '486 system:

EMM386.EXE
HIMEM.SYS

Two other .SYS files should never be used with the DEVICE command:

    COUNTRY.SYS
    KEYBOARD.SYS

Also, other device drivers may be available, including alternative ANSI .SYS drivers and mouse device drivers such as MOUSE.SYS.

DEVICEHIGH

The DEVICEHIGH command is essentially the same thing as DEVICE. The difference is that DEVICEHIGH loads a device driver into high DOS memory, as opposed to the conventional 640K of RAM. The net effect is that, with the driver now in high DOS memory, you have that much more memory in which to run your applications.

The format for DEVICEHIGH is similar to that of DEVICE:

    DEVICEHIGH [size = n]pathname

Pathname is the name of a device you want to load into high DOS memory. Most of the time, that's all you'll need to specify. But some applications require more memory, in which case you must tell DEVICEHIGH how much space they need. For example, if your driver BLORT.SYS uses up some 20K of RAM, you'd use the following:

    DEVICEHIGH size = 5000 C: \ DEV \ BLORT.SYS

Oops! Five thousand isn't 20K. Actually, it is in a way. DEVICEHIGH (for some reason) wants you to list the size value in hexadecimal, base 16. So 20K, which is 20,480, is really 5000 hexadecimal. (Silly, silly.) To find out these secret numbers, do the following:

1. Load the driver using the standard DEVICE command in CON FIG.SYS.
2. Reset your system.
3. Use DOS 5's MEM command with the /CLASSIFY switch to locate the driver in memory.
4. Take note of the driver's size.

Specify that value with DEVICEHIGH's size option and you're set to go.

Note that you must specify the following commands in your CON FIG.SYS file to use DEVICEHIGH:

    DEVICE = C: \ DOS \ EMM386.EXE
    DOS = umb

Also, and I hate to mention this last, but you can only pull this trick on an 80386 or '486 equipped PC.

DOS

The DOS directive is another memory saving DOS 5 command you can stick in your CONFIG.SYS file. The magic it does is to load DOS's files and information into your PC's HMA (the High Memory Area), an extra 64K of memory that's only found on 286 and 386 PCs. The format is:

```
DOS = [umb ¦ noumb][high | low]
```

The defaults are NOUMB and LOW, meaning DOS will not create UMBs (Upper Memory Blocks, memory locations in high DOS memory) and it will load itself in low RAM, just as every previous version of DOS has done.

Specifying DOS = UMB means that DOS will maintain "links" between upper and lower memory, allowing other device drivers to be loaded in upper memory. But note that this is only possible if you have some sort of device driver (such as EMM386) to map high DOS memory.

Specifying DOS = HIGH allows DOS to load itselft into the High Memory Area (HMA), which is created by the HIMEM.SYS device driver. {The most common implementation of . . . .}

The most common implementation of the DOS directive is with the HIGH switch. If you have a 286 or 386 system, often you'll use the following two commands in CONFIG.SYS:

```
DEVICE = C: \ DOS \ HIMEM.SYS
DOS = HIGH
```

The HIMEM.SYS driver allows DOS to use an extra 64K of RAM in 286 and 386 systems that have at least 350K of extended memory. After this is done, you specify DOS = HIGH to force DOS to load itself into that high memory. Now you should be swimming in conventional memory, up to the full 640K free.

Unfortunately, though, this function doesn't work on the older 8088-level of PCs.

DRIVPARM

DRIVPARM sets up a "block driver" that allows you to install an external disk drive in your system (or add a 720K drive to an older type of PC). The format for the DRIVEPARM command is:

```
DRIVPARM = \ d:number[/c][/f:type][/h:heads][/i][/n][/s:sectors]
[/t:tracks]
```

All that—those options—targets a specific type of drive you're installing in your system. (They're all listed in your DOS manual if you're curious about the details.) As an example, consider the following line in a CON FIG.SYS file that would set up an external drive D, a 720K drive on an older PC:

```
DRIVPARM = /D:3 /F:2 /I
```

The external drive is no. 3 (D:), the drive type (form factor) is 2 for a 720K drive; and the /I switch is specified because it was specifically put there for this situation (a 720K drive on an older PC system).

FCBS

FCBS is used to set the maximum number of files (actually File Control BlockS) that DOS can have open at one time:

    FCBS = *max, close*

max is the maximum number of FCBS that can be opened at one time. It can be any value from 1 through 255.

An option with DOS 3.3 and 4 is *close*, specified after *max* and a comma. It's a number from 0 through 255. It specifies the number of FCBS that will not be closed by DOS, should the total number of FCBS opened by DOS exceed *max*. *close* is used to protect a given number of FCBS from being automatically closed by DOS when an application tries to open more than *max* files. *close* should always be less than *max*.

If you don't set FCBS in your CONFIG.SYS file, DOS automatically assigns values of 4 and 0 to *max* and *close* respectively.

FILES

FILES specifies the maximum of files that DOS can have open at a time:

    FILES = *n*

n sets the maximum number of files that can be open. Its value ranges from 8 through 255. If you don't set FILES in your CONFIG.SYS file, DOS uses 8.

FILES is similar to BUFFERS. It's generally a good idea to set FILES to a high number, generally equal to the value of BUFFERS. (After all, if DOS won't let you open that many files, why have the BUFFERS?)

A question that usually comes up concerning FILES is "Why set them at all?" The answer is that DOS controls access to all files on disk. If a program asks to create or access a file and there are already the maximum number of files open (according to FILES), your program gets an error. These errors are rather uncommon because DOS automatically gives you eight files whether FILES is set by CONFIG.SYS or not. But just to be on the safe side, FILES should be set to a high number, with values greater than 20 being the most common. For example:

    FILES = 32

This command would make a perfect companion to a BUFFERS = 32 command (as any good maitre d' would let you know).

INSTALL

Starting with DOS 4, INSTALL allows you to load memory-resident applications in a CONFIG.SYS file rather than during execution of your AUTOEXEC.BAT file:

INSTALL *filename*

filename is the full path and name of your memory-resident program. INSTALL will load and execute that program, leaving it in memory for later use. Using INSTALL, as opposed to including the memory-resident program's installation in AUTOEXEC.BAT, makes more efficient use of memory.

At present, four DOS programs can be used with CONFIG.SYS's INSTALL command:

FASTOPEN
KEYB
NLSFUNC
SHARE

Other, third-party memory-resident applications should also work with INSTALL. Refer to their manuals to see if it's okey-dokey.

LASTDRIVE

LASTDRIVE is used to set the maximum number of disk drives your system can have:

LASTDRIVE = *n*

n is the highest drive letter your system can have. It can be any letter from A to Z (which implies that your system can only handle 26 drives max.). The default minimum value is the number of drives you have in your system. If you have a hard disk, then it's drive C. If LASTDRIVE isn't specified, DOS gives you up to drive E.

LASTDRIVE comes in handy when you're assigning "fake" drives using the SUBST command (see chapter 4). If you want to SUBST a number of drive letters for directories, simply specify LASTDRIVE equal to the maximum number of drives you want substituted. As long as your system isn't short on memory, make it drive Z:

LASTDRIVE = Z

This command lets DOS know that your system can handle up to Z drives. You don't need to use all those drives—it's just the letters you want.

REM

REM allows you to include comments in your CONFIG.SYS file, starting with DOS 4:

REM *comment*

comment can be anything—any string of characters. This allows you to comment the operation of your CONFIG.SYS file, to include important notes, or to "comment out" certain CONFIG.SYS commands that no longer apply to your system (without deleting them entirely). CON FIG.SYS will not execute any commands after a REM.

Aside from REM, you may also include blank lines in your CON FIG.SYS file to "clean it up" a bit.

SHELL

SHELL allows you to specify another command interpreter instead of COMMAND.COM, or to specify a different location for COMMAND.COM. Additionally, by using COMMAND.COM with SHELL, you can adjust the size of your computer's environment:

SHELL = *pathname*

pathname is the full filename, including drive letter, colon, and path, for an alternate COMMAND.COM file, or an alternate location for COMMAND .COM.

When you specify COMMAND.COM as your shell, two optional switches can be used: /P and /E.

The /P switch instructs DOS to load and execute a batch file named AUTOEXEC.BAT in the root directory of your boot disk after COMMAND .COM is executed. Otherwise, without the /P switch specified, COMMAND .COM will simply display a copyright message and then the default command prompt. (It won't even ask for the date and time.)

The /E switch is used to change the size of COMMAND.COM's environment. An optional value *n* sets the size of the environment and it ranges from 160 to 32,768 bytes. For example:

SHELL = C: \ COMMAND.COM /P /E:2048

This command directs DOS to use the COMMAND.COM file found in the root directory of your hard drive, load and run AUTOEXEC.BAT after it's finished, and allocate 2K, or 2,048 bytes of space, for the environment. This example is a must for your CONFIG.SYS file if you want more environment space.

Also, as was mentioned in the previous chapter, SHELL doesn't change the COMSPEC= value in your default environment. That needs to be done in AUTOEXEC.BAT with the SET command.

STACKS

STACKS allows you to increase internal stack storage space used by DOS:

STACKS = *number,size*

number is a value ranging from eight through 64. It indicates the number of stack frames DOS is to allocate. The default value for a PC/XT computer is zero, for AT and faster computers, DOS sets *number* to 9 unless otherwise specified.

size indicates the size (in bytes) of each stack. It can be a value from 0 through 512, with the default value for PC/XTs equal to zero and AT computers equal to 128.

Normally, DOS uses an internal stack to keep track of return addresses from interrupt calls. So what does that mean to you? Not much, unless you see a very rare error message: "Out of stack space, System Halted." This can be devastating. (I almost fainted when I first saw it.)

On AT machines that can run multiple processes (or so they claim), it may be a good idea to allocate a few internal stacks. Otherwise, unless your software application mentions using the STACKS command in CONFIG.SYS, set is as follows:

    STACKS = 0,0

SWITCHES

SWITCHES suppresses the use of extended keyboard functions:

    SWITCHES = /K

/K is used to suppress the extended keyboard functions, preventing them from being used.

Some older software packages may not properly interpret the extended keyboard's functions. When SWITCHES /K is specified in your CONFIG.SYS file, the computer is forced to use the older, conventional keyboard functions. This will make your system more compatible with older applications.

The second format of the SWITCHES command is

    SWITCHES = /W

This tells DOS and Windows that the file WINA20.386 isn't in the root directory. Where is it? You must edit your Windows' SYSTEM.INI file and, under the section starting "[386enh]", add a line as follows:

    DEVICE = C: \ WINDOWS \ WINA20.386

Specify the proper location for the WINA20.386 file; C: \ WINDOWS is assumed. Also, to remove that painful sucker from the root directory, you must peel away its read-only attribute with the following command:

    ATTRIB −R C: \ WINA20.386

You should also do this if you don't have a 386 or later PC.

CONFIG.SYS

One of the best ways to become familiar with advanced CONFIG.SYS files is to take a look at some. The following are CONFIG.SYS files that I use on my computers and that various friends employ. Each of them is followed by an explanation of what they do and why.:

Standard CONFIG.SYS

```
BUFFERS = 32
FILES = 20
DEVICE = C:\DOS\ANSI.SYS
```

Two of the most common commands you'll see in CONFIG.SYS are BUFFERS and FILES. Most databases want you to have at least 20 of each. The CONFIG.SYS file above is configured for a "worst-case scenario." Just about any program, no matter how disk intensive it is, will probably not want more than 32 buffers and 20 files.

Even if you're sour to the entire idea of a CONFIG.SYS file, you should always include the FILES and BUFFERS statements. Having extra files and buffers available not only makes certain programs run smoothly, it also speeds up DOS in certain instances. For example, DOS takes a long time to display the last few files of a long, fragmented directory (one with, say more than 200 files in it). Increasing the BUFFERS and FILES values will alleviate this problem.

ANSI.SYS is also thrown into this CONFIG.SYS file to give the system the extra control that ANSI.SYS offers. Note that the full pathname, including drive letter, was given for ANSI.SYS. Again, this avoids having to keep the file in your root directory.

My favorite CONFIG.SYS   Figure 5-1 shows the CONFIG.SYS I use on my old, original IBM PC. Two REM statements start my CONFIG.SYS, telling me which computer the CONFIG.SYS file is on (I call my PC "Denise"), and the date the file was last updated. FILES, BUFFERS, and ANSI.SYS are specified, as are the device drivers DRIVER.SYS and MOUSE.SYS.

5-1 This is the CONFIG.SYS on my original PC.

```
REM CONFIG.SYS File for Denise
REM September 9, 1988

BUFFERS = 32,8
FILES = 20
DEVICE = C:\SYSTEM\DOS\DRIVER.SYS /D:1 /T:80 /S:9 /H:2 /F:2
DEVICE = C:\SYSTEM\DOS\ANSI.SYS
DEVICE = C:\SYSTEM\MOUSE\MOUSE.SYS
```

DRIVER.SYS is used to establish my second internal floppy drive as a 720K 3½-inch drive. Originally, I had two 5¼-inch drives, but replaced drive B with a 3½-inch drive for compatibility with the new PS/2 machines, as well as laptops. Also, the disk holds more information and makes backing up less tedious.

The DRIVER device driver configures my drive B as an "external" logical drive D that can hold 720K. When I access the drive as D, it's a 720K drive. But the same drive, logically accessed as B, is only a 320K drive. This is because DOS (and IBM and the gang) assumes that you cannot have a 720K drive in a PC/XT. Therefore, anything that's 720K must be an "external" drive, hence it's drive D. Confusing? Yes. But the DRIVER.SYS command in CONFIG.SYS allows me the 720K drive (as D).

MOUSE.SYS is the Microsoft Mouse driver. You need to load the mouse driver into memory in order to use your mouse hardware. (Because the mouse isn't a part of the normal system, you must load its BIOS routines.) There are two ways you can load the mouse driver: MOUSE.COM and MOUSE.SYS.

MOUSE.COM is a memory-resident program that installs the mouse BIOS. You type MOUSE.COM, or just "MOUSE," at the DOS prompt right before you run a mouse-operated program. Once it's in memory, it stays there, so you don't need to type MOUSE a second time. (If you do, you get an "already installed" message.)

MOUSE.SYS is the same mouse driver that's packaged in MOUSE .COM. The difference is, it's a device driver and can be loaded when CON FIG.SYS runs.

By using MOUSE.SYS in CONFIG.SYS, you never have to worry about typing MOUSE before you run a mouse-driven program, and then having that program not work. The mouse driver is always in memory when you use MOUSE.SYS, so it's an easier way to do things.

Multi-drive CONFIG.SYS

```
BUFFERS = 32
FILES = 20
LASTDRIVE = Z
DEVICE = C:\DOS\ANSI.SYS
SHELL = C:\DOS\COMMAND.COM /P
```

Aside from BUFFERS, FILES, and ANSI.SYS, this user's CONFIG.SYS file adds the LASTDRIVE and SHELL configuration commands.

LASTDRIVE allows up to Z drive letters to be assigned. Normally, DOS will give you 5, A through E. But by setting LASTDRIVE to Z, this user can take advantage of the SUBST command and have up to 23 subdirectories substituted as disk drives (the other three are drives A, B, and C).

SHELL is used here to specify a new location for COMMAND.COM. Normally, SHELL is used to specify a new command processor. Here, the command simply directs SYSINIT to look for COMMAND.COM in the \ DOS subdirectory. Also, the /P switch was added, allowing the user's AUTOEXEC.BAT file to run. There is one drawback to this command, the user must place the following line into their AUTOEXEC.BAT file:

```
SET COMSPEC=C:\COMMAND.COM
```

That will patch up the minor faux pas of DOS not recognizing from whence it loaded COMMAND.COM.

RAM disk example

```
BUFFERS = 32
FILES = 32
DEVICE = C:\DOS\ANSI.SYS
DEVICE = C:\DOS\RAMDRIVE 360 512 64
```

The only new addition to this CONFIG.SYS file is the new device, RAM-DRIVE. RAMDRIVE is DOS's idea of a RAM disk. (A RAM disk is a super-fast, electronic disk drive that uses memory instead of a physical diskette.) There are much better RAM disk drivers out on the market than RAM-DRIVE, most of which come with memory upgrade boards. (But RAM-DRIVE is free with DOS, so what the heck?)

This RAMDRIVE driver has the options "360 512 64" tagged on. This directs RAMDRIVE to create a 360K disk from memory with 512 byte sectors. The disk will allow up to 64 entries in the root directory.

If your system has extended memory, you can specify the /E switch to place the RAM disk there. The following CONFIG.SYS command would place a one megabyte RAM drive into extended memory:

```
DEVICE = C:\DOS\RAMDRIVE 1000 512 64 /E
```

The /A switch can likewise be used to put the RAM drive in expanded memory.

Yet another personal CONFIG.SYS Figure 5-2 shows the CONFIG.SYS file on my 386, multitasking system. There is strong evidence of QEMM, Quarter-deck's 386 memory management program (which comes with the DESQview/386 extended DOS environment).

5-2 The CONFIG.SYS file on a multitasking 386 system.

```
DEVICE=C:\SYSTEM\DV\QEMM.SYS RAM EXTMEM=2048
BUFFERS = 32
FILES = 40
LASTDRIVE = Z
SHELL=C:\SYSTEM\DOS\COMMAND.COM /E:1024 /P
DEVICE = C:\SYSTEM\DV\LOADHI.SYS C:\SYSTEM\DOS\ANSI.SYS
DEVICE = C:\SYSTEM\DV\LOADHI.SYS C:\SYSTEM\MOUSE\MOUSE.SYS
DEVICE = C:\SYSTEM\DV\LOADHI.SYS C:\SYSTEM\DOS\VDISK.SYS 2048 /E
```

The first line in the CONFIG.SYS file fires up QEMM, the 386's memory control program. The RAM option is specified, which allows memory-resident programs and device drivers to be loaded into "high DOS memory," or secret memory areas above the 640K DOS boundary. QEMM performs the memory mapping that makes that possible, and in the end result you have more RAM in your computer for programs.

QEMM converts all of this PC's Extended memory into Expanded memory, which can be used under DOS. (DOS cannot directly access Extended memory.) The EXTMEM option is used to retain two megabytes (2048K) of Extended memory for use as a RAM disk.

The next three lines are standard: BUFFERS specifies 32 file buffers; FILES allows for 40 files maximum to be open at a time; and LASTDRIVE is set to Z. You may think FILES and BUFFERS are high in this system—and they are. But this guarantees that they'll probably never need to be reset by some file happy, demanding program. (Also note that QEMM can do special things with FILES, BUFFERS and LASTDRIVE, stuff which isn't shown in FIG. 5-2.)

The next line is the SHELL directive, which sets a new location for COMMAND.COM, sets aside 1024 bytes for the environment, and indicates that AUTOEXEC.BAT should be run (the /P switch).

The last three lines are the most peculiar, especially to someone who's unfamiliar with QEMM, QRAM, or any of the noble DOS memory management utilities. LOADHI.SYS is a QEMM device driver that loads DOS device drivers into high DOS memory (as specified by QEMM's RAM switch). Here, three devices, ANSI.SYS, MOUSE.SYS, and VDISK.SYS, are loaded into high memory. (Though VDISK's two megabyte RAM drive is placed into Extended memory, via the /E switch.)

The net effect of using LOADHI.SYS is that all three programs aren't placed in the main, 640K of RAM. How much memory is saved? Only about 14K. But for large spreadsheets, graphics, and other memory-mad programs, that's 14 more kilobytes you have to play with. (Other memory-resident programs, such as those you run in AUTOEXEC.BAT, can also be stuffed into high DOS memory using QEMM's LOADHI.COM. Refer to the QEMM manual for additional information.)

DOS 5's suggestion   When you run the DOS 5 INSTALL program, it builds a suggested CONFIG.SYS file for you and places it on your hard drive. (DOS 4 did the same thing.) When I first installed DOS 5 on my test machine, it decided I needed the CONFIG.SYS file shown in FIG. 5-3.

5-3   This is the CONFIG.SYS file DOS 5 gave me.

```
DEVICE=C:\SYSTEM\DOS\HIMEM.SYS
DOS=HIGH
FILES=32
BUFFERS=30
STACKS=0,0
```

DOS 5 is smart about its CONFIG.SYS file, a lot smarter than DOS 4 was when it created a CONFIG.SYS file during installation. Everything is brief—and enough. DOS 4 only gave me 25 BUFFERS and 8 FILES. DOS 5 is smart enough to know most applications require more than that. DOS, the installation program detected that I have a 386 system and installed HIMEM.SYS and DOS=HIGH for me. It was a shock to boot the system and find a whopping 640K free under DOS.

After tinkering with the system for a while, I settled on the CON FIG.SYS file shown in FIG. 5-4. It's more detailed, plus it shows the inclu-

5-4 Here is my final CONFIG.SYS file under DOS 5.

```
 1:REM This is my DOS 5 CONFIG.SYS file
 2:REM Dell 320LT, 386SX system
 3:REM September 20, 1990
 4:
 5: Device=c:\system\386max\386max.sys
    pro=c:\system\386max\386max.pro
 6:REM DEVICE=C:\SYSTEM\DOS\HIMEM.SYS
 7:
 8:DEVICE = C:\SYSTEM\386MAX\386LOAD.SYS
   PROG=C:\SYSTEM\MOUSE\MOUSE.SYS /C1
 9:
10:SHELL=C:\SYSTEM\DOS\COMMAND.COM /P /E:1024
11:DOS=HIGH
12:FILES=32
13:BUFFERS=32
14:STACKS=0,0
```

sion of Qualitas' 386 memory manager, 386MAX. Note how HIMEM.SYS was REMmed out in line 6? It's not needed when you run 386MAX. Other commands are pretty much the same as they were in the original, save for the REM statements I added. ("REMming out" is covered later in this chapter.)

DOS 5's INSTALL program also configured an AUTOEXEC.BAT program for my system. That's displayed later in this chapter.

All told

CONFIG.SYS is an important part of your system and you should know what to put into it. Above all, be very careful of programs that do self-modification to your CONFIG.SYS file. As long as you stick by some of the recommendations mentioned previously, you should be doing okay.

AUTOEXEC.BAT

AUTOEXEC.BAT is your system's startup file. It's also the most common batch file, and the most important. Its primary function is to set up your system and customize your operations. Because of this, you must be careful about what you place into AUTOEXEC.BAT. Also, there might be a few things your AUTOEXEC.BAT is missing. Keep reading.

Behind the scenes

Reviewing how DOS is loaded, first comes IBMBIO, the DOS BIOS, followed by IBMDOS, the "kernel." This is followed by CONFIG.SYS (if present), and finally COMMAND.COM. The COMMAND.COM that comes with DOS will look for and execute a batch file named AUTOEXEC in the root directory of your boot disk. (If you use the SHELL command to place COMMAND.COM in a subdirectory, the /P switch must be specified in order for AUTOEXEC.BAT to be executed.)

If AUTOEXEC.BAT isn't found, COMMAND.COM asks for the date and time to be entered, displays a copyright notice, and displays the default system command prompt, as shown in FIG. 5-5.

5-5 This is Scott M's AUTOEXEC.BAT.

```
Current date is Tue   1-01-1980
Enter new date (mm-dd-yy): 7-17-89
Current time is 0:01:06:07
Enter new time: 15:54

IBM DOS Version 4.00
   (C)Copyright International Business Machines Corp 1981,1988

   (C)Copyright Microsoft Corp 1981-1986

C>
```

Things to do:
Setting the clock, PATH, PROMPT, and MODE

What you put in AUTOEXEC.BAT is up to you. Some people write complex AUTOEXEC files that spiff-up their entire system (and take about fifteen minutes to run). Other people only include the name of a program they want to run immediately after booting their computer. Both examples are fine because both express how you can personalize your system using AUTOEXEC.

But for the majority of people, AUTOEXEC does some "standard" operations, more or less. Consider that AUTOEXEC is the first program that does anything on your computer. (CONFIG.SYS just loads drivers and initializes system settings.) Because it gives you control over your system each time you start your computer, there are some things you can do in your AUTOEXEC that should be done first.

Most people develop an AUTOEXEC strategy. There are always a certain number of things that should be done by the AUTOEXEC.BAT file. These include:

- Setting the system clock
- Setting a search path via the PATH command
- Setting a system prompt with the PROMPT command
- Setting the screen mode, or setting up the printer with the MODE command
- Changing the screen color
- SUBSTituting or JOINing drives and subdirectories
- Setting environment variables via the SET command
- Executing startup programs
- Executing applications programs or user "shells"

These are only a few of the many things that could be done in an AUTOEXEC file. Additionally, you can use any of the regular DOS commands (after all, they were why batch files were originally invented). For example, you can use CLS to clear the screen, TYPE to list a text document (rather than use repeated ECHO statements), CD to change directories—any of the DOS commands are legal in AUTOEXEC, and in some cases, necessary.

The following descriptions go into more detail on the above categories:

Setting the system clock Because DOS asks you to if you don't have an AUTOEXEC file, the first thing most people put in their AUTOEXEC file is a command to set the system clock. DOS offers two commands, TIME and DATE, that get it up to speed:

```
DATE
TIME
```

These two commands in AUTOEXEC.BAT will prompt the user to enter the date and time—just as DOS normally would had AUTOEXEC.BAT not been present.

However, most PC/XTs can have internal clocks added to them, either on a special clock card or a multi-function card that has a"real-time" clock and battery backup.

If your PC has such an internal clock, you'll need to issue the command to read the time from the clock in your AUTOEXEC file. For example, with the AST Six-pac multi-function card, the command is ASTCLOCK. Other real-time clocks may use programs such as GET CLOCK or TIMER. These programs simply read the time from the real-time clock hardware and set DOS's internal clock.

So, depending on your hardware, you would add a command in AUTOEXEC.BAT that looked something like the following:

```
ASTCLOCK
```

or

```
GETCLOCK
```

or

```
TIMER/S
```

AT-class computers (including all 286, 386, 486 and ?86 computers of the future) don't need a time-setting command in their AUTOEXEC file. The reason is that the AT BIOS automatically reads the time from the AT's battery backed-up RAM. So for an AT computer, a set-the-time command in the AUTOEXEC file is unnecessary.

Setting a search path Typically, the next command to be issued by

AUTOEXEC.BAT is the PATH command. This sets up the search path for any program that might be included later in the batch file, as well as the programs you want on the path while you run the computer:

PATH = C: \ DOS;C: \ UTILITY;C: \ 1-2-3

Of course, this isn't a "must have" command early on in a batch file. As long as full pathnames are specified for any programs AUTOEXEC.BAT may run, there's no need to set a path until later.

Setting a system prompt After the PATH is set, the next command most users include is the PROMPT command. This sets the system prompt, though the system prompt may not be visible until AUTOEXEC.BAT finishes running:

PROMPT pg

Or, you can choose from a variety of interesting prompts, all covered in chapter 4.

Setting the MODE Mode is one of those totally useful and confusing commands. It started out rather innocently. In the fine tradition of all-purpose commands, MODE has mushroomed into an ugly, multipurpose mess.

The MODE command has several functions, ten with DOS 5. With MODE you can do the following:

- Control the printer
- Control the display
- Control the serial port
- Redirect printer output to the serial port
- Manage code pages
- Select a code page
- Display current code page
- Refresh the code page
- Request a status
- Set the keyboard's "typematic" rates

Most of these are things you might need to do in AUTOEXEC.BAT. Two of the most common are setting the screen mode (only needed for color monitors) and creating a serial printer port:

MODE Co80

This enables your color monitor to display color on an 80-column screen. If you are vision impaired, you could try:

MODE Co40

This sets up a color monitor in the 40-column mode, which is far more readable.

Though not related to the MODE command, users with Hercules

Monochrome Adapter cards may want to issue a command to set up their monochrome monitors. HGC is the command to enable a Hercules graphics card. It could easily replace, or serve the same function as, the MODE command would for a color monitor:

```
HGC FULL
```

This command enables the Hercules Graphics Card (HGC) to its full graphics potential.

A few users need MODE to set up a serial printer. This involves setting up the serial port, and redirecting printer output from the printer port to the serial port.

This takes two steps with the MODE command as well:

```
MODE COM1:1200,N,8,1
MODE LPT1 = COM1
```

The first command sets the first serial port (COM1) to 1200 bps (bits per second), No parity, an 8-bit word length, and 1 stop bit. (See the DOS manual for other settings.)

The second command reassigns output from LPT1, the first printer port, to COM1, the first serial port. These two MODE commands enable the user to use COM1 and a serial printer as any other user would use LPT1 (or the PRN device).

Before moving on, it should be noted that MODE (and HGC) is a program on disk. If used in AUTOEXEC.BAT, a full pathname should be specified—or the PATH should be set to include the subdirectories where those programs are located.

Changing colors   This only works if your system has a color display (naturally). There are many ways to change the color of the screen. The first, and cheapest, is with the ANSI.SYS driver the nice people who sold you DOS have given you. (You do have ANSI.SYS in your CONFIG.SYS file, don't you?)

If you create or edit your AUTOEXEC.BAT file with EDLIN, it's possible to ECHO an ANSI display string in AUTOEXEC.BAT, allowing you to start up with a colorful display:

```
ECHO ^[[37;44m;
```

This command would give you that prestigious white on blue screen that so many users clamor for. The problem with this is that some programs will change the color back to boring white on black. To get around this, there are several screen color programs available. The most popular of which comes with the highly touted Norton Utilities.

In Norton's BE, Batch Enhancer, utility there is SA option. SA stands for Screen Attributes. BE SA allows you to change screen color to any foreground or background color that your monitor is capable of. For example:

```
BE SA white on blue
```

This sets the foreground (character) color to white and the background color to blue. (It sure beats the heck out of remembering what the ANSI numbers stand for.)

Of course, you could always put the color changing commands into your system prompt, via PROMPT's $e meta command—but why do that when you can buy the Norton Utilities? (More information on Norton's batch file enhancers is covered in chapter 11.)

SUBST or JOIN commands   Those users who make use of SUBST and JOIN will want to make their substitutions early on. AUTOEXEC is the perfect place to make drive substitutions and to JOIN disk drives as subdirectories. In some instances, these commands should be issued before the PATH statement is set:

```
SUBST U: C:\UTILITY
SUBST W: C:\WP\WORDSTAR
SUBST T: C:\RELAY
JOIN A: C:\DEV\DRIVEA
```

These substitutions help prepare your system. It might even be helpful to ECHO a substitution message to the console (especially if you've turned ECHO OFF). So the above commands may be followed by:

```
ECHO Drives substituted:
SUBST
ECHO Drives joined:
JOIN
```

The SUBST and JOIN commands by themselves simply list out the substituted and joined drives.

Setting environment variables   Quite a few programs rely on environment variables: Borland's Turbo C, the design package AutoCAD, the Clipper database, and on and on. This is the ideal place to set them:

```
SET TEMP=C:\WINDOWS\TEMP
```

The environment variable "TEMP" is used by DOS 5, as well as Microsoft's *Windows* environment and a few other programs, to specify the location of a temporary files subdirectory. Above, the directory C:\WINDOWS\TEMP is put into the environment. Now DOS 5 and *Windows*, et al, will know where to stuff its temporary files.

You can and should set a whole slew of environment variables in your AUTOEXEC.BAT file. (Refer to chapter 4 for additional information.)

Executing startup programs   This is perhaps the most diverse area of AUTO EXEC.BAT: the ability to run other programs that help to set up your system. These programs are usually of two types, *utility* and *memory-resident*.

The *utility* programs are run to do various things with your system. For example, the *VOpt* program from Golden Bow Systems will quickly unfragment your hard drive. Unfragmenting the hard drive means your system will run faster and more efficiently. It's something that should be done regularly, so why not do it each time you start your computer?

Another utility comes as part of the *Mace* hard disk utilities. The RXBAK program will make a duplicate of your hard disk's boot sector, as well as your system's root directory—a safety copy if you will. This safety copy is used by another one of the *Mace Utility* programs to successfully recover from the hard disk being accidentally reformatted. *PC Tools* from Central Point Software, has the MIRROR utility, which also monitors drive access and eases recovery of accidentally deleted files.

The second type of program is a *memory-resident* program. These programs include RAM disks and print spoolers, as well as the popular memory-resident utilities. There's no problem with setting up your system with these "goodies"—as long as you've got the memory for it.

Another point is that certain memory-resident utilities insist upon being loaded last. The greatest offender is Borland's *SideKick* (or "suicide-kick" as it's been dubbed). *SideKick* must always be the last program to be loaded in your AUTOEXEC.BAT file—according to Borland. Also, the manual specifies that you must be in your *SideKick* directory when you load the program:

```
CD \ MEMRES \ SIDEKICK
SK
CD \
```

These commands move you to the *SideKick* directory, load the program, then return you to the root directory.

DOS 5 has added the LOADHIGH command to place a memory-resident program into high DOS memory (providing you have an 80386 or '486 system and have installed the proper memory device drivers and commands). To use LOADHIGH, you simply stick it in front of the program you want to stick in high DOS memory. For example:

```
LOADHIGH C: \ DOS \ DOSKEY
```

This command loads DOS 5's command line editor, DOSKEY, into high DOS memory. The end result is, with DOSKEY up there you have more memory down in low DOS to run your programs.

Other, third-party software packages can do the same thing as LOADHIGH. Putting their equivalent commands into your AUTOEXEC .BAT file is also a good idea.

Executing applications programs Applications programs can be of two types. The first is a program that you normally use when you start your computer. The second type is a DOS shell program.

Quite a few users will stick to the basics when writing an AUTOEXEC-.BAT file. However, they never pay attention to what they type after they run AUTOEXEC. For some, the next thing they type is:

```
CD \ WORDSTAR
WS
```

If they're so consistent, why not include those two commands as the last two in AUTOEXEC?

Sure, by not adding an applications program at the end of AUTOEXEC you're affording yourself with a tiny bit more freedom—but if you can save the keystrokes, why not?

The second type of program that can be run immediately by AUTOEXEC is a DOS shell. These are the infamous "User-Friendly" programs that supposedly make using DOS a snap. They offer menus for choosing programs, or pretty graphic interfaces that are supposed to take the pain away from using DOS.

Bah!

If you bought a DOS computer, learn DOS.

This doesn't mean you can't buy the shell and install it at the end of someone else's AUTOEXEC.BAT file. Just in case, there are a few shell programs that do rank quite high in their usefulness, and you may consider one if another user or yourself would rather use the computer that way.

One of many benefits you get with DOS 5 is a shell program. *DOS SHELL* is graphic "windowing," menu-driven shell program. With that program, you can use an optional mouse to control your computer, manipulate files, and even run several programs at once. (It's not multitasking; instead DOSSHELL simply swaps the programs you're running in and out of memory.)

My overall impression of the program is that it's quite capable. However, I prefer to use the command prompt or a shell system such as PCTools' PC Shell or the Norton Commander rather than *DOSSHELL*.

Another situation that arises is *Windows*. If you're using a lot of graphics programs that require the *Windows* environment, then you might as well customize your AUTOEXEC batch file to setup and end with the WIN command. But do you think running *Windows* leaves you dry for exciting batch file material? *Au contraire, mon frère*. Check out chapter 17.

AUTOEXEC strategies

Your AUTOEXEC.BAT file can get a lot done. Yet, you don't really need to toss the kitchen sink into the works just to get your system up and running. There is a certain strategy to composing your own, personal AUTOEXEC file. Not all of the previous section's examples need to be used. Instead, this section concentrates on some strategies you might want to take to make your AUTOEXEC.BAT file more personal.

Here are some tips on creating effective AUTOEXEC.BAT files:

First things first   The first command in most people's AUTOEXEC.BAT file is ECHO OFF, or @ECHO OFF. This shuts off the echoing of the various commands, which may confuse some users. Also, it pleases the advanced user who enjoys a "clean" display when his computer starts.

Some systems forego the initial ECHO OFF. In fact, one of the computers I use has ECHO OFF omitted intentionally. Because this system has a long, detailed AUTOEXEC.BAT file, I want to be certain that everything is executing properly. (Batch files don't stop if a program errs unless you direct them to—more on that later.)

More importantly, the echoing of some commands may be necessary during some intense disk operations, or long pauses, just to let you know things are proceeding. An alternative to turning ECHO off, of course, is to use ECHO to display what's going on. Such as:

```
ECHO Optimizing Hard Drives . . .
ECHO (this takes a few seconds)
VOPT C: /N
VOPT D: /N
```

No ECHO   Sometimes you might want to suppress the output of all commands. For example, using some commands in any batch file might display only brief and sometimes confusing messages:

```
11 file(s) copied
Memory-resident portion installed
CF (C)Copyright 1988 Nice 'n' Soft, Inc.
```

To suppress these types of messages from being displayed you can use an old, old DOS 2.1 trick. This involves I/O redirection to send the file's output to the NUL device:

```
COPY C: \ WORD \ SPELL.DAT E: \ > NUL
```

This command copies a word processor's spelling checker data to drive E: \ (possibly a RAM disk). The > NUL portion of the command redirects the normal DOS message "1 file(s) copied" to the NUL device, effectively concealing it from view.

> NUL can be used with a variety of commands, and in just about any batch file, to suppress the superfluous display of trivial information.

REMming out   Another popular AUTOEXEC trick is using the REM statement to "comment out" some commands that may not always be necessary. (This trick applies to all batch files, but is used most often in AUTOEXEC.)

Normally, you'd use REM to comment exactly what your AUTOEXEC .BAT file is doing. Believe me, I've looked at dozens of them to research this chapter. I've given several people phone calls asking them "what does CL/I mean?" It would have helped a lot if they would have put a REM command in there telling everyone what the CL program is and what the /I switch does.

```
REM HGC FULL
MODE CO80
BE SA white ON blue
```

or

```
HGC FULL
REM MODE CO80
REM SA white ON blue
```

These are two snippets from an AUTOEXEC file. The first is for a system with a color monitor. The REM statement blocks out the HGC FULL command, normally used for a monochrome Hercules-compatible system. Then the MODE command is used to set the 80-column color mode, and the *Norton Utilities* Batch Enhancer SA command is used to change screen color.

The second example is from the same AUTOEXEC file. In this case, a monochrome monitor is used. Notice how the color statements are now REMmed out and the Hercules command is included? This shows an effective use of the REM command to temporarily block out commands without having to totally rewrite your AUTOEXEC.BAT file.

Positioning crucial commands   Another interesting strategy is to place the set-time, path, and prompt commands at the top of your AUTOEXEC.BAT file. This allows you to "break out" of the AUTOEXEC.BAT file if you'd like and still have a useful system.

Some people crowd their AUTOEXEC.BAT file with a lot of trivial displays, backflips, twists and turns. If you've ever had to reset your system a few times during a programming session, you know how annoying it can be waiting for your AUTOEXEC.BAT file to dazzle you with screen displays. However, with all the important commands at the top of your AUTO EXEC.BAT file, you could press CTRL – BREAK to stop the file and still have a working system (complete with TIME, PATH and PROMPT) without having to wade through a bunch of meaningless display material.

An occasional pause   In several of the above examples, messages were displayed, indicating exactly what was going on. There may be a time when you would actually want AUTOEXEC.BAT to stop after displaying some information. For example, the following snippet from an AUTOEXEC.BAT file runs a program called SCHEDULE that creates a TO-DO file:

```
SCHEDULE < SINPUT
TYPE TO-DO
ECHO ^G
PAUSE
```

This snippet of code shows the SCHEDULE file running using standard input from the SINPUT file. SINPUT probably contains the keystrokes used to create the TO-DO file, a list of things that need to be done that day.

The next step is to display TO-DO, this list of things the user needs to do. This is followed by a BEEP (the ECHO ^G command sends the ^G character, the bell, to the console), and the PAUSE command. This allows the user to see what needs to be done, acknowledge it, and then move on.

Time savers   The first time you type DIR on a hard drive it takes a long time to return to the command prompt. The reason is that the DIR command must calculate how much space is left on the hard drive as the last part of its display (see FIG. 5-6). This happens when you first start your system, or after you use any disk utility that also calculates how much space is on the hard disk (such as CHKDSK).

5-6 This is the display when you first DIR a hard drive.

```
ALPHA                6603    7-03-89   12:11p
DEBUG1    FIG        2010    7-01-90   10:00p
SCHEDULE  EXE       88051    5-15-86    1:00a
        36 File(s)    9754624 bytes free
```

You can avoid the wait easily, by including the following command in AUTOEXEC.BAT:

    DIR > NUL

Or, you can eliminate the > NUL if you're interested in seeing your directory displayed. By "pulling a directory" in your AUTOEXEC file, you're making the next directory you display move a lot quicker (because the initial, slow display was already done).

Memory saving tips   Generally speaking, it's a good idea to save any modifications to the environment for the last part of your AUTOEXEC file.

The reason for saving environment modifications for last—especially after you run memory-resident programs—is that each memory-resident program makes a copy of the environment. If the environment is already full of variables (besides COMSPEC, PATH, and PROMPT), each one of those variables is copied to a new environment when the memory-resident program exits.

In a worst-case scenario, suppose you have boosted the size of your environment to 2 or 3K to allow for a ton of environment variables. After you load your first memory-resident program, a copy is made of that 3K environment. Theoretically, what used to take 3K now occupies 6K in your system (the original 3K environment is still there). Add two more memory-resident programs and you've used 12K, 9K of which is useless to you.

So, if you're going to use SET to create a lot of environment variables, save it for last—after the memory-resident programs are loaded.

Directory strategies   In several instances, your AUTOEXEC batch file will be running other programs. In the case of DOS commands and common utilities, those should already be on your path. But some commands may be of the run-only-once type and you wouldn't want to include their directories on your path. In those instances you have two choices: Use the file's full pathname (only under DOS 3), or use CD to move to the file's directory and run the file there.

Full pathnames are the preferred way to run these programs. After all,

DOS 3 allows you to specify a program by its full pathname—so why not do it?

```
C:\UTILITY\GOLDNBOW\VOPT C: /N
```

This causes the VOPT program in \UTILITY\GOLDNBOW to run. The alternative method, using CD, would be a little more involved:

```
CD \UTILITY\GOLDNBOW
VOPT C: /N
```

It's important to note that some programs may insist that you be in their directory when you run them. A good example is *SideKick* which insists, among other things, that you be in your *SideKick* directory when you first start the program. In that case, you must CD to that directory to run the program in your AUTOEXEC batch file:

```
CD \MEMRES\SIDEKICK
SK
```

Before moving on, there are some cautions when dealing with the CD command in a batch file. First, make certain that you're on the drive the directory is on. In some cases, this involves using the drive letter before the CD command. For example, if you've substituted the drive letter U for your \ UTILITY subdirectory, you might need to do the following:

```
U:
CD GOLDNBOW
VOPT C: /N
```

Also, after using CD in a batch file, remember to return yourself to whichever directory you would like to start from. For most cases, that's the root directory on drive C. So the final command in the batch file may be:

```
C:
CD \
```

AUTOEXEC examples

The following are AUTOEXEC.BAT files I've collected. The most amazing thing about this assignment was the reaction I got from most people when I told them I wanted a printout of their AUTOEXEC file. Most people thought theirs were boring. In fact, no two of them were alike (except in an office situation, and then only two from the same dealer were alike).

The line numbers used in each of the following figures are for reference and are not a part of the batch file.

Scott's AUTOEXEC is pretty simple (FIG. 5-7). He starts with the traditional ECHO OFF (1) and then sets his path (2). The three directories on his path are DOS, DB# (dBASE) and PCW (*PC Write*). These are the only three programs he uses so it makes sense to have them on the path.

5-7 This is Scott M's AUTOEXEC.BAT.

```
1: ECHO OFF
2: PATH=C:\DOS;C:\DB3;C:\PCW
3: PROMPT $t$_$d$_$p$g
4: AUTOTIME
5: CD\UTILITY\SIDEKICK
6: SK
7: CD\
8: CLS
```

Scott's prompt setup is typical of others found in the same office: display the time, a new line, the date, a new line, and the standard directory and greater-than prompt (3):

```
12:36:24.97
Tue 7-21-1992
C:\DB3\JUNE>
```

AUTOTIME (4) is the real-time clock setting program for Scott's computer. Again, this varies from PC/XT system to system depending on who made the clock.

To run the memory-resident program *SideKick*, first you need to log to the *SideKick* directory (5) and then load the program (6). This is part of the loading procedure described in the SideKick manual. After loading *SideKick*, CD changes back to the root (7) and clears the screen (8).

Kent has a pretty complex AUTOEXEC.BAT file (he's read this book), as shown in FIG. 5-8. After the initial ECHO OFF (1), Kent has REMmed out his time-setting command (2). I asked him why and he said because the battery on his real-time clock was dead and he hasn't gotten around to changing it. After he replaces the battery, he can edit out the REM.

5-8 This is Kent's AUTOEXEC.BAT.

```
 1: ECHO OFF
 2: REM \SYSTEM\UTIL\TIMER/S
 3: PROMPT . $A
 4: PATH = C:\SYSTEM\DOS;C:\SYSTEM\UTIL;C:\SYSTEM\BATCH
 5: SUBST E: C:\ETC
 6: SUBST F: C:\ISSUES\FUTURE
 7: SUBST G: C:\GAMES
 8: SUBST I: C:\ISSUES
 9: SUBST M: C:\WORDP\BB\MAIN
10: SUBST T: C:\TALK
11: \SYSTEM\MACE\RXBAK
12: DIR
13: CLS
14: GREET Kent!
15: VER
16: BANNER HELLO THERE, KENT
17: DATE
18: TIME
```

Kent's prompt is a cryptic dot prompt, ala dBASE (3). The "$A" is used as a placeholder for the space character after the cryptic dot. Kent's path is set to three directories, a DOS directory, a UTILity directory, and a special BATCH file directory. (This technique is covered in Part Five.)

Lines 5 through 10 contain SUBSTitution commands to set up Kent's directory the way he wants. Note that, unlike line 2, here he can just use the SUBST command without a path prefix because the PATH command has already set the path.

Line 11 runs the RXBAK program, part of the *Mace Utilities*. RXBAK is kept in the \SYSTEM\MACE subdirectory.

Line 12 pulls a directory, speeding up any further DIR commands Kent may issue. From here on, the AUTOEXEC file gets "pretty." All the work is done, and now it's time for Kent to bemuse himself, starting with a clear screen (13).

The GREET program (14) is included on the supplemental disk you can order with this book. Basically, it reads the real-time clock and displays "Good Morning," "Good Afternoon," or "Good Evening," followed by whatever is on the command line. In Kent's case, he'll see:

Good Morning, Kent!

(He'll always see Good Morning because, remember, his real-time clock is broken.)

Next, DOS displays its version number (15) and this is followed by huge letters scrolling up the screen displaying, "HELLO THERE, KENT" (16). (BANNER is a program with many variations, one of which displays huge messages on the screen.)

Finally, because the real-time clock is broken, Kent must enter the date and time manually (17, 18) to finish out his AUTOEXEC.BAT file.

Tina's AUTOEXEC file, shown in FIG. 5-9, is rather uncomplicated, doing only the necessary commands and then running a shell program (6). This computer's real-time clock setting command is RCLK (3) and before Tina runs her shell, she runs a special program in her \LIBRARY subdirectory, CL. This program displays a list of "things to do today."

5-9 This is Tina's AUTOEXEC.BAT.

```
1: PROMPT $P$G
2: PATH C:\DOS;D:\;D:\LIBRARY;C:\UTIL
3: RCLK
4: CD \LIBRARY
5: CL/I
6: SHELL
```

Sean's AUTOEXEC batch file, in FIG. 5-10, is unique in that it doesn't have an ECHO OFF command. Instead, Sean relies entirely on DOS 3.3's @ command to suppress the listing of his batch file to the screen.

SET COMSPEC (1) really isn't necessary here because DOS does it automatically (unless there is a SHELL command in Sean's CON FIG.SYS). Sean sets a pretty long path (2), but again, as in line 5, doesn't need to use the SET command for either PATH or PROMPT.

5-10 This is Sean's AUTOEXEC.BAT.

```
 1: @SET COMSPEC=c:\command.com
 2: @SET PATH=E:\;C:\;C:\BIN;C:\DOS;C:\POINT;C:\NORTON;
    C:\WORD;C:\TURBOC;C:\FONTS;C:\MENUS;C:\LUCID;C:\GAMES
 3: @chkdsk c:/f
 4: @chkdsk d:/f
 5: @SET PROMPT=$P$G
 6: @sfreak 0400
 7: @timer/s
 8: @SUPERSPL LPT1:/M=256/EXTM=2560
 9: @SET term=ibmpc-ega
10: @SET PCPLUS=C:\PROCOMM
11: @SET LUCID=C:\LUCID
12: @CED -fc:\bin\ced.cnf
13: @kcsetpal
14: @egafont c:\fonts\thin.ega
```

Two CHecK DiSKs are run (3, 4) to look for bad files on both Sean's hard drives. SFREAK slows down the computer's RAM refresh rate (6). TIMER is used to set the system clock (7). And a print spooler is activated in line 8.

Lines 9 through 11 set environment variables for game software, *Pro Comm* (a telecommunications package), and *Lucid* (spreadsheet). CED (12) is a program that Sean claims "makes DOS a little less inconvenient" (it's a command line editor). KCSETPAL (13) sets the computer's EGA monitor to the standard color palette and EGAFONT (14) loads a "readable" font into the EGA display.

Sean's AUTOEXEC.BAT file is a perfect example of customization. He knows exactly what he wants, and uses AUTOEXEC to set his computer up that way.

When I asked my friends to send me their AUTOEXEC.BAT files, I received a whole slew of them. Some I really don't have the room for (there is one that's over 2K in length—a monster!). Figures 5-11 to 5-14 are several more AUTOEXEC.BAT files, without the liberal comments I gave on the previous examples.

Look at FIG. 5-11. Note how full paths are used to run certain programs in lines 4, 5, and 6. And check out that prompt! The COMSPEC is reset to drive D: in line 9, which follows since COMMAND.COM is copied there in line 9. This batch file demonstrates the \BIN philosophy of running a computer, which you'll read more about in Part Five.

5-11 This is Mike's AUTOEXEC.BAT.

```
1: echo off
2: mouse
3: cpanel
4: \bin\util\setdos
5: \bin\util\respro
6: \bin\util\l 48
7: prompt $e[1;1H$e[7m Date  $d    $e[1;30H Directory  $p  $e[0m
   $e[25;1HCommand
```

```
 8: copy c:\command.com d:\ >nul
 9: set comspec=d:\command.com
10: set procomm=c:\usr\telecom\prcm\
11: path d:\;c:\;\bin;\bin\sys;\bin\util;\etc\filefix;\usr\ws
12: search d:\;c:\usr\ws;\usr\telecom\aems;\usr\telecom\prcm;\tn
13: cd\bin\util
14: ced
15: pf k 5
16: mark >nul
17: \usr\ws\wf
18: echo Moving job files into RAM drive D:
19: copy c:\etc\dev\*.bat d:\ >nul
20: copy c:\etc\dev\*.exe d:\ >nul
21: copy c:\etc\dev\*.com d:\ >nul
22: cls
23: echo  E n v i r o n m e n t  i s:
24: echo ----------------------------
25: chkdsk /f
26: echo Standby while defragging hard disk
27: vopt
28: cls
29: cd\
```

In FIG. 5-12, BACKSCRL is a back-scrolling utility, allowing you to review data that has already scrolled off your screen. Note that the ECHO ON (12) is never necessary at the end of a batch file.

5-12 This is Jim's AUTOEXEC.BAT.

```
 1: echo off
 2: prompt .
 3: path
 4:
c:\;c:\bin;c:\dos;c:\batch;d:\turbo;d:\utils;d:\norton;d:\games;
    d:\dfedit;d:\vi;
 5: timepark 5
 6: backscrl 5
 7: scrnsave
 8: set PROCOMM=\TERM\PRO-COMM
 9: set TC=D:\TURBO
10: set DFEDIT=D:\DFEDIT
11: cls
12: echo on
```

Notice the nice use of REMs in FIG. 5-13. With all the REMs in there, it makes commenting Scott O's AUTOEXEC.BAT file a little redundant. (See how nice remarks can be?)

5-13 This is Scott O's AUTOEXEC.BAT.

```
1: echo off
2: cls
3: REM echo Switching to monochrome monitor...
4: \dos\mode mono
5: echo Setting system defaults, please wait...
```

```
 6: set user=SAO
 7: REM
 8: REM ---- Set path information for DOS & UTILITY commands
 9: REM
10: path c:\;c:\batch;c:\dos;c:\util;c:\db3
11: REM
12: REM ---- Run Vopt to optimize hard disk.
13: REM
14: vopt
15: if not errorlevel 4 goto ok
16:     echo There are hard disk errors!  Check HARD DISK!
17:     pause
18: :ok
19: REM
20: REM ---- Set prompt for "\dir >"
21: REM
22: prompt $p$g
23: REM
24: REM ---- Install PRINT with a 20 file queue
25: REM
26: rem print /b:1024 /q:20 /d:prn > nul
27: REM
28: REM ---- Install Video-7 CGA Emulation & Screen Saver
29: REM
30: rem vega save:8 > nul
31: REM
32: REM ---- Set hard disk park for 5 minutes
33: REM
34: timepark 5 > nul
35: REM
36: REM ---- Install Mouse driver
37: REM
38: rem mousesys > nul
39: REM
40: REM ---- Set keyboard repeat rate
41: REM
42: REM quickeys
43: REM
44: REM ---- Set-up DOS EDIT feature
45: dos-edit > nul
46: REM
47: REM ---- Turn keyclick OFF
48: REM
49: mode: cli=0
50: REM
51: REM ---- Install PC-193A Okidata TSR setup
52: REM
53: REM PC-193A > nul
54: REM
55: REM ---- All done, return to user
56: type \dos\logo.ans
57: C:\quicken2\billmind /c=C:\QUICKEN2
```

As with Scott M's AUTOEXEC.BAT file, Donald (in FIG. 5-14) needed to go to his *SideKick* subdirectory in order to run *SideKick*. Did you notice the batch file subdirectory in line 3? This idea crops up again in Part Five.

5-14 This is Donald's AUTOEXEC.BAT.

```
 1: @echo off
 2: ver
 3: path=c:\mouse;c:\batch;c:\msdos;c:\util;c:\util\norton;
    c:\util\sideways
 4: set clipper=c:\clipper
 5: fast
 6: mode co80
 7: sa bright yellow on black
 8: prompt $v$_Current Directory $p$_$n$g
 9: getclock
10: menu
11: click
12: cd\
13: fastopen c:=100
14: cd\util\sidekick
15: sk
16: cd\
17: cls
18: C:\QUICKEN2\BILLMINDER /C=\QUICKEN2 /P
```

DOS 5 suggests . . .

Earlier you read about how DOS 5's INSTALL program created a suggested file for my laptop system's CONFIG.SYS file. It did the same thing with AUTOEXEC.BAT. That file is shown in FIG. 5-15.

5-15 INSTALL created this AUTOEXEC.BAT file.

```
1: @ECHO OFF
2: PROMPT $P$G
3: PATH C:\SYSTEM\DOS
4: SET TEMP=C:\TEMP
```

This is nothing impressive. It's not as detailed as the suggestion DOS 4 gave with its install program, but it's enough—and it works well with my CONFIG.SYS file DOS 5 also suggested. PROMPT, PATH and TEMP are the only things this batch file does. The INSTALL program does ask you if you want to run DOSSHELL immediately after starting the computer. If you indicate "yes," then the AUTOEXEC.BAT file ends with DOSSHELL. Otherwise, DOS 5 will probably create something similar to FIG. 5-15 for your system.

Just as I did with CONFIG.SYS, however, I modified my DOS 5 AUTOEXEC.BAT to become what you see in FIG. 5-16.

Line 3 runs a program that makes the characters larger on the laptop's screen, easier to read. The next group of lines, from 5 through 10, sets various system variables, the PROMPT, PATH, TEMP and COMSPEC variables. MPATH is used as a backup for the PATH variable in line 8.

The final group sets my DOSKEY command line macros, from lines 12 through 16. (This is covered in depth in chapter 16.) And lastly, as a safety measure, backup copies of AUTOEXEC.BAT and CONFIG.SYS are saved in the \TEMP subdirectory.

5-16 Here is my final AUTOEXEC.BAT file under DOS 5.

```
 1: @ECHO OFF
 2:
 3: C:\SYSTEM\DELL\SEMISTRT
 4:
 5: REM Set system variables...
 6: PROMPT $p$g $a
 7: PATH C:\SYSTEM\BATCH;C:\SYSTEM\UTIL;C:\SYSTEM\DOS
 8: SET MPATH=%PATH%
 9: SET TEMP=C:\TEMP
10: SET COMSPEC=C:\SYSTEM\DOS\COMMAND.COM
11:
12: REM Set your DOSKEY macros
13: c:\system\386max\386load size=5504 prgreg=3
    flexframe prog=DOSKEY
14: DOSKEY D=DIR /W
15: DOSKEY H=DOSKEY /DHIST
16: DOSKEY M=DOSKEY /DMACS
17:
18: COPY \AUTOEXEC.BAT TEMP > NUL
19: COPY \CONFIG.SYS TEMP > NUL
```

Non-booting disk example

Some older computers, and some computers with special types of fixed disks (such as the older Bernoulli drives), could only boot from the first floppy drive. This can be annoying—requiring you to keep a system disk in the first floppy drive even when you use a hard disk. But there's a way around it with only a simple change to your AUTOEXEC.BAT file.

The object is to fake a "boot" from the hard drive. This is done by loading a second copy of the command processor from the floppy boot disk.

Essentially, your system would have two COMMAND.COMs and two AUTOEXEC.BATs. The first set would be on a bootable floppy disk. The AUTOEXEC.BAT file would look something like this:

```
@ECHO OFF
C:
COMMAND C:\ /P
```

This directs your system to log to drive C, then reload COMMAND.COM (a secondary shell). The C:\ option tells COMMAND.COM to reload itself from the root directory on drive C. The /P switch directs COMMAND.COM to execute the AUTOEXEC.BAT file, this time on the root directory of drive C. Now you can safely remove the boot disk from drive A and use the system as a hard disk system should be used (and much faster, as well).

This strategy also applies to flaky and marginally operational hard disks. In fact, it would be a good idea to keep a boot disk around with an AUTOEXEC.BAT file just like the above example. This way, if ever the boot sector on your hard drive went south, you'd still be able to boot your system, then back up all your files before you rushed out to buy a new hard disk. (Of course, it's always best to have a backup handy "just in case.")

SHUTDOWN.BAT

An interesting concept in system batch files is a SHUTDOWN.BAT file. Just like AUTOEXEC.BAT is the first batch file your system runs, SHUT DOWN.BAT should be the last file your system runs. The designers of the original PC (and of DOS) didn't see fit to include such a program. So you must write it yourself.

Before continuing, it should be noted that a few computers do come with SHUTDOWN routines. For example, the Epson PC runs a special BIOS routine when the "off" button is pressed. Rather than turning itself off immediately, an Epson first parks the hard drives and then shuts itself off. This is a nice safety feature, but frustrating because there should be some way to access and modify those routines so you could perform other functions at shutdown time.

Because there is no official SHUTDOWN.BAT file, let's make one up. The following tasks should be done by a SHUTDOWN batch file:

- Erase any unneeded files/clear out "junk" directories
- Print any files in a "spool" directory
- Back up most recently worked on, or important, files
- Optimize the hard drive
- Park the hard drive

Generally speaking, SHUTDOWN.BAT should take care of all the things that you normally do at the end of the day, just before shutting down the computer (or just turning the monitor off, which is what I usually do).

The SHUTDOWN.BAT file in FIG. 5-17 tries to accomplish most of the above strategies. This SHUTDOWN file accomplishes most of the things that I typically do at the end of my computing session. I've spiced it up a bit, adding some variety and showing some examples that apply to just about everyone's situation.

First comes the traditional ECHO OFF (1), followed by messages informing the user what's going on (3, 4). If the SHUTDOWN file takes a while to perform its duties, you may want to add a message here telling the user how long the operating will take, or give them the option to cancel the shutdown procedure.

The batch file removes temporary files (6) from the \TEMP directory on drive C (7, 8). (Some users name this directory \JUNK.) Line 9 removes all the files and uses I/O redirection to first provide the input for the "Are you sure?" question that DEL *.* always asks, and second to redirect the output to the NUL device, reducing possible confusing by the user.

Next, the SWEEP utility is used to clean through all directories and remove all *.BAK (12), KILL*.* (13), and TEMP*.* (14) files. If SWEEP is used starting at the root directory (11), it looks through all subdirectories. Otherwise, you could use it to sweep only selected subdirectories.

Line 16 checks drive E (possibly a RAM disk) for any files that need to

5-17 The SHUTDOWN.BAT file.

```
 1: @ECHO OFF
 2: REM Display shut down message
 3: ECHO ^G
 4: ECHO System Shutdown
 5: ECHO Cleaning directories...
 6: REM Remove temporary files...
 7: C:
 8: CD \TEMP
 9: DEL *.* < C:\SYSTEM\BATCH\YES >NUL
10: REM Use SWEEP utility to remove temporary files
11: CD \
12: SWEEP DEL *.BAK > NUL
13: SWEEP DEL KILL*.* > NUL
14: SWEEP DEL TEMP*.* > NUL
15: ECHO Printing spooled files...
16: IF NOT EXIST E:\SPOOL\*.* GOTO SKIP1
17: E:
18: CD \SPOOL
19: COPY *.* PRN > NUL
20: DEL *.* < C:\SYSTEM\BATCH\YES >NUL
21: :SKIP1
22: REM Backup most recently worked on stuff/important files
23: ECHO Backing up spreadsheet data
24: HOLD Put spreadsheet backup disk in Drive A and
25: CD \LOTUS
26: BACKUP C:\LOTUS\*.* A: /S/M
27: HOLD Put word processing backup disk in Drive A and
28: CD \WORDP
29: BACKUP C:\WORDP\*.* A: /S/M
30: REM Optimize the hard drive
31: ASK Optimize the hard drive now? (y/n)
32: REM ERRORLEVEL 1 IS "NO"
33: IF ERRORLEVEL 1 GOTO SKIP2
34: VOPT /N
35: :SKIP2
36: REM all done, park the hard drive
37: CLS
38: ECHO Shutdown completed, parking hard disk
39: GREET Dan
40: PARK
```

be spooled to the printer. If there are any files (16), they are copied one by one to the printer (19) and then deleted (20). You should also note any files in a RAM disk if you're using a laptop. Typically, laptop users will employ a RAM disk as a battery-saving step. But before turning off the juice, it's a good thing to check the RAM disk for any valuable files that should be copied to more permanent storage.

About the most important thing a SHUTDOWN.BAT file can do is ensure that crucial files are backed up. As opposed to backing up your entire system, which should be done once a month or so, backing up recently worked-on files should be done every day. Lines 23 through 26 and lines 27 through 29 back up all the spreadsheet and word processing files on this system that have been modified since the last backup.

The HOLD command (24 and 27) is part of the program disk available with this book. It's a "smart" version of the DOS pause command, which doesn't always display a message before the "press any key to continue" prompt.

Lines 30 through 35 are for optimizing the hard drive. As you saw with the AUTOEXEC.BAT examples, many users opt to do this before they run their computer. However, there's nothing wrong with putting an optimizing utility in a SHUTDOWN.BAT file. In this instance, the ASK command (31) is used to determine if the user wants to optimize now or not. If so, the hard drive is optimized (34), otherwise execution skips to the SKIP2 label (35).

Finally, the screen is cleared (37), the user is informed that SHUT DOWN.BAT is done running (38), and the user is presented a friendly greeting (39). Line 40 parks the hard drive. Depending on the parking program, the system may "lock up" and the user may be forced to shut off the system. Other parking programs may simply return to DOS, in which case the user can shut off the system at that time.

You'll notice in this batch file how " > NUL" was used in several places to repress the display of some messages. Also, the ASK command could have been used more liberally to control what SHUTDOWN.BAT does and doesn't do.

The BACKUP commands are really rather simple. A more realistic example might have the user enter specific directories to backup as part of the batch file's replaceable parameters (covered in Part Two). And over all, this file would take a long time to run, even on a fast computer. Still, with all its drawbacks, this example provides an excellent base upon which you could build your own SHUTDOWN.BAT file.

The killer

Paul is one of the world's true batch file zanies. I met him through Compu-Serve, and since then he's sent me all sorts of batch file goodies through E-mail—including his own incredible AUTOEXEC file, as well as other must-have batch file utilities.

For a SHUTDOWN.BAT-type of program, Paul has written QUIT.BAT. This is an amazing piece of work, obviously not your typical beginner batch file.

QUIT.BAT is shown in FIG. 5-18. But rather than give you a blow-by-blow of its duties, note the following items:

- See how ANSI codes and extended ASCII graphics are incorporated into ECHO statements? This makes for interesting displays, as opposed to dull, text-only statements.
- Notice how the RAM drive is checked? See how the RAMDISK and HAVERAM variables are used, and then what happens to the contents of the RAM drive if it's detected.
- The WHAT utility is interesting. It returns the status of several

items in your system (the disk drives, printer, etc.) into the WHAT environment variable. (I would love to include this on the supplemental diskette, but I'm not certain of its source.) Using the results from WHAT, this batch file determines if any substantial changes have been made during the PC's uptime. If so, a message urging a backup is displayed.

- Subdirectories that should be empty are tested in QUIT.BAT using extensive IF EXIST tests. Nothing is really done with them, in fact, the batch file really contains no handling of the situations other than to display a warning message. A more complete (and complex) version may have ways to deal with the situation, but the way Paul has set things up now, the user still has an iota of control.

Not every SHUTDOWN.BAT file needs to be as complex as QUIT.BAT. But notice how informative it is? Note how third-party utilities are used to gather information about the system and display the results. Essentially, this is a good SHUTDOWN batch file because it takes care of tasks that need to be attended to at the end of the workday.

5-18 This is Paul's mondo QUIT.BAT program.

```
ECHO OFF
CLS
DPATH GET > NUL
ECHO
ECHO ^[[1;36m
ECHO   ┌─────^[[1;33m QUIT.BAT^[[1;36m ─────────────────────────────┐
ECHO   │ Before QUITting this file will │
ECHO   │ check for any loose ends you   │
ECHO   │ may wish to correct.  Please   │
ECHO   │ wait...                        │
ECHO   └────────────────────────────────┘
WAITS 3
IF %HAVERAM%X==NOX GOTO NORAM
IF %RAMDISK%X==X GOTO NORAM
IF NOT EXIST %RAMDISK%:*.* GOTO NORAM
CLS
ECHO
ECHO ^[[1;36m
ECHO   ┌─────^[[1;33m QUIT.BAT^[[1;36m ─────────────────────────────┐
ECHO   │ Checking the ram drive %RAMDISK% for   │
ECHO   │ files other than COMMAND.COM.          │
ECHO   │ Please wait...                         │
ECHO   └────────────────────────────────────────┘
ECHO
WAITS 3
FOR %%f IN (%RAMDISK%:*.*) DO IF NOT %%f==%RAMDISK%:COMMAND.COM
    GOTO MAKEDIR
GOTO NORAM
:MAKEDIR
ECHO ^[[1;33m
DIR %RAMDISK%:
ECHO
ECHO ^[[1;36m
```

```
ECHO      ┌──────^[[1;33m QUIT.BAT^[[1;36m ──────────────────────┐
ECHO      │   Since there are files on ram     |
ECHO      │   disk %RAMDISK% other than COMMAND.COM   |
ECHO      │   you may wish to dispose of
ECHO      │   those files now.  Press CTRL-C
ECHO      │   to abort QUIT.
ECHO      └───────────────────────────────────┘
ECHO
ECHO ^[[1;33mTo continue nevertheless, press any key...^[[1;36m
PAUSE > NUL
:NORAM
CLS
ECHO
ECHO ^[[1;36m
ECHO      ┌──────^[[1;33m QUIT.BAT^[[1;36m ──────────────────────┐
ECHO      │   Checking hard drives C and D
ECHO      │   usage.  Please wait...
ECHO      └───────────────────────────────┘
ECHO
ECHO
SET WHAT=
WHAT K C
SET STOPC=%WHAT%000
WHAT K D
SET STOPD=%WHAT%000
SET WHAT=
IF %STARTC%==%STOPC% ECHO No change in free space available on
     Hard Disk C since boot.
IF NOT %STARTC%==%STOPC% ECHO ^[[1;33mChanges were made in the
     free space available on Hard Disk C since boot.^[[1;36m
IF %STARTD%==%STOPD% ECHO No change in free space available on
     Hard Disk D since boot.
IF NOT %STARTD%==%STOPD% ECHO ^[[1;33mChanges were made in the
     free space available on Hard Disk D since boot.^[[1;36m
IF %STARTC%==%STOPC% IF %STARTD%==%STOPD% GOTO NOCHANGE
ECHO
ECHO      ┌──────^[[1;33m QUIT.BAT^[[1;36m ──────────────────────┐
ECHO      │   The bytes available on hard
ECHO      │   drives C and/or D indicate that
ECHO      │   changes have been made.  If you
ECHO      │   have not made backups for the
ECHO      │   changes you may wish to do so
ECHO      │   now.  Press CTL-C to abort.
ECHO      └───────────────────────────────────┘
ECHO
ECHO
ECHO ^[[1;33mTo continue nevertheless, press any key...^[[1;36m
PAUSE > NUL
:NOCHANGE
CLS
ECHO
ECHO ^[[1;36m
ECHO      ┌──────^[[1;33m QUIT.BAT^[[1;36m ──────────────────────┐
ECHO      │   Testing for files in the
ECHO      │   normally empty subdirectories
ECHO      │   (ARCING, DOWNLOAD, HOLDING,
ECHO      │   and WORKING) of hard drive C,
ECHO      │   (WORK) of hard drive D, and
ECHO      │   also for files by MORE and
ECHO      │   other DOS functions in C:\ and
ECHO      │   D:\.
```

5-18 Continued.

```
ECHO  └─────────────────────────────────────────┘
ECHO
IF EXIST C:\ARCING\*.* ECHO     ^[[1;33mThere are files in
    C:\ARCING.
IF EXIST C:\DOWNLOAD\*.* ECHO    ^[[1;33mThere are files in
    C:\DOWNLOAD.
IF EXIST C:\HOLDING\*.* ECHO    ^[[1;33mThere are files in
    C:\HOLDING.
IF EXIST C:\WORKING\*.* ECHO    ^[[1;33mThere are files in
    C:\WORKING.
IF EXIST C:\0*. ECHO   ^[[1;33mThere are 0*. files in C:\.
IF EXIST C:\FILE*.* ECHO   ^[[1;33mThere are FILE*.* files in
    C:\.
IF EXIST C:\*.CHK ECHO    ^[[1;33mThere are *.CHK files in C:\.
IF EXIST D:\WORK\*.* ECHO    ^[[1;33mThere are files in D:\WORK.
IF EXIST D:\0*. ECHO    ^[[1;33mThere are 0*. files in D:\.
IF EXIST D:\FILE*.* ECHO   ^[[1;33mThere are FILE*.* files in
    D:\.
IF EXIST D:\*.CHK ECHO    ^[[1;33mThere are *.CHK files in D:\.
IF NOT EXIST D:\WORK\*.* IF NOT EXIST C:\ARCING\*.* GOTO MAYBE
GOTO FILES
:MAYBE
IF NOT EXIST C:\DOWNLOAD\*.* IF NOT EXIST C:\HOLDING\*.* IF NOT
    EXIST C:\WORKING\*.* GOTO CLEARED
:FILES
ECHO
ECHO ^[[1;36m
ECHO  ┌────^[[1;33m QUIT.BAT^[[1;36m ───────────────────────────┐
ECHO  │ Since there are files in some
ECHO  │ of the normally empty subdir-
ECHO  │ rectories of hard drives C
ECHO  │ and/or D, you may dispose of
ECHO  │ those files now.  Press CTRL-C
ECHO  │ to abort QUIT.
ECHO  └──────────────────────────────┘
ECHO
ECHO ^[[1;33mTo continue nevertheless, press any key...^[[1;36m
PAUSE > NUL
:CLEARED
CLS
ECHO
ECHO ^[[1;36m
ECHO  ┌────^[[1;33m QUIT.BAT^[[1;36m ───────────────────────┐
ECHO  │ ^[[5;1;32mCleared to shut down.  Goodbye!^[[0;1;36m │
ECHO  └────────────────────────────┘
:END
ECHO
DPATH SET > NUL
EXIT
```

Summary

CONFIG.SYS and AUTOEXEC.BAT are the two most important files you control on your system.

CONFIG.SYS sets up your system, allowing you to customize and configure it to your tastes. Only three CONFIG.SYS commands are important to batch file programming. They are: DEVICE, LASTDRIVE, and SHELL.

AUTOEXEC.BAT is the first program your computer system runs—and you get to write it. There are many things you can do in AUTOEXEC, some of which are important and others can simply be your own strategy on how you want your system to start. The important thing to remember is that a well-written AUTOEXEC.BAT file will do wonders for your system.

SHUTDOWN.BAT is not an official DOS batch file, but it can come in handy. The SHUTDOWN batch file can take care of all sorts of miscellaneous duties that you normally perform before turning your system off. Just remember to type SHUTDOWN.BAT, as unlike CONFIG.SYS and AUTOEXEC.BAT, DOS will not run it automatically.

6
OS/2

Just when you thought you knew everything about DOS, along comes OS/2.

Actually, OS/2 is nothing to be afraid of. In fact, it's quite an impressive piece of work. Regardless of what all the doomsayers have to say, most of whom have a vested interest in keeping DOS alive, OS/2 will eventually be "the" future operating system for PCs. (But maybe not in our lifetime . . .)

OS/2 has many powerful features and, just to put all your fears aside, it's very, very similar to DOS. In fact, they should have called DOS 3.0, 3.1, 3.2, 3.3 and 4.0, Versions 2.2, 2.3, 2.4, and 2.5. OS/2 is really DOS 3.0. It's an improvement. It's better. You'll like it.

The problem with OS/2 is that there's really no reason to buy it right now. Sure, I spent several hundred dollars for it to write this book. But I have no OS/2 software other than OS/2 itself and a scant few utilities. The OS/2 software that does exist has equally capable DOS counterparts. And the current trend shows that people won't be rushing out to buy OS/2 for at least a few years, especially given the popularity of the so-called DOS extenders, *Windows* and *DESQview*.

This chapter scratches the surface of OS/2. It's not designed as a comprehensive tutorial, nor is there space to explain all the details of OS/2. Instead, this should help get those few of you who use OS/2 off to a better start writing OS/2 batch files. If you don't own OS/2, the information here is optional reading.

History of OS/2

The history of OS/2 starts with IBM's decision to put Intel's 80286 microprocessor in their PC/AT. The 80286 was a giant technological leap up from the old 8088 in the original PC and the PC/XT. It was also a leap up from the 8086 chips (a true, 16-bit version of the 8088) used in some of the faster PC clones, such as Compaq.

The 80286 could address much more memory than the 8088. Also, it offered a special "protected" mode. In this mode the processor can restrict access to certain areas of memory. Hence, when run in the protected mode, an 80286 program couldn't just go out and grab memory like an 8088 program could. Instead, the 80286 program must ask for the memory. (Under normal circumstances, the 80286 behaves just like a fast 8088—so this memory control stuff is trivial if you're just running DOS programs on your AT clone.)

The protected mode meant the 80286 chip could offer programs a lot more flexibility when running. It also meant that a crude form of multitasking would be possible. That is, in the protected mode, the 80286 could conceivably run two or more programs at the same time. While it sounds a bit much for a microcomputer (which, after all, is based on the one computer-one human concept of getting work done), multitasking opens up a whole new area of capable computer programs.

The problem with the 80286, and really all computer hardware advances, is that it takes the software a long, long time to catch up. Developing hardware and getting the bugs out is an involved process. But once it's done, it's done.

Software, on the other hand, takes a lot longer. Because of this, software specifically for the 80286 chip lagged. Also, software developers weren't anxious to write 80286-only programs with the abundance of 8088 computers. Software for the 8088 can run on the 80286 (and run quickly). But 80286-specific software cannot run on the 8088.

Because of the power of the 80286, Microsoft set out to write what was internally called "DOS 3." It would be a multi-tasking version of DOS that took advantage of the 80286's protected mode. In the course of events, DOS 3 (the MS-DOS version) was released instead. Then the older DOS 3 project became DOS 4, and then DOS 5. Finally, coupled with IBM's introduction of their new PS/2 computers, Microsoft decided to start the whole numbering shebang over with OS/2, for Operating System Two.

It took the team at Microsoft, working closely with IBM, quite some time to develop OS/2. But the results are worth it. It takes advantage of the power of the 80286 chip. And because the newer 80386 and '486 chips can run 80286 programs, users with those computers can run OS/2 as well. (The 80386-specific version of OS/2 should be introduced right after this book goes to press.)

Additionally, OS/2 allows compatibility with DOS via the "DOS 3x box." This is a special operating mode of OS/2 that allows it to "fake" MS-DOS Version 3.3, albeit slowly. The DOS 3x box is also referred to as the OS/2 "real" mode.

Concerns

As I said in the introduction, there are few OS/2 software packages available. In fact, there probably won't be anything OS/2-specific that everyone *must* have for some time to come. (OS/2 is undergoing a long infancy, contrasting with DOS which was very quick to start in the early '80s.) Because of this, OS/2 needed to be very compatible with existing computer systems. The DOS 3x box plays a leading role in this. But there are other items of importance as well. They are:

Hardware compatibility
File structure compatibility
Memory compatibility
Program compatibility

Hardware

Hardware compatibility determines the success of the operating system. DOS was successful for three reasons, two hardware and one software: It ran on a lot of computers; you could read diskettes formatted on another DOS computer, regardless of who made that computer; and DOS programs could run on any "compatible" computer. All this has to do with hardware compatibility. For OS/2 to follow successfully in DOS's footsteps, it needs to incorporate those three items.

Hardware compatibility also refers to which systems can run OS/2. As you might know, just about everyone and anyone can make a DOS compatible computer. What about OS/2?

It turns out that most 80286, 80386 and '486 computers that are DOS compatible are also OS/2 compatible. (Older 8088 and 8086 computers cannot run OS/2.) In fact, most major IBM compatible manufacturers now offer a version of OS/2 for their AT-class computers. I have tested OS/2 on an 80286 "clone" computer and it ran fine. You cannot "buy" OS/2 like you can MS-DOS. So if you're looking for a copy to run on your clone computer, you'll need to locate a version distributed by a national manufacturer, or visit your local IBM authorized dealer to buy a copy.

You also need at least 1.5 megabytes of RAM to run OS/2. The more RAM you have, the more OS/2 can do for you. Presently, about four megabytes seems to be a "comfortable" amount. By the way, most AT computers come with 512K of RAM. That's the ".5" part of 1.5 megabytes. To run OS/2, you'll need to add that extra megabyte of memory. You'll also need to specify that extra megabyte as "extended memory." (Only DOS uses expanded memory.)

OS/2 requires a hard drive, and will use from six to eight megabytes of storage on that drive. Presently, OS/2 comes on either 1.2 megabyte 5$\frac{1}{4}$-inch or 1.44 megabyte 3$\frac{1}{2}$-inch diskettes. So you need that sized disk drive to read the OS/2 diskettes and install it on your system.

With the introduction of the graphical Presentation Manager (PM) interface, OS/2 now requires an EGA or VGA graphics setup, plus an optional mouse. Don't kid yourself with either of these items: If you want to do OS/2 correctly, you need VGA graphics (or better) and a mouse.

Fortunately, all of the above items are presently available on quite a few DOS machines. Cost might be the only thing keeping you from turning your standard DOS PC into a screaming OS/2 monster. (This is, of course, assuming that you need OS/2 in the first place.)

File structure

OS/2 uses the same file structure as DOS. Presently, that means OS/2 uses eight character filenames with an optional three character extension, pathnames with the backslash separator, drive letters with colons—the whole nine yards. You can install OS/2 on a hard disk that already has DOS on it, no changes are necessary.

Starting with OS/2 Version 1.2, however, a new hard drive format was used. This format, the HPFS (High Performance File System), is totally DOS-incompatible. It has the advantage of giving you longer filenames under OS/2 (up to 255 characters), plus faster disk access. But if you want to run DOS and OS/2 on the same computer, you need to reformat your hard drive under OS/2, then back up DOS onto the OS/2-formatted disk. It will work okay, but then again such a drastic step should only be taken if you consider OS/2 to be your primary operating system.

Memory

OS/2 requires a minimum of 1.5 megabytes of RAM to run. But this is like saying you need .25 gallons of gas to drive to the store. You *need* at least four megabytes of RAM to run OS/2, more if you can afford it. Regardless of your memory configuration, the first megabyte of RAM under OS/2 is configured roughly the same as a DOS computer, as shown in FIG. 6-1.

Memory above the one megabyte mark is used exclusively by OS/2 programs. Remember, OS/2 will need one megabyte of extended memory to run. That's memory in the address space between one and two megabytes in FIG. 6-2. Beyond two megabytes, it's all just extra playground space for OS/2. But you need that basic 1.5 megabytes for OS/2 to get up in the morning.

Program compatibility

A major question many users ask about OS/2 is "Can I run my DOS programs under OS/2?" The answer is a qualified yes. OS/2 will run DOS programs in its compatibility box, its "real" mode. But consider the following:

Why would you go to the time and expense of getting OS/2 just to run

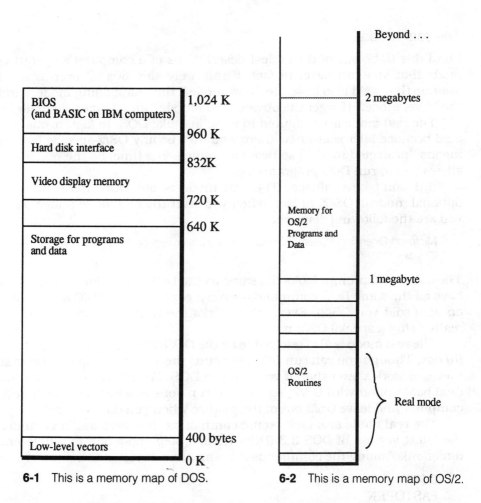

BIOS (and BASIC on IBM computers)	1,024 K
Hard disk interface	960 K
	832K
Video display memory	
	720 K
	640 K
Storage for programs and data	
Low-level vectors	400 bytes
	0 K

6-1 This is a memory map of DOS.

Beyond . . .

	2 megabytes
Memory for OS/2 Programs and Data	
	1 megabyte
OS/2 Routines	

Real mode

6-2 This is a memory map of OS/2.

DOS programs? If you buy OS/2, then it should be your primary operating system. All your software, the stuff you need to run, should be under OS/2. The only reason you would want DOS compatibility would be to interact with those few programs or people who still operate under DOS.

OS/2 isn't a DOS solution. It's a new operating system. The silly part is, currently all the OS/2 software you can buy has equally capable counterparts that work under DOS—and are widely supported. If and when you need something that specifically runs under OS/2, then switch. Otherwise, stay with DOS for now.

Real and protected modes

OS/2 comes in two flavors, real and protected modes. Eventually, the protected will be the only OS/2 mode. The real mode was added to maintain compatibility with DOS and many applications programs that can only run under DOS. The protected mode is where the real power of OS/2 lies.

The real mode

I find this to be one of the oddest descriptions of a computer's operating mode that you can have. In fact, if this were the '60s all over again, I assume that we'd also have the "now mode," the "happening mode," and the "like, mode." (Forget the obvious "ala mode" and "super slo-mode.")

The real mode is configured to work just like DOS. In fact, it was created because Microsoft knew there wouldn't be any OS/2-specific (which means "protected mode") software for quite some time. So the real mode allows you to run DOS programs.

But don't be confused. The real mode is not DOS. It's simply an optional mode of OS/2. In fact, when you start the real mode under OS/2, you see the following displayed:

```
Microsoft Operating System/2 Command Interpreter Version 1.10 - DOS Mode
C: \ >
```

The command prompt looks the same as the DOS command prompt. You have all the same DOS commands—even a copy of GW BASIC (depending on who sold you OS/2). Everything works the same as DOS, but you're really using a special OS/2 mode.

The real mode is also referred to as the *DOS 3x box*, or the *compatibility box*. Though you can run DOS programs there, some people claim that they will work slower than if you just use DOS. My advice is to install the dual-boot option with OS/2, so you can run your machine as a DOS-only computer and leave OS/2 out of the picture when you don't want it.

The real mode also lacks some commands that were available under the latest version of DOS 3.3 (DOS 4.0 is a step-and-a-half in a different direction). Among the commands missing are:

CTTY
FASTOPEN
KEYB (though there is a protected mode version of this command)
NLSFUNC
SELECT

(There's a complete commands reference listed later in this chapter.)

The protected mode

I don't find the title "protected mode" as silly as the real mode's title. The protected mode is a nice title, in fact. It means that your software is protected by the processor from other programs. The memory used by one program can never be interfered with by another program. Everything is protected.

The protected mode is what OS/2 is all about. It's where you can run multiple programs and perform multitasking. The protected mode offers a new face and looks quite different from DOS. For example, the default prompt is the current drive and path enclosed in brackets:

```
[C:\OS2]
```

(Though, as with DOS, you can change the prompt using the OS/2 PROMPT command.)

Also, some of the commands are souped up. You can now type:

```
DIR *.COM *.EXE
```

to display a directory of all your COM and EXE files.

You cannot run DOS programs in the protected mode, however. Only OS/2-specific programs will run. If you try to run a DOS program, you'll get an error message like:

```
SYS1107: The system cannot complete the process.
```

If you're running under the Presentation Manager, you'll see a graphic error displayed in a box on the screen. It's a little more explanatory than the command line version, as seen in FIG. 6-3.

Eventually, there will be some OS/2 protected mode software. Until then about the only programs you can run are (can you guess?) batch files.

```
+---------------------------------------+
|              File System               |
|                                        |
| PMV1004: Cannot run EDLIN.COM. Make    |
| sure that the file is an OS/2 program, or |
| that it is associated with one. There may |
| not be enough memory available to run the |
| program.                               |
|                                        |
|      (Cancel)    (Help)                |
+---------------------------------------+
```

6-3 The Presentation Manager's friendly error message is shown here.

Sessions

Using OS/2, you can have multiple "sessions" running at a time. A session is an independent process. For example, you could be formatting a disk in one OS/2 session, and then use another session to run a text editor. Both operations work at the same time and are independent of each other.

An example of running multiple sessions would be to have a word processor working in one session while a database is sorting a long list in a second session and you're connected with a mainframe computer downloading a program in a third session. (You don't need to be present, monitoring each activity for it to work.) All processes are running independently of each other. From the operator's point of view, everything is happening at once—and with no loss of speed. This is the primary purpose behind the new operating system.

The real mode is also considered an OS/2 session, though you can (currently) only run one copy of the real mode at a time. In the protected mode, you can run as many sessions as you like, or until whenever your system's memory fills up. You can switch back and forth between the real mode session and the protected mode sessions, but once you leave the real mode, its actions are suspended. (Protected mode sessions continue to run after you leave them.)

One nice thing about these independent sessions is that if a program crashes in one session it doesn't bring down the whole system. You simply return to OS/2's Program Switcher and start up a new session. The old, crashed session still stays in memory, but it doesn't stop you from using your computer.

To start a new session, you press ALT – ESC. That activates the OS/2 Task Master, a program selector/switcher where a list of programs and running sessions are displayed. You choose a new program to run, or a new session to switch to, using the arrow keys and the ENTER key or a mouse.

To finish a session, type EXIT at the protected mode command prompt or just close the PM window. (You cannot end the real mode session.) To switch between two running sessions, press CTRL – ESC. Or if you're using the graphical Presentation Manager, you use the mouse to switch from one program to another by clicking on the appropriate window.

The presentation manager

Since the introduction of the Macintosh in 1984, all types of computers have gravitated toward the graphical user interface (GUI), as opposed to the command line interface DOS uses. Some believe this is a better, more intuitive and friendlier way to use a computer. But it doesn't hold much promise for batch files.

The first version of OS/2, 1.0, used only a command line interface, similar to DOS's. But starting with OS/2 1.1, it's grown graphical. Closely resembling Microsoft's *Windows* application, OS/2's Presentation Manager gives OS/2 users a graphical way to interact with their computers. Now, each session runs in its own window. And everything is controlled with a mouse. Eek, eek!

The OS/2 command line interface is still there. It exists in two modes: On the graphics side, the command line interface appears in a window as the *windowed command prompt* (see FIG. 6-4). The second mode is the traditional, "text mode" command prompt, called the *full screen command prompt*. Either mode operates the same, though in the windowed command prompt you can see and use other windows on the PM's screen at the same time. The full screen command prompt requires you to switch modes to get back to the PM.

In either mode, things work just like DOS. OS/2's batch files still func-

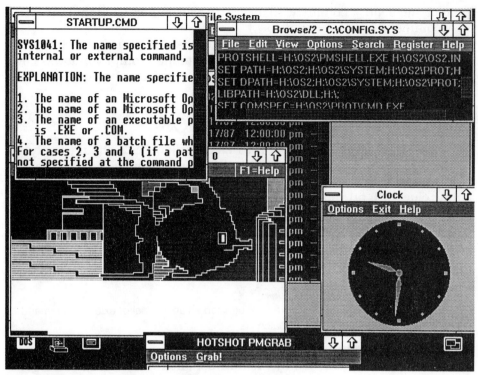

6-4 OS/2's graphical Presentation Manager is shown here.

tion. But they offer you no control for the graphics side of the operating system. And since it looks like the PM isn't going away, the future is pretty grim for OS/2 batch files.

Batch files

Both the real and protected modes of OS/2 use batch files. The real mode runs the same batch files that run under DOS. All the same commands are used and the batch files end with the .BAT file extension.

In the protected mode, batch files behave the same as they do in protected mode. The only difference is that the CMD extension is used rather than BAT:

.BAT   Real
.CMD   Protected

There are additional, OS/2-only batch file commands that work only in the protected mode. If you don't use these new protected mode commands, however, you can still run any protected mode (.CMD) batch file in the real mode—and vice versa. Simply rename the batch file from CMD to BAT. Both mode's batch files are text files, and as long as you omit any real or protect mode-only commands, they'll run in either environment. (The new commands are covered below.)

Again, note that the big drawback here is that your batch files only work and can only control files from the command prompt windows. They cannot manipulate PM programs or the PM interface. But they still have value, as you'll read later.

Similarities between OS/2 and DOS

OS/2 and DOS are really close. As I said earlier, OS/2 should really be called DOS 5.0 or 6.0 or 7.0 (or *SuperWindows*). Anyone who's comfortable with DOS or *Windows* will learn OS/2 in no time. In fact, only a few subtle clues will tip you off that you're not running DOS.

Error messages

One annoying thing I've found with OS/2 is its cryptic error message handling. Rather than getting a simple "File not found" message, OS/2 confronts you with the following:

SYS1041: The name specified is not recognized as an internal or external command, operable program or batch file.

Is this supposed to be friendly?

If you type HELP followed by the number (after SYS above), you'll get a more detailed explanation of what went wrong, as shown in FIG. 6-5.

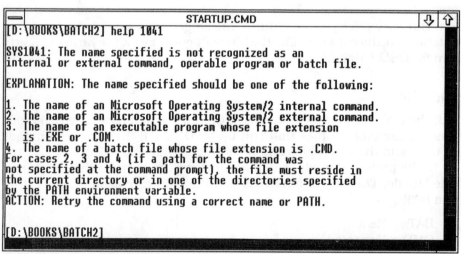

```
┌─────────────────── STARTUP.CMD ────────────────── ⇩ ⇧ ┐
│[D:\BOOKS\BATCH2] help 1041                             │
│                                                        │
│SYS1041: The name specified is not recognized as an     │
│internal or external command, operable program or batch file.│
│                                                        │
│EXPLANATION: The name specified should be one of the following:│
│                                                        │
│1. The name of an Microsoft Operating System/2 internal command.│
│2. The name of an Microsoft Operating System/2 external command.│
│3. The name of an executable program whose file extension│
│   is .EXE or .COM.                                      │
│4. The name of a batch file whose file extension is .CMD.│
│For cases 2, 3 and 4 (if a path for the command was     │
│not specified at the command prompt), the file must reside in│
│the current directory or in one of the directories specified│
│by the PATH environment variable.                       │
│ACTION: Retry the command using a correct name or PATH. │
│                                                        │
│[D:\BOOKS\BATCH2]                                       │
└────────────────────────────────────────────────────────┘
```

6-5 The detailed explanation of error SYS1041 is shown here.

Of course, this is a definite improvement over some earlier operating systems that merely displayed a single question mark, leaving you totally in the dark as to what you did wrong.

Fatal error handling has been "improved" as well. Instead of the now "classic" Abort, Retry and Fail message, OS/2 displays a fancy box with a help screen and detailed instructions. This is a definite improvement over the old "Abort, Retry, Ignore, and Fail" error message, perhaps one of my most favorite computer error messages of all time.

OS/2 commands

Tables 6-1 and 6-2 list a comparison of DOS 3.x and OS/2 commands. (DOS 3.x was chosen over DOS 4.0 because OS/2 claims compatibility with DOS 3.3—not DOS 4.0.) The OS/2 commands have been grouped into real and protected modes in TABLE 6-1.

Table 6-1

DOS 3.x command	Real Mode OS/2 command	Protected Mode OS/2 command
—	—	ANSI
APPEND	APPEND	DPATH
ASSIGN	ASSIGN	—
ATTRIB	ATTRIB	ATTRIB
BACKUP	BACKUP	BACKUP
BREAK	BREAK	—
CHCP	CHCP	CHCP
CHDIR (CD)	CHDIR	CHDIR
CHKDSK	CHKDSK	CHKDSK
CLS	CLS	CLS
COMMAND	COMMAND	CMD
COMP	COMP	COMP
COPY	COPY	COPY
CTTY	—	—
DATE	DATE	DATE
DEL	DEL	DEL
—	—	DETACH
DIR	DIR	DIR
DISKCOMP	DISKCOMP	DISKCOMP
DISKCOPY	DISKCOPY	DISKCOPY
—	—	DPATH (see APPEND)
ERASE	ERASE	ERASE
FASTOPEN	—	—
FIND	FIND	FIND
FORMAT	FORMAT	FORMAT
GRAFTABL	GRAFTABL	—
GRAPHICS	—	—
—	HELPMSG	HELPMSG
JOIN	JOIN	—
KEYB	—	KEYB
LABEL	LABEL	LABEL

Table 6-1 Continued.

DOS 3.x command	Real Mode OS/2 command	Protected Mode OS/2 command
MKDIR (MD)	MKDIR	MKDIR
MODE	MODE	MODE
MORE	MORE	MORE
NLSFUNC	—	—
—	PATCH	PATCH
PATH	PATH	PATH
PRINT	PRINT	PRINT
PROMPT	PROMPT	PROMPT
RECOVER	RECOVER	RECOVER
RENAME (REN)	RENAME	RENAME
REPLACE	REPLACE	REPLACE
RESTORE	RESTORE	RESTORE
RMDIR (RD)	RMDIR	RMDIR
SELECT	—	—
SET	SET	SET
—	SETCOM40	—
SHARE	—	—
SORT	SORT	SORT
—	—	SPOOL
—	—	START
SUBST	SUBST	—
SYS	SYS	SYS
TIME	TIME	TIME
TREE	TREE	TREE
TYPE	TYPE	TYPE
VER	VER	VER
VERIFY	VERIFY	VERIFY
VOL	VOL	VOL
XCOPY	XCOPY	XCOPY

Special directories

Like all complicated software, OS/2 must be installed. Depending on the version of OS/2, there will be several installation strategies. My advice (for everyone) is to use the automatic installation the first time. Later, as you get to know OS/2, you can move the files around. But when you start, it's frustrating not knowing which files do what and where you can put them.

OS/2's installation program will also tell you if your system has what it takes to run OS/2. For example, you need that one megabyte of extended memory to run OS/2. If you don't have it, the installation program will simply sit there and be stubborn.

OS/2 creates for itself a number of directories into which it places its files (see FIG. 6.6).

Table 6-2

Renamed commands:

APPEND is called DPATH in the protected mode
OS/2's COMMAND.COM is called CMD.EXE

New commands:

Command	What it does
ANSI	Turns the extended screen and keyboard control on or off.
DETACH	Sends a process off into the background. You can "detach" a command that will function while you're doing something else. When the command is finished, the process "dies."
HELPMSG	A program that displays helpful information about OS/2's cryptic error messages. You type the error message number after HELPMSG. (This program works with a batch file named HELP.CMD or HELP.BAT depending on which mode of OS/2 you're using.)
PATCH	Used to alter or update the code of a program. You can apply a "patch" to the program by specifying a file containing the patching code.
SETCOM40	Controls access to the serial ports for the real mode. Because some real mode programs will just "take control" of a serial port, SET COM40 is used to avoid conflicts with protected mode programs and to make the port available to the real mode program.
SPOOL	Starts a background printer spooler.
START	Starts a new protected mode process. You can use START to begin a new protected mode session.

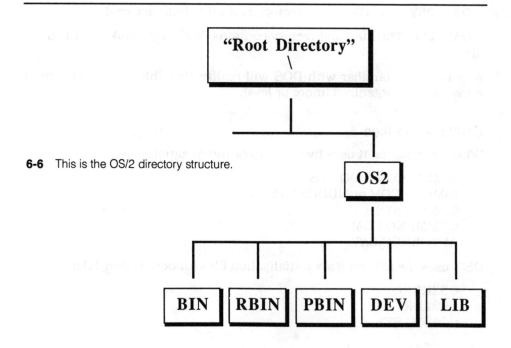

6-6 This is the OS/2 directory structure.

In the root directory are CONFIG.SYS and AUTOEXEC.BAT (for the real mode). Additionally, OS/2 will place a bunch of .SYS and a few .COM and .EXE files into your root directory, disobeying the law of "keeping the root clean."

If you're running a dual mode computer, your DOS CONFIG.SYS and AUTOEXEC.BAT files will be named *.DOS while you run under OS/2. When you run under DOS, your OS/2 files will be renamed CONFIG.OS2 and AUTOEXEC.OS2. The dual-booting program (DBMON.COM, which is invisible) will rename the files when you select one or the other operating system at boot time.

The subdirectories listed in FIG. 6-6 are really only one way of approaching an OS/2 system setup strategy. Actually, the locations for any or all of the files can be set in your OS/2 CONFIG.SYS file. But above, the subdirectories are laid out as follows:

\ **OS2**   The OS2 subdirectory holds all the OS/2 commands, program and data files. It can have five directories under it: BIN, RBIN, PBIN, DEV, and LIB.

\ **OS2** \ **BIN**   The BIN subdirectory holds all the executable files that run under both the real and protected modes.

\ **OS2** \ **RBIN**   The RBIN subdirectory holds only those files and programs used by the OS/2 real mode.

\ **OS2** \ **PBIN**   The PBIN subdirectory holds only those files and programs used by the OS/2 protected mode.

\ **OS2** \ **DEV**   The DEV subdirectory is used to hold device drivers.

\ **OS2** \ **LIB**   The LIB subdirectory contains OS/2's dynalink (.DLL) library files.

Anyone who's familiar with DOS will realize that this makes for quite a mess. Yet, it's organized (more or less).

OS/2 startup files

When DOS starts, it uses five startup or initialization files:

> IBMBIO.COM or IO.SYS
> IBMDOS.COM or MDDOS.SYS
> CONFIG.SYS
> COMMAND.COM
> AUTOEXEC.BAT

OS/2 uses the following six initialization files (under Version 1.1):

> OS2KRNL
> OS2LDR
> CONFIG.SYS

OS2.INI
CMD.EXE
STARTUP.CMD

The OS2KRNL and OS2LDR files are invisible and serve similar purposes as IBMBIO.COM and IBMDOS.COM. They're followed by CONFIG.SYS, the last required file in the boot sequence, and the most important.

The heart of OS/2 is really its CONFIG.SYS file, which works just like DOS's CONFIG.SYS file. Under OS/2, however, CONFIG.SYS takes on *both* the functions of DOS's CONFIG.SYS *and* AUTOEXEC.BAT files. This is important to remember from a batch file programming standpoint: under OS/2, CONFIG.SYS is the big, set-up-your-computer file. Though an AUTOEXEC-like equivalent exists, all the heavy-duty stuff under OS/2 is done in its CONFIG.SYS file.

Table 6-3 is a brief list of OS/2 Version 1.1's CONFIG.SYS commands. If a "Yes" appears in the second column, it means that command applies only to the real mode. Otherwise, most of the commands are specific to the protected mode or a combination of both modes.

One of the big commands shown in TABLE 6-3 is PROTSHELL, roughly the equivalent to the DOS CONFIG.SYS SHELL directive. PROTSHELL is used to identify a shell for OS/2's protected mode. For example:

```
protshell = c: \ os2 \ pbin \ pmshell.exe c: \ os2 \ pbin \ os2.ini
            c: \ os2/pbin \ cmd.exe
```

The above command directs OS/2 to use PMSHELL.EXE (the Presentation Manager) as its primary protected mode shell. The OS2.INI file is the PM setup file, which is required after PMSHELL. Following that is the name of the text mode shell, CMD.EXE, which is covered below. That's how OS/2 knows what to do after its basic three startup files are run. (The rest of the files are covered after this mini-section on CONFIG.SYS.)

Some other interesting commands you should note in TABLE 6-3 are the SET commands and RUN. Note that SET is used here, in OS/2's CON FIG.SYS file, just like you would in AUTOEXEC.BAT under DOS. In fact, you can use SET to create any or all of your OS/2 environment variables (which is why an OS/2 equivalent AUTOEXEC.BAT isn't needed over here—too bad for batch files).

Table 6-3

Command	Real Mode	Description
BREAK	Yes	If set equal to YES the system will check for Control-C (break) to halt programs.
BUFFERS		Specifies the number of buffers to be used by OS/2 for file reading and writing.
CODEPAGE		Selects the code page to be used by your system (for foreign language computers).

Table 6-3 Continued.

Command	Real Mode	Description
COUNTRY		Selects time, date and currency display formats for different countries.
DEVICE		Loads a device driver into memory.
DEVINFO		Prepares a specified device for use with code pages.
DISKCACHE		Allocates space for a disk cache.
FCBS	Yes	Specifies the number of file control blocks that can be open at a time.
IOPL		Controls access to hardware, such as screen memory.
LIBPATH		Specifies the path of OS/2's dynamic-link library modules.
MAXWAIT		Specifies the maximum number of seconds a process will be ignored before OS/2 gives it some time.
MEMMAN		Sets memory management options.
PAUSEONERROR		If set equal to YES, the system will pause if there is an error in the CONFIG.SYS file.
PRIORITY		Specifies how priority will be allocated to different processes.
PROTECTONLY		If set equal to YES, then only OS/2 protected mode programs will be allowed to run.
PROTSHELL		Specifies a program shell and a command processor for the protected mode, such as the Presentation Manager (PMSHELL.EXE) and command interpreter (CMD.EXE for the command prompt mode).
REM		Used to include comments in the CONFIG.SYS file.
RMSIZE		Sets the real mode's memory size.
RUN		Specifies a program or background process to run during system initialization.
SET COMSPEC		Specifies the location of the command line command interpreter (CMD.EXE).
SET DPATH		Sets a search path for data files.
SET PATH		Sets the system PATH, the same as the PATH command under DOS.
SET PROMPT		Sets the system prompt, the same as the PROMPT command under DOS.
SHELL	Yes	Specifies a real mode command processor.
SWAPPATH		Specifies the location for a "swap" file, used when swapping memory to disk or vice versa.
THREADS		Specifies the maximum number of threads (individual processes) allowed.
TIMESLICE		Selects the minimum and maximum number of milliseconds allowed per timeslice (time allocated to each thread).
TRACE		Monitors the trace buffer.
TRACEBUF		Sets the size of the trace buffer.

Similarly, the RUN directive is used to automatically start programs under OS/2. Unlike DOS, where you'd use AUTOEXEC.BAT to run memory resident, startup programs, or just to launch applications, you do all that under OS/2 using CONFIG.SYS and the RUN directive.

A final friendly face to notice is the traditional DEVICE directive. As with DOS, there are a lot of OS/2 device drivers and such that you can load using CONFIG.SYS. Table 6-4 lists a few of them included on the OS/2 installation diskettes.

Table 6-4

Device driver	What it does . . .
ANSI.SYS	Loads the ANSI.SYS console driver into memory for use in the real mode only.
COM01.SYS	A device driver that controls the serial port.
COM02.SYS	A serial port device driver for PS/2 systems.
EGA.SYS	Used to support a mouse in the various EGA (Enhanced Graphics Display) screen modes and resolutions.
EXTDSKDD.SYS	A device driver that allows the addition of external floppy drives.
MOUSEA??.SYS	Loads device drivers for support of the various mouse pointing devices made by Microsoft or IBM.
POINTDD.SYS	Creates a pointer image (from the mouse pointing device) on the screen.
VDISK.SYS	A device driver used to configure parts of memory as a RAM disk.

After CONFIG.SYS runs, another setup file used by OS/2 is OS2.INI. It's actually an initialization file required by the Presentation Manager (and it's specified after PMSHELL.EXE in the PROTSHELL directive). Unlike similar *.INI files you'd find under Microsoft's *Windows*, OS2.INI isn't a text file. Yet it's important to the way the PM behaves, and changes you make while using the PM are saved in your OS2.INI file all the time. Before the PM can appear on the screen, it must first read OS2.INI, which is why it's placed here in the chain of command.

After OS2.INI comes CMD.EXE, the COMMAND.COM of OS/2. It serves virtually the identical function as COMMAND.COM and also contains the OS/2 batch file interpreter. CMD.EXE is specified after the PM using the PROTSHELL directive in CONFIG.SYS.

CMD has two optional switches, /C and /K.

/C works exactly like the /C switch for COMMAND.COM. You follow /C with the name of a program to run, such as a batch file. CMD.EXE executes that command, then returns. (So you could use CMD /C with a batch file to "call" the batch file. However, the CALL batch file command works in the protected mode, so this would be unnecessary.)

/K works like /C, except after the optional program runs, OS/2 stays in the new shell created by CMD.EXE. To return to the previous shell, simply type EXIT just as you would exit from a COMMAND.COM shell. (This is explained a little bit down the road.)

Under the PM, CMD.EXE is rarely used. It's only in a command prompt window that you'll find CMD.EXE fired up.

Finally we have STARTUP.CMD, the AUTOEXEC.BAT of OS/2. But given the importance and versatility of CONFIG.SYS—why bother? If you do want to use it, however, simply create a batch file with the commands you want, place it into the root directory of your boot disk, and name it STARTUP.CMD. Each time OS/2 starts it will open a windowed command prompt and run the STARTUP.CMD batch file.

STARTUP.CMD only runs once, when the system first starts. A second type of batch file, OS2INIT.CMD, used to be run each time you opened a new session. Since the PM came along, however, OS2INIT is no longer automatically run each time you start a new session. Even when you fire up a new command prompt (windowed or full screen), OS2INIT isn't run.

The only way to get OS2INIT to run each time you open a command prompt window is by specifying it using CONFIG.SYS's PROTSHELL command. If you list CMD's /K switch followed by the full path to OS2INIT.CMD, it will run every time you open a command prompt window. For example:

```
protshell = c: \ os2 \ pbin \ pmshell.exe c: \ os2 \ pbin \ os2.ini
            c: \ os2 \ pbin \ cmd.exe /k c: \ os2init.cmd
```

The final part of that line will cause OS2INIT.CMD to run for each windowed or full screen (text) command prompt you run under OS/2. Remember, however, that OS2INIT.CMD will not run for each window you open up in the PM. Again, OS/2 is a graphic operating system and the need for batch files in that environment is slight.

OS/2 batch files

So where does all this leave us with OS/2 batch files? Not very far. Thanks to the Presentation Manager, the usefulness of batch files under OS/2 is questionable. But they still exist. And there are still interesting things we can do with them.

Like everything else with OS/2 (well, the command line version at least), its batch files are remarkably similar to the old DOS batch files. The only visible difference is that the protected mode batch files have the extension .CMD rather than .BAT.

OS/2 can only run three different types of programs, all based on the program's filename extensions. Just as DOS has .COM, .EXE and .BAT, OS/2 has .COM, .EXE, and .CMD. And, yes, the CMD files work under the

PM. If you click on a CMD file with the mouse, OS/2 just opens up a windowed command prompt, and the batch file runs in there. No problem.

Besides the new .CMD filename extension, OS/2 adds the following batch file commands to protected mode batch files:

ANSI	Turns extended keyboard and screen control on or off.
ENDLOCAL	Restores the drive, directory and environment to what they were when the SETLOCAL command was issued.
EXTPROC	Defines an external batch file processor.
SETLOCAL	Saves the current drive, directory and environment. These can then be altered by the batch file and subsequently restored to their original states via the ENDLOCAL command.

A final difference with OS/2 is how it reacts to a user pressing CTRL – BREAK to halt a batch file. In the real mode, this works just like it does under DOS; you see the famous "Terminate batch file (Y/N)?" prompt and are allowed to press "N" to continue the batch file or "Y" to stop it. However, under OS/2's protected mode, pressing CTRL – BREAK immediately stops the batch file and returns you to the OS/2 command prompt (which is better).

The only two official OS/2 batch files are STARTUP.CMD and OS2INIT.CMD. STARTUP.CMD is the AUTOEXEC.BAT, running each time you start OS/2 if it's present. (You can see the STARTUP.CMD window in FIG. 6-4.) OS2INIT.CMD is run each time you start a windowed or full screen command prompt, and then only if it's specified by the PROT SHELL directive in your CONFIG.SYS file (see above).

Now what can you do with these batch files? As with most of OS/2, the answer is "not much." Because CONFIG.SYS lets you run programs and set environment variables, that leaves little for a STARTUP.CMD file to do—not to mention a negative reaction we all have to a text program running under a graphic interface.

On my system I wrote the following STARTUP.CMD file:

```
1: @ECHO OFF
2: REM STARTUP.CMD, run when OS/2 first starts
3: REM in a PM windowed command prompt
4: ECHO This is OS/2
5: VER
6:
7: OS2INIT.CMD
```

Very simply, this displays the message "This is OS/2" followed by the OS/2 copyright notice (VER—the same as the DOS VER command):

```
This is OS/2
The Microsoft Operating System/2 Version is 1.10
```

The final thing my STARTUP.CMD file does is to run OS2INIT.CMD. Realistically, this should be an automatic operation. You must specify OS2INIT if you want it to run for your initial protected mode session.

My OS2INIT.CMD file looks like this:

```
1: @ECHO OFF
2: REM OS2INIT.CMD, run each time you start a
3: REM command line interface
4: ANSI ON > NUL
5: ECHO Welcome to OS/2
6: ECHO Now whatcha gonna do?
```

The ANSI ON command turns on the ANSI.SYS driver for this OS/2 session; > NUL redirects the output to the NUL device, which suppresses the "ANSI is on" message. Finally I display a funny little rhyme:

```
Welcome to OS/2
Now whatcha gonna do?


[C:\]
```

This is in reference, of course, to the fact that I own no OS/2 software and having nothing to do with OS/2 other than write silly little batch files.

Because I've specified OS2INIT.CMD in my CONFIG.SYS file, each new command prompt session runs OS2INIT.CMD executes, displaying that silly, yet accurate, rhyme.

Summary

OS/2 is the next-generation operating system for IBM compatible computers. It runs only on computers with an 80286 or later microprocessor. Older, 8088 and 8086 systems are unable to run OS/2. Also, your 80286 or 80386 system will need at least 1.5 megabytes of RAM to accommodate OS/2, preferable four or more megabytes if you're serious.

There are two operating modes in OS/2. The *real* mode, also called the DOS 3x box, operates similar to DOS Version 3.3. Older DOS programs can run in the real mode, though they cannot take advantage of OS/2's true power.

The *protected* mode is the true OS/2 mode. In this mode, several programs can be run simultaneously. Each program is called a session and you can run as many sessions as your system allows.

Since Version 1.1, OS/2 comes with a graphic interface, the *Presentation Manager*. It looks a lot like Microsoft *Windows* (who would guess?) and it's a new approach to running a computer—yet it limits the uses for batch files under OS/2.

Speaking of which, OS/2's real mode batch files are identical to DOS batch files. In the protected mode, batch files end with the .CMD extension. Also, there are four new batch file commands you can use in the protected mode: ANSI, ENDLOCAL, EXTPROC, and SETLOCAL.

Most of the heavy-duty functions of batch files, specifically AUTO-EXEC.BAT, are handled by OS/2's CONFIG.SYS file. However, a START-UP.CMD batch file will be run the first time OS/2 boots (only once). A second type of batch file, OS2INIT.CMD, will be run each time you start a new windowed or full screen command prompt, but then only if you specify that file in your CONFIG.SYS.

Part Two

Batch file programming

Now that you should be all boned up on DOS, you're ready to apply that knowledge to your batch files. That's what Part Two is all about: programming batch files. Because batch files use DOS (or is that make DOS easier to use?), after wading through all the information in Part One, you should come up with some interesting concoctions. The information in this part of the book will help.

7
Programming tools

All programming languages, even batch files, have many parts. In all cases, the end result is a program you've written that instructs your computer to do something. How you get from the basic idea in your head—the "Hey, I need a program (or batch file) that does blah blah"—to the actual program that does blah blah—is what this chapter is all about.

Of primary concern here are programming tools: those things you need to write, edit and run batch files. The tools include a text editor or some other method of writing the batch file; the batch file commands themselves; the DOS commands that are used with batch files; and the variables that batch files employ. Put them all together and you have advanced batch file programming.

Standard procedures

Perhaps the best thing about computers is that you can tell them exactly what to do—and they'll do it (even when it's wrong). For most people, this means telling the computer that they want to use a word processor to write a letter. But for others, it means that you can program the computer, instructing it to do exactly what you want it to.

There are varying degrees of programming languages, depending on how "friendly" you want them, or how close you want to get to programming the computer hardware directly. Just about the friendliest programming language around is the batch file programming language. Another friendly language is BASIC. Pascal is a bit more rigid in its structure than BASIC, but still friendly (and popular). C is getting toward the obscure yet powerful end of the spectrum, but is the preferred language for PC programming. And assembly language is as close as you can get to telling the computer's microprocessor exactly what it is you want it to do (almost like grunt and point).

All these languages and more can be grouped into two types: interpreted and compiled. Only BASIC and the batch file programming languages are interpreted. This means, simply, that the computer examines each instruction one at a time, then carries out that task.

Compiled languages involve a few more steps. First, a compiled language has source code, written with a text editor. The source code contains all the programming instructions and information for a compiler. The compiler translates the source code, which is basically English text, into an "object" format, or sometimes directly into machine-readable code. The object format is then run through a "linker" that creates the final program (see TABLE 7-1).

Table 7-1

Compiler steps	Interpreted steps	Tools used
Edit/Create	Edit/Create	Editor
Compile	(not needed)	Compiler/Assembler
Link	(not needed)	Linker program
Run	Run	DOS

The extra steps, compile, link and then run, make a compiled program run much faster than an interpreted one. But compiled programs take longer to write, test and debug. Interpreted programs, on the other hand, are easy to write and run. For example, you simply write the text for a batch file, then type the batch file's name at the command prompt and it runs. However, because it's interpreted, batch files can be really slow— especially because they fetch each line of text from the disk one at a time.

Compiled programs might offer speed of execution and interpreted programs offer quick development. For batch file programming, all you need are tools to create the programs. These are editing tools to write the batch file; the batch file programming language, which consists of DOS commands, batch file directives, and third-party utilities; and DOS itself to translate, or interpret, each line of the batch file. Fortunately, you get most of these items free with DOS.

Editors

Batch files must be text files, composed solely of ASCII characters.

The ASCII limitation isn't really a hard and fast rule. After all, as seen in chapter 3, it's possible to embed control characters in batch files. It's also possible to have the extended ASCII character set used, for example, to display line graphics. If a non-ASCII character is used in a batch file, for example, a word processing code, chances are that the batch file won't work properly.

So, the first step to writing a batch file is to find the proper tool to do the job. As was discussed in chapter 1, there are three popular methods of creating a batch file:

- A Word Processor
- DOS
- A Text Editor

These are listed in order here from "worst" to "best" based on my recommendations. The end result always must be the same: a text file on disk with the .BAT filename extension. How you get there is up to you.

Word processors—not the best way

If you're going to be doing any serious batch file programming, or any programming, you'll need to get a text editor. Word processors are nice for writing, composing letters, writing stories, book and plays—creative verbal stuff. But programming requires only text. You don't need all the pretty margins, headers, footnotes, spell checkers, underline printing and whatnot. Just plain text.

For example, most word processors "wrap" a line of text, rather than insisting that you press ENTER at the end of each line (like a typewriter). The batch file interpreter needs that ENTER character to signal an end of line. Actually, it really needs the combination carriage return and line feed characters. Some word processors may simply put a carriage return character at the end of a line. If you ever encounter a "Bad Command or Filename" error message, or notice that not all your batch file's commands are executing, it's probably because you're missing a line feed character somewhere.

Some word processors save their files in a unique format, keeping their formatting codes, font changes, and other pretty things intact. You don't want that in a batch file. So, in order to save a batch file program in a word processor, you'll need to specifically save the file as a nondocument, text, or ASCII formatted file. Further, some word processors have different formats for ASCII files. If so, you'll want the "DOS" text format, with a carriage return and line feed character at the end of every line: a major bother.

If you like using a word processor, by all means stick with it. Just make sure that you save your batch files in the text mode. Also, be prepared to wait, seeing that most word processors take longer to load and save text files than any of the text editors discussed later in this section.

Quick and dirty: Using DOS

I would estimate that 100 percent of the batch files that are less than four lines in length were created using DOS. It's the quickest and easiest way to create any text file, and you don't even need a program.

On the other hand, using DOS to create a batch file means no editing. Once a line of text is entered and sealed with the ENTER key, it's done! I don't need to tell you how many times I've used DOS to create a batch file, then absentmindedly pressed the up-arrow key to fix a previous line. No matter how hard I try, it just doesn't work.

This quick and easy way, of course, is using the famous COPY CON "function" of DOS. Actually, this is simply using DOS to copy a file from the CONsole device to a batch file name. Because DOS is device driven, this is possible:

```
C> COPY CON TEST.BAT
```

DOS is now ready for you to type your text. The characters you enter will be copied to a DOS file named TEST.BAT. If TEST.BAT doesn't exist, it will be created. If it does exist, DOS will overwrite it with the new information.

If you've never done this before, or even if you have, here are the rules for creating a text file using COPY CON:

- You are allowed to edit each line up until the time ENTER is pressed. The DOS editing keys (see below) are available for working on the current line only. Once ENTER is pressed, the line is locked into memory.
- Pressing CTRL–Z ends input and creates the file. You must follow CTRL–Z with ENTER. CTRL–Z can be at the end of a line or on a line by itself.
- Pressing CTRL–Z cancels the COPY CON operation and returns you to DOS.

The following is an example of a short batch file created with COPY CON:

```
C> COPY CON SHORT.BAT
@ECHO OFF
VOL
VER
^Z
        1 File(s) copied
```

On the last line, CTRL–Z was pressed to end input. The final file was "copied" from the console to disk and named SHORT.BAT. Presto! You have created a batch file.

Using COPY CON isn't as limited as it might appear. For one, you have access to the DOS editing keys. These are the often ignored function key commands for manipulating information in DOS's input buffer. (They're also available at the command prompt.)

By using the editing keys in TABLE 7-2, you can have limited control over the line you're currently working on. Also, because DOS retains the previous line in the input buffer's "template," you can edit or reuse it as well. Further explanation of the function keys in TABLE 7-2 is provided in appendix F.

Table 7-2

DOS Editing Function Keys

F1	Right Arrow	Move cursor right, display next character in the template (if any)
F2		(Followed by a character) Search for character, display template up to that character
F3		Display the rest of the template
F4		(Followed by a character) Delete up to the character
F5		Reset the template, replacing it with the Characters entered so far
F6	Control-Z	End input, write file after pressing ENTER
ENTER	Control-M	Accept current line, begin new line
ESC	Control-[	Cancel current line, start over
Backspace	Left Arrow	Move back one character
DEL		Remove character from template
INS		Insert characters into the template (can be toggled on and off)

Most people would probably use COPY CON more often if they were aware of these function keys and what they could do. For creating fast batch files, nothing beats it. But, when you need more sophistication, one step above COPY CON (actually, a giant leap toward batch file writing nirvana) is the text editor.

Text editors

Text editors differ from word processors because they only edit text. There are rarely any text formatting abilities, and only a handful of the popular text editors have any printing facilities. You can forget underline, bold, superscript and italics. Instead, text editors were designed to create and edit text files. This is ideal for programming and any other type of work where text files are required.

Like all microcomputer software, there are dozens of text editors on the market. Some are free, some shareware, and some cost more than most word processors do. The power and capability of the text editor determines its price. Believe it or not, just because a text editor isn't a word processor doesn't mean it's short on features. For programming work, there are a lot more goodies you'll require than when you're writing prose.

Recommendations

If you don't already have a text editor, there are two that I recommend (in addition to the EDIT program that comes with DOS 5, and EDLIN that comes with all DOS versions). They are *QEdit*, which I consider to be the ultimate text editor; and *PC Write*, which is really a full featured word processor but serves well as a text editor. There are other text editors on the market and a few of them are discussed later in this section.

QEdit

I found *QEdit* when I was looking for a small, fast, and useful text editor for my laptop. It's small, under 50K in size. And it's fast, making it an ideal text editor or word processor.

QEdit is really one neat program. It works a lot like *WordStar*, yet it can be configured so that you can assign its commands to any Function, Alt, or Control key you want. It uses multiple windows, so you can edit or view a number of documents at a time. You have the option of using key commands or *QEdit*'s pull-down menu system (though it doesn't yet support a mouse). And *QEdit* is surprising; when I brought it up on a screen that was 132 columns by 43 rows, *QEdit* filled in everything perfectly; the odd screen size didn't phase the program at all.

All *QEdit*'s power is available for only $54.95 plus $3 shipping. A shareware version is available for test driving, and there's even an OS/2 text version for writing those all-important OS/2 batch files.

> QEdit
> SemWare
> 4343 Shalowford Road, Suite C3
> Marietta, GA 30062
> (404) 641-9002

PC Write

PC Write isn't just a text editor. It's a full-fledged word processor, but still a favorite for writing *dBASE*, assembly language, C, and batch file programs.

Also, *PC Write* is an interesting computer software success story. Offered since the early days of the PC as "shareware," QuickSoft eventually became a full-fledged and thriving company that now sells its product commercially.

Even though it's a word processor, *PC Write* saves its text in ASCII format. As long as you turn wordwrap off (SHIFT – F7), *PC Write* is quite a handy editor to have. In fact, you may want to incorporate it as the default editor for programs such as *ProComm* and *dBASE* that allow a secondary editor program.

PC Write can be obtained from a number of sources and usually for free. As part of the shareware agreement, you can use the program for a while to test it. Then, if you keep on using it, you're asked to pay a nominal fee for registration. Full registration for *PC Write* is $129, which includes the manual and full support.

PC Write
QuickSoft, Inc.
219 1st Ave N #224-B
Seattle, WA 98109-9911
(800) 888-8088

DOS 5's EDIT command

After nine years of never upgrading its text editor, DOS 5 finally introduces EDIT, a nice, full-screen, mouse-supported, text editor. It even has pull-down menus and dialog boxes (if you're into that sort of thing).

EDIT is nice. Unlike *QEdit*, though, it can't edit more than one file at a time. But it beats the pants off of the old EDLIN. Also, another drawback is that EDIT has no ready way to enter the ESC character, so editing ANSI codes in a batch file is difficult. (And even EDLIN lets you enter the ESC character!)

EDIT is free with DOS 5, and until you get something better it will suit you just fine for editing batch files. DOS 3.3 and 4 users will have to be stuck with—you guessed it—EDLIN until they get something else.

Speaking of EDLIN

No one ever has anything nice to say about EDLIN. Well, how about this: it's free. Everyone has it (even DOS 5 users). And, as pointed out earlier in this book, it's one of the few word processors that will let you enter the ESCape character into the text (and other control characters as well).

There are two problems with EDLIN that make everyone hate it. The first is its confusing command structure. Sure, it's easy to remember that I is insert and D delete. But do the line numbers come before or after the command? Here's a hint:

> In EDLIN, the line number comes *before* the command.

1D means to delete line 1. D1 means delete the current line, then edit line one. Confusing? Yes.

Also, the second problem with EDLIN is that it's line-oriented. You can only edit one line of text at a time—and you're limited to DOS's function key editing, meaning you can't really see what you're working on.

On the bright side, EDLIN, automatically makes a backup copy of your work, so you'll never likely lose any originals. Of course, some people don't like their disks littered with .BAK files.

The DOS manual has a complete reference and a brief tutorial on EDLIN. Also, appendix G of this book has a command summary and reference.

Other text editors

Other popular text editors are *Brief*, the *Norton Editor*, *SideKick*, and *WordStar*.

Brief Brief is the most sophisticated programming editor you can buy—and the most expensive. Its abilities go beyond what I could describe here. Because of Brief's advanced features, and the fact that it's really designed for C, assembly language, or *dBASE* compiling efforts, a few would accuse it of being too powerful for writing batch files. Though this may be the case, you should seriously look into purchasing *Brief* if you plan to be doing any extensive programming.

Brief
Solution Systems
541 Main Street Suite 410
South Weymouth, MA 02910
(800) 821-2492

The Norton Editor Contrary to popular belief, master programmer Peter Norton did not write the *Norton Editor*. Someone else did. Still, now that you're crushed, the *Norton Editor* is a handy text editor, written for only one purpose: writing programs. (What else would you expect from Peter Norton Computing?)

The Norton Editor
Peter Norton Computing, Inc.
10201 Torre Avenue
Cupertino, CA 95014
(800) 441-7234
(800) 626-8847 (CA only)

SideKick *SideKick* is the venerable "good buddy" program. Not only does it have an editor that you can pop up and use at any time, but it has other memory-resident utilities as well, including a handy calculator.

SideKick is nice because, once loaded, it's always there. The only drawback to the *SideKick* editor is that it has a clumsy way of saving and loading files. Also, it sucks up a great deal of memory and might conflict with some of your other programs.

SideKick
Borland International
1700 Green Hills Road
Scotts Valley, CA 95066
(800) 331-0877

WordStar *WordStar* is an official, deluxe word processor. The current version even supports spell checking and offers a thesaurus—things you rarely need when batch file programming. By the way, I'm talking about the old *WordStar*, the unfriendly, cursor-diamond pattern, control-key *WordStar* of the CP/M days of computing. This isn't the behemoth slug *WordStar 2000* (or whatever they're calling it nowadays).

Believe it or not, *WordStar* was every famous programmer's first text editor. Even *SideKick* and *dBASE* use its famous key commands. Back in the good old days, *WordStar* was all a programmer had to write long expanses of code. Today, with *WordStar*'s added features, it would make an excellent choice as both a text editor and word processor.

> WordStar
> Department C58
> PO Box 9000
> San Fernando, CA 91341-9000
> (800) 227-5609

There are other editors as well, including a whole slew of editors that mimic the UNIX-style editors "vi," VEDIT, and EMACS (or JOVE). Because I can't stand UNIX, I didn't bother with any of these. However, if you must, several of these public domain/shareware editors are available from the PC-SIG library. (Their number is in appendix L.)

Batch file commands

Besides an editor to create batch files, another tool you'll need is the batch file programming language itself. Batch file commands are a mixture of DOS's commands and the special batch file directives included with DOS. This section covers an introduction to the batch file commands. The following section covers some interesting DOS commands than augment the batch file commands. Of course, any DOS command names as well as any programs on your computer can be part of a batch file.

Batch file commands are those DOS commands and functions that were written to specifically aid in the writing of batch files. Some of these commands can be used at the command prompt. Others only have meaning in batch files.

Table 7-3 briefly describes the various batch file commands and what they do. (Yes, there are only eight official batch files commands.) Part Six of this book contains a complete "cookbook" of all the batch file commands, along with descriptions and examples.

There are other elements of batch files, certain functions and variables such as EXIST, ERRORLEVEL, DO, NOT and "= =", which are also incorporated into the batch file language. The following descriptions elaborate on those batch files commands that use them. Again, refer to the cookbook section for more details.

Table 7-3

Batch file directives	Description
CALL	"Runs" a second batch file, like a BASIC subroutine
ECHO	Turns ECHO on/off, sends strings to the console
FOR	Repeats a command for a given group of files
GOTO	Transfers execution to a label
IF	Executes a command on a given condition
PAUSE	Displays a pause message and waits for any key
REM	Allows REMarks in batch files
SHIFT	Rotates, or shifts, replaceable parameter variables

FOR

The FOR command is used by both batch files and on the DOS command line. Like the BASIC programming language's FOR-NEXT loop, the batch file statement FOR allows you to do a number of commands at a time. The format is:

FOR %*variable* in (*file selection*) DO *command*

variable is a one character variable. In DOS, *variable* is preceded by a single percent sign; in batch files, there must be two percent signs.

file selection is a list of files, including wildcards, full pathnames, or just a list of individual filenames. (It can also be a list of items, as shown in chapter 9.)

command is a DOS command. Usually *command* incorporates *variable* to perform some action on the list of files in *file selection*.

In a nutshell, FOR repeats the DOS command listed after DO for as many times as there are files in *file selection*. The *variable* is used to represent each individual file.

FOR %A IN (MENU*.* SUB*.* CTRL*.*) DO COPY %A B:\STOW

The above FOR command operates on three groups of files, MENU*.*, SUB*.* and CTRL*.*. For each of those files, FOR will DO the command:

COPY %A B:\STOW

Each time FOR executes the DO command, %A is replaced by one of the three filenames. So the single FOR command does the same thing as the following three commands:

```
COPY MENU*.* B:\STOW
COPY SUB*.* B:\STOW
COPY CTRL*.* B:\STOW
```

Fundamentally, that's the extent of the FOR command. It performs a single DOS command on a variety of files as specified between the parenthesis. Later chapters will show you some nifty tricks you can pull with the FOR command. But for now keep in mind that, when used in a batch file, two percent signs are used instead of one.

IF

IF is used in batch files to evaluate a condition—just like the IF statement found in many programming languages (specifically, BASIC). The only difference is that there is no THEN or ELSE statement to follow IF:

IF [NOT] *condition command*

condition is an evaluation or comparison. If *condition* is true, then *command* is executed. Otherwise, batch file execution continues with the next line.

NOT is a logical switch that can be placed before *condition*. When NOT is specified and *condition* is false, then *command* is executed—the opposite of IF's normal operation.

command is another batch file command. Typically it's a GOTO, though it could be any DOS command or program name—even another IF statement.

condition is evaluated using two batch file commands, the EXIST test and the ERRORLEVEL variable. Also, a double equal sign operator is used for string comparisons.

EXIST tests the existence of files:

IF EXIST *.* . . .

If any files exist (*.*), then *condition* is true and *command* is executed.

IF EXIST JUNE.DAT . . .

If the file JUNE.DAT exists in the current directory, *condition* is true and *command* is executed.

NOT can be used to see if a file doesn't exist:

IF NOT EXIST JUNE.DAT . . .

condition is evaluated as true here only if the file JUNE.DAT does not exist. If it exists, then *command* isn't executed and the batch file continues with the next line.

ERRORLEVEL is used to test the return code from certain programs.

When programs return to DOS, they can do so in four manners (see chapter 1). If they return properly (according to *Microsoft*), they'll return a code value from 0 to 255. The ERRORLEVEL variable is used to hold the program's return code.

ERRORLEVEL is followed immediately by a comparison code value. If ERRORLEVEL is greater than or equal to that value, the *condition* is true and *command* is executed. This is important to remember:

> ERRORLEVEL tests "true" if the return code is greater than or equal to its value

Consider the following:

    IF ERRORLEVEL 1 . . .

If an ERRORLEVEL value of 1 or greater is returned by the previous program, *command* is executed. (Appendix I contains a list of DOS programs and their return codes.)

= = (double equal signs) are used to compare string values. These can include environment variables or replaceable parameters, as well as string constants. Incidentally, both strings must be exact, uppercase for uppercase and lowercase for lowercase. If both strings are identical, *condition* is true and *command* is executed.

    IF %LOGIN% = = STEVE . . .

This command tests to see if the value of the environment variable LOGIN is equal to the string "STEVE". If so, *command* is executed. To see if the strings are not equal, use NOT:

    IF NOT %LOGIN% = = STEVE . . .

Keep this rule in mind:

> When comparing strings with IF, two equal signs are used

This is to avoid confusion with BASIC, where only one equal sign is used when comparing variables. (It is, however, the same as the C language, where two equal signs test equivalence.)

command is executed in this case only if the contents of the environment variable LOGIN is not equal to "STEVE".

The batch file example in FIG. 7-1 shows how the IF statement is used to test for the existence of a file. The batch file simply scans two directories on disk, \TEMP (5) and \ASM\BATCH (7) and deletes any *.BAK files found. IF EXIST is used to first test if any *.BAK files exist. If so, the *command*, DEL *.BAK is used to remove those offending files.

DOS commands

The following is a list of several DOS commands that work quite well with batch files. In fact, some of them have become "hall of fame" tricks used with most advanced batch file programming.

7-1 An IF statement tests for the existence of a file.

Name: `KILLBAK.BAT`

```
 1: @ECHO OFF
 2: REM Remove .BAK files from where they may be lurking
 3: ECHO Removing ugly .BAK files...
 4: C:
 5: CD \TEMP
 6: IF EXIST *.BAK DEL *.BAK
 7: CD \ASM\BATCH
 8: IF EXIST *.BAK DEL *.BAK
 9: ECHO Done
10: :END
```

This is not a list of all DOS commands that can be used with batch files (because, well, all DOS commands can be used with batch files). Instead, the following are some DOS commands that you can use to enhance your batch files.

A TYPE of short cut

One of the worst examples of batch file programming is the overuse of the ECHO command. I cringe each time I see an entire screen full of text scroll up one line at a time, meaning some clown used 24 ECHO statements to get his point across.

Rather than use multiple ECHOes to get the job done, use the DOS TYPE command. TYPE will quickly and nicely display an entire screen of text—a lot faster than ECHO (which needs to go to the disk each time it executes).

The only drawback to using TYPE is that you must know the exact name and location of the file you'll be typing. However, as long as you specify a full pathname (and are certain that the file exists), TYPE really makes displaying text a lot smoother than overusing ECHO.

Speed trick

When displaying a long file, for example, with TYPE, information might scroll off the screen before the user has a chance to read it. You can solve this problem by putting at the top of the file:

ECHO Press Control-S to pause the display, Control-Q to continue

But most users won't see that message until it's too late. Instead, you can use the MORE filter that came with DOS. There are two ways to use MORE:

TYPE MESSAGE.TXT | MORE
MORE < MESSAGE.TXT

Both of these methods will display the contents of the text file MES SAGE.TXT. Each method correctly uses the MORE filter to pause the display of text after each screen. The second method is faster than the first, however.

The first method uses the TYPE command to send the contents of MESSAGE.TXT to the MORE filter. This takes time because both TYPE and MORE are being used at once. Because the second method uses I/O redirection to send the contents of MESSAGE.TXT directly into the MORE filter, it's faster.

IF EXIST

So many users write batch files that run quite smoothly—except for those occasional "File not found" error messages. There's a simple way around this: use IF EXIST. In fact, adding the IF statement to any command that deals with a file is easy. For example:

```
DEL *.BAK
```

This command can be used in a batch file to delete all those terrible .BAK files that accumulate all over your hard disk. But what if they're all gone? Then your batch file will display a string of those "File not found" messages. Instead, you can modify the above line as follows:

```
IF EXIST *.BAK DEL *.BAK
```

Painless—and no more phantom error messages.

>NUL

This is a popular trick you might have seen at various locations in this book. The NUL device is the "door to nowhere." Though it's a real device and can be used with I/O redirection like any other device, it really doesn't put anything anywhere. So, it's a safe bet that when you redirect output to the NUL device it will be invisible.

>NUL is most often used in "silent" batch files. When you don't want the user to see something, or when the results of a command need not be displayed, simply redirect them to the NUL device. For example:

```
COPY *.* E:\SPOOL
```

This command copies a whole squad of files to the directory \SPOOL on drive E (assume it's an electronic disk). If this line were in a batch file and ECHO were turned off, either one of the following may be displayed on the screen:

```
3 File(s) copied
```

or

```
File not found - ????????.????
    0 File(s) copied
```

(The number of files copied varies depending on how many files *.* represents.)

Needless to say, those messages, especially the latter, will be confusing. So, rather than risk confusion, simply use >NUL to redirect any output to the NUL device. Whatever the results of the COPY command, the screen will remain clean.

By the way, you can avoid the above situation by using the IF EXIST command as shown in FIG. 7-2.

7-2 To keep the screen clean, use the IF EXIST command and I/O redirection to the NUL device.

```
1: @ECHO OFF
2: CD \WS\PRINT
3: IF EXIST *.* GOTO COPYTHEM
4: ECHO No files found to copy
5: GOTO END
6: :COPYTHEM
7: COPY *.* C:\TEMP >NUL
8: ECHO Files copied to spool directory
9: :END
```

IF EXIST tests for the existence of any files in the directory \WS \PRINT (3). If any file (*.*) is found, the EXIST test proves true and execution branches to the COPYTHEM label (6). Otherwise, the "No files found to copy" message is echoed (4) and the program stops (5, 9).

>NUL is used in line 7 to suppress the listing of the files as they are copied, as well as the final DOS message telling you how many files were copied. Line 8 ECHOes a message to the screen telling the user what has happened. This is always a wise idea after any potentially long disk activity.

YES, NO, ENTER, and ENTERN

Another I/O redirection trick is the use of small files that contain the answers to some familiar questions:

Are you sure (y/n)?
Press ENTER to continue
Why is the sky blue?

When running a batch file, you may want to perform some actions that make it necessary for the user to type a "Y" or press ENTER to confirm some choice. This is risky. First, who really knows what a user will press? Second, why risk them messing up your batch file by insisting that they press "Y" when they don't even know why (or wouldn't understand the reason even if you told them)?

The trick is to use I/O redirection to provide the answer for them. They'll never know the difference.

Somewhere on your system you should have several small files. (I put them in my \BATCH subdirectory.) The first file should contain a "Y" followed by a carriage return/line feed; the second should contain an "N" followed by a carriage return/line feed; and the third should contain only the carriage return/line feed. These files should be named YES, NO, and ENTER respectively. You can use DOS to create them (see FIG. 7-3).

7-3 To create files YES, NO and ENTER . . .
```
C> COPY CON YES
Y
^Z

C> COPY CON NO
N
^Z

C> COPY CON ENTER

^Z

C>
```

A fourth file can be named ENTERN. It's to be used with I/O redirection to replace pressing ENTER and then the "N" key:
```
C> COPY CON ENTERN
N
^Z

C>
```

Remember to press ENTER after Y and N. ^Z is obtained by pressing CTRL – Z or F6. These files are now ready to be used to answer common questions that pop up during batch file execution.

As an example, I use the batch file in FIG. 7-4 to an update disk at the end of my work day. I don't want to use the BACKUP program because it saves the files in a funky format that I can't use. A disk created with BACKUP can only be undone by the RESTORE command (and from the

7-4 This batch file I use to back up my files.
```
 1: @ECHO OFF
 2: REM Program files update
 3: REM can be run from any subdirectory on drive
 4: C:
 5: ECHO Updating program files subdirectory
 6: ECHO Insert diskette "ONE" in drive A and
 7: PAUSE
 8: ECHO Formatting . . .
 9: REM "ENTERN" must be cr/lf + "N" + cr/lf or
    keyboard locks
10: FORMAT A: <C:\SYSTEM\UTIL\ENTERN >NUL
11: ECHO Done!  Copying files . . .
12: COPY \BATCH\DISK\*.* A: >NUL
13: ECHO Done!
```

same version of DOS). So I just want a disk full of files. As long as my files don't occupy more space than is on the disk, that's fine.

Also, I want to make sure no other files are on the disk before I copy my files to it. There are two ways I could ensure this. The first is to reformat the disk each time before I copy the files to it. And the second is to delete all files already on the disk. The first is safer, the second is quicker. The batch file in FIG. 7-4 shows both versions.

This is a "silent" batch file (see lines 1, 10, and 12 in FIG. 7-4). Because of that, there are quite a few ECHO statements to let the user know what's going on. The first two ECHO statements (5, 6) direct the user to put the diskette ONE into drive A, then press any key to continue (7). Line 10 formats the disk, which is where the first tricky input redirection technique takes place.

The REM statement in line 9 reminds you that the data in ENTERN must contain a carriage return/line feed plus the "N" character followed by another carriage return/line feed. This is supplied to answer the two questions that FORMAT (10) asks: "Strike ENTER when ready" and after the formatting, "Format another (y/n)?" If you forget to supply the "N", DOS will sit and wait for input. Because input is redirected from the file, if the N isn't there, your keyboard is locked and you may have to reset to get control of your computer. Also, the output of the FORMAT command is redirected to the NUL statement. This way, a user will not know that the diskette is being formatted (unless they have a good ear and can "hear" it being formatted).

The final step is to copy the files from the special subdirectory (12) to drive A. Again, the ECHO command is used (11, 13) to tell the user exactly what's going on.

The batch file in FIG. 7-4 is time-consuming because it always reformats the diskette before continuing. The example in FIG. 7-5 is faster. This program is a slight modification of the first batch file. The difference takes place in line 8, where DEL A:*.* is used instead of format to clean the disk of any files. The redirected input for the DEL command is provided by the YES file. YES contains a "Y" followed by a carriage return/line feed. This input will answer the question "Are you sure?" and the redirected output will make the entire operation invisible to the user.

7-5 This batch file is a faster backup program.

```
 1: @ECHO OFF
 2: REM Program files update
 3: REM can be run from any subdirectory on drive
 4: C:
 5: ECHO Updating program files subdirectory
 6: ECHO Insert diskette "ONE" in drive A and
 7: PAUSE
 8: DEL A:\*.* <C:\SYSTEM\UTIL\YES >NUL
 9: ECHO Copying files . . .
10: XCOPY \BATCH\DISK\*.* A: >NUL
11: ECHO Done!
```

If redirected input were not provided in line 8, the batch file would stop and wait for either "Y" or "N" to be pressed. Because output is redirected to the NUL device, the user wouldn't have a clue what was going on. Also, unlike the FORMAT command example, the YES file need only contain a "Y" and a carriage return/line feed. There are no further questions asked by DEL *.*, so the "Y" is sufficient to erase all the files.

Finally, to add some zip to this batch file, the XCOPY command is used to copy a whole slew of files at a time. Unlike COPY, which reads and copies one file at a time, XCOPY reads as many files as will fit into RAM at a time, then writes them out at once. Combined with >NUL, this makes the updating procedure run extremely fast.

Oh, and the sky is blue because of light refraction.

CTTY

The CTTY command is one of those strange, last-minute things *Microsoft* probably threw into DOS just to confuse people. It's an interesting command, but a dangerous one. Still, with the right technique, you can translate that danger into something extremely useful.

As any UNIX fiend can attest, any command ending in *TTY is something a novice shouldn't mess with. CTTY is the same. What it does is to change the CONsole device. Primarily, it allows you to change the console device to the AUX, or serial port device. (Any serial port, from AUX or COM1, up to COM4).

To demonstrate this, I hooked up a null modem cable between my PC and a Macintosh. After running a communications program on both systems (and making sure the BPS, or Baud, was set properly and other things were working), I "shelled out" of the PC's communications program and typed:

    CTTY AUX

This transferred the console device from the screen and keyboard to the serial port and, indirectly, to the Macintosh. The screen and keyboard on the PC were no longer used for input or output. In fact, the keyboard was frozen. Even pressing CTRL – BREAK had no effect. Yet, when I turned to the Macintosh—there was DOS! I typed all the commands, DIR, COPY, even used EDLIN. They all worked. (Only DOS programs would work. Other programs that don't use the DOS functions will "hang" the computer.)

Incidentally, I called in a friend and said I had an IBM Emulator program running on the Macintosh. I had them going for a while (see FIG. 7-6).

To surrender control of the PC away from the Macintosh (or whatever you have hooked up to your serial port), you must type:

    CTTY CON

I typed this on the Macintosh and, voila, control was returned (gladly) by the Macintosh to the PC. So what does this have to do with batch files?

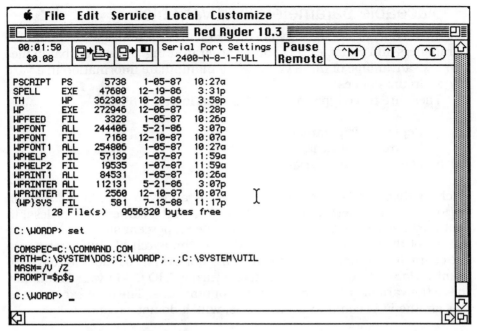

```
 ⌘  File  Edit  Service  Local  Customize
≡□≡═══════════════ Red Ryder 10.3 ═══════════════□≡
┌──────────┬──────┬──────┬─────────────────────┬──────┐
│ 00:01:50 │ ▯▶🖨 │ ▯▶💾 │ Serial Port Settings │Pause │  (^M)  (^I)  (^C)  ⬆
│  $0.08   │      │      │   2400-N-8-1-FULL    │Remote│
└──────────┴──────┴──────┴─────────────────────┴──────┘

PSCRIPT  PS     5738   1-05-87  10:27a
SPELL    EXE   47680  12-19-86   3:31p
TH       WP   362303  10-20-86   3:58p
WP       EXE  272946  12-06-87   9:28p
WPFEED   FIL    3328   1-05-87  10:26a
WPFONT   ALL  244406   5-21-86   3:07p
WPFONT   FIL    7168  12-10-87  10:07a
WPFONT1  ALL  254806   1-05-87  10:27a
WPHELP   FIL   57139   1-07-87  11:59a
WPHELP2  FIL   19535   1-07-87  11:59a
WPRINT1  ALL   84531   1-05-87  10:26a
WPRINTER ALL  112131   5-21-86   3:07p
WPRINTER FIL    2560  12-10-87  10:07a
{WP}SYS  FIL     581   7-13-88  11:17p
       28 File(s)   9656320 bytes free

C:\WORDP> set

COMSPEC=C:\COMMAND.COM
PATH=C:\SYSTEM\DOS;C:\WORDP;..;C:\SYSTEM\UTIL
MASM=/V /Z
PROMPT=$p$g

C:\WORDP> _
```

7-6 This is a Macintosh communications program "running" an IBM PC after CTTY AUX.

Ever run a batch file and want the user absolutely not to break out of it? How about AUTOEXEC.BAT? Ever want that to run uninterrupted? The answer is to turn off the keyboard using CTTY AUX. But always remember to return control back again with CTTY CON. In fact, using a batch file is the only way you can issue these two commands using only one computer.

There is a problem, however. The problem is with CTRL–BREAK. When you press CTRL–BREAK from the keyboard, that character is still generated (actually, an interrupt is generated and it's the interrupt that causes the problem).

For example, when I was typing DOS commands on my Macintosh's screen, I was also typing on the PC's keyboard to see what would happen. CTRL–C didn't do anything, but pressing CTRL–BREAK caused the ^C character to appear on the Mac's screen:

    C:\WORDP> ^C
    C:\WORDP>

Also, after I typed CTTY CON on the Macintosh, all those characters I typed on the PC appeared on the screen. They had been buffered.

I tried a few more batch files to use CTTY AUX and CTTY CON to shut off the keyboard. While they do work, there is a drawback: if the user types a CTRL–BREAK, the system will hang.

Replaceable parameters and variables

The final concept of "tools" you can use with batch files are replaceable parameters and variables. Like other programming languages, batch files can take advantage of these variables to manipulate information in a variety of circumstances.

There are three types of variables used in batch files:

1. Replaceable parameters
2. Environment variables
3. FOR command variables

Each of these variable types are different and you should distinguish between them. Unfortunately, all of them look the same (more or less) in that they are designated as variables by the %, percent sign.

All of these variables are expanded by the batch file interpreter into the character strings they represent. This works just as it does for environment variables (see chapter 4). You can turn ECHO ON in your batch files to see the variables expanded as the program runs. The only exception to this are the FOR command's variables, which do not expand.

Replaceable parameters

Replaceable parameter variables are used to represent "arguments," or the text typed after your batch file command. Other programming languages, for example the C language compilers that are available under DOS, also take advantage of these parameters. This way, you can pass instructions to your batch file commands. For example:

```
C> UPDATE \SYSTEM\UTIL\LOTUS\JUNE
```

The name of the program is UPDATE. The first argument is \SYSTEM \UTIL and the second argument is \LOTUS\JUNE. Batch files allow you to use up to nine arguments and represent them by the replaceable parameter variables %1 through %9. When your batch file runs, using the above as an example, %1 will be replaced by "\SYSTEM\UTIL" and %2 will be replaced by \LOTUS\JUNE.

There are ten replaceable parameter variables that your batch files can take advantage of:

%0 is the command file name, the name of your batch file
$1 is the first word after the batch file name
$2 the second word
$3 the third word
$4 the fourth word
$5 the fifth word
$6 the sixth word

$7   the seventh word
$8   the eighth word
$9   the ninth word

"Words" in this instance are a series of characters surrounded by a space. The characters could be a group of command switches, a filename, a drive letter, a pathname, or a word of English text. Surrounding a string of text with quotes will not make it all one word. Also, anything beyond the ninth word cannot be referenced unless the SHIFT command is used (see below).

The examples in FIG. 7-7 show how the replaceable parameters would represent various arguments on the command line.

7-7 This is how replaceable parameters represent various arguments on the command line.

```
   %0   %1      &2
C> MOVE A:\*.* C:\SYSTEM\UPDATE

%0=MOVE
%1=A:\*.*
%2=C:\SYSTEM\UPDATE

   %0   %1     %2      %3
C> LOGIN 10:12 LITTLE HENRY

%0=LOGIN
%1=10:12
%2=LITTLE
%3=HENRY
```

The batch file in FIG. 7-8 can be used to display all the replaceable parameters on the command line. You can use it when writing batch file to see how the parameters will fall and in what order. When this program runs it displays the contents of each of the parameters, as shown in FIG. 7-9. Notice that I didn't use "ECHO %1 = %1"; this is because the batch file interpreter would translate both %1s into the variable's value.

7-8 This displays all replaceable parameters on the command line.
Name: BATARG.BAT

```
 1: @ECHO OFF
 2: REM Batch file to display replaceable parameters
 3: ECHO Parameter 0 = %0
 4: ECHO Parameter 1 = %1
 5: ECHO Parameter 2 = %2
 6: ECHO Parameter 3 = %3
 7: ECHO Parameter 4 = %4
 8: ECHO Parameter 5 = %5
 9: ECHO Parameter 6 = %6
10: ECHO Parameter 7 = %7
11: ECHO Parameter 8 = %8
12: ECHO Parameter 9 = %9
```

7-9 The result of running FIG. 7-8 is shown here.

```
C> BATARG C: THIS IS A TEST "HELLO, TOM"
Parameter 0 = BATARG
Parameter 1 = C:
Parameter 2 = THIS
Parameter 3 = IS
Parameter 4 = A
Parameter 5 = TEST
Parameter 6 = "HELLO,
Parameter 7 = TOM"
Parameter 8 =
Parameter 9 =
```

You can use any information on the command line simply by specifying the replaceable parameter variable in your batch file, as shown in FIG. 7-10. This batch file moves a group of files from one place to another. A move is actually a copy then delete. So this batch file first copies the files (4) and then deletes the originals (5). Notice how the I/O direction tricks from the previous section are used to suppress the warning messages and whatnot. ECHO is used often (3, 6) to let the user know what's going on.

7-10 Any information on the command line can be used in a batch file.

```
Name: MOVE.BAT

1: @ECHO OFF
2: REM MOVE FILES FROM %1 TO %2
3: ECHO Moving Files...
4: COPY %1 %2 >NUL
5: DEL %1 <C:\SYSTEM\UTIL\YES >NUL
6: ECHO Files moved
```

A typical run of this batch file might look like this:

```
C> MOVE A:\*.* C:\TEMP\UPDATE
Moving Files . . .
Files moved

C>
```

All the files from the root directory on drive A (A:*.*) are first copied to subdirectory \TEMP\UPDATE on drive C, and then deleted from drive A. The replaceable parameter %1 is given the value "A:*.*", and %2 is given the value "C:\TEMP\UPDATE". If you change @ECHO OFF to @ECHO ON and run the batch file again, you'll see FIG. 7-11.

See how %1 and %2 were replaced as the file ran? That "Y" between the last two commands was supplied by the \SYSTEM\UTIL\YES file. (Because ECHO is on, it was echoed to the console.)

There is a problem with this batch file.

If you don't supply any arguments, you'll get the following:

```
C> MOVE
Moving Files . . .
```

Invalid number of parameters
Invalid number of parameters
Files moved

C>

Doesn't look right, does it?

7-11   This is the run of FIG. 7-10 with ECHO ON.
```
C> MOVE A:\*.* C:\TEMP\UPDATE

C> REM MOVE FILES FROM %1 TO %2

C> ECHO Moving Files...
Moving Files...

C> COPY A:\*.* C:\TEMP\UPDATE >NUL

C> DEL A:\*.* <C:\SYSTEM\UTIL\YES >NUL
Y
C> ECHO Files moved
Files moved
```


Testing for nothing

Because not everyone is going to know if a command needs parameters or not, you'll need to test for their existence. To do this, you'll use the IF command and the equals assignment operator, = =.

Testing for nothing sounds difficult, yet it's an easy technique to remember. Just keep in mind that the batch file interpreter expands variables out to their string values when the batch file is run. If a variable isn't assigned to anything, then it will be expanded into nothing.

The common format for testing for nothing is:

IF *parameter string constant* = = *string constant*

If the above statement is true, then *parameter* doesn't exist. Remember, if there is no variable for *parameter*, it's not expanded. So, when the batch file is run, you'll have:

IF *string constant* = = *string constant*

This evaluates as true. For example:

IF %1TEST = = TEST

If %1 is equal to "A:*.*" then the statement on page 205 will be expanded to:

IF A:*.*TEST = = TEST

That statement is false. Otherwise, if there is no replaceable parameter

%1, you'll get:

```
IF TEST = = TEST
```

You can use any value for string constant. Most popular is:

```
IF %1! = = !
```

This is nice because it's brief. However, it tends to be confusing. A novice batch file programmer may wonder if ! doesn't mean something. Instead, try using "nothing" as your string constant:

```
IF %1NOTHING = = NOTHING
```

If that statement is true, there is no replaceable parameter %1. You can also check for the reverse:

```
IF NOT %1NOTHING = = NOTHING
```

This statement will come out true if there is a replaceable parameter %1 (the opposite of the previous example).

To incorporate these examples in the MOVE.BAT file, you only need to add two lines (see FIG. 7-12). Just to be nice about things, the batch file now displays an informative message if the first parameter is left out (the second parameter is optional, as it is with the COPY command).

7-12 A few more changes are made to MOVE.BAT.

```
 1: @ECHO OFF
 2: REM MOVE FILES FROM %1 TO %2
 3: IF %1NOTHING==NOTHING GOTO WARNING
 4: ECHO Moving Files...
 5: COPY %1 %2 >nul
 6: DEL %1 < C:\SYSTEM\UTIL\YES >NUL
 7: ECHO Files moved
 8: GOTO END
 9: :WARNING
10: ECHO Please specify a source filename
11: :END
```

Line 3 tests for the existence of the first parameter. If it doesn't exist, and NOTHING = = NOTHING, execution branches to the WARNING label (9). Line 10 echoes an error message and then the program ends:

```
C> MOVE
Please specify a source filename

C>
```

If a source filename (%1) is supplied, the test in line 3 fails and execution continues with the rest of the program. Line 8 skips over the warning message (9, 10) and ends the program with the :END label.

You don't need to specify NOTHING = = NOTHING each time you want to test for nothing. In this book, that's the example used because it's also easy to remember. Most of the time, you can get by using a single letter, character or number. The following are all acceptable methods of testing for nothing:

```
IF %1X==X . . .
IF %1!==! . . .
IF "%1"=="" . . .
IF NUL%1==NUL . . .
IF X%1==X . . .
```

SHIFT

SHIFT is used primarily with replaceable parameters. It shifts the variable assignments of parameters %0 through %9—and beyond. SHIFT moves the value of the next highest replaceable parameter into the new lowest. Parameter %0 is SHIFTed away (goes bye-bye) and any parameters after %9 are shifted into %9, one for each use of the SHIFT command.

For example, after SHIFT is issued, the value of %2 becomes the new value of %1, %3 becomes %2, %4 becomes %3 and on and on until %9. For the value of %9, the batch file interpreter assigns any "words" to the left of %9 to %9. This way, you can read in arguments well beyond %9—but at the cost of losing the original values of %1, %2 and so on.

The batch file program in FIG. 7-13 shows how SHIFT alters the contents of the replaceable parameters %0 through %9. This program looks complex, but there's a lot of repeat. First, a GOTO statement (3) causes execution to jump to the :START label (7). The next line tests to see if argument %0 is equal to nothing. The first time through it will be equal to SHIFTARG, the name of the program. But each time after that, its value will change until it's equal to the final word typed on the command line. When this happens, %1 will equal nothing and the statement, evaluated to true, will branch to the :END label (29). A similar test is performed on the first replaceable parameter, %1 (10). This ensures a short program run in case no arguments were typed after SHIFTARG.

7-13 This program shows how SHIFT alters parameters %0 through %9 and beyond.
Name: SHIFTARG.BAT

```
 1: @ECHO OFF
 2: REM Shift and display parameters
 3: GOTO START
 4: :LOOP
 5: ECHO ==== Shifting ====
 6: SHIFT
 7: :START
 8: IF %0NOTHING==NOTHING GOTO END
 9: ECHO Parameter 0 = %0
10: IF %1NOTHING==NOTHING GOTO END
11: ECHO Parameter 1 = %1
12: IF %2NOTHING==NOTHING GOTO LOOP
13: ECHO Parameter 2 = %2
14: IF %3NOTHING==NOTHING GOTO LOOP
```

7-13 Continued.

```
15: ECHO Parameter 3 = %3
16: IF %4NOTHING==NOTHING GOTO LOOP
17: ECHO Parameter 4 = %4
18: IF %5NOTHING==NOTHING GOTO LOOP
19: ECHO Parameter 5 = %5
20: IF %6NOTHING==NOTHING GOTO LOOP
21: ECHO Parameter 6 = %6
22: IF %7NOTHING==NOTHING GOTO LOOP
23: ECHO Parameter 7 = %7
24: IF %8NOTHING==NOTHING GOTO LOOP
25: ECHO Parameter 8 = %8
26: IF %9NOTHING==NOTHING GOTO LOOP
27: ECHO Parameter 9 = %9
28: GOTO LOOP
29: :END
```

After line 12, each IF statement tests for the existence of each replaceable parameter. If it exists, it's displayed. Otherwise, execution branches back to the :LOOP statement (4). The ECHO statement in line 5 breaks up the output of the program and lets the user know when a SHIFT statement has taken place. Line 6 contains the SHIFT command that shifts the variable's values.

The best way to see how the file works is to run it. A sample of the program's output is shown in FIG. 7-14 using the command line "this is a test." Graphically, you see how SHIFT moves the values from each replaceable parameter. Because the program tests for the existence of a variable, and bases its "looping" on it, not a lot of space is wasted with the display.

7-14 This is a test run of SHIFTARG.BAT.

```
C> SHIFTARG this is a test
Parameter 0 = SHIFTARG
Parameter 1 = this
Parameter 2 = is
Parameter 3 = a
Parameter 4 = test
==== Shifting ====
Parameter 0 = this
Parameter 1 = is
Parameter 2 = a
Parameter 3 = test
==== Shifting ====
Parameter 0 = is
Parameter 1 = a
Parameter 2 = test
==== Shifting ====
Parameter 0 = a
Parameter 1 = test
==== Shifting ====
Parameter 0 = test
C>
```

An excellent example of how the SHIFT statement can be used appeared earlier in this book. The COPY2 program uses SHIFT to move several files (as many as can fit on the command line) from one place to another. It uses SHIFT to read in all the filenames—a feat that wouldn't be possible had only variables %1 through %9 been available (see FIG. 7-15).

The program in FIG. 7-15 works along a loop structure (between lines 6 and 11). Also, you'll see a test for no parameters in line 3 and a warning message in lines 13 and 14.

7-15 This is COPY2.BAT, which makes practical use of the SHIFT command.

Name: COPY2.BAT

```
 1: @ECHO OFF
 2: REM A 'Gang Copy' batch file example
 3: IF %1NOTHING==NOTHING GOTO HELP
 4: SET DISK=%1
 5: ECHO Copy a group of files to drive %DISK%
 6: :LOOP
 7: SHIFT
 8: IF %1NOTHING==NOTHING GOTO END
 9: COPY %1 %DISK% >NUL
10: ECHO %1 copied to %DISK%
11: GOTO LOOP
12: :HELP
13: ECHO COPY2 Command format:
14: ECHO copy2 [drive:[\path]] [file1] [file2] .... [fileN]
15: :END
16: SET DISK=
```

The SET instruction in line 4 is used to "remember" the original starting disk location. This location will eventually be SHIFTed off into oblivion. So the variable %DISK% is used to remember the target destination in line 9, also in line 10 for display.

The NOTHING = = NOTHING test in line 8 determines the end of the loop. And finally, being good users of the DOS environment, the program releases its environment variable in line 16.

This program can easily be modified to delete a group of files, or to move files from one drive to another. See if you can do so on your own. Examples are listed at the end of this chapter.

Environment variables

The environment and environment variables were discussed in chapter 4. However, they are variables that can be used in batch files, and as such, fit nicely into the format of this chapter.

Environment variables are different from replacement parameters in that their values are set, and remain, in the system's environment table. Also, the way they're used is different. Unlike replaceable parameters, environment variables are surrounded by percent signs:

%VARIABLE%
%STATUS%
%USER NAME%

Environment variables are created by the SET command. They consist of any characters, letters, numbers—or even spaces—up to an =, equal sign. The variable is translated to uppercase by DOS, though you can use upper- or lowercase when specifying the environment variable between percent signs.

The variable name will be replaced by the string assigned to it when a batch file runs. This is part of the batch file interpreter's variable expansion that also takes place with replaceable parameters. Using the SET command, you assign the environment variable to any string of characters (after the equal sign), though the string will not include the carriage return character at the end of the line.

```
SET DRIVE = A:
SET STATUS = ON
SET USER NAME = Orville the Robot
```

Though the variable name is translated to uppercase, DOS uses whichever case you typed for the variable's data. So, for the above examples:

```
ECHO %STATUS%
```

displays: ON

```
ECHO %USER NAME%
```

displays: Orville the Robot

You should note that the expansion will not take place on the command line. It is assumed that the previous two examples would be used in a batch file.

The nice thing about environment variables is that you can create them on the fly. Only remember to reset them when you're through, otherwise you may run out of environment space. To reset the variable, simply reassign its contents to nothing:

```
SET VARIABLE =
SET STATUS =
SET USER NAME =
```

Environment variables are good for storing data. As was previously shown, you can use them to temporarily save replaceable parameters:

```
SET TEMP = %1
```

This assigns the variable TEMP to whatever the parameter %1 is set to. However, you cannot "swap" the contents of two environment variables. For example, observe the following:

```
SET LOGIN = JULES
SET NAME = LOGIN
```

This creates two variables in the environment. The first is LOGIN, which has the value "JULES", and the second is "NAME" which has the value

"LOGIN". To give NAME the same value as LOGIN, you'll need to use LOGIN as a variable (and remember, this only works in a batch file):

```
SET NAME = %LOGIN%
```

When the batch file containing that line runs, %LOGIN% is replaced (expanded) by the batch file interpreter with "JULES". So the end result is that both NAME and LOGIN will equal "JULES".

This can make for a nifty application that saves the system's path:

Name: SAVEPATH.BAT

```
1: @ECHO OFF
2: SET TEMP = %PATH%
3: PATH = C: \ SYSTEM \ DOS;C: \ LOTUS;U:
4: CD \ LOTUS
5: 123
6: SET PATH = %TEMP%
```

This batch file runs the program 123 in the \ LOTUS subdirectory. But, before that, it saves the PATH in a temporary variable, TEMP. The PATH is reset in line 3, presumably to something that the 123 program likes better than the standard path. Then, after 123 is run (5), the old path is restored.

Before going off and creating batch files like this, be forewarned: you will run out of environment space quicker than you can believe. If that happens, you can always add the SHELL command to your CONFIG.SYS file and specify a larger environment. (Refer to chapter 4.)

FOR variables

The third type of variable you'll encounter in a batch file is used by the FOR command. FOR uses two types of variables, depending on if you use FOR in a batch file or in DOS:

```
% (one percent sign)      DOS
%% (two percent signs)    Batch files
```

In either case, the %, percent sign, is followed by a single character to represent the variable.

The FOR variable is used twice in the FOR command. The first time is to assign the variable to a group of files; the second time is as a wildcard in a DOS command:

```
C> FOR %V IN (*.*) DO TYPE %V | MORE
```

The first use of the variable %V (in DOS) assigns it to the set of files in parenthesis. In this case, %V is equal to every file in the current directory.

The second use of the variable %V is in the DO command. In this case, %V will represent each file on disk, one at a time. FOR repeats the command TYPE %V | MORE for each file found that matches (*.*). The FOR command will singularly take each file it finds via *.* and place it into the

TYPE %V | MORE command. This is the only way you can list the contents of all files in a directory with a single DOS command.

```
C> FOR %F IN (*.BAT *.COM *.EXE) DO XCOPY %F A:
```

The variable %F will be assigned to three values, *.BAT, *.COM and *.EXE. The second part of the FOR command will then be executed three times, each time %F will be replaced by those three file definitions. This is the same as issuing the three separate commands:

```
C> XCOPY *.BAT A:
C> XCOPY *.COM A:
C> XCOPY *.EXE A:
```

The important things to remember about FOR's variables are:

- In a batch file, two percent signs are used
- In DOS, only one percent sign is used
- The variable name is only one letter long and, with versions of DOS prior to 4.0, cannot be a number
- The FOR command's variable is only used with the FOR command

For extra credit

The following two batch files in FIG. 7-16 and FIG. 7-17 are modifications to the COPY2.BAT program discussed earlier. Figure 7-16 deletes a group of files and the batch file in FIG. 7-17 moves a group of files.

7-16 This batch file deletes a group of files.

```
Name: DEL2.BAT

 1: @ECHO OFF
 2: REM A 'Gang Delete' batch file
 3: IF %1NOTHING==NOTHING GOTO HELP
 4: ECHO Delete a group of files
 5: :LOOP
 6: IF NOTHING%1==NOTHING GOTO END
 7: DEL %1 <C:\SYSTEM\UTIL\YES >NUL
 8: ECHO %1 is/are gone . . .
 9: SHIFT
10: GOTO LOOP
11: :HELP
12: ECHO DEL2 Command format:
13: ECHO del2 [file1] [file2] .... [fileN]
14: :END
```

Notice how each file makes use of SHIFT, testing for nothing, as well as I/O redirection to suppress messages. The only thing that isn't tested for in these programs is the existence of the files. To test for that, you can use the IF EXIST %1 statement, and then skip over the COPY or DELETE statement if that particular file isn't found. (See, there are always ways to improve upon things.)

7-17 This batch file moves a group of files.

Name: MOVE2.BAT

```
 1: @ECHO OFF
 2: REM A 'Gang Move' batch file
 3: IF %1NOTHING==NOTHING GOTO HELP
 4: SET DISK=%1
 5: ECHO Moving a group of files to path %DISK%
 6: :LOOP
 7: SHIFT
 8: IF %1NOTHING==NOTHING GOTO END
 9: COPY %1 %DISK% >NUL
10: DEL %1 <C:\SYSTEM\UTIL\YES >NUL
11: ECHO %1 moved to %DISK%
12: GOTO LOOP
13: :HELP
14: ECHO MOVE2 Command format:
15: ECHO move2 [drive:[\path]] [file1] [file2] .... [fileN]
16: :END
17: SET DISK=
```

Summary

There are quite a few "tools" used to create batch files. The first is the tool you use to write the batch file. This can be with a word processor, text editor, or use DOS and the COPY CON function. Overall, the best way to write a batch file is with a good text editor.

Other tools for creating batch files are the batch file commands themselves. These include special batch file directives, of which there are only a few, plus all the DOS commands and your program and application's names.

The final set of tools are the % (percent) variables that you can use in batch files. These variables come in three flavors: replaceable parameters, or those items you type after the name of your batch file on the command line; environment variables; and variables used with the FOR command.

8
Batch file structure

Most hard-core programmer types will really get a laugh over the title of this chapter. The reason is that batch files inherit a lack of structure simply because of their nature (the way they began). However, there are a few elements of structure—call it style, call it esthetics—that come in handy when writing batch files. Mostly, these are hints that allow you to better modify your batch files in the future—but, for the purposes of conversation, and just to make Pascal programmers irate, I'll refer to it as batch file structure.

The purpose of this chapter is to acquaint you with those threadbare elements of structure that apply to batch file programming. This includes three areas: general structure, or how best to assemble a batch file (perhaps this can best be described as "consistency among batch files"); labels and the GOTO statement which are used to bring order and a flow to a batch file; and finally subroutines and batch file chaining are also elements of structure that are covered here.

Is it really a programming language?

Yes, batch file programming is a real programming language. By definition, a programming language is a form of communication between a human and a computer. The human uses the programming language to tell the computer what to do. In this sense, batch file programming more than qualifies.

Batch file programming is similar to other programming in that you compose a source code file consisting of instructions that the computer understands. Unlike compiled languages, batch file programs are interpreted. Some of the hard liners may claim that any interpreted language is not really a programming language at all. Wrong. It still qualifies.

Second, batch file programs can make use of variables, albeit only string variables and it really can't do much with the variables other than display them or compare them. (No searches, no direct input from the user.)

Third, batch file programs can make decisions and take action. Through use of the GOTO statement and labels, different parts of the batch file program can be executed. Using IF and variables, loops can be performed in batch files—and those loops can be executed and exited by evaluating certain conditions.

How is batch file programming unlike other programming? For starters, no one will ever write a commercial application using batch files. Sure, you could try. But will people buy it? There are just better and faster ways to communicate with a computer than batch file programming.

Also, batch files have no inherent math functions. A lot of programming derives from simple math, addition, subtraction, division and multiplication. For batch files, this is impossible (and really out of the scope of things).

Batch files were never intended to be a substitute for real programming. But this doesn't mean that they don't come in handy. Even the most sophisticated applications will use a batch file to help you install the program. Later in this book, you'll see a complete DOS ''shell'' program implemented entirely by batch files.

The only way to summarize this is by saying that batch files are limited by their design, yet unlimited in application. There is only so much that batch files were designed to do, only certain things that they do best. Yet, they do those things well. On the other hand, because of the unlimited amount of software available to DOS (including batch file utilities), the things that batch files can do is virtually unlimited.

Structure

Believe it or not, you can do a lot to help your batch files along by writing structured programs. This isn't in the classic sense of structured programming. For example, some programming languages insist you follow a structure along these lines:

1. Use massive amounts of ''remark'' or ''comment'' statements, tell what the program is going to do, remembering to add your name, date, class section and teacher's name. (That was added as a joke because the only time anyone really cares about this is when you're in school.)
2. Define all the variables used in this program. (Does anyone really do this *before* they write the program?)

3. Write all the modules, or subroutines, used by this program.
4. Write the program itself.
5. Exit properly.

Fortunately, batch files can be programmed a little more loosely than that. Actually, most of that "structured" approach was from the old mainframe computer days. Because actual computer time was limited, programmers would write an entire program on paper before keying it in (or using punch cards). They would turn the program into the computer center and the staff would place it on a stack with a bunch of other programs to run.

Then, during the midnight hour, the staff would run the program. They would place the output (if any) in a box, along with the list of errors. Then the programmer would have to rewrite the entire thing, or just the parts that didn't work.

In a nutshell, that's how structure evolved. The same lunatics who implemented that regimen, sought to apply it to microcomputers. Alas, the concept of "one person/one computer" never occurred to them. It took geniuses like Bill Gates of Microsoft to write a BASIC programming language that better understood the one person/one computer concept.

With one computer/one person, you can write your programs and run them at the same time. It's more of an on-the-fly operation. You could go in and modify your code as you were working on it. Add variables as you need then, modify routines, make adjustments. This is the way most microcomputer programming is done today. Most of the old timers, and those who were educated by them, will say this is "bad programming." Yet the most popular and fastest microcomputer applications written today are developed that way. The worst programs? The slow ones? The ones no one likes? They're done the old way.

Batch file structure

An example of a type of batch file structure is shown in the following batch file program skeleton:

```
1: @ECHO OFF
2: REM this is a description of the program
3: ECHO tell them what's going on
4: . . .
5: . . .
6: :END
```

That's a simple structure. First comes the initial ECHO OFF statement (1), followed by a REM statement (2). For shorter batch files, you probably will leave out the REM statement. But they're a must for longer batch files, especially when a batch file is using replaceable parameters and variables.

The ECHO statement (3) is optional. I use them to tell the user that a batch file is running and what the batch file does. Before DOS 3.3, you could always tell a batch file was running because you'd see:

ECHO OFF

on your screen. But with the implementation of the @ sign to suppress batch file listings, you no longer see the initial ECHO OFF. So I usually put an ECHO statement in a batch file to either give the name of the batch file, or tell what the program is about to do. Optionally, you could follow the ECHO statement with a PAUSE command, allowing the user to "break out" of the batch file if necessary:

ECHO This program erases your hard disk;
ECHO Press Control-Break to stop or
PAUSE

This gives them the option of pressing CTRL – BREAK to stop the batch file, or "Strike a key when ready . . ." to continue.

Finally, an :END label is added to the end of the batch file. END is not a reserved batch file word (though it should be; allowing you to exit from a batch file at any point). I've used it throughout this book and in my own batch files "just in case." If you were to modify this batch file, having an END label would help in case you wanted to "leave early."

As batch files grow more complex, and you start using IF to make decisions, you'll add labels and subroutines. In most cases, you will evaluate decisions to either execute one part of your batch or another. For example, say you're writing a batch file to decide whether to print a group of files or simply save them in a temporary directory.

The program in FIG. 8-1 has two parts that will be executed depending on the results of the IF statement (4). If the environment variable DESTINATION equals "PRINTER", lines 8 through 10 are executed. If not, lines 5 through 7 are executed. After the first routine (5, 6, 7) is executed, it "jumps over" the second routine to the :END label (11).

8-1 Here is a batch file that decides whether to print or save files.

```
 1: @ECHO OFF
 2: REM To Print or To Temp?
 3: ECHO Print/Store files; One moment
 4: IF %DESTINATION%==PRINTER GOTO PRINTIT
 5: REM This code saves the files to disk
 6: IF EXIST C:\WS\DATA\SPOOL\*.* COPY C:\WS\DATA\SPOOL\*.*
    C:\TEMP >NUL
 7: GOTO END
 8: :PRINTIT
 9: IF NOT EXIST C:\WS\DATA\SPOOL\*.* GOTO END
10: FOR %%F IN (C:\WS\DATA\SPOOL\*.*) DO COPY %%F PRN >NUL
11: :END
```

Jumping over routines, as in the above example, is common in batch files—and a source of confusion. Some batch files will make a lot of decisions and have many routines. Jumping around in these batch files and following their flow can drive you mad. Of course, there is one possible solution; pretty printing.

Pretty printing

Pretty printing is a term (I don't know where it came from) that applies to writing program source code. It's used by BASIC programmers for the most part because, like batch files, most BASIC interpreters lack any type of structure.

When you take a programming language like C and compare its source code to BASIC, you become amazed at how "neat" the code looks. C is interesting to read because it has an elegant structure (see FIG. 8-2). (Actually, the structure is not required by the C compiler. Yet, tradition dictates that the above type of format be used for C programs.)

8-2 This is an example of C program source code.

```
/* C example */
#include <stdio.h>

#define MAXSIZE      20

main( )
{
     int list[MAXSIZE];
     int size=0,num;

     do {
         printf("Type number: ");
         scanf("%d",&list[size]);
     } while ( list[size++] != 0 );
     size--;
     num = max(list,size);
     printf("Largest number is %d",num);
}

max( list,size )
int list[],size;
{
     int dex,max;
     max = list[0];
     for ( dex = 1; dex<size; dex++)
          if( max < list[dex] )
               max = list[dex];
     return(max);
}
```

BASIC, on the other hand, really has no structure. It's all one long list of commands. The BASIC program in FIG. 8-3 does the same thing as the C source code in FIG. 8-2. Isn't it gross looking?

Seeing how hard that was to read, certain BASIC programmers would take advantage of spaces and REM statements to make the listing a bit easier on the eyes. Cleaning it up with pretty printing helps. Figure 8-4 shows

8-3 This is an example of a BASIC program.

```
 10 REM BASIC EXAMPLE
 20 DIM MAXSIZE(20)
 30 LET SIZE=0: LET DEX=0: LET NUMBER=1
 40 WHILE NUMBER<>0
 50 INPUT "Type number:",NUMBER
 60 MAXSIZE(SIZE)=NUMBER
 70 SIZE=SIZE+1
 80 WEND
 90 DEX=MAXSIZE(0)
100 FOR X=1 TO SIZE
110 IF DEX<MAXSIZE(X) THEN DEX=MAXSIZE(X)
120 NEXT
130 PRINT "Highest number was";DEX
```

8-4 This is FIG. 8-3 done the pretty printing way.

```
 10 REM BASIC EXAMPLE
 15 '
 20 DIM MAXSIZE(20)
 30 LET SIZE=0: LET DEX=0: LET NUMBER=1
 35 '
 40 WHILE NUMBER<>0
 50     INPUT "Type number:",NUMBER
 60     MAXSIZE(SIZE)=NUMBER
 70     SIZE=SIZE+1
 80 WEND
 85 '
 90 DEX=MAXSIZE(0)
100 FOR X=1 TO SIZE
110     IF DEX<MAXSIZE(X) THEN DEX=MAXSIZE(X)
120 NEXT
125 '
130 PRINT "Highest number was";DEX
```

the same BASIC program, but using REM statements and indents to make it more legible.

Apostrophes are abbreviations for the REM statement. Here they are used in lines 15, 35, 85 and 125 to break up the various sections of the program. The two loops, the WHILE/WEND loop in lines 40 through 80 and the FOR/NEXT loop in lines 100 through 120, have their contents indented. This makes it easy to see where the loop starts and ends. If "nested" loops were used, their contents would be further indented.

The BASIC interpreter (or compiler) doesn't give a hoot about extra spaces or tab characters in the listing. It won't speed up or slow down the program any. However, it makes it easier to read and follow the program flow. The same can be done with batch files, as shown in FIG. 8-5.

The batch file interpreter doesn't care about extra spaces on the line (but note that line 8 in FIG. 8-5 was split because it was too long; you can't do that with a "real" batch file). Also, you can include blank lines in a batch file—no problem. COMMAND.COM interprets them as if you just pressed *ENTER* alone on the command line. The only thing that may hap-

8-5 Extra spaces can make batch files easier to read.

```
 1: @ECHO OFF
 2: REM To Print or To Temp?
 3: ECHO Print/Store files; One moment
 4:
 5: IF %DESTINATION%==PRINTER GOTO PRINTIT
 6:
 7:     REM This code saves the files to disk
 8:     IF EXIST C:\WS\DATA\SPOOL\*.*
        COPY C:\WS\DATA\SPOOL\*.* C:\TEMP >NUL
 9:     GOTO END
10:
11: :PRINTIT
12:     IF NOT EXIST C:\WS\DATA\SPOOL\*.* GOTO END
13:     FOR %%F IN (C:\WS\DATA\SPOOL\*.*) DO COPY %%F PRN >NUL
14:
15: :END
```

pen is if you have ECHO ON, you will see the command prompt displayed a few times. That's it. Otherwise, you can liberally use blank lines in your program to clean up their appearance.

Labels and GOTO

This book has shown you a lot of labels and quite a few GOTO statements, but still has yet to explain them. Sorry about that.

Basically, the GOTO statement works with labels to give your batch files a smidgen of structure. Using both GOTO and labels, you can execute specific portions of your batch file, avoid others, and ''bail out'' quickly if need be.

Labels

A label in a batch file is designated by the :, colon character. The label doesn't include the colon, but follows it. Labels can be up to 127 characters long but only the first 8 are important.

:label

label is eight or fewer characters, including letters and numbers, but not the period (.) character or a space. (Other characters are allowed, but it's wise to only use letters and numbers.) Upper- and lowercase are treated the same.

A space denotes the end of the label and the start of optional comments (see below):

:LOOP

''Loop'' is the perfect name for a well-used label.

:10

Numbers are also okay for labels. Though it's best to make your labels descriptive where possible:

```
:PRINT
:GETINPUT
:ALARM
:ERROR
```

Remember that only the first eight characters are important, so:

```
:ZEDDIDIAYA
```

and

```
:ZEDDIDIAYO
```

Are both considered the same label, though they might be in different parts of the batch file.

In FIG. 8-6, lines 4 and 6 are labels. The GOTO in line 2 will branch to the matching *label*. In this case, line 4. (All characters after the space are ignored, so "Label One" equals "LABEL" according to the batch file interpreter.) The output of the program will be:

```
after one
after two
```

Essentially, what happened in the above example is that the second label was ignored. In all cases where a program has two identical labels, the second one will be ignored (more on this below).

8-6 Lines 4 and 6 are labels.

```
1: @ECHO OFF
2: GOTO LABEL
3: REM where will it go?
4: :Label One
5: ECHO after one
6: :LABEL
7: ECHO after two
```

When the batch file interpreter encounters a line starting with a colon, it assumes the line is a label and skips it. In fact, any line in a batch file starting with a colon is skipped; it's not even displayed when ECHO is turned ON:

```
1: :FIRST LABEL
2: :SECOND LABEL
3: :THIRD LABEL
```

Running the above batch file example would produce no output—even though ECHO is not used and therefore, ON.

Labels are only used by the GOTO command. Otherwise, you can use labels as a form of comment within your batch file, or as a combination of both:

    :LABEL This is a comment after the label "LABEL"

Anything after the colon is ignored by the batch file interpreter. The rest of the line can be used for comments.

GOTO

Normally, batch files execute one line at a time, one line after the other. However, there are times when you might want to execute a specific part of the batch file or skip other parts. That's where GOTO comes in handy.

GOTO is a batch file statement Microsoft borrowed from its BASIC. In fact, it behaves a lot like the BASIC GOTO statement. What it does is to transfer batch file execution to the line containing a label specified by GOTO:

    GOTO *label*

label is up to eight characters long and specifies a label somewhere else in the batch file. After the GOTO statement, the batch file interpreter will look for the *label* and then start executing commands after that line. If *label* isn't found, you'll see the following error message:

    Label not found

and the batch file immediately stops executing.

    GOTO END

After the above statement, the batch file interpreter will begin reading lines in the batch file, searching for those lines starting with a colon, signaling a label. As each label is found, the interpreter will compare that label with the one after GOTO. If found, execution transfers to that new line.

GOTO searches from the beginning of the batch file all the way to the end. Then, if the label isn't found, the "Label not found" error occurs, and the batch file will stop. This is important to remember if you use the identical label twice. The second label appearing in the program will never be used (see FIG. 8-7).

Before running this program, try to look at it and figure what it would do. The output is as follows:

    PASSED LABEL1
    Strike a key when ready . . .
    PASSED LABEL1
    Strike a key when ready . . .

(And on and on.) GOTO will only find the first of two identical labels.

8-7 The second label in the program will never be used.

```
 1: @ECHO OFF
 2: REM GOTO TEST PROGRAM
 3: :LABEL1
 4: ECHO PASSED LABEL1
 5: PAUSE
 6: GOTO LABEL1
 7: ECHO THIS LINE IS AFTER THE GOTO STATEMENT
 8: :LABEL1
 9: ECHO PASSED THE SECOND LABEL1
10: PAUSE
11: GOTO LABEL1
```

Using GOTO with IF

Because so much of batch file programming is borrowed from the BASIC programming language, it's important to note the differences. One that will pop up from time to time is using GOTO with the IF statement:

IF *condition* GOTO *label*

IF is basically a testing statement. It tests *condition* to see if it's either true or false. If true, then whatever follows *condition* is executed. In the above example, the GOTO *label* statement would be executed.

The important thing to remember here is that:

The IF command does not use "THEN"

So don't catch yourself using the following syntax:

IF *condition* THEN *label*

It won't work.

Endless loops

One of the hazards of using GOTO, or any looping statement in any program, is the possibility of entering an endless loop. That happens when the same set of instructions are executed repeatedly:

```
1: @ECHO OFF
2: :ETERNITY
3: REM A lot going on, but nothing happening
4: GOTO ETERNITY
```

In the above example, lines 2 through 4 are executed repeatedly; an endless loop. Most good programmers will introduce some code into the loop to determine an end point. Otherwise, you can stop a batch file the traditional way by pressing CTRL – BREAK:

```
Terminate batch job (Y/N)?
```

Pressing Y stops your computer from repeatedly executing the same commands over and over.

Sometimes an endless loop might be necessary. If so, you might want to add some lines to the program to let the user know how to get out of it:

```
ECHO The following might take a long time
ECHO If you want to stop, press Control-Break
ECHO and answer "Y" to the question.
```

Or, you can use ECHO with the PAUSE command to give the user a chance to think in the middle of the loop:

```
ECHO This might take a few more times.
ECHO Press Control-Break to stop, or
PAUSE
```

That second ECHO command is used a lot before the PAUSE statement. The net effect on the screen reads:

```
This might take a few more times.
Press Control-Break to stop, or
Strike a key when ready . . .
```

Both the ECHOed message and the PAUSE command flow together nicely, giving the message a good consistency.

Is GOTO bad?

Don't let the programming gurus kid you about GOTO; you can't write a program without it. Some of the Pascal programmers (yes, them again) claim that GOTO is the bane of programming. "Good programmers never use GOTO." Bah! Look at assembly language: it's full of GOTO statements (though they're called "jumps" instead). Because every other language eventually is translated to machine code (just like assembly), you can firmly attest to the programming prudes that you can't program without GOTO. So use it freely, but wisely.

Subroutines and chaining

Batch files can run other batch files. In fact, quite a few AUTOEXEC batch files will end with another batch file. After all, the name of a batch file is a command, so why not include other batch files in your batch files?

The answer lies in a flaw of logic that most beginning batch file programmers soon discover. Suppose you're writing a batch file called MENU .BAT. In the middle you want to use a second batch file, LOCATE.BAT, to position the cursor on the screen:

```
1: @ECHO OFF
2: REM Main Menu batch file
3: CLS
4: LOCATE 1 12
5: ECHO Main Menu
6: . . .
```

Assuming that LOCATE is a batch file to move the cursor (and 1 and 12 are parameters), what will happen is that the screen will clear (3), and then the LOCATE.BAT file will be run. LOCATE will move the cursor to row 1, column 12, and then return to DOS.

Huh? Most users assume execution would return to line 5. It doesn't. When batch files quit, they return to DOS. They don't "remember" who called them or how they were started. Real applications, .COM and .EXE programs, return execution to the batch file interpreter. But using one batch file inside another stops the first and starts the second. This is known as chaining.

Chaining

Chaining happens when one batch file "runs" another, the first one stops and the second takes over. This could be quite advantageous and avoid a lot of GOTO structures, as in the example of FIG. 8-8. This program could be called LOGIN.BAT. After LOGIN, the user types their name on the command line (in caps). Then, this program runs other batch files depending on which user has logged in. Because all the files specified in lines 5 through 8 are batch files, execution will not return to this batch file. This avoids a whole multitude of GOTO statements.

8-8   This is an example of "chaining."

```
 1: @ECHO OFF
 2: REM Program to run individual user's batch files
 3: IF %1NOTHING==NOTHING GOTO HELP
 4: ECHO Welcome to the machine, %1
 5: IF %1==STEVE LOTUS.BAT
 6: IF %1==DIANE DIANE.BAT
 7: IF %1==BILL WORD.BAT
 8: IF %1==PEGGY ACCOUNT.BAT
 9: :HELP
10: ECHO Sorry, I don't know you, %1
11: ECHO Contact the machine coordinator for help
12: :END
```

For the majority of batch file programmers, however, chaining batch files is not what life is all about. Fortunately, IBM came to the rescue with the addition of the CALL batch file directive, added in DOS 3.3.

CALL

CALL works like the BASIC programming language's GOSUB statement. It allows you to run a second batch file from your current batch file, then, when the second batch file is done, execution returns to the first batch file.

CALL *batchfile*

batchfile is the name of a batch file, including the optional drive letter and pathname. After CALL *batchfile* is executed, the batch file program *batchfile* is run. When *batchfile* stops, control returns to the first batch file.

Using the example from the previous section, the program can now "call" the LOCATE.BAT file by editing line 4 of his program to read:

4: CALL LOCATE 1 12

This will execute the LOCATE.BAT file, then return to the original batch file, line 5, and pick up where it left off.

In FIG. 8-9, the first batch file calls the second batch file in line 5. In the second batch file, control returns to the first after line 6. What you'll see on the screen is shown in FIG. 8-10.

8-9 The first program calls the second.

```
Name: FIRST.BAT

1: @ECHO OFF
2: REM First batch program
3: ECHO This is the first batch file program
4: ECHO Transferring control to SECOND.BAT...
5: CALL SECOND.BAT
6: ECHO Back in the first program
7: :END


-------        --------        --------


Name: SECOND.BAT

1: REM Second batch program
2: REPT = 20
3: ECHO Now we're in the second program
4: REPT = 20
5: PAUSE
6: :END
```

8-10 This is the visual result of running the batch files in FIG. 8-9.

```
C> FIRST
This is the first batch file program
Transferring control to SECOND.BAT...
====================
Now we're in the second program
====================
Strike a key when ready . . .
Back in the first program
C>
```

Control passes from one batch file to another as seen by the output. If ECHO is OFF in the first batch file, it will be off in the second as well. This is why the second file doesn't have (nor need) an initial ECHO OFF statement.

By the way, the REPT command (SECOND.BAT, lines 3 and 5) is a supplemental program included on the diskette available with this book. It REPeaTs a single character the specified number of times. In this case, it displays twenty equal signs. For some reason, and in some versions of DOS, ECHO will not display 20 equal signs and does one of these:

    ECHO is off

That's why I wrote REPT and made it available on the supplemental programs diskette.

Breaking out

You should note that if you press CTRL – BREAK in a secondary batch file, control returns to DOS—not the first batch file. CALL doesn't act like the command processor shell's EXIT command. Any time a batch file is canceled with CTRL – BREAK the following message is displayed:

    Terminate batch job (Y/N)?

If Y is pressed, control returns to DOS.

COMMAND

For DOS versions prior to 3.3, the CALL command isn't available. However, this doesn't mean that you can't "call" one batch file from another. The secret is to use a second copy of the command processor, COMMAND .COM. (This method still works under later versions of DOS as well.)

    COMMAND /C *batchfile*

batchfile is the name of a batch file, including the optional drive letter and pathname. After COMMAND /C *batchfile* is executed, the batch file program *batchfile* is run. When *batchfile* stops, control returns to the first batch file.

You can change line 5 in FIRST.BAT (FIG. 8-9) to read:

    5: COMMAND /C SECOND.BAT

COMMAND /C uses COMMAND.COM to invoke a second copy of the command processor, like a shell. That's the only difference between COM MAND /C and CALL. Oh, and COMMAND /C is a lot slower than CALL. Otherwise, if you're still using an older version of DOS, replace all occurrences of CALL in this book with COMMAND /C.

And remember to specify a full path to COMMAND.COM for your batch files. An interesting trick, however, is to take advantage of the COM

SPEC environment variable, which should always show the proper location of COMMAND.COM. So you could use the following as well:

```
%COMSPEC% /C SECOND.BAT
```

Remember, %COMSPEC% is expanded to the path for COMMAND.COM when the batch file runs. This is yet another neat-o trick you probably weren't aware of.

Summary

Though batch files really lack any type of formal structure, there are things you can do that will bend them that way. The first is to use a consistent program "skeleton," use REM comments liberally, and always have an END label. The second method involves indenting lines and using blank lines to create a "pretty printing" effect. And the third method is using the batch file directives GOTO and CALL to implement specific portions of code or to call external batch files. Though it isn't officially a structure, it is one step closer to writing better batch files.

9
Interactive batch files

Yet another complaint the programming priesthood has with batch files is their limited communications ability. Other programming languages employ all sorts of neat tricks—ways to send information from one "module" to another, secrets for retaining values in memory, and other manipulative and sneaky acts. On the surface, it looks like batch files lack these tricks—"bah," I say. Look beneath the surface. If you spend the time with them, you'll realize that there are all sorts of ways you can share information between batch files.

This chapter covers interactive batch files. That is, batch files that can communicate with each other. Talk. Chat. Ramble. Right away, this is putting one foot outside of the realm of what many people expect batch files to do. The purpose of this chapter (and this book) however, is to show you that there is very little batch files can't manage, and no limit to how clever you can be with DOS.

How batch files communicate

Communications is a key element of computer programming. As the programmer, you must communicate what it is you want the computer to do. You do this by instructing the computer via some programming language (or yelling at it, if all else fails). You must write your program so that it communicates with the user. This is most important. Gone are the days of cryptic programs, multiple command line switches, backwards syntaxes, and baffling interfaces that left most computer users in the dark.

Batch files really lack a fancy method of presentation. They don't have graphics, there are no decorative colors, panels, windows, zips, bleeps, or zooms. Of course, third-party utilities may allow you to add these features to a batch file (which is covered in Part Three). But the basic batch file is DOS-like text. And that's the way we have to deal with things as batch file programmers.

Communicating with the user as far as batch files is concerned is just supplying a lot of ECHO statements (or TYPEing a text file), letting the user know what's going on when appropriate. Or you can use ECHO OFF and redirect output to the NUL device if you prefer the silent approach. That handles the second form of program communications: with the user. The first form of communications, within the program itself, is really the subject of this chapter.

How the real languages do it

Real programming languages have many methods of communicating:

- Using variables
- Passing parameters
- Saving data in memory
- Saving data to disk

In the "real world," programming languages primarily use variables to communicate. The variables store information, strings input by the user, values calculated, and other interesting stuff. There are two general types of variables, regardless of what they contain: *Local* and *global*.

A *local* variable is one that's used only in one part of the program. For example, suppose a programmer wrote a subroutine that calculates and prints the result of two values. That result could be held in a local variable, just one you'd see and use around the local neighborhood. The only time a local variable is needed is in that subroutine. As far as the rest of the program is concerned, the variable doesn't exist.

A *global* variable is one used throughout the program, a worldly traveler. (It may also be referred to as a *public* variable.) For example, if you're playing a war game and you set the computer to do battle with you at level nine, the value 9 is probably held in some global variable. It's available for all the subroutines in the program to examine or change as need be.

Passing parameters is another form of communications used in real programming languages. When you call a subroutine you may often *pass* it a value. Say a subroutine figures out your weight in kilograms given that value in pounds. The value in pounds is passed to the subroutine, which then *returns* the value in kilograms (along with some nasty dieting comments). Depending on the language, one or more values may be passed or returned in this manner.

Finally, saving data to memory or disk is another important part of real world programming. Saving information to memory is similar to using variables, but not necessarily the same. A real life programmer may designate a "block" of memory and put a graphics image there. That's not really a type of variable (though it could be). Disk storage is permanent, more long term than memory storage. Sure, you could keep your graphics image in memory, but only by saving it to disk will you be able to access it at a later time.

The purpose of these examples is to show you just what batch files *can't* do: They can't define a variable that holds a value, and though they can hold strings, you cannot manipulate the strings; you cannot define a global or public variable in a batch file for use by other batch files; you cannot save information to memory and retrieve it later; and you cannot save information to disk in a batch file. Can't! Can't! Can't!

Or can you?

Batch file communications is something few people think about. Yet batch files can be incredibly interactive. This diatribe is designed to get you thinking about batch files and communications. Why? Again, to expand your knowledge of DOS and to make you a better, advanced batch file programmer.

All of the above examples are possible with batch files. In fact, the only thing a batch file can't do is math. (And you cannot manipulate variables in memory, at least not without some third-party utility designed to do so.) Here are the solutions:

How do you define variables? Use the environment. The environment is permanent storage in memory (as long as you don't run out of environment space). Variables and other strings of information can be kept there until your batch file stops running. True, you cannot manipulate them once they're there. But it is a type of local—and global—storage.

How do you pass parameters? Use the CALL command, or COMMAND /C. Just specify your parameters after CALL. The next batch file will interpret them just like command line variable arguments.

Want to return a parameter? This is the best trick of all: Use I/O redirection to create a temporary file on disk. The name of the file can clue in your batch file as to the result of the operation. (An example is provided later in this chapter.)

Want to retain other information? Temporary files are the key here. Not only the name of the files, but their contents as well. Using batch files and I/O redirection you can create other files on disk—some of which could even be batch files that other batch files can call.

Isn't this nuts? When you really look at it, there are lots of things batch files can do to pass information back and forth between them. Where you might think batch files lack any communications abilities at all, it turns out they're just ripe with them.

Using the environment

The environment is often overlooked by most typical DOS users. When you think about it, Microsoft was really nice to give us any environment at all in DOS. Sure, they could have just tossed the PATH, PROMPT and

COMSPEC off into some undocumented memory pool somewhere, allowing only dedicated routines to change their values. Instead, we have an environment and the handy SET command. Why not take advantage of it?

The first example for saving items into the environment you've already seen. The MOVE2.BAT program (covered in chapter 7) is again shown in FIG. 9-1. It uses the environment variable DISK to store the value of the first replaceable parameter.

This is an example of what can be considered a *local variable*. The environment variable DISK is created in line 4, set equal to the first command line word. It's used again in line 9 for the COPY procedure. Finally, in line 17, DISK is erased, freeing up space in the environment pool.

DISK is local. No other program sees it, uses it, or needs it. In FIG. 9-1, DISK is only used during execution of the program. Since SHIFT is used to copy a whole gang of files from one place to another, we need to save that first parameter. The best way to do that is in the environment. Essentially this is a local variable.

9-1 MOVE2 uses an environment variable to store a temporary value.

Name: MOVE2.BAT

```
 1: @ECHO OFF
 2: REM A 'Gang Move' batch file
 3: IF %1NOTHING==NOTHING GOTO HELP
 4: SET DISK=%1
 5: ECHO Moving a group of files to path %DISK%
 6: :LOOP
 7: SHIFT
 8: IF %1NOTHING==NOTHING GOTO END
 9: COPY %1 %DISK% >NUL
10: DEL %1 <C:\SYSTEM\UTIL\YES >NUL
11: ECHO %1 moved to %DISK%
12: GOTO LOOP
13: :HELP
14: ECHO MOVE2 Command format:
15: ECHO move2 [drive:[\path]] [file1] [file2] .... [fileN]
16: :END
17: SET DISK=
```

A global, or public, variable could be an environment variable shared between two batch file programs. Actually, all environment variables you create are global. They'll stay in the environment until you erase them. The ideal way to see that demonstrated is when you CALL one batch file from another.

The two batch files (in FIG. 9-2) are actually doctored up versions of the same batch programs shown in chapter 8. This time an environment variable is passed from one to the other. The variable TEMP is created in line 5 of FIRST.BAT. It's set to "second batch." After, CALL SECOND.BAT (line

9-2 Here FIRST.BAT and SECOND.BAT share a global environment variable.

Name: FIRST.BAT

```
 1: @ECHO OFF
 2: REM First batch program
 3: ECHO This is the first batch file program
 4: ECHO Creating the environment variable TEMP
 5: SET TEMP=second batch
 6: ECHO Transferring control to SECOND.BAT...
 7: CALL SECOND.BAT
 8: ECHO Back in the first program
 9: ECHO Clearing TEMP variable
10: SET TEMP=
11: :END
```

Name: SECOND.BAT

```
1: REM Second batch program
2: REPT = 20
3: ECHO Now we're in the %TEMP% program
4: REPT = 20
5: PAUSE
6: :END
```

7), the variable will still be in the environment and available to SECOND .BAT.

In SECOND.BAT, line 3 uses the ECHO statement to display the environment variable. After that, we return to FIRST.BAT, where the TEMP variable is cleared in line 10. The output for this program will look something like this:

```
C:\ > first
This is the first batch file program
Creating the environment variable TEMP
Transferring control to SECOND.BAT . . .
= = = = = = = = = = = = = = = = = = = =
Now we're in the second batch program
= = = = = = = = = = = = = = = = = = = =
Strike a key when ready . . .
Back in the first program
Clearing TEMP variable
C:\ >
```

There's nothing mystical here; environment variables cannot be removed from the environment unless you do so with the SET command. So passing an environment variable to a second batch file program is no major secret. In fact, you can change the variable in the second batch file program and that change will be reflected when you get back to the first program. You can even create a variable in the second program and then have that variable intact when control returns to the first program.

In a way, environment variables are eternal. (Or at least as eternal as the reset switch allows.) To sum it all up, note the following:

> Any environment variable you set in any batch file is available to all other batch files and to DOS

It doesn't matter when or where the variable was created, it's always available. (The reason for this is that, internally, DOS places all environment variables into a *master environment*. While each program has its own, mini-copy of the environment attached, SET sticks all new variables into the master environment. So they're available to all programs under DOS.)

There is, however, one time variables will not be retained. If you run a second copy of the command processor or "shell out" of a program. Any variables created after that will not live past the EXIT command. But using CALL doesn't cause that problem.

Creating an environmental MODE

The typical DOS user will do more than one thing with their PC. Most computer owners have a minimum of three to five programs they use quite often. But the exceptional DOS user (meaning you) has lots of programs. You may even have several different *modes* under which you run your computer: The word processing mode; the spreadsheet mode; the database mode; the programming mode; the utility mode; not to mention possible graphics modes and modes associated with certain operating environments (*Windows, DESQview*, etc.). You can change modes via batch files, and you can keep track of them via an environment variable.

On my machine I use the MODE variable:

    SET MODE = STARTUP

I have four or five modes in which I use the PC. There's the STARTUP mode; the C programming mode; the assembly language programming mode; and, though I'm reluctant to admit it, a game playing mode. For each mode, I run a batch file that customizes my PATH, PROMPT and MODE variables to reflect the mode I'm in.

Consider the three batch file examples in FIG. 9-3. Each one changes the computer's mode, depending on what the computer is being used for. The first batch file sets the PC to the standard, startup mode. The PATH is set to the MPATH variable (covered later in this chapter), the PROMPT is set to the standard pg, and the MODE variable is set to equal "START UP." The other two batch files do the same thing, but for their individual modes. Note how the PATH and PROMPT are changed, as well as the MODE variable, to reflect the computer's current mode.

9-3 These three batch files change the computer's MODE.

```
@ECHO OFF
REM This changes the PC to startup MODE
SET PATH=%MPATH%
SET PROMPT=$p$g
SET MODE=STARTUP
REM Other commands could go here ...

@ECHO OFF
REM This changes the PC to wordprocessing MODE
SET PATH=C:\WP;C:\DOS;C:\BATCH
SET PROMPT=[WP]$_$p$g
SET MODE=WP
REM Other commands could go here ...

@ECHO OFF
REM This changes the PC to programming MODE
SET PATH=C:\QBASIC;%MPATH%
SET PROMPT=*$p$g
SET MODE=PROG
REM Other commands could go here ...
```

In all three files, the "other commands" could change directories, run programs, load memory-resident software, clean up files, configure other aspects of the system or printer, and so on. The object here is to change the computer's operating mode, but to keep track of it using an environment variable.

You can do the same with your own system or the systems you manage at work. Even with beginners, who may be running some sort of "idiot" shell or menu system, it's a good idea to keep a MODE variable. A batch file such as the following could be used to determine the current mode:

```
@ECHO OFF
REM Display the current mode
ECHO The current MODE is %MODE%
```

Name the batch file ISMODE.BAT (because "MODE" is already a DOS command). Now each time you or some other user is in a dilemma, type ISMODE at the batch file and you'll get a response. It saves a lot of time over typing SET or CD or just sitting down and trying to figure out what's been going on. And if you find ISMODE handy, you can add other commands that will help you quickly analyze the problem and devise a solution.

Saving environment variables

On some systems you know environment space is tight. You want to keep dozens of environment strings, but realistically only a few of them are used from time to time. Rather than set or reset the variables, or risk running out of environment space, it's possible to save an environment variable to disk and recall it later.

I know it sounds crazy. But consider this:

```
ECHO %VAR% >FILE
```

This saves the contents of the environment variable %VAR% to a file on disk, FILE. Suppose VAR was set to a command line parameter, something like: "C:\WIN\TEMP." After the above command, the file FILE will contain "C:\WIN\TEMP." The contents of the variable have been saved to disk.

The problem immediately obvious is that, while the information is saved on disk, how can a batch file retrieve it? Sure, a program might want and need that information in that format in a file on disk. But for batch files, the information in the file is of little use (other than using TYPE to display the information later on).

But consider the following:

```
ECHO SET VAR=%VAR% >FILE.BAT
```

This creates a batch file with a single line:

```
SET VAR=contents of VAR
```

Because the batch file expands %VAR% into its contents, we now have a one-line batch file (FILE.BAT) that contains a SET command to recreate the VAR variable. Resurrecting the VAR variable is now as easy as using CALL FILE.BAT in any other batch file.

A similar thing can be done with the PATH. Suppose you want to keep your current path—but don't exactly know what it is. Then use the following in a batch file:

```
PATH > SETPATH.BAT
```

The PATH command by itself displays your current path in the following format:

```
PATH=C:\SYSTEM\DOS;C:\SYSTEM\UTIL\;C:\SYSTEM\BATCH
```

That also happens to be the same format you use to set the PATH. CALLing SETPATH.BAT from another batch file will reset your path.

As long as you can ECHO or output a full DOS command line in a batch file, you can use I/O redirection to create a secondary batch file. That batch file can be called by any other batch file to reset a certain condition. The above examples used an environment variable and PATH. But many more can be done as well.

There is, however, one caveat: You cannot use I/O redirection-append, > >, to create a single command line. For example:

```
ECHO SET VAR= > FILE.BAT
ECHO %VAR% >> FILE.BAT
```

This creates a *two line* batch file, FILE.BAT. The first line clears the VAR variable from the environment, the second is just the contents of VAR on a line by itself. That probably won't do what you want it to.

Other unusual examples

There are many other interesting things you can use environment variables for in batch files:

Informative strings of text   A batch file can evaluate a condition or simply create a mode and save that information in a variable. Later batch files can display that information (whatever it is) simply by ECHOing the variable.

Status variables   If you're operating in a number of different MODEs, then keeping a MODE or STATUS variable is a handy thing to have. Especially when you're writing a batch file menu program, a LEVEL variable will tell you which level of menu you're at, or which to return to after some sub-menu batch file is done running.

PATHs, PROMPTs, etc.   While PATH and PROMPT are traditional batch file variables, you may consider making backups. My favorites are MPATH and MPROMPT. Each of those variables contains copies of my Master PATH and PROMPT configurations. So when I want to return to them, I use the following:

```
SET PATH = %MPATH%
SET PROMPT = %MPROMPT%
```

Now I can reset my PATH and PROMPT to the originals at any time, simply by issuing the above commands.

Program options   Programs that start with optional switches can have those switches set into environment variables. You could even have several sets of switches, one for each mode the computer is in. By first examining the MODE, you can use the proper switches for that program. An example would be some type of high-resolution screen mode, where certain programs would require a graphics compatibility switch be set before they start.

Filenames   Environment variables can contain the names of programs. These can then be used with IF EXIST tests, or to when you start certain applications to load a specified document or data file.

Program names   Finally, consider that environment variables can contain the names of programs. A good example is COMSPEC, which holds the location for COMMAND.COM and can be run in a batch file:

```
%COMSPEC%
```

Other program names can be SET into environment variables and used in your batch files.

The only drawbacks to using the environment are as follows:

- You cannot manipulate variables already in the environment. You can put them there, you can take them out. But you cannot rearrange some string already inside the environment.
- It's easy to run out of environment space. If this happens when you run a batch file or SET a new variable, something in the environment gets corrupted. DOS is diseased when it comes to running out of environment space, so don't expect anything already in there to be intact. Also, you must reset COMMAND.COM in your CONFIG.SYS file to have a larger environment space, which requires that you reboot.
- Matching strings is time-consuming. Saving information in an environment variable is a snap. But using a series of IF commands to figure out which string is there isn't so snappy. Information in environment variables can be commands, informative text, or status variables. But don't expect trying to examine the variable's contents to be easy.

But, over all, the environment does play a major role in making batch files more communicative.

Passing parameters

Anything you stick in the environment will stay there, even when you CALL a second batch file. But there's a more natural way to send information off to a second batch file.

The CALL command runs a second batch file just as if you typed that batch file's name on the command line. Of course, this is true for all lines you type in a batch file. The difference is CALL allows control to return to the first batch file when the second is done. (CALL can also be used with those stubborn programs that won't return to a batch file; just stick CALL in front of the offending application's name instead of using that name by itself.)

Because you're CALLing a second batch file just like you typed its name on the command line, you can also pass *command line parameters* to that batch file. The second batch file will pick them up and treat them just like variables %1 through %9, even allowing you to use the SHIFT command to examine any extras.

No, this isn't anything new. But few people pause to think that it could work, and it saves memory over stuffing several items in the environment.

Figure 9-4 shows two batch files. CALL-A calls batch file CALL-B, sending to it three variables. In this example, the three variables happen to be CALL-A's own command line variables—but they could be anything: environment variables, constants, etc. The CALL command in line 6 simply sends them off to CALL-B.

9-4 CALL-A passes three parameters to CALL-B.

Name: CALL-A.BAT

```
 1: @ECHO OFF
 2: REM CALL-A, calls CALL-B
 3: REM First test for three parameters
 4: IF $%3==$ GOTO ERROR
 5: ECHO Now calling with our parameters: 1=%1, 2=%2, 3=%3
 6: CALL CALL-B %1 %2 %3
 7: ECHO Back in the first batch file.  All done.
 8: GOTO END
 9: :ERROR
10: ECHO Enter up to three parameters for the best effect
11: :END
```

Name: CALL-B.BAT

```
1: @ECHO OFF
2: REM CALL-B, called from CALL-A
3: ECHO Call-B has picked up these parameters: 1=%1, 2=%2, 3=%3
4: PAUSE
5: :END
```

The interesting part is that CALL-B interprets these variables as its own command line variables. In CALL-B, line 3 displays the variables passed. This is only an example, but a real batch file could further examine those variables and act upon them. Or, if you want to get really crazy, you could pass them down the line to another batch file.

The output of these two programs is shown below:

```
C:\> CALL-A ONE TWO THREE
Now calling with our parameters: 1 = ONE, 2 = TWO, 3 = THREE
Call-B has picked up these parameters: 1 = ONE, 2 = TWO, 3 = THREE
Strike a key when ready . . .
Back in the first batch file. All done.
C:\>
```

Making decisions

Starting with DOS Version 2.0, the IF command gives us decision-making power in batch files. There are three ways the IF command is used:

IF *variable* = = *value command*
IF ERRORLEVEL *value command*
IF EXIST *filename command*

In each of the above three formats, IF tests something and then performs the DOS *command* that follows. *Variable* tests environment and command line variables; ERRORLEVEL compares return *values* from programs; and EXIST tests for the existence of a *filename*. In all three examples, the NOT operator can be positioned just after IF to reverse the conditions of the test. (IF is discussed at length in chapter 7.)

If you just read the DOS manual, you'd be totally convinced this was the only way to make a decision in a batch file. But that's just not the case. There are two other tools you can use (sometimes in conjunction with IF) to make comparisons. The first is GOTO, the second is the FOR command.

Using GOTO to make decisions

Practically all decision making in a batch file is done by the IF command. Other programming languages share the IF command, using it to make simple either-or decisions. But often in programming, we encounter more multiple choice type of questions than simple true-false.

A multiple choice problem can be handled in a batch file. You just use a slew of IF statements. Consider FIG. 9-5.

9-5 This shows how not to handle a multiple choice question in a batch file.

```
 1: @ECHO OFF
 2: REM Password detecting program
 3: IF %1!==! GOTO ERROR
 4: IF %1==LIZ GOTO LIZ
 5: IF %1==LIz GOTO LIZ
 6: IF %1==LiZ GOTO LIZ
 7: IF %1==Liz GOTO LIZ
 8: IF %1==lIZ GOTO LIZ
 9: IF %1==lIz GOTO LIZ
10: IF %1==liZ GOTO LIZ
11: IF %1==liz GOTO LIZ
12: :ERROR
13: ECHO Type your password after PASSWD and try again
14: GOTO END
15: :LIZ
16: ECHO Hi Liz!
17: :END
```

This is your typical password batch file. You type in the name of the batch file, then your password. Here, we go through some eight permutations of the password "LIZ" to find a correct match. After all, to some humans, "Liz" is the same thing as "liz" or "LIZ."

There are many faults with this approach. First, it takes a long time for the batch file to test for all possibilities of L-I-Z. For each IF test, DOS must access a new line from the batch file on disk. Second, LIZ is only three letters long. It takes eight lines to cover all the possibilities. To test for all permutations of STEVE you'd need over 30 lines of IF statements. Third, consider adding more users to the single password file. It would be a mess.

Instead of using IF, however, you can use GOTO and various labels. When GOTO hunts for a label, it doesn't care whether or not it's UPPER-, lower-, or mixed-case. GOTO matches characters, and it can also be used with a command line parameter or an environment variable.

In FIG. 9-6, GOTO is used in line 4 to figure out whose password was entered. For all permutations of LIZ and STEVE, GOTO branches to the

9-6 Using GOTO with variables narrows down the decision-making processing.
Name: PASSWD.BAT

```
 1: @ECHO OFF
 2: REM Password detecting program
 3: IF %1!==! GOTO ERROR
 4: GOTO %1
 5: REM Label Not Found error here if no match
 6: :ERROR
 7: ECHO Type your password after PASSWD and try again
 8: GOTO END
 9: :LIZ
10: ECHO Hi Liz!
11: GOTO END
12: :STEVE
13: ECHO Welcome aboard, Steve!
14: GOTO END
15: REM (Et cetera . . .)
16: :END
```

appropriate label. But there is one major flaw, as described in line 5 of the program.

If you enter an unknown password, or you misspell a password, you'll see a "Label not found" error. While GOTO will solve the problem of using multiple IF statements to match UPPER- or lowercase, it won't solve the problem of finding an unknown word.

Of course, you don't have to limit your use of GOTO to locating passwords. An environment variable can be set to any label in your program and you can then branch to it via:

GOTO %LABEL%

But be reminded of the "Label not found" error. There's no way to trap for it or get around it. (More information on batch file errors is in chapter 10.)

Using FOR to make decisions

The FOR command has long been left out in the cold as far as DOS and batch files are concerned. Face it: It's a confusing little command with limited purpose. There are a few tricks you can pull with FOR, things that you may not have thought of by looking at the examples in the DOS manual.

As a review, the format of the FOR command is:

FOR %*variable* in (*file selection*) DO *command*

The "*file selection*" above is really misleading. You can put any number of items between the parenthesis. FOR will then execute its *command* for that number of times. Consider the following:

FOR %%A IN (1 2 3 4 5) DO ECHO HELLO!

The above line in a batch file displays "HELLO!" on the screen five times.

If you typed it on the command line (and remember to use only one percent sign before the "A" if you do), you'd see something like FIG. 9-7.

9-7   Here is how the FOR command says "hello" five times.

```
C:\> FOR %A IN (1 2 3 4 5) DO ECHO HELLO!

C:\> ECHO HELLO!
HELLO!

C:\> ECHO HELLO!
HELLO!

C:\> ECHO HELLO!
HELLO!

C:\> ECHO HELLO!
HELLO!

C:\> ECHO HELLO!
HELLO!

C:\>
```

FOR processes each of the elements in the "file selection." There are five elements. Yet, the variable is never used in the command part. This is perfectly fine as far as DOS is concerned. The net effect is that something is done five times—a loop.

Granted, the above has little practical use, other than giving you the ability to repeat a certain command a given number of times (which some may find practical enough). A better use for the FOR command is to choose one item out of many. Consider the following:

```
FOR %%A IN (1 2 3 4 5) DO IF %%A = = 3 ECHO %%A
```

Here we're still using FOR with a group of constants. But this time the constants are used with IF in the command part. When the variable %%A is equal to 3, the batch file will ECHO that variable to the screen. If you typed this as the DOS prompt (and used only one percent sign), you'd see something like FIG. 9-8:

Notice how the "3" is ECHOed (midway down FIG. 9-8)? This same logic can be applied to the ERRORLEVEL command, covered later in this book. Consider the following:

```
FOR %%A IN (1 2 3 4 5) DO IF ERRORLEVEL %%A GOTO %%A
```

If you designed a batch file that had labels based on the ERRORLEVEL return values, the above statement would both examine the ERROR LEVEL and branch to the proper label. This eliminates several IF ERRORLEVEL tests in a single batch file, as well as makes the batch file run faster.

9-8 Here FOR is used with constants to make a decision.

```
C:\> FOR %A IN (1 2 3 4 5) DO IF %A==3 ECHO %A

C:\> IF 1==3 ECHO 1

C:\> IF 2==3 ECHO 2

C:\> IF 3==3 ECHO 3
3

C:\> IF 4==3 ECHO 4

C:\> IF 5==3 ECHO 5

C:\>
```

Using temporary files

Earlier in this chapter, you read how ECHO can be used with I/O redirection to create files on disk. I'm now going to take that concept and go way overboard with it. There are some truly amazing tricks you can pull with ECHO and I/O redirection. And they all have interesting consequences in batch files (not to mention how useful they can become).

This first example extends a theme throughout this chapter, returning information from a called batch file. So far, you know of only one way to do this: Create or change an environment variable. The variable can then be examined and a decision made. But what if you want to return more than one variable? Or what about running out of environment space? These are risks you must deal with in the environment, but not when you create a temporary file to indicate your return value.

There are two ways you can use temporary files to return a value from a batch file subroutine. The first is via the file's name, the second is via the file's contents.

Unique filenames

Returning information from a CALLed batch file can be done by using ECHO and I/O redirection. You simply create some unique filename on disk in the called batch file. When you return to the main batch file, you use IF-EXIST to test for the existence of that filename. Based on the results, your batch file can complete some action or start a particular activity. (And later you should delete the uniquely-named file from disk, just to keep things clean.)

Figure 9-9 shows two batch files, CALL-1 and CALL-2, which demonstrate creating a unique filename. As with a previous example, parameters are passed to this batch file in line 6 of CALL-1.BAT. CALL-2.BAT receives those parameters and then evaluates whether one or two were sent in lines 3 and 4. Note how NOT is used to reverse the test in those two lines.

9-9 These two batch files communicate via temporary filenames on disk.

Name: CALL-1.BAT

```
 1: @ECHO OFF
 2: REM CALL-1, calls CALL-2
 3: REM test for parameters
 4: IF %1$==$ GOTO ERROR
 5: ECHO Calling batch file CALL-2
 6: CALL CALL-2 %1 %2
 7: ECHO Back in the first batch file.
 8: IF EXIST &&TWO GOTO TWO
 9: IF EXIST &&ONE GOTO ONE
10: ECHO No parameters returned by second batch file
11: GOTO END
12: :ONE
13: ECHO Batch file CALL-2 returns one parameter
14: DEL &&ONE
15: GOTO END
16: :TWO
17: ECHO Batch file CALL-2 returns two parameters
18: DEL &&TWO
19: GOTO END
20: :ERROR
21: ECHO Enter one or two parameters
22: :END
```

Name: CALL-2.BAT

```
 1: @ECHO OFF
 2: REM CALL-2, called from CALL-1
 3: IF NOT %2!==! GOTO TWO
 4: IF NOT %1!==! GOTO ONE
 5: REM nothing received
 6: GOTO END
 7: :ONE
 8: ECHO One parameter found > &&ONE
 9: GOTO END
10: :TWO
11: ECHO Two parameters found > &&TWO
12: :END
```

Depending on whether one or two parameters were found, CALL-2.BAT creates one of two unique files on disk. If one parameter was found, the file &&ONE is created in line 8. If two parameters are found, the file &&TWO is created in line 11.

When control returns to line 7 in CALL-1.BAT, either of those two files are tested for in lines 8 and 9. If one or the other is found, batch file execution branches to the appropriate subroutine. Note how IF-EXIST is used here to test for those unique filenames. Also note how the unique files are deleted (lines 14 and 18) when they're found.

This is a good example of how information can be passed between batch files. Normally, you'd only think about using IF EXIST to test for a file before deleting it, running it, or TYPEing it to the screen. But here, IF EXIST is used to test for a condition.

File contents

The previous section's example has some definite advantages over using environment variables. One is permanence. Temporary files will exist even when you've turned off or reset your machine. This has advantages in creating unique AUTOEXEC.BAT files that can react on situations that happened last time you reset the computer. But for now, consider another approach.

Creating a temporary file is a practical way of passing information between batch file programs. But sometimes, too many temporary filenames creates a long series of IF-EXIST tests, which slows down your batch file performance. To cure this, consider making the contents of a temporary file more important than its name (see FIG. 9-10).

9-10   Here the contents of the temporary file are more important than its name.

```
Name: CALL-1A.BAT

 1: @ECHO OFF
 2: REM CALL-1a, calls CALL-2a
 3: REM test for parameters
 4: IF %1$==$ GOTO ERROR
 5: ECHO Calling batch file CALL-2a
 6: CALL CALL-2a %1 %2
 7: ECHO Back in the first batch file.
 8: IF EXIST &&PARAMS GOTO COUNT
 9: ECHO No parameters returned by second batch file
10: GOTO END
11: :COUNT
12: ECHO Batch file CALL-2a returns:
13: TYPE &&PARAMS
14: DEL &&PARAMS
15: GOTO END
16: :ERROR
17: ECHO Enter one or two parameters
18: :END


Name: CALL-2A.BAT

 1: @ECHO OFF
 2: REM CALL-2a, called from CALL-1a
 3: IF NOT %2!==! GOTO TWO
 4: IF NOT %1!==! GOTO ONE
 5: REM nothing received
 6: GOTO END
 7: :ONE
 8: ECHO One parameter found > &&PARAMS
 9: GOTO END
10: :TWO
11: ECHO Two parameters found > &&PARAMS
12: :END
```

CALL-1A.BAT and CALL-2A.BAT are subtle rewrites of CALL-1 and CALL-2. In CALL-2A you'll note that both strings are sent to the same filename, as opposed to unique files. Then when we return to CALL-

1A.BAT, only one file need be tested. That file's contents are then displayed (line 13) and it's quickly deleted.

This example only works best if its the contents of the file that are important. Batch files cannot access or evaluate the contents of any files. They can examine the file's name, they can TYPE the file's contents, or they can execute the file (providing it's a .COM, .EXE, or .BAT file).

Building batch files with batch files

This final example is really neat and rather frivolous, though I assume someone somewhere may come up with some practical use for it. The idea here is to use I/O redirection in one batch file to create a second batch file. Then you CALL that newly created second batch file. (There's lots of potential for usefulness here. But most of those examples would be too long to list in this format.)

Again, the second batch file is created via ECHO and I/O redirection. You subsequently ECHO each line of the new batch file to it's file name, first using > and then > > to append each line (see FIG. 9-11).

9-11 This batch file creates and runs a second batch file.
Name: 1.BAT

```
1: @ECHO OFF
2: REM First batch program
3: ECHO Now creating second batch program
4: ECHO REM Second batch program > 2.BAT
5: ECHO ECHO Now we're in the second batch program >> 2.BAT
6: CALL 2.BAT
7: ECHO Back in the first program
8: :END
```

Carefully notice lines 4 and 5 (in FIG. 9-11). They use ECHO followed by the lines that will go into the secondary batch file, 2.BAT. Note how line 4 uses a single > character, and line 5 uses the double > > characters to append. This creates the secondary batch file, and then it's CALLed in line 6. The output on the screen will look something like this:

```
C: \ > 1
Now creating second batch program
Now we're in the second batch program
Back in the first program
C: \ >
```

Remember that ECHO OFF doesn't need to be respecified in a CALLed batch file. That's how you can get away with a minimum number of lines in an I/O redirection-created batch file.

Practical uses for this technique would involve creating a unique batch file, or at least different unique parts of a batch file, and then running it. For example, you could already have a file, RUNME.BAT, on disk.

But RUNME.BAT leaves off rather hurriedly, lacking a proper ending. The end to RUNME.BAT is actually supplied by a second batch file using I/O redirection. A batch file could append those final lines using something like the following:

```
COPY RUNME.BAT RUNME.BAK
ECHO CD \ WIN > > RUNME.BAT
ECHO WIN > > RUNME.BAT
CALL RUNME
COPY RUNME.BAK RUNME.BAT
DEL RUNME.BAK
```

First, a backup copy of the original RUNME is made. Then two lines are appended to RUNME.BAT, and RUNME is CALLed. After it's done, the original file is restored with another COPY command, and the backup deleted. In practice, a batch file may have several decision points and possibly append a number of different endings to RUNME.BAT.

Summary

The subject here is batch file communications, making them more interactive. Now you know there are several ways to make that possible.

Batch files can make extensive use of environment variables, to hold temporary values, to pass information from one batch file to another, or to save a variable for later use by other programs or batch files.

When you CALL a second batch file, you can send information to it either via an environment variable or a command line parameters after the CALL command. Those parameters are interpreted by the second batch file as %1 through %9, and can be evaluated, shifted, or returned to the original batch file via the environment.

GOTO and FOR can be used to sift through a number of possible comparisons. This is much more efficient than using multiple IF statements. If you use a GOTO-LABEL structure instead of IF xxx = = xxx, you save time and make the batch file easier to read. It's hard, however, to avoid a "Label not found" error in case there is no match. FOR, can also be used to select one option from a list of many.

Finally, I/O redirection can be used in batch files to create unique temporary file names, interesting contents in those temporary files, as well as to create secondary batch files on disk.

10

Troubleshooting

Isn't "troubleshooting" a wonderful word? Think about it. It's so violent. When you think about the word (more specifically the two words trouble and shooting) a vision comes to mind of sitting down in a harshly lit room, shirt sleeves rolled up, pencil in hand, ready to track down some annoying problem. Not a pleasant situation.

But, when I think about "troubleshooting," I think of this beast, trouble. It's lurking out there somewhere. And I have a gun. A big one. That's what makes troubleshooting interesting. You don't even need a license.

Fortunately, troubleshooting batch files doesn't require a gun (and will probably never receive an "R" rating). Instead, this chapter contains everything having to do with batch file "trouble." This isn't limited to batch file errors and how to fix them. I've also included the ERRORLEVEL statement. Even though it has nothing to do with a batch file error, you can use ERRORLEVEL to aid in troubleshooting some common batch file problems—and to make your batch files smarter.

Things DOS won't let you do with batch files

No one ever accused batch files of being all-powerful. Yet, there are some things that you would think work in a specific manner, but they don't. Some things DOS just won't let you do with batch files. Prominent among them is using I/O redirection on the same command line as the batch file name.

There are also certain reserved filenames that DOS won't let you use with batch files. Actually, you can't even name .COM and .EXE files these names. Though this isn't really a no-no, just don't be scratching your head wondering why your COPY.BAT file won't run.

Also, the ECHO command hasn't been known to be particularly predictable. Because ECHO sometimes doesn't behave the way you think it would, it's also been included in this section.

I/O redirection

One thing that would be nice would be to pipe the output of a running batch file to the printer. Or, to automatically provide input to a batch file. This could be used effectively for self-running demonstration programs. I/O redirection is not allowed by the batch file interpreter. Any of the following characters are ignored after you type the name of a batch file program:

> < |

You might experience some peculiarities if you try to use these. First of all, don't expect them to work. However, in some cases, it might appear that they work. For example:

C> TEST > TEMP

TEST is a batch file and TEMP will (hopefully) be a file on disk that contains TEST's output. Of course, this will never happen. However, a brief attempt will be made to create a TEMP file as you can see by listing the DIRectory:

```
Volume in drive C is MISSING
Volume Serial Number is ABCD-1234
Directory of C: \ BATCH \ DISK
TEMP              0 8-01-92 8:39p
       1 File(s) 9584640 bytes free
```

Unfortunately, TEMP contains nothing. However, this doesn't mean that the batch file didn't run. Batch files will operate if you attempt to use I/O redirection—it's the I/O redirection that won't work.

A possible solution

Though I/O redirection isn't possible on the command line, DOS lets you use it freely inside a batch file. If you want output of a batch file to be sent to a file, a solution would be to use I/O redirection inside the batch file to redirect the output. You could even write a special version of the batch file that would provide the output automatically.

Take one of the directory sorting programs discussed earlier in this book:

Name: DSN.BAT

```
1: @ECHO OFF
2: REM Sort directory by name
3: DIR | SORT > ZIGNORE.ME
4: MORE < ZIGNORE.ME
5: DEL ZIGNORE.ME
```

You could write a modified version, call it DSNDISK.BAT. That version will use replaceable parameters to send its output to a disk file as well as the screen. Or you could just delete line 5 above, but study FIG. 10-1 before you start editing.

10-1 This program uses replaceable parameters.
Name: DSNDISK.BAT

```
1: @ECHO OFF
2: REM Sort directory by name--disk output version
3: IF %1N==N GOTO NORMAL
4: DIR | SORT > %1
5: ECHO Data saved in %1:
6: :NORMAL
7: DIR | SORT > ZIGNORE.ME
8: MORE < ZIGNORE.ME
9: DEL ZIGNORE.ME
```

This is the same program—from line 7 on. The difference is in a test for a replaceable parameter (3). If there is no parameter, the batch file performs the same as DSN.BAT, with no errors. Otherwise, the sorted output is sent to the file specified after DSNDISK on the command line (4). Then a message is displayed letting the user know that the file was saved (5).

```
C> DSNDISK TEMP
Data saved in TEMP:
```

(A sorted directory listing would follow.)

Lines 3 through 6 could be added to any program where you wanted optional I/O redirection to disk. Just remember to type the filename after the command.

Some clever readers might think about testing for the > character on the command line using IF. For example:

```
IF "%1" = = ">"
```

This won't work. Remember, DOS ignores >, < and | if they're typed on the command line after a batch file. ">" will never be read as a parameter. Also, using > with the IF statement is not allowed. Again, DOS assumes you want to redirect the output of the IF command. If you try this, you'll get a "File creation error" message.

Doing I/O redirection on the input side is next to impossible. It's best to use the replaceable parameters on the command line than attempt any tricky input redirection. Unless, of course, you're using the YES, NO, ENTER, and ENTERN files covered in chapter 7.

Reserved names

The following are names of internal DOS commands. If you name a .COM, .EXE or .BAT file any of these names, those files will never run. Internal

DOS commands always take priority over all other program names on disk:

BREAK	FOR	SET
CALL	GOTO	SHIFT
CD	IF	TIME
CHCP	MD	TYPE
CHDIR	MKDIR	VER
CLS	PATH	VERIFY
COPY	PAUSE	VOL
CTTY	PROMPT	
DATE	REM	
DEL	REN	
DIR	RENAME	
ECHO	RD	
ERASE	RMDIR	

% signs

The percent sign, %, is a valid character in a filename, but you should be aware of using the character % in your batch files.

Have you ever wondered why the FOR command requires only one percent sign when used at the DOS prompt and two of them when used in a batch file? You can tell why if you turn ECHO ON and look at the FOR command as it's displayed. The batch file contains:

```
FOR %%F IN (*.*) DO DIR %%f
```

But you will see (with ECHO ON):

```
FOR %F IN (*.*) DO DIR %f
```

The batch file interpreter uses the percent sign to identify a variable. However, you can use "%" as the percent character by specifying it twice. When the batch file interpreter sees two percent characters, it translates them both into a single percent sign character.

```
ECHO %%
```

This command echoes one percent sign to the display. ECHO will echo only one "%" for every two you have listed. So:

```
ECHO %%%
```

displays only one, whereas:

```
ECHO %%%%
```

displays two.

If a filename contains a percent sign, such as:

ANNUAL%

Specify the percent sign twice when you reference the file in your batch file program:

ANNUAL%%

ECHO oddities

The ECHO command has three distinct functions:

1. Turn the echoing of batch file commands on or off
2. Echo character strings to the display
3. Display the status of the ECHO command.

In my humble opinion, the third function of the ECHO command is utterly useless. ECHO, without any arguments, displays the current status of the ECHO command. So:

ECHO

all by itself yields:

ECHO is on

or:

ECHO is off

Most users assume that ECHO by itself will "echo" a blank line. It doesn't. Instead, it displays one of the above status messages. This is perhaps the most annoying thing about ECHO.

Lost in spaces

Some enterprising users figured that you could follow ECHO with some spaces. After all, spaces are characters and ECHO followed by spaces should just ECHO those spaces to the screen. The result would be a blank line, right? Wrong:

ECHO is off

Depending on the version of DOS, ECHO followed by spaces is interpreted the same as the ECHO command along on the line. (Earlier versions of DOS might display the spaces.) In fact, all spaces up to the first non-space character are ignored by some versions of DOS:

ECHO test

This command might just display "test" as the first four characters on the next line. Using the TAB key with some versions of DOS will not work either.

Generally, you should include some non-space character to start a blank line, or a line without any text on it:

```
ECHO !
ECHO ! test
ECHO !
```

This always displays:

```
!
! test
!
```

Another character to use is character 255. This extended ASCII character is actually a blank, but it's also a non-space character. (Use the ALT-keypad trick to enter character 255.)

If you follow ECHO with a space, and then type character 255, a blank line is displayed.

Dot commands

In earlier versions of DOS, you could use a period to "echo" a command:

```
.You may now turn off your computer.
```

DOS versions prior to 3.0 ignored the dot character and anything after it. So this served well as a substitute for ECHO. However, this trick should be avoided if you want to be compatible with later versions of DOS.

Long lines

Each line of a batch file can contain 128 characters. Actually, that's 127 characters, plus the ENTER key. ECHO and the space that follows it takes up five characters, which leaves you 122 to get your message across. If you exceed the 122 character limit, DOS might do one of two things: Truncate the string, or totally hang.

By the way, you can get more than 122 characters after the ECHO statement is one of three ways (or a mixture of all three):

1. by using an environment variable (or more than one) that expands out to a long string
2. by using a replaceable parameter (more than once) that expands out to a long string
3. by using a text editor and writing a long string after the ECHO command

ON and OFF

Because ECHO ON and ECHO OFF are two ways of using ECHO, any string you try to display that starts with "on" or "off" will not be displayed. Instead, ECHO will be turned either on or off. (That makes sense.)

A way around this is to use character 255 as described earlier. If you precede the word ON or OFF with character 255, ECHO will not interpret it as the ON or OFF switch.

I/O redirection (again)

ECHO sends its output to a device, normally the console. However, you can use I/O redirection with ECHO for some special effects. My favorite is:

```
ECHO ^L > PRN
```

This ejects a page from the printer, and it comes in quite handy.

Because ECHO allows I/O redirection, you cannot use any of the following characters in an ECHO string:

```
> < |
```

DOS will interpret those characters as I/O redirection symbols and the results of your ECHO command will not be what you expect. For example:

```
ECHO Insert backup disk ONE and press <Y> at the prompt.
```

This will send the string "Insert backup disk ONE and press" to a file called "AT" and redirect input from a file called "Y"—not what you wanted.

With DOS 4 and later, you can enclose the I/O redirection characters in double quotes and use them. For example:

```
ECHO The greater-than symbol is " > "
```

This displays:

```
The greater-than symbol is " > "
```

All three of the I/O redirection symbols can be used within double quotes in this manner.

Forbidden characters

Besides the above quirks, ECHO also acts funky when used with the following characters in the manner noted:

```
=
```

ECHO followed by any number of equal signs is the same as typing ECHO by itself; the equal signs will be echoed to the screen. However, if you follow the equal signs with any other non-space character, they will be displayed. A possible solution instead of using the equal sign is to use character 205, which is similar looking.

%

The percent sign is not displayed by itself. Instead (in a batch file), you need to specify two percent signs for every one you want displayed.

;

The semicolon works along the same lines as the equal sign. When used by itself or in any number it's the same as typing ECHO by itself. The solution is to follow the semicolon with a non-space character.

,

Comma operates the same as the equal sign and semicolon. Follow it by a non-space character if you want it to be displayed.

Using ERRORLEVEL

ERRORLEVEL is used to test a program's return code. When certain programs quit, they optionally send a return code back to DOS. This code value can be used by other programs, or by the batch file command ERRORLEVEL.

ERRORLEVEL, or more specifically, a program's return code is a primitive form of communications between that program and DOS. The sad part is that most programs, including most DOS programs, fail to take advantage of the return code.

ERRORLEVEL *value*

value is a value compared with the previous program's return code. It can be any number from 0 through 255. The meaning of the value depends on the program, though a value of zero typically means a success (or that the program didn't offer a return code).

ERRORLEVEL is used with IF to test *value*. If the return code from a program is greater than or equal to *value*, then the IF statement is true. Note that in this instance an equal sign after ERRORLEVEL is optional:

IF ERRORLEVEL 6 GOTO OOPS

If the preceding program returned an ERRORLEVEL value of 6 or more, batch file execution will continue at the label :OOPS.

IF ERRORLEVEL 0 ECHO That was smooth

This statement causes "That was smooth" to be echoed to the console. Why? Because ERRORLEVEL will always be greater than 0.

ERRORLEVEL testing

Only five programs that come with DOS return ERRORLEVEL values (see appendix I):

BACKUP   DISKCOPY   RESTORE
FORMAT   GRAFTABL   XCOPY
DISKCOMP   KEYB

Several applications programs return ERRORLEVEL values. But for the most part, only third-party utility programs take advantage of ERROR LEVEL values.

From the DOS utilities mentioned previously, BACKUP offers five return code values as follows:

0   Normal Exit
1   No files were backed up (all were already backed up or none existed)
2   File sharing conflicts. Not all files were backed up
3   CTRL–BREAK was pressed, halting the backup
4   Error, program stopped

The batch file example in FIG. 10-2 shows how ERRORLEVEL can be used to communicate these messages to a user. (Remember, "BACKUP" is already used as the name of the BACKUP program. If you named your

10-2   This program shows how error levels can be communicated to the user.

Name: BACK.BAT

```
 1: @ECHO OFF
 2: REM Backup the hard drive
 3: ECHO Backing up the hard drive ...
 4: ECHO Have a stack of disks handy, then
 5: BACKUP C:\*.* A: /S/M
 6: IF ERRORLEVEL 4 GOTO ERROR4
 7: IF ERRORLEVEL 3 GOTO ERROR3
 8: IF ERRORLEVEL 2 GOTO ERROR2
 9: IF ERRORLEVEL 1 GOTO ERROR1
10: ECHO Backup was successful
11: GOTO END
12: :ERROR4 -- error, program stopped
13: ECHO Some kinda error took place
14: GOTO END
15: :ERROR3 -- Control-Break pressed, stopping the backup
16: ECHO Backup halted!  (You pressed Control-Break)
17: GOTO END
18: :ERROR2 -- File sharing conflicts
19: ECHO There are file sharing conflicts.
20: ECHO Please contact the network administrator for assistance
21: GOTO END
22: :ERROR1 -- Nothing to backup
23: ECHO No files found to backup, no need to proceed
24: ECHO Bye!
25: :END
```

backup batch file BACKUP, the BACKUP.EXE (or .COM) program would be run instead.)

The batch file (FIG. 10-2) backs up a hard drive, C to diskettes in drive A (5). The BACKUP switches are set to back up the entire drive, but only those files modified since the last backup. The ECHO statement in line four ends with "then" because the first line displayed by BACKUP is "Insert a disk . . ." (It makes for a smooth display.)

After the BACKUP command come the ERRORLEVEL tests—from highest to lowest (6 through 9). You'll also see how each label is used as a REM statement to explain what the various return codes mean (12, 15, 18, 21). When ERRORLEVEL 0 is returned, execution falls through to line 10, then branches to the :END label. Otherwise, messages particular to each return code are displayed.

Even better uses

Perhaps the most useful purpose of the ERRORLEVEL variable comes with two utility programs on the supplemental programs diskette: ASK and READKEY. These are two variations on some popular public domain utilities. In fact, some similar batch file utility programs come with popular packages such as the Norton Utilities.

ASK is used to display a line of text and then wait for Y or N to be pressed. If Y is pressed, an ERRORLEVEL of 0 is generated. If N is pressed, an ERRORLEVEL of 1 is generated. This way you can get feedback from the user in your batch file:

```
ASK Is it okay to go on?
IF ERRORLEVEL 1 GOTO END
```

ASK displays the string "Is it okay to go on?" and then waits for either Y or N to be pressed (upper- or lowercase). If the user presses N, ERRORLEVEL 1 is returned and the program ends. Otherwise the program goes on.

READKEY comes in many variations. In chapter 11 you will use DEBUG to create a READKEY program (called RKEY) that returns the ASCII code value of a key pressed on the keyboard. The READKEY program available on the supplemental programs diskette does that, as well as return relative values for the function keys, number keys, and alpha keys.

In FIG. 10-3, after the string is displayed (4), READKEY will accept any single character input (5). That character's ASCII code value will then be available to your batch file via ERRORLEVEL (6, 7, 8). In this case, the values you want are 49 for "1" and 50 for "0". The first ERRORLEVEL statement eliminates any characters out of range (6) and goes to the :RANGE label (9) to display a warning (10). The program then repeats (11). This also happens for ASCII code values less than "1" or "2"; the ERROR LEVEL test fails in line 8 so the message is displayed.

Each of the messages displayed by ECHO (10, 13, 16) are preceded by

10-3 This program accepts a 1 or 2 key press.
Name: RANGE.BAT

```
 1: @ECHO OFF
 2: REM An example of READKEY
 3: :START
 4: ECHO Type a 1 or a 2
 5: READKEY
 6: IF ERRORLEVEL 51 GOTO RANGE
 7: IF ERRORLEVEL 50 GOTO TWO
 8: IF ERRORLEVEL 49 GOTO ONE
 9: :RANGE
10: ECHO --That number is out of range
11: GOTO START
12: :ONE
13: ECHO --You typed the number 1!
14: GOTO END
15: :TWO
16: ECHO --You typed the number 2!
17: :END
```

two dashes. This offsets the message from the character entered. (A side effect of the READKEY utility is that it does not display the character just entered followed by a space or a linefeed.)

Error trapping

There are two ways to "trap" potential errors in batch files. The first is to anticipate what an error might be. You will notice that the two preceding batch file examples used ERRORLEVEL and some fancy branching to detect errors and display error messages. If you know what a potential error could be, it's easier to program around it.

The second type of error to trap for is a bit harder to catch. These are batch file errors that occur because of simple typos, or some errors DOS might throw at you. In batch files, these errors are hard to predict and next to impossible to remedy. However, a list with explanations is provided here to assist you in tracking down causes.

IF EXIST

One of the most common errors encountered in a batch file is "File not found." It means you either mistyped something when you created the batch file, or something actually happened to the file in question. In either case, the prescription is to always use IF EXIST to see if the file is there.

```
IF EXIST DATAFILE.001 ECHO It's there!
```

If the file DATAFILE.001 exists, "It's there!" is displayed on the console.

```
IF NOT EXIST E:\SPOOL\*.* GOTO SKIP
COPY E:\SPOOL\*.* C:\TEMP
:SKIP
```

The above snippet of code might be part of a SHUTDOWN batch file. Assume E: is an electronic disk. This code is used to remove all files from the electronic disk and place them in the \TEMP directory on the hard drive. If only the middle line were used in a batch file and E:\SPOOL was empty, then an error message would be displayed. This way, IF NOT EXIST tests to see if the directory is empty. If no files exist, the line containing the COPY command is skipped.

You can test for any file on disk using IF EXIST. However, you cannot check for subdirectories. If a subdirectory exists and it's full, then a statement such as:

```
IF EXIST C:\SUB\*.*
```

will work. However, if \SUB exists and it's empty, then the above statement will be false. Even if you try:

```
IF EXIST C:\SUB
```

the test will be negative. So it's better to specify files within a subdirectory rather than the subdirectory's name when using IF EXIST.

Batch file errors

There are quite a few batch file-specific errors you might come across. Additionally, you could change any of the by-now-familiar DOS error messages from the classic "File not found" (which IF EXIST will catch) to "Abort, Retry, Fail, Ignore."

The following are error messages that you might see when running your batch files:

Batch file missing
Cannot start COMMAND, exiting
FOR cannot be nested
Label not found
No free file handles—Cannot start COMMAND, exiting
Out of environment space
Syntax Error
Terminate batch job (Y/N)

Fortunately, most of these errors have specific causes. When you do see them, the following explanations will come in handy.

Batch file missing   The batch file you're running can no longer locate itself to load in the next line. This might happen if you accidentally deleted or renamed the batch file, if the batch file contains unusual characters (it was made by a word processor and saved improperly) or if you changed drives or diskettes. Sometimes, if you change your PATH statement, the batch file can get lost. Also, if you're accessing your batch file via a SUBSTituted drive and you unassign the drive, then the batch file can get lost.

Cannot start COMMAND, exiting This error occurs if you're using COM MAND /C to "call" other batch files and there are too many files already open. The solution is to increase the number of files that can be open at a time by increasing the number specified with the FILES statement in your CONFIG.SYS file.

FOR cannot be nested You attempted to use a second FOR as the *command* portion of a FOR command. For example:

    FOR %F IN (*.*) DO FOR %A IN (*.BAK) DO . . .

The solution is to try to figure out another way to implement the FOR command.

Label not found This is one of the few commands that will halt a batch file instantly. If the batch file interpreter cannot locate a label associated with a GOTO statement, the above message is displayed and the batch file immediately stops. The solution is to check your spelling, or add the label where it should go. (See chapter 8 for more information on labels.)

No free file handles/Cannot start COMMAND, exiting This is the same type of error that happens when you call another batch file with COMMAND /C. (This error happens with earlier versions of DOS.) See "Cannot start COM MAND, exiting" above.

Out of environment space You attempted to alter the environment and there is no more room. This can happen with the PATH, PROMPT, or SET commands. The solution is either to reset certain environment variables to zero, or to give yourself more room in the environment by using the /E switch of the SHELL command in your CONFIG.SYS file. You can also run a second copy of COMMAND.COM with the /E switch specified, but remember to EXIT back to your original copy before the batch file is through.

Syntax error This is one of the most common batch file errors, but not that serious. It won't halt your batch files like "Label not found" does, but if you have ECHO OFF, it can be frustrating. Generally speaking, a "Syntax Error" only crops up when you forget to type something. In batch files this happens a lot when one equal sign is used instead of two with the IF statement:

    IF %STRING% = TEST ECHO "Syntax Error"

Other DOS commands might use the "Syntax Error" message from time to time, though the majority of DOS commands have their own unique and confusing error messages. To hunt down Syntax Errors, first check for single equal signs. Turn ECHO ON and watch your batch file as it executes. You should be able to find the offending command and then edit it.

There is another, trickier error associated with the IF statement. Suppose you fix your IF statement with two equal signs:

IF %STATUS%= =ON GOTO MAIN

If you still get "Syntax Error" with the above format, what DOS is telling you is that the environment variable STATUS isn't equal to anything (it's undefined). Essentially, the batch file interpreter expands it to:

IF = =ON GOTO MAIN

Because there is nothing on one side of the double equal sign, you have a syntax error. To fix this you can use the old quote trick:

IF "%STATUS%"= ="ON" GOTO MAIN

The statement will still evaluate true if %STATUS% is equal to ON. However, if %STATUS% isn't equal to anything, the batch file interpreter will see:

IF ""= ="ON" GOTO MAIN

and you won't get your Syntax Error.

Terminate batch job (Y/N) Although not really an error message, "Terminate batch job" isn't the friendliest way to stop a batch file from executing.

What this message means is that either CTRL – C or CTRL – BREAK was pressed. The batch file interpreter asks the user if they want to stop the batch file or continue. Pressing Y continues—pressing N stops.

But where does it stop?

As a rule of thumb, whichever line is being executed when CTRL – C or CTRL – BREAK is being pressed will not be executed. Figure 10-4 demonstrates how CTRL – BREAK stops a batch file:

10-4 This program demonstrates how CTRL — BREAK stops a batch file.
Name: HALT.BAT

```
 1: @ECHO OFF
 2: ECHO Press Control-Break to stop me!
 3: ECHO This is line 1
 4: ECHO This is line 2
 5: ECHO This is line 3
 6: ECHO This is line 4
 7: ECHO This is line 5
 8: ECHO This is line 6
 9: ECHO This is line 7
10: ECHO This is line 8
11: ECHO This is line 9
12: ECHO Be faster next time ...
```

Run the program in FIG. 10-4 and then press CTRL – C or CTRL – BREAK to stop it. Answer N to the question, then see where the batch file picks up. It usually ignores the line being executed when CTRL – BREAK was pressed (see FIG. 10-5). Line 7 in FIG. 10-5 was never executed. Keep this in mind when you halt long batch files—especially with ECHO OFF—because you don't really know what you're stopping.

10-5 This is the test run from HALT.BAT.

```
C> HALT
Press Control-Break to stop me!
This is line 1
This is line 2
This is line 3
This is line 4
This is line 5
This is line 6
T^C

Terminate batch job (Y/N)? n
This is line 8
This is line 9
Be faster next time ...
C>
```

If you're concerned about users messing up a batch file, give them a good place to break out by using the PAUSE command. The following is a common technique:

```
ECHO Press any key to go on, or press Control-Break to stop
ECHO and answer "Y" to "terminate batch job"
PAUSE
```

Here PAUSE is used to allow the user to press CTRL–BREAK. This way, a serious operation won't be interrupted. Also, remember that pressing CTRL–BREAK in a called batch file returns control to DOS, not to the calling batch file.

One last thing/one last thing

No, I typed two of those titles on purpose. Occasionally you might get a double command at the end of your batch file. Say the final command in your batch file is:

```
ECHO All Done!
```

But you see on the screen:

```
All Done!
All Done!
```

The reason for the double display is an oddity with some versions of DOS. The problem is a missing carriage return/line feed character combination. (You probably used a text editor to create the document and forgot to press ENTER after the final line.)

To fix things up, go in and add ENTER using your text editor.

But it's too slow

One "trouble" area you can't control is batch file speed. Batch files are slow. Doubly slow, in fact. Sure they're slick, and you can fool a few first-time computer users into thinking they're running a "real" program. But batch files still must fetch each line from disk. On a hard drive system, this is tolerable. But on a floppy: crunch, crunch, crunch. It's slow.

There are a number of ways to make your batch files run faster. One trick mentioned already is to use a text file and the TYPE command as opposed to multiple ECHO statements. (Though if you want to cut down on the number of files in your system, this isn't viable.)

TYPE versus ECHO is pretty well known. But another trick, not so common knowledge, is to lean on the FOR command for running multiple DOS commands.

FOR is used to process a number of files into a given DOS command. As a refresher, the format is:

FOR %*variable* in (*file selection*) DO *command*

Here, *file selection* is a list of files or wildcards. Each file will be represented by the *variable* in the DOS *command* that follows DO. Most people look at this, do a "ho-hum," and move on to the more interesting batch file commands. But consider that *file selection* also means program names in addition to standard files or wildcards. For example:

FOR %P in (VOPT NDOSEDIT PROMPT = PG \ HERCULES \ HGC) DO %P

This FOR command takes each of the programs listed and runs them via DO %P. Here, the DOS command following DO is the program name itself.

The advantage to this is twofold. First, it saves space in the batch file. The above FOR command replaces the following four lines in your batch file:

```
VOPT
NDOSEDIT
PROMPT = $P$G
\ HERCULES \ HGC
```

Instead of four command lines you now have one. That saves space.

The second advantage is speed. Now DOS will access only one line in the batch file. The FOR command itself will process the four programs. When DOS accesses the disk once instead of four times your moving four times as quickly through the batch file. The speed improvement isn't great (because each program will still take time to load and run), but it's there.

There are restrictions to this, however. The most important is that your programs must all be only one word long. You cannot use a program with options or switches because those options and switches would each be interpreted as a command by FOR.

```
FOR %P in (PROMPT $P$G  \ HERCULES \ HGC FULL) DO %P
```

Here, FOR will process four—not two—DOS commands: PROMPT, PG, \ HERCULES \ HGC and FULL. If your DOS commands have parameters, then they cannot be bundled into the FOR command.

Another speedup trick, one that can apply to just about any program, is to run your batch files from a RAM disk. Again, the speed gained here comes in the faster access time a RAM disk gives to batch files. (Any disk-intensive software will run faster from a RAM disk.)

Because DOS will always read a batch file one line at a time, the slowest place you can run a batch file is from a floppy drive. Hard drives are the next fastest place. But the fastest of all is a RAM drive.

To run your batch files from a RAM drive you can pull two tricks:

The first trick is to create a RAM drive and then copy your entire collection of batch files there. (Later in this book you'll be introduced to the concept of a batch file subdirectory. Just copy the whole subdirectory to the RAM drive.) Put the RAM drive on your path and all your batch files will then run faster.

A second trick would be to create a RUN.BAT batch file. RUN's job would be to transfer a batch file to your RAM drive and then run that batch file. It only needs to be a few lines long:

Name: RUN.BAT

```
1: @ECHO OFF
2: COPY %1 D: \
3: D: \ %1
```

Assuming drive D is your RAM drive, the above copies the batch file to the RAM drive and then runs that batch file. For example:

```
RUN WP
```

This command runs the WP batch file, first transferring it to your RAM drive.

The RUN.BAT approach is more complex than just transferring your entire batch file throng to a RAM drive. After all, you now have to type two commands at the DOS prompt instead of one. But for specific and time-consuming batch files, it's an interesting trick.

Remember that copying the files to a RAM drive is a temporary thing. You want to keep the originals around in a permanent place. Only copies are sent to the RAM drive, so that when the power goes off and the RAM drive disappears into Bit Heaven, you still have the original version of your batch files.

And one final trick to making batch files run faster: Buy a faster computer.

I know, this is a bad joke. (And no reader of this book can claim not to like spending money on computers!) Some major software developers actually offer that piece of advice when you complain about the speed of their applications. While a math co-processor or faster RAM won't speed up batch files, a faster PC or hard drive will. So if you're really getting bogged down, consider them. But have other reasons than speeding up batch files in mind before you pay the cash.

Summary

Troubleshooting batch files is not as scary as it sounds. Instead, it involves minding your Ps and Qs and paying attention to several rules.

The restrictions DOS places on your batch files are that you cannot do I/O redirection on the same line as you start your batch file and you cannot name a batch file using the name of an internal command.

The ECHO command behaves rather oddly at times. It can be doubly frustrating because ECHO seems to vary with each release of DOS. However, there are alternative ECHO programs available (including SAY on the supplemental programs diskette) that solve most of these problems.

Two batch file directives, ERRORLEVEL and EXIST, can be used to detect certain conditions in batch files. ERRORLEVEL contains a return code from a previously run DOS program or utility—and it can additionally be used to get a single character of input from the user. EXIST is used to test for the existence of files and can be used to avoid "File not found" errors.

There are several batch file-specific errors that can occur. The most common is using a single equal sign with the IF statement (rather than the required double equal sign, = =). Other errors can best be detected by turning ECHO ON and observing your batch file as it runs.

Finally, to speed up a batch file you can use the FOR command to run multiple, single-word DOS commands, and a RAM drive helps to speed up some long, disk-intensive batch files.

Part Three

Beyond batch files

When you go beyond batch files you're breaking the limits of what batch files can do. After all, batch files were only designed with a limited purpose in mind. Yet, as most users discover how useful they can be, they want more.

Sadly, DOS doesn't provide that extra power that most advanced batch file programmers want. Instead, you'll have to turn to other sources: utility programs; third-party programs, and batch file enhancement languages. It's these sources that complete batch files, making them more useful and powerful than DOS does.

11
Beyond batch files

There are quite a few layers of "beyond batch file" techniques. Most of them covered in this chapter deal with supplemental batch file programs. First up to bat (what a horrid pun!) are utility programs—both public domain and third party.

This chapter is about utilities you can use to boost batch file performance. These are programs outside of DOS that can help you do numerous batch file things. Because DOS has been around a few years, enterprising programs have had a chance to examine the problem and come up with these program solutions. The ones discussed here only scratch the surface of what's possible.

Additions to batch file commands

Besides the limited number of batch file commands DOS gives you, there are virtually thousands of supplemental programs and utilities, all of which can be added to your batch file command repertoire. You can use these programs to enhance your batch file performance, as well as to make your batch files more interesting and capable.

There are two sources for these batch file command additions. The first is the public domain. (Where is that anyway?) That's a place where programmers and philanthropists deposit programs and utilities free of charge for everyone to use. You can locate these programs on an electronic bulletin board system, or on national on-line systems such as GEnie or CompuServe. Or you can order disks full of these programs from places like PC-SIG.

The second source consists of third-party software or utility programs. These are the programs you buy off the shelf and pay money for.

Though some public domain programs call themselves "shareware," meaning that they want a donation, they are not the same as these "real" programs. For one thing, third-party programs usually come with a money-back guarantee and phone support. They're thoroughly tested and, in most cases, well worth the money.

Public domain utilities

There are so many DOS public domain utilities it would be futile to attempt to list them all. Some books try, but seeing that new and better utilities are constantly being written, it's not worth the effort. As a bit of advice, just keep your eyes open, attend user group meetings, and keep in touch with other PC enthusiasts and you'll catch wind of most of them.

Generally speaking, I divide all batch file utilities into five groups:

- The Display Group
- The Q&A Group
- The Chron Group
- The Test Group
- The General Group

The display group is batch file utilities that do something to the display—usually something exciting. They could be as simple as a replacement for the ECHO command, or they could do fancy animation, display big letters, or give you fancy graphics.

The Q&A group is a popular—and sorely needed—category of batch file utilities. They allow you to enter information in a number of ways. The most common Q&A type utility is ASK, which displays a prompt and waits for a Y or N response. That response, or any of the responses from a Q&A-type utility is then translated into an ERRORLEVEL value, which your batch file can then examine.

The Chron group consists of utilities that deal with time. These are time-stamping utilities for creating log files, as well as pausing and waiting programs that will wait a certain duration or until a certain time before continuing batch file execution.

The Test group is composed of programs that test various items in your computer, usually files and disk drives. For example, IF EXIST is a powerful file test, but better utilities are available that test for the existence of subdirectories—even the size of diskettes in your floppy drives.

Finally, the General group consists of batch file and non-batch file utilities you may find come in handy. Together, all these programs build upon the base of commands DOS gives you, and they allow you to create bigger, better, and smarter batch files.

Sad to say, however, there are two problems with all these utilities. The first is trying to find them. The second problem is that there are too many of them. I've helped out with both problems by putting as many as I can on the diskette offered with this book. In the next few sections, I've listed some of the creme de la creme. This isn't by any means all of them, just some that I've found particularly useful. Yet all of these (and more!) have been supplied on the supplemental programs diskette.

The display group

Display batch file helpers is the most common group of utilities. There are many ways to visually spice up your batch files, from giving it big letters to colorful ANSI animations. All of these utilities fit into the display group.

BIGTITLE.COM BIGTITLE is a fun program that will really WAKE UP some early morning PC snoozers. What it does is to display an eight character (or less) message in huge, colorful characters on the screen:

    BIGTITLE Wake up!

Because you're limited to eight characters or less, BIGTITLE can't be used for displaying menus or any informative text. But does make for splashier title screens and reminders, such as BACKUP!, or VDisk?, or just Hello!

ECOH.COM ECOH works like DOS's ECHO function with a twist, the string echoed is displayed in reverse:

    ECOH I am in inverse type.

This displays "I am in inverse type" on the screen using black letters on a white background. Astute readers will recognize that you can do this using the ECHO command with ANSI escape characters as follows:

    ECHO ESC [7m I am in inverse type. ESC [7m

(Remember to replace ESC with ^V[, or ^[, or whatever your text editor accepts as the ESCape character.) The advantage to ECOH, however, is that it doesn't rely upon ANSI to produce inverse type.

The Q&A group

There aren't as many Q&A-type batch file utilities as there are display helpers. The reason is variety. All Q&A-type utilities typically ask a question and supply the answer to your batch file via some ERRORLEVEL value. Some of them get fancier than that, some of them are quite limited. But there's not much else you can do given the nature of batch files.

ANSWER.COM ANSWER is one of those batch file utilities you've been searching for all your life. It's at a level way beyond the simple ERROR LEVEL return code utilities listed in this group.

What ANSWER does is to display a prompt and allow for input. That input is then placed into the *environment* in the ANSWER environment variable. From there, you can use the variable for whatever purpose you wish.

    ANSWER What is your name?
    ECHO %ANSWER%

The above batch file asks the user to input their name and then displays it via the ECHO command.

Note that if you want to save the contents of the ANSWER variable, you'll need to save it:

    SET DISK = %ANSWER%

Each time ANSWER is used, the response is placed into the same ANSWER variable. So, as above, create a new variable using SET to save some of your earlier ANSWERS.

FAKEY.COM   What FAKEY does, as its name suggests, is to fake certain keystrokes. The casual DOS users will wave this aside, "Oh, but you can do that with I/O redirection." True, but FAKEY works at the *BIOS* level. This means you can send keystrokes to just about any program—not just DOS utilities.

    FAKEY "hello"

The above sends the characters h-e-l-l-o off into the BIOS keyboard buffer. The next program that runs will fetch those characters, just as if they were typed from the keyboard.

FAKEY has numerous options and controls that allow you to place any key on the keyboard into the BIOS keyboard buffer. This includes all the cursor control keys, function keys, and keys on the numeric keypad.

INPUT.COM   INPUT is a program that reads the keyboard and returns an ERRORLEVEL return code relative to the key pressed. Unlike other, similar programs, if the user presses ESCape, ERRORLEVEL 255 is generated, which can come in handy.

INPUT, is followed by a string of characters to scan for:

    INPUT "ABCDE"

Pressing "A" (upper- or lowercase) returns ERRORLEVEL 1; pressing B returns ERRORLEVEL 2 and so on.

REPLY.COM   REPLY is another in a series of "get input" programs that reads one character from the keyboard and translates that character somehow into an ERRORLEVEL code. The advantage of REPLY is that it waits ten seconds for input and if there isn't any, it returns an ERRORLEVEL of zero. Of course, you might not think of this as an advantage. If so, there are similar utilities you can use.

With REPLY you can narrow down the keys the user can press by listing valid key combinations after the REPLY command:

REPLY ynq

Here, REPLY waits ten seconds for either "Y", "N" or "Q" to be pressed (upper- and lowercase are treated the same. If "Y" is pressed, an ERRORLEVEL of 1 is returned; if "N" is pressed, ERRORLEVEL 2 is returned; and if "Q" is pressed, ERRORLEVEL 3 is returned. REPLY assigns ERRORLEVEL values based on the position of the responses. So for:

REPLY abcdefghijklmnopqrstuvwxyz

"A" generates an ERRORLEVEL of 1 and "Z" generates an ERRORLEVEL of 26.

The chron group

With something as slow as a batch file you'd think there would be little need for waiting around. But waiting for something or until a specific time is important for many batch files. The chron group includes those commands that pause for a given duration of time or until a specific time. Also thrown in are time displaying programs, which are handy for generating log files.

STIME, ETIME, NOW and TSTAMP   These are a series of time displaying programs, each of which displays the time in a different format:

STIME	Start time = (the current time)
ETIME	End time = (the current time)
NOW	It is now (the current time)
TSTAMP	(Military time format)

STIME and ETIME display "Start time" and "End time" each followed by a full time and date format. The output of these two commands can be used with I/O redirection/append (> >) to create a log file of your computer activity.

NOW and TSTAMP offer other variations on the time display. NOW simply displays "It is now" followed by the current time, which allows you to show the current time in any batch file. And TSTAMP uses an abbreviated, military time format.

All of these programs may seem redundant. After all, DOS has a TIME command. But TIME doesn't just display the time, it prompts for a new time. By using the above utilities, you can incorporate a time display into any of your batch files.

WAIT.EXE   WAIT is a utility I wrote for the *Enhanced Batch File Programming* book. It combines the functions of two previously "must have" batch file utilities, WAITN and WAITUNTIL.

WAIT has five different formats:

    WAIT

When used by itself waits approximately 1 second.

    WAIT *n* SECONDS

In this format, WAIT will wait for *n* seconds.

    WAIT *n* MINUTES

Above, WAIT waits for *n* minutes.

    WAIT FOR *hh:mm*

Here, WAIT waits for *hh* hours and *mm* minutes to pass. This differs from the following format:

    WAIT UNTIL *hh:mm*

Here, WAIT will wait until the time is *hh:mm*. The time is 24-hour military time.

   If a key is pressed while the computer is WAITing, WAIT returns to DOS with an ERRORLEVEL value of one. Also, note that WAIT does not wait for a specific date—only the time.

The test group

The test group consists of batch file enhancers that determine some condition in your PC and then relate that condition back to your batch file. As usual, this is done via the ERRORLEVEL value, though both of the utilities mentioned here also offer optional text output.

ACCESS.EXE   ACCESS is a program that determines whether or not you can access a file on disk. It sounds like IF EXIST and it works just like it, except that ACCESS also determines the accessibility of subdirectories and hard drives.

    ACCESS c:\temp

If the subdirectory \TEMP exists on drive C, ACCESS returns an ERROR LEVEL of zero. If it doesn't exist, an ERRORLEVEL of one is returned. In either case, ACCESS displays "EXISTS!" or "NOT FOUND!", which means you should redirect output to NUL if you want a silent display.

DPATH.COM   DPATH is a great little utility by Lawrence Spiwak, a good friend of Paul Heim (who is one of the world's true batch file zanies). Larry wrote DPATH to solve the problem of "how do I return to my original drive and subdirectory after running a batch file?" DPATH does that in two ways:

   The DPATH GET command creates a DPATH variable in your environment, a variable equal to your currently logged drive and subdirectory. Because that information is saved in the environment, you can move to another drive, switch diskettes, or do just about anything in your batch file you'd like.

The DPATH SET command is used at the end of your batch file. It reads the DPATH variable from the environment and resets your drive and sub-directory accordingly. After that, you just use SET DPATH= to clear the variable, and you're back where you started.

DTEST.EXE DTEST is a utility I wrote based on the old DSIZE utility. DSIZE would return the size of the diskette in a floppy drive via an ERRORLEVEL value. But DSIZE was written before the 1.2-megabyte diskette. Also, DSIZE would hang if a diskette wasn't in the drive. DTEST (a punny name) improves on both those points.

    DTEST A

The above command tests drive A for a diskette. If one is found, its size is returned according to the following ERRORLEVELs:

    10   160K   5^1/$_4$-inch diskette
    11   180K   5^1/$_4$-inch diskette
    12   320K   5^1/$_4$-inch diskette
    13   360K   5^1/$_4$-inch diskette
    14   1.2M   5^1/$_4$-inch diskette
    15   720K   3^1/$_2$-inch diskette
    16   1.4M   3^1/$_2$-inch diskette
    17   Hard drive
    18   Unknown format

In addition, DTEST returns the following ERRORLEVELs:

    0   Help message was displayed
    1   Diskette missing
    2   Diskette unformatted
    3   Diskette write-protected

An optional /V switch (which must be specified after the drive letter) will display a "verbose" listing. Otherwise, DTEST returns an ERRORLEVEL which your batch files can examine.

Why use this? Because sometimes you want to know if a diskette is in the drive. DOS returns the ugly "Not ready error reading drive A, Abort, Retry, Fail?" message. DTEST is silent, letting you know by ERROR LEVEL if a diskette is there and formatted, ready for use. Further, DTEST tells you the size of the diskette. So you can let your user know if they've inserted a low capacity diskette into a high capacity drive.

The general group

General utilities don't have to be batch-related. They can be normal, every-day utilities, any of which you can use in a batch file, but they don't actually replace or augment any batch file commands.

Each of the following are in my "treasure chest" of utilities. These aren't all of them, yet each does have potential to boost batch file performance.

GLOBAL.EXE   Global is my own personal rewrite of that all-time favorite SWEEP. As with SWEEP, GLOBAL is followed by a DOS command, such as:

    GLOBAL DEL *.BAK

What GLOBAL does is to issue the command for the current directory, plus all subdirectories on all hard drives in your computer system or over your network. Optional switches control GLOBAL's behavior, restricting it to either the current drive only, or just all subdirectories under the current directory.

MORE.COM   MORE is just a better interpretation of DOS's own MORE filter. It works independently of DOS version, accounts for unusually sized screens, and it erases its own "more" display so your listing doesn't foul up. You use MORE just like any filter:

    MORE < TEXT.TXT

or:

    TYPE TEXT.TXT | MORE

NDOSEDIT.COM   is one of the two classic DOS command line editors, the other being CED. As far as batch files go, NDOSEDIT doesn't really help you much. However, it does give you command line editing abilities at the DOS prompt, as well as a "history" of your last few DOS commands. It makes using DOS more tolerable.

RENDIR.COM   RENDIR is a utility that renames subdirectories. It uses the same format as the REN command, except it works with DIRectories (hence, RENDIR). The following command renames the subdirectory TEMP to JUNK:

    RENDIR TEMP JUNK

RENDIR has some limitations. For example, you can't rename an entire subdirectory PATH. You must be in a parent directory to rename one of its subdirectories. Better versions of this command come in virtually all of the popular DOS shell applications, though RENDIR is the only one accessible via a batch file.

Norton Utilities

Aside from the public domain goodies discussed above, there are programs you can buy that contain all sorts of batch file utilities. Perhaps the best all around is the "Norton Utilities," put out by Peter Norton Computing. There are two versions of the program: the Norton Utilities and the Norton Utilities Advanced Edition. You want the Advanced Edition.

The Norton Utilities, is actually a series of small, individual programs that serve to enhance your computer. Several of the commands deal with disk management, unfragmenting the hard drive, scanning and repairing files, and, most famous of all, the undelete program that has saved many a user's life.

Out of the 24 utilities that come with NU Advanced Edition, you'll find BE for Batch Enhancer. BE actually used to be five little files that were each extremely useful in batch files. However, starting with Version 4.5 of the Norton Utilities, four of them—plus five additional commands—have all been bundled into the single BE command.

The format for BE is:

BE *command* [*parameters*]

There are nine *commands* that can be used with BE, each of which are described as follows.

ASK   ASK is yet another in a long series of programs that takes a single keystroke of input and translates it into an ERRORLEVEL value. The Norton ASK, however, has the following options:

- You can specify a prompting string
- You can specify the keys to scan for
- A "default" key can be specified
- A timeout value can be defined (after which the default key is selected)
- The return value can be adjusted
- A color can be assigned to the prompting text as well as the answer

BEEP   BEEP is a handy program that beeps your computer's speaker. Of course, ECHOing a CTRL–G will do the same thing, but not in the many ways that the NU's BEEP command will.

BEEP is followed by a number of optional switches or, if you'll believe it, a filename containing pitches and durations that will play a small tune. Text in the file can optionally be displayed as beep is singing its song. BEEP's switches set the duration, frequency, repetition and wait factors of a tone, giving you quite some harmonic freedom. In fact, you could even alert the dog with some of the possible pitches.

BOX   The BOX command allows a number of boxes, or panels, to be drawn on the display. It's really quite fancy, and can make your batch files look impressive.

BOX has a number of parameters that make the box do all sorts of delightful things. Aside from being different colors, the box can explode, have a shadow, or have any of a number of exciting things happen to it. The manual hesitates to document some of these things. Note that the command to get a box to explode is (surprisingly) EXPLODE. If you want a shadow box, specify SHADOW. Both of these options are put last in the list.

CLS   CLS is a command you can use to clear your screen. It's not documented in the manual. It works just like CLS.

DELAY   The DELAY command is used to pause batch file execution for a number of "ticks." A tick is $1/18$ of a second, so:

    BE DELAY 18

will pause for one second.

PRINTCHAR   The PRINTCHAR command is interesting. Like REPT on the supplemental programs diskette, it repeats a specific character a certain number of times—and in an optional color.

    BE PRINTCHAR * 60 GREEN

The above displays a row of 60 green asterisks on a color display.

ROWCOL   ROWCOL is a positioning command. It displays an optional string of text at a given ROW and COLumn position on the screen.

    BE ROWCOL 7 10 Hello? RED

The above displays "Hello?" at row 7, column 10, and in the color red.

SA   SA stands for Screen Attributes and it's the famous Norton Utility command that will permanently change the color characteristics of your display. The nice thing about SA is that it uses plain English commands:

    BE SA BRIGHT WHITE ON BLUE

As you might have guessed, this command changes the screen colors to a bright white foreground (letters) on a blue background.

WINDOW   WINDOW is another box-drawing command, but also fills in the center of the box. (BE BOX just draws an outline.) The format of the command is the same, though WINDOW adds SHADOW and ZOOM options to give the window a shadow or "explode" it when it opens. Neat.

The Batch Enhancer can also be used to "run" a file composed of BE commands. You simply specify the file containing the commands after BE on the command line:

    BE FILE.BAT

FILE.DAT can contain BE commands—but without the leading BE. It can also contain batch file commands, so in essence you can use BE to run your batch files similar to the way most batch extenders work (refer to chapters 12, 13, and 14).

Another Norton Utility that can help batch files is TM, the Time Mark program. Time Mark (TM) is one of the most interesting commands. It works like a stopwatch, keeping track of elapsed time:

TM START

This command starts the stopwatch. Now your batch file could execute, or a certain activity could take place.

TM STOP

This command halts the stopwatch and displays the elapsed time since the TM START command was issued.

TM operates up to four independent clocks and keeps track of the elapsed time. It can be quite useful for log entries or billing purposes when computer time is important.

The Norton Utilities contains several other nifty little programs that will make life under DOS easier. Especially good are the Directory Sort, File Find, and Speed Disk commands. But only BE and TM have any potential for batch files directly.

Supplemental programs diskette

Windcrest Books is offering a supplemental programs diskette—a companion disk—to go along with this book. On the diskette you'll find all the batch file examples listed here, as well as some of the public domain and shareware batch file utilities, and some programs that I've written myself.

One of the best parts of writing this book has been sitting down and thinking about which utilities would be the best to go with batch files. As I completed each chapter, a new utility would pop up in my head. I'd think, "Yeah, that would come in handy." Then I'd sit down, fire up the assembler or C compiler, and write the utility.

Granted, my first profession is a writer, not a programmer. But all the programs have been tested and they all work. They're not public domain programs, nor are they third-party. Instead, the only way to get them is to order the companion diskette that comes with this book. (There is a form near the back of this book.)

If you order the disk, and I encourage you to, you'll get the following programs I've written. I think all of them will help you to write better batch files. (Complete documentation for all of these files is included on the supplemental programs diskette.)

ASK.COM ASK is yet another one of those read key/return ERRORLEVEL utilities. But, unlike the Norton Utilities' ASK, this one comes on the supplemental diskette for far less than you'd pay for the complete *Norton Utilities*.

ASK optionally displays a string that asks a yes or no question. The user can then type only a Y or N (either case). For "Y", ERRORLEVEL 0 is returned; for "N", ERRORLEVEL 1 is returned.

ASK Continue?

This displays the word "Continue?" and waits for either Y or N to be pressed.

BLANKS.COM I wrote BLANKS because of the inadequacy of the ECHO statement to display a blank line. If you use BLANKS all by itself in a batch file it will display a single blank line. Otherwise, you can follow blanks with any value (up to 255) and it displays that many blank lines.

    BLANKS 6

This command causes six blank lines to be displayed.

BOX.COM BOX is one of my pride-and-joys, though few people understand how to use it to its full extent. Basically, I wrote it for menu-generating batch file commands to make the screen look prettier.

What BOX does is to draw a box, using either block graphics, single or double lines, at any position on the screen.

    BOX ALL

This command draws a box around the edge of the screen. If anything is already drawn on the screen it will not be erased by the box.

Also, BOX will draw a box around a specified string. In this instance, BOX only encloses the string; it does not draw a box elsewhere on the screen:

    BOX "Hackers do it on computers"

If you add a /C, the box will be centered on the screen (see FIG. 11-1), adding another interesting effect.

```
┌──────────────────────────────┐
│ Hackers do it on computers   │
└──────────────────────────────┘
```

11-1 BOX encloses a text string.

CLZ.COM CLZ is a program a friend sent me—I don't know where he got it. What it does is to clear the screen in an interesting fashion. I took the original CLZ program, cleaned it up, and rewrote it, leaving the original flavor intact. (I added a proper exiting routine and made the cursor go to position "1,1" when the program was finished.)

CLZ is just an alternative to CLS, though it's more visually interesting.

GREET.COM GREET is a program I include in all my batch files that others use around the office. GREET displays one of three messages depending on the time of day:

    Good morning,
    Good afternoon,
    Good evening,

If any text follows GREET on the command line, that text is echoed after the above greeting:

GREET Dan

displays, "Good morning, Dan" depending on the time of day. People really get a kick out of that one.

HOLD.COM HOLD was written to counter the lameness of the batch file PAUSE command. What PAUSE does is to display "Strike a key when ready . . ." and then wait for a key press. What it should do is allow you to include an optional message after PAUSE, a message that would be displayed a line above the "Strike a key" message. The DOS manual says PAUSE does this—but only when ECHO is turned off. Why didn't I think of that?

HOLD can be used in two ways. The first is just like PAUSE. HOLD by itself displays the message "Press any key to continue . . .". But when HOLD is followed by an optional string, it first displays that string, then the "Press any key" message:

HOLD Insert the diskette "OLDFILES" in Drive A and

This displays the following:

Insert the diskette "OLDFILES" in Drive A and
Press any key to continue

That's what PAUSE should have done in the first place.

ISANSI.COM This program was mentioned back in chapter 4. It's of the test group of batch utilities, and what it tests for is whether or not you have an ANSI-type of drive installed. If so, an ERRORLEVEL of one is returned. If no ANSI screen driver is present, zero is returned.

LOCATE.COM I wrote LOCATE.COM after writing LOCATE.BAT (in chapter 3). LOCATE.COM does the same thing—position the cursor anywhere on the display:

LOCATE 5,10

This positions the cursor at column 5, row 10 (the coordinates are in X-Y order). If no coordinates are given, LOCATE homes the cursor. (Also, if bad coordinates are given, LOCATE returns an ERRORLEVEL code of 1.)

You can follow LOCATE with an ECHO statement to position a string of characters at any spot on the screen:

LOCATE 20,5
ECHO Main Menu

READKEY.COM Yes, here's yet another read key/return ERRORLEVEL program. But this one has some interesting advantages that none of the others offer. All by itself, READKEY simply returns the ASCII value of a key pressed as the ERRORLEVEL value. However, READKEY has three optional switches that allow you to narrow down the choices.

The A switch limits READKEY's input to only the alphabet characters, A through Z (case doesn't matter). When /A is specified, READKEY returns an ERRORLEVEL value relative to the characters offset within the alphabet, so A is ERRORLEVEL one, B is ERRORLEVEL two and so on.

The N switch limits READKEY's input to only the numbers, 0 through 1. Again, as with the /A switch, the "1" returns an ERRORLEVEL of one, "2" returns ERRORLEVEL two, and on up to "9". A special case is the "0" key which returns ERRORLEVEL zero.

The F switch does something no other "read key" utility does: it reads the function keys, F1 through F10. For "F1", an ERRORLEVEL of one is returned, for "F2", an ERRORLEVEL of two is returned, and so on.

The E switch determines whether the key pressed will be displayed or not. Normally, the key is displayed, but when /E- is specified, the key will not be displayed.

Also, an optional prompting string can be specified after the switches:

    READKEY /F Enter function key:

This displays "Enter function key:" then waits for F1 through F10 to be pressed. READKEY then returns a corresponding ERRORLEVEL value depending on the key pressed.

REPT.COM REPT was written to spiff up the display, and take care of one of the shortcomings of the ECHO command. What REPT does is to repeat a specific character a certain number of times, similar to the BASIC language STRING$ statement.

    REPT * 20

This reads, "Repeat the * (asterisk) character twenty times." After the above command, you'll see twenty asterisks on your screen.

Some users like to use a string of equal signs to separate items in their batch files:

    REPT = 80

This command displays 80 equal signs.

RESTPATH.COM RESTPATH was written to solve a problem that batch file programmers have puzzled over for years: how to restore your original drive and subdirectory after running a batch file. It does the same thing as DPATH (covered previously), but doesn't use the environment.

RESTPATH uses the CD command and I/O redirection to remember from which drive and path you started your batch file. For example, at the top of your batch file, put the following command:

    CD > C:\TEMP

This redirects the output of the CD command to the file TEMP in your root directory (on drive C). TEMP will contain something like:

C:\WP\WORD

When the batch file is over, the RESTPATH command can be used:

RESTPATH C:\TEMP

RESTPATH reads the TEMP file, then restores the drive to C and the path to \WP\WORD. (You can then add a second line to the end of your batch file to delete C:\TEMP.)

RESTPATH does its job quickly and silently. Because it has no output, it returns the following ERRORLEVEL values: 0, meaning everything went okay; 1 meaning that a file wasn't found; and 2 meaning that the path could not be restored (the file probably wasn't created with CD >).

SAY.COM SAY was another program written to solve some of my frustrations with the ECHO command. In fact, SAY works just like ECHO but with two exceptions.

You can SAY anything—even nothing—and SAY repeats exactly what you want. Just like ECHO, type SAY followed by any string and that string is displayed to the console—even a blank line, or the word ON or OFF or anything.

Secondly, SAY has optional cursor positioning power, making it a combined LOCATE and ECHO statement. If you follow SAY with an @ sign and a row and column position, SAY will echo its text at that location.

SAY @1,1 Enter your selection:

The above displays "Enter your selection:" at the top of the screen.

VERNUM.COM VERNUM might come in handy someday—if DOS ever changes radically. What it does is to return the current version number of DOS as an ERRORLEVEL value. Version numbers are returned as shown in TABLE 11-1.

Table 11-1

Version	ERRORLEVEL
5.0	50
4.0	40
3.3	33
3.2	32
3.1	31
3.0	30
2.1	21
1.0	0

The batch file example in FIG. 11-2 shows how VERNUM.COM might be used.

11-2 VERNUM.BAT is an example of how VERNUM.COM can be used.

Name: VERNUMT.BAT

```
 1: ECHO off
 2: ECHO This tests vernum
 3: VERNUM
 4: IF ERRORLEVEL 40 GOTO VER40
 5: IF ERRORLEVEL 33 GOTO VER33
 6: IF ERRORLEVEL 32 GOTO VER32
 7: IF ERRORLEVEL 31 GOTO VER31
 8: IF ERRORLEVEL 21 GOTO VER21
 9: ECHO You have a *very* early edition of DOS
10: GOTO END
11: :VER40
12: ECHO DOS Version 4.0 is in use
13: GOTO END
14: :VER33
15: ECHO DOS Version 3.3 is in use
16: GOTO END
17: :VER32
18: ECHO DOS Version 3.2 is in use
19: GOTO END
20: :VER31
21: ECHO DOS Version 3.1 is in use
22: GOTO END
23: :VER21
24: ECHO DOS Version 2.1 is in use
25: :END
```

Summary

For a start, going beyond batch files means using more than what DOS gave you to write interesting and useful batch file programs. You can do this with public domain, shareware, or third-party utilities (quite a few of which come on the supplemental programs diskette).

Public domain and shareware utilities worth using in batch files can be divided up into five groups: the display group, which handles the displaying of text and fancy screen stuff; the Q&A group, which gets information from the user while a batch file is running, returning it to you as an ERRORLEVEL value; the chron group, which deals with pausing, waiting, and time-stamping utilities; the test group which examines conditions on your PC and returns the results; and the general group, which includes everything else.

Quite a large number of these programs, as well as custom utilities written specifically for this book, are available on the supplemental programs diskette. Another source is third-party vendors, including the Norton Utilities, which offers a few batch file enhancing utilities in their repertoire of programs.

12
Rolling your own

There are quite a few interesting though obscure programs that come with DOS—programs that let you write other programs. These are the BASIC programming language and DEBUG.

BASIC integrates quite nicely with batch file programs for picking up and taking care of a few simple, mundane tasks. DEBUG can be a powerful (and deadly) program. But in this instance, DEBUG can be used to build some useful utilities.

This chapter is about writing your own batch file helpers—utilities—using the brief, yet limited tools DOS gave you. There are other languages and programming tools you can use as well. But here we're sticking with DOS, trying not too hard to tread on the sacred ground of the "real" programmer. (If you find the subject of writing batch file enhancers exciting, consider Windcrest's *Enhanced Batch File Programming*, by your's truly.)

Batch files and BASIC

The original IBM PC, and all versions since, have had the BASIC programming language built into their ROM. This was because, back in the good old days, every computer came with a built-in version of BASIC, and IBM wanted to be just like everyone else. In most cases, the BASIC programming language also served as the computer's operating system! But today, with inexpensive software widely available, learning to program your computer in BASIC is an all-but-forgotten art.

BASIC integrates nicely with batch files. In the first place, BASIC comes with most versions of DOS. (It's a disk-based version of BASIC called GW BASIC, or QBASIC for DOS 5. IBM computers have a special "supplemental" version of BASIC that comes on PC-DOS diskettes; that version won't run on any other computers.) As long as the BASIC interpreter is on your system's path, you can access and run BASIC programs from anywhere on your system.

There is a problem, though: don't get carried away with writing supplemental BASIC programs for your batch files. In other words, if you start writing more and more of your batch files using a "supplemental" BASIC program, then you should question why you're writing the batch file in the first place. If a BASIC program would better suit your needs, write the program in BASIC.

Also, this book doesn't offer any programming tips on BASIC. If you'd like to learn BASIC programming, or need a reference, refer to the books mentioned in the introduction of this book. You don't need to know how to program BASIC to type in the routines in this section. But if you intend on further using BASIC, I'd recommend picking up those books.

Manipulating the environment

BASIC is perfect for writing quick little routines—time savers and other functions that batch files are incapable of. Of primary interest to batch file programming is BASIC's ability to assign and manipulate the environment. Two BASIC functions do the work:

    ENVIRON
    ENVIRON$

ENVIRON is used like the SET command from DOS:

    ENVIRON("*variable* = *string*")

variable becomes an environment variable and *string* becomes the variable's data. This works just like:

    SET *variable* = *string*

ENVIRON$ is used to display the contents of environment variables, or to list them by their number (relative to the top entry in the environment table):

    ENVIRON$(*value*)

value is a number from 1 to 127. It represents the variables in the environment in order, from first through 127th. Because this is a function, you'll need to assign ENVIRON$ to a variable or use it with the PRINT statement (it won't work by itself):

    PRINT ENVIRON$(1)

This command displays the first variable's data in the environment table. Or you can use the following format:

    PRINT ENVIRON$("PATH")

This command displays the contents of the PATH variable—or any variable listed in the quotes. But remember to put the variable name in UPPER CASE. ENVIRON$ won't match lowercase environment variables.

There is one minor drawback to using ENVIRON and ENVIRON$. For some reason, assigning variables with ENVIRON is only a temporary thing. During the research for this book I tested both functions. ENVIRON continually produced "Out of Memory" errors no matter how long the variables were. Also, when I was able to assign a variable, once I quit BASIC and returned to DOS, that variable was gone. (The SET command did not display it.)

On other computers and with other versions of DOS and BASIC, these functions might behave differently. But for the purposes of researching this book, I didn't get them to work properly.

If they did work, a BASIC program along the lines of the following could be in order:

Name: GETDATA.BAS

(All BASIC programs have the .BAS filename extension.)

```
10 REM Program to assign an environment variable
20 LINE INPUT "Variable data:",VD$
30 VD$ = "DATA = " + VD$
40 ENVIRON(VD$)
50 SYSTEM
```

This BASIC program asks for a string of text (20). Then it creates the string "DATA = " plus whatever text you entered (30). If you typed in My Name, the string created in line 30 would be "DATA = My Name". Line 40 uses ENVIRON to pass the variable DATA and the string you entered to the environment table. Line 50 exits BASIC and returns to DOS.

To incorporate this BASIC program into your batch files, add the line:

```
BASICA GETDATA
```

That's the name of the BASIC language interpreter, BASICA, followed by the name of the BASIC program you want to run. Note that other, non-IBM versions of BASIC go by different names: GWBASIC, QBASIC, and a whole line of *.BASICs depending on your version of DOS.

Because the BASIC program returns to DOS (line 50 above), this line would execute just like any other program in a batch file—with the added advantage of assigning an environment variable.

A possible solution

As I pointed out earlier, I never could get ENVIRON or ENVIRON$ to work with my IBM PC. But still, I have batch files where it would be nice to include some method of assigning environment variables. BASIC provided a solution.

One of the most frustrating things when dealing with BATCH files is not being able to accept input from the keyboard. (Pretend for a moment that the ANSWER utility doesn't exist.) But what about a BASIC solution?

The solution works like this: the problem is to get input from the user and assign that input to an environment variable, NAME. To do this we'll go through three steps:

1. Run a batch file that needs the data for NAME.
2. Run a BASIC program that gets the input, then creates a second batch file to SET the value of NAME.
3. Call the second batch file that sets the NAME variable, then return to the first batch file.

This is tricky, so pay close attention.

First, we write a batch file that needs the input. The input will be handled jointly by BASIC and the second batch file, SETVAR.BAT. The first batch file is shown in FIG. 12-1.

12-1 This is the first half of a dual-program batch file.

Name: READNAME.BAT

```
1: @ECHO OFF
2: REM This batch file will read your name
3: ECHO Just like magic, this batch file knows who you are!
4: REM Clear old NAME variable...
5: SET NAME=
6: BASICA SETVAR
7: CALL SETVAR
8: ECHO Pleased to meet you, %NAME%
```

The batch file in FIG. 12-1 is straightforward, with a few ECHOes and REMs tossed in to let us and the user know what's going on. The secret tricky part is in lines 6 and 7. Line 6 runs the BASIC program interpreter, BASICA, and runs the BASIC program SETVAR. After BASIC is done, control returns to DOS and, in line 7, the batch file SETVAR is called.

Figure 12-2 is a listing of the BASIC language program SETVAR.BAS. This program actually creates the batch file program, SETVAR.BAT (it writes it out to disk).

To type in the program, enter BASIC by typing BASICA at the DOS command prompt. Remember to type in the line numbers and carefully watch your work. Do not run the program until you've saved it to disk! To save the file type:

    SAVE "SETVAR.BAS"

and press ENTER. To run the program, type RUN. This program automati-

12-2 This program creates a batch file.

Name: SETVAR.BAS

```
100 REM BASIC program to build a call-able batch file
110 REM disable Control-C and Control-Break for no interrupts
120 KEY 15,CHR$(4)+CHR$(46) 'CONTROL-C
130 KEY 16,CHR$(4)+CHR$(70) 'CONTROL-BREAK
140 ON KEY (15) GOSUB 240: KEY (15) ON
150 ON KEY (16) GOSUB 240: KEY (16) ON
160 REM ask for input
170 LINE INPUT "Enter your name: ";N$
180 OPEN "SETVAR.BAT" FOR OUTPUT AS 1
190      PRINT #1,"@ECHO OFF"
200      PRINT #1,"REM BASIC-created batch file"
210      PRINT #1,"SET NAME=";N$
220 CLOSE 1
230 SYSTEM
240 RETURN 230
```

cally returns to DOS. Otherwise, to manually return to DOS, type the BASIC command "SYSTEM".

Lines 120 through 150 disable CTRL–C and CTRL–BREAK. This is necessary because if the user pressed them while the BASIC program was running control would return to BASIC, not DOS. Here, if either of these two keys are pressed, they execute the subroutine at line 240. Line 240 returns the user to line 230, which dumps them back into DOS. This way the program cannot ever exit to BASIC.

Line 170 asks for input from the user and stores the input in the BASIC variable N$ (pronounced N-string). Next comes the tricky part.

Lines 180 through 220 create the batch file program SETVAR.BAT. (Only a twisted genius would think of creating a batch file for the sole purpose of assigning an environment variable. No—it wasn't me.)

Line 180 "opens" SETVAR.BAT for output. The "output" mode erases any file already called SETVAR.BAT, so we know we won't be appending or messing with any file already on disk. The next three lines create the contents of SETVAR.BAT.

Line 190 writes the first line of SETVAR.BAT using the PRINT statement. As usual, the first line is your typical "@ECHO OFF" statement.

Line 200 writes a REM statement. This is rather useless, but it does let you know where the batch file came from.

Line 210 is the key. It writes a line in the batch file that contains "SET NAME=" and then N$, which is whatever string you typed in line 170. The command line is then created just as it would be in any other batch file, but in this instance, it's *customized*!

Line 220 CLOSEs the batch file, writing it out to disk, and line 230 returns to DOS.

Now that BASIC is done, the next line in the batch file (READNAME .BAT) is executed, line 7:

```
7: CALL SETVAR
```

The newly created batch file SETVAR is called. SETVAR looks something like this:

```
1: @ECHO OFF
2: REM BASIC-created batch file
3: SET NAME = winston mcgillicutty
```

BASIC created this batch file. The user typed in "winston mcgillicutty" and BASIC created a batch file incorporating that string. After SETVAR runs, "NAME = winston mcgillicutty" is in the environment table. Control returns to READNAME.BAT (the original batch file) and the following is ECHOed on the display:

```
Pleased to meet you, winston mcgillicutty
```

BASIC can be used in a variety of ways like this, creating and writing custom batch files that take advantage of the SET statement. There's only one warning (which was stated earlier): just make sure you don't get carried away.

Also, you should know that when you enter BASIC to run a BASIC program, such as:

```
BASICA SETVAR
```

the BASIC interpreter will first clear the screen. Keep this in mind if there's a message you want the user to read before the BASIC program runs. You may want to add a PAUSE statement before a line such as that above.

Writing .COM programs with BASIC

Aside from supplementing batch file programs, BASIC can be used to create utility programs. These aren't BASIC programs, but .COM programs that are originally written in assembly language. BASIC is used in this case as a catalyst, a tool by which you can transform the raw data of the .COM program into a .COM file on disk.

This technique is really far removed from batch file programming. Yet, quite a few of the magazines use it to allow everyone to duplicate their utilities.

For an example, I'm using the GREET.COM utility mentioned earlier. GREET.COM simply displays a friendly message followed by any optional data on the command line. It was originally written in assembly language. However, using BASIC we can recreate the program. This works sort of like Dr. Frankenstein creating his monster from bits and pieces of dead people (sort of).

By the way, no .COM program or utility starts out this way. This technique simply makes those programs and utilities available to anyone who wants to type them in using BASIC.

The technique works like this: first the .COM program is written and debugged. Then its contents, the individual bytes that make up the machine language instructions, are "dumped" in hexadecimal format. These bytes are then placed in BASIC language DATA statements.

The BASIC program then opens a .COM file on disk (similar to what was done with SETVAR earlier). The bytes are read from the DATA statement and then written to the .COM file on disk. When the last byte is ready, the .COM file is CLOSEd and the BASIC program ends.

This technique allows anyone with a BASIC interpreter to write the program, copying down all the DATA bytes, then run that program to create the .COM program.

The following is a BASIC program that creates the GREET.COM utility. It employs a checksum method to determine that all the DATA values that the user enters are the same as printed in FIG. 12-3. Remember to type in the program exactly as listed, including line numbers. To save the program, type:

SAVE "GREET.BAS"

and press ENTER. To return to DOS, type SYSTEM.

12-3 This BASIC program creates the GREET.COM utility.

Name: GREET.BAS

```
100 REM A BASIC program to build GREET.COM
110 CLS
120 PRINT "Building GREET.COM"
130 PRINT"(C) Copyright 1988, TAB Books"
140 DEFINT V,C
150 C=0
160 OPEN "R",#1,"GREET.COM",1
170    FIELD #1,1 AS VALUE$
180    FOR X=1 TO 117
190       READ A$
200       V = VAL("&H"+A$)
210       C=C+V: LOCATE 3,1: PRINT "Checksum =";C
220       LSET VALUE$ = MKI$(V)
230       PUT #1
240    NEXT X
250    IF C=11382 THEN PRINT "Checksums match--file okay!":
       GOTO 270
260    PRINT "Bad checksum--check your DATA statements!"
270 CLOSE
280 DATA EB, 27, 90, 47, 6F, 6F, 64, 20
285 DATA 24, 4D, 6F, 72, 6E, 69, 6E, 67
290 DATA 2C, 24, 45, 76, 65, 6E, 69, 6E
295 DATA 67, 2C, 24, 41, 66, 74, 65, 72
300 DATA 6E, 6F, 6F, 6E, 2C, 24, 0D, 0A
305 DATA 24, BA, 03, 01, B4, 09, CD, 21
310 DATA B4, 2C, CD, 21, 80, FD, 0C, 73
315 DATA 06, BA, 09, 01, EB, 0F, 90, 80
320 DATA FD, 11, 73, 06, BA, 1B, 01, EB
325 DATA 04, 90, BA, 12, 01, B4, 09, CD
330 DATA 21, A0, 80, 00, 3C, 00, 74, 11
335 DATA 98, 8B, C8, BB, 81, 00, 8A, 07
340 DATA 8A, D0, B4, 02, CD, 21, 43, E2
345 DATA F5, BA, 26, 01, B4, 09, CD, 21
350 DATA B8, 00, 4C, CD, 21
```

Be extra careful typing in the DATA statements (280 through 350). The program will let you know if you've made a mistake by displaying the "Bad checksum" message. If that happens, double-check the values you typed in.

Most of the details of this program tend more toward a BASIC language tutorial rather than anything to do with batch files. Briefly, lines 160 through 270 are responsible for creating the file. The FOR-NEXT loop between lines 180 and 240 uses the READ statement to read in the values from the DATA statements. Line 210 calculates and displays the checksum value, and lines 220 and 230 write the value to disk.

To run the program, type RUN. You'll see a numeric display as the program builds its checksum. When the program is done, it writes GREET .COM out to disk. When you see the BASIC "Ok" prompt, type SYSTEM to return to DOS. Now you can test your GREET.COM utility.

Batch files and DEBUG

DEBUG can be a useful tool. But like all useful tools, it can also be a deadly weapon. Use it cautiously.

DEBUG has many faces. It can be a memory peeker, a disk peeker, a program peeker, a mini-assembler, a debugger, a tracer, and a million other things.

The problem with DEBUG is that it's cryptic in its command structure and that scares a lot of people away from using it. And, of course, it has the ability to really muck up your hard drive. That, too, will scare some people away.

In this section you're going to see how DEBUG can be used to write programs. The first example is another self-creating program, similar to the BASIC program SETVAR.BAT. The second example shows how to use DEBUG to write a simple version of the READKEY.COM program discussed in the previous chapter.

Finally, you'll see how DEBUG can be used to "patch" programs, and how batch files can be used to remove some of the deadliness of some DOS commands.

DEBUG as assembler

Like BASIC, DEBUG can be used to write programs. In this instance, the programs can be written using a mini-assembler built into DEBUG. This assembler is quite limited, yet for quick-and-dirty purposes—especially batch files—it can come in quite handy.

Some users' first encounter with DEBUG is with their hard drive. Some hard drives need to have a low-level format performed on them. To do this, you need to access the hard drive's ROM which is located on its controller card. DEBUG allows you to access that ROM and run the low-level formatting code that's written in the controller card's BIOS.

The controller card's BIOS is located in memory segment C800 (hexadecimal). This is true for all PC/XT compatible hard drives. Most Western Digital hard drive controllers have their low-level formatting routine located at offset 5 within memory segment C800. Other hard drive controllers might use a different location, CCC (hex) also being popular.

You enter DEBUG by typing DEBUG at the DOS command prompt:

```
C> DEBUG
```

The hyphen is DEBUG's prompt. Here you can examine memory, load programs, examine raw data on disk, and disassemble or assemble programs. The command to perform a low-level disk format (the Western Digital version) is as follows (please don't type this in):

```
-GC800:5
```

This reads Go memory segment C800 and start executing the machine code instructions at offset 5. You can optionally specify an equal sign after the G:

```
-G=C800:5
```

Be careful not to try this command on your computer's hard drive: it will perform a low-level format and erase your disk's data.

If you want to goof around in DEBUG, then enter the following for kicks. Type this at the hyphen prompt:

```
FB800:0 L2000 21 CE
```

Press ENTER. If nothing happens, type FB000 instead of FB800 above. Exciting, isn't it?

Press Q to exit DEBUG and get back to DOS.

Booting examples

A better demonstration for using DEBUG is a small batch file I picked up off a national computer network. This batch file works similarly to the BASIC program SETVAR in that it creates a second program and then runs that program. In this instance, it's a batch file that creates an assembly program using DEBUG.

If you recall from the first part of chapter 2, the Intel 8088 microprocessor starts its day by executing the instruction at memory segment FFFF (hex), offset 0. Using a technique similar to the low-level disk format, a batch file can be written that will execute that instruction, which will reset your computer. See RESET.BAT in FIG. 12-4.

Before running RESET.BAT, type it in and take a look at it. The first instruction (1) branches to the :BEGIN label (9). Here the batch file performs a sort of cannibalization, using itself to create the assembly language pro-

12-4   This batch file will reset your PC.

Name: RESET.BAT

```
 1: GOTO BEGIN
 2:
 3: RCS
 4: FFFF
 5: RIP
 6: 0000
 7: G
 8:
 9: :BEGIN
10: DEBUG < RESET.BAT
```

gram through I/O redirection. Line 10 uses that data from the batch file as input for DEBUG. (Be sure to include a complete pathname before RESET .BAT or DEBUG, unless they're already on the PATH.)

With I/O redirection, DEBUG will attempt to interpret the batch file as DEBUG instructions. Line one will be meaningless to debug, so it will produce an error message. The second line is blank, and will provide the ENTER character needed to continue DEBUG.

Lines 3 through 7 provide the code that will reset the computer.

Line 3 resets the code segment register, and line 4 supplies the memory segment address, FFFF (hex).

Line 5 sets the instruction pointer, and line six supplies the instruction pointer's address, the offset from memory segment FFFF (hex) where our "program" will execute.

Line 7 is the "G" that sets everything in motion . . . and the system reboots.

"Code segment register," "Memory segment address," "Instruction pointer," "Memory offset." These terms are not required to know batch file programming. If you'd like to learn more about them, you can try understanding DEBUG by using the DOS reference manual, or refer to the book list in the introduction.

If you haven't tried it already, run the RESET program to make sure it works. Because ECHO is never turned off, you'll see the batch file as it runs—briefly, because the system will reset before you know it.

The only problem with RESET.BAT is that it's a "hard" reset. The reset behaves similarly to (but not exactly the same as) a cold boot; your PC will start all over again with a memory test and system check. This is time-consuming.

To avoid the memory test and system check, you can create and run a second batch file program, REBOOT.BAT, which is shown in FIG. 12-5.

Here, I've modified RESET.BAT, adding an extra DEBUG command at line 3. The E command changes the contents of the two bytes at memory location 40:72. When these bytes equal 1234 hexadecimal (which must be entered as 34 12), the computer will skip the memory test when it reboots. The end result is still a reset, but it's faster.

12-5 REBOOT.BAT resets your PC faster than RESET.BAT.

Name: `REBOOT.BAT`

```
 1: GOTO BEGIN
 2:
 3: e 40:72 43 12
 4: RCS
 5: FFFF
 6: RIP
 7: 0000
 8: G
 9:
10: :BEGIN
11: DEBUG < REBOOT.BAT
```

Creating RKEY

Besides using a batch file to execute a program via DEBUG, you can use DEBUG to write useful utilities. The following is the assembly language source code for a RKEY.COM program. This utility is similar to READKEY .COM that comes on the supplemental programs diskette. The difference is that this RKEY.COM accepts any key press and then translates that key press into an ERRORLEVEL value equal to the key's ASCII code value.

Name: RKEY.ASM

(You don't need to type this in)

```
mov ah,1       ;read/wait for key press
int 21h        ;DOS function call
mov ah,4Ch     ;Exit to DOS
int 21h        ;DOS function call
```

The first duty of this program is to read the keyboard. DOS function call number one waits for a character from the keyboard (actually, from the standard input device). That key's ASCII code value will be returned in register AL.

DOS function 4C (hex) is used to return to DOS with an ERRORLEVEL code value. The code value is in register AL. The previous function puts the code value of the key press in the AL register for us so we simply return to DOS with the ERRORLEVEL intact.

There are two ways to create this program. The first is to write it in DEBUG and then save it to disk. The second is to write a batch file program that does the same thing.

To compose the program using DEBUG, enter DEBUG and type the A command, directing DEBUG to go into the mini-assembler mode:

```
C> DEBUG
-A
234D:0100
```

The number 234D might not appear on your screen, but some other four-digit hex number will. This is the memory segment in which you're writing your program. The other four numbers are an offset within the segment. All programs written in DEBUG start at offset 100 (hex). Incidentally, all numbers in DEBUG are in hex, base 16, notation.

Type the rest of the commands as follows:

```
234D:0100 MOV AH,1
234D:0102 INT 21
234D:0104 MOV AH,4C
234D:0106 INT 21
234D:0108 ^C
```

(Press CTRL–C on the last line to stop input.)

You've now entered four lines of assembly language code. To save this code to disk, you'll first need to tell the assembler how many bytes to write. The code above is eight bytes long. To tell the assembler this you need to modify the CX register. Type the following:

```
-RCX
```

DEBUG responds by displaying the current value of the CX register and a colon prompt. Enter the new value for CX at the colon prompt:

```
CX 0000
:8
```

Type 8 and press ENTER.

Next you need to give the file a name. So as not to confuse it with the original READKEY (which might be on your disk), name it RKEY. Type:

```
-N RKEY.COM
```

Now you can use the W command to write the file to disk:

```
-W
Writing 0008 bytes
```

DEBUG responds by telling you it's written eight bytes to disk. Press Q to leave DEBUG:

```
-Q

C>
```

Now that you're back in DOS you can try out your new RKEY command. You can type RKEY on the command line, in which case DOS will wait for you to press a key, then redisplay the command prompt. (Who ever knew this could be so simple?)

Better still, type in the batch file program in FIG. 12-6 to test RKEY. This program uses RKEY (5) to read in a character from the keyboard. That character's ASCII code value is then compared with the ASCII code values of "1" and "2". The program uses IF-ERRORLEVEL tests to determine whether the key was in range, and if so it displays a message and then quits. Other-

12-6 This program uses RKEY to read in a character from the keyboard.

Name: RANGE.BAT

```
 1: @ECHO OFF
 2: REM An example of RKEY
 3: :START
 4: ECHO Type a 1 or a 2
 5: RKEY
 6: IF ERRORLEVEL 51 GOTO RANGE
 7: IF ERRORLEVEL 50 GOTO TWO
 8: IF ERRORLEVEL 49 GOTO ONE
 9: :RANGE
10: ECHO --That number is out of range
11: GOTO START
12: :ONE
13: ECHO --You typed the number 1!
14: GOTO END
15: :TWO
16: ECHO --You typed the number 2!
17: :END
```

wise, an "out of range" message is displayed (10) and the program loops through the same routines over again (3 through 9).

Figure 12-7 shows a batch file program that also creates RKEY. If you were a little reluctant to create the batch file using DEBUG, then MAKERKEY.BAT does the same thing—but safely. This program borrows some technique from RESET.BAT. The difference is that this program will return you to DOS rather than reset your computer. Also, once completed, you'll have the RKEY.COM program on disk.

12-7 This batch file creates RKEY.

Name: MAKERKEY.BAT

```
 1: GOTO BEGIN
 2:
 3: A
 4: MOV AH,1
 5: INT 21
 6: MOV AH,4C
 7: INT 21
 8:
 9: RCX
10: 8
11: N RKEY.COM
12: W
13: Q
14:
15: :BEGIN
16: DEBUG < MAKERKEY.BAT
```

When you run MAKERKEY.BAT, your screen will show output that looks something like FIG. 12-8.

12-8 This is a test run of MAKERKEY.BAT.

```
C> MAKERKEY

C> GOTO :BEGIN

C> :BEGIN

C> DEBUG < MAKERKEY.BAT
-GOTO BEGIN
   ^ Error
-
-A
234D:0100 MOV AH,1
234D:0102 INT 21
234D:0104 MOV AH,4C
234D:0106 INT 21
234D:0108
-RCX
CX 0000
:8
-N RKEY.COM
-W
Writing 0008 bytes
-Q

C>
```

Patching

Another thing you can do with DEBUG is to patch programs. That is, you load the programs into DEBUG and then modify them. Needless to say, this is a very dangerous thing to do. Some users will go so far as to patch their COMMAND.COM file, replacing the names of DOS commands with their own commands.

Usually what happens when you patch a program using DEBUG is that it won't run. Worse, sometimes it will crash your system. (Now you can imagine why it would be folly to "patch" COMMAND.COM.)

So why do it? One reason is for security. For example, using DEBUG, you can load COMMAND.COM into memory and search for the DEL command (an internal command). You can then manually rename DEL to something odd, like T-Z. The T-Z command now replaces DEL, but the users of that computer don't know that offhand. Instead they continue to type DEL to erase files. The difference? A batch file named DEL has taken over the internal DEL command's place. The DEL.BAT file might look like this:

```
1: @ECHO OFF
2: REM DEL batch file, replaces DEL command
3: IF %1NOTHING=NOTHING GOTO ERROR
4: COPY %1 C:\JUNK > NUL
5: ECHO %1 Files deleted
6: GOTO END
```

```
7: ERROR
8: ECHO No filename(s) given
9: :END
```

This batch file command doesn't delete anything. Instead, it copies all the files that DEL would erase to a \JUNK directory on drive C. This way, the system manager could walk by at another time, examine the files, and then delete them using T-Z. This also saves a lot of heartache for those times when users delete files and then want them back. In this case, the system manager could simply copy the "deleted" files back from the \JUNK directory.

Internal commands need to be patched by using DEBUG with COMMAND.COM. However, external commands can be fixed simply by renaming them.

As an example, consider FORMAT. You can rename FORMAT.COM to something no one would ever type: ZGBLQZFM.COM. Then, somewhere else on the disk, have a FORMAT.BAT file that actually does the formatting job, but checks to see if drive C or some other important drive is about to be formatted. If so, an error message could be displayed, or the program might just refuse to format. (Or it could beep very loudly and let everyone else in the office know that someone just made a dumb mistake.)

But overall, patching programs is a task too risky to undertake, even at this level. It's just too easy to botch things up. If you do take a stab at it, remember to experiment first with the file on the floppy drive system. Then, if everything checks out, copy the file to your hard drive. I'm not offering any guarantees and the publisher of this book, myself, and your computer store cannot be held accountable for anything that might happen because of your patching.

Summary

This chapter continues the theme of going beyond batch files, but this time concentrating on writing your own utilities and batch file extensions using BASIC and DEBUG, two programs that come with DOS.

BASIC can be used to write quick routines—even to write batch files themselves. You can also interact with BASIC programs by including the name of your BASIC interpreter followed by the BASIC program's name in your batch file. This is a handy way to augment your batch files.

DEBUG can be used for many purposes. For example, you can use I/O redirection with DEBUG to access internal computer routines, such as those that reset the PC. DEBUG can also be used to write small utility programs that supplement batch files. But be careful with DEBUG; like any good tool, if used sloppily, it can cause some damage.

13
EBLplus

Out there in computer entrepreneur land are lots of folks writing batch file extenders. These programs add power to batch files, augment their features, and pull a whole barrel full of fancy tricks. Two of them covered in the first edition of this book were Beyond*Bat and EBL. Beyond*Bat has, sadly, been discontinued. But EBL is still around and thriving for us to enjoy.

EBL is Frank Canova's Extended Batch Language, a batch file enhancer that's now in its "plus" incarnation. EBLplus offers a complete extension to the DOS batch file language, plus it allows DOS batch file commands to be intermingled with EBLplus commands.

EBLplus offers an advanced programming language, user input, advanced string handling, arithmetic operations, comparisons, advanced control structures, tracing facilities, error trapping, and it's not that hard to get used to. In fact, it's quite similar to the BASIC programming language and, although I'm not familiar with it, the manual states that it's similar to the EXEC2 language that comes on a VM/370 computer.

Behind the scenes—what you get

Programs augmenting the way batch files work can operate in two manners:

- Memory-resident
- Interpreted.

(This doesn't apply only to EBL, but to any batch file enhancing language.)

A memory-resident batch file enhancement program works like any other memory-resident program: it loads itself into memory and then waits until it's needed. In the case of a batch file modification program, the memory-resident portion monitors the command line, waiting for a batch file to be interpreted. When a batch file is run, the program takes over, adding its power to the batch file commands executed.

An interpreted batch file enhancement program must be called before the batch file is run. Typically, the name of the program is listed, followed by the name of the batch file to be run (sort of like running the BASIC interpreter from the previous chapter). The interpreter then reads in the batch file commands and executes them one by one.

Memory-resident batch file enhancers have the advantage of always being in memory. Because they're always there, any batch file you run at any time will automatically be executed without having to type an extra command. Interpreted batch file enhancers have the advantage of not taking up the memory required by the memory-resident programs. Fortunately, EBLplus lets you have it both ways.

The main program behind EBLplus is BAT.COM. BAT.COM acts as an interpreter. You specify EBLplus commands after typing BAT to start a line in a batch file. This way, you can mix EBLplus's extended batch file commands with regular DOS batch file commands in the same program.

There are two ways to run an EBLplus batch file. The first is to start each line of the batch file with BAT, as follows:

```
BAT * This is an EBLplus batch file
BAT * These lines are comments
BAT READ What is your name:> %0
BAT TYPE Howdy, %0
```

"BAT" essentially runs the BAT.COM program (so make sure BAT.COM is on your path). BAT then interprets the information that follows it. In this example, you will be prompted for your name and that information will be saved in the variable %0. The next line uses the TYPE command (EBLplus's version—not the DOS TYPE command) to display "Howdy," followed by your name. For example:

```
What is your name: HAVEN
Howdy, HAVEN
```

The second method of running an EBLplus program is to make BAT.COM permanent by specifying the /P switch. This avoids the necessity of starting each line with the word "BAT":

```
@BAT /P * This is an EBLplus batch file
* These lines are comments
READ What is your name:> %0
TYPE Howdy, %0
```

BAT /P tells EBLplus to make the BAT.COM interpreter resident. This way the rest of the batch file can contain EBLplus commands with the word BAT. You'll also note that the initial BAT is prefixed by an @ (at) sign. This suppresses the EBLplus commands from being displayed. (Normally, EBLplus is always in ECHO OFF mode, however the first line is still displayed—unless it starts with an @.)

To mix DOS batch file commands with EBLplus's commands, you have two choices. If you're using EBLplus by starting each line with "BAT" then simply specify a DOS command (don't start the line with BAT):

```
BAT * This is an EBLplus comment
BAT TYPE Here's your directory of drive C:
DIR C:
```

In this example, the first two lines are interpreted by EBLplus. The third is simply a DOS command.

If you're using the /P switch to make BAT permanent, you'll need to use the LEAVE command to exit EBLplus and return to the normal DOS batch file mode:

```
BAT /P * This is an EBLplus comment
TYPE Here's your directory of drive C:
LEAVE
DIR C:
```

The LEAVE command in the third line suspends EBLplus and allows the rest of the file to be interpreted using DOS's batch file interpreter. To continue with EBLplus, simply start it up again on a later line using BAT or BAT /P.

A second command, SHELL, can be used to issue only one DOS command. For example:

```
BAT /P * This is an EBLplus comment
TYPE Here's your directory of drive C:
SHELL DIR C:
* We're still in EBLplus
```

Only line 3 is a DOS command, issued via the EBLplus SHELL command. EBLplus picks up immediately after line 3 with another comment.

EBLplus comes on a diskette full of programs and examples. The main program is BAT.COM. Additional external functions are available in two library files, BATFUNC1.COM and BATFUNC2.COM. There is also a floating point (mathematical) function library called BATMATH3.COM, and if you have an 8087 math co-processor, you can even use BMATH87.COM.

The demos on the diskette are the most impressive. BATDEMO.BAT will be the first one you probably will run. It will amaze you that all the functions and fancy displays are available via a batch file language. To amaze yourself even further, TYPE the batch file on the screen to see how easy it looks.

The only drawback to picking up EBLplus (either from an electronic BBS or from a user group's software library) is that there is no on-line documentation. Typing BAT on the command line by itself lists the commands and functions, but doesn't explain what any of them do. So in order to be fully proficient at EBLplus, you'll need to pick up the manual. For that, you must pay the shareware fee of $79, plus $3 shipping. (*See* the end of this chapter for more information.)

An EBLplus example

As an example, I'll use the RANGE.BAT program, demonstrated in chapter 12 with RKEY.

RANGE.BAT asks the user to type either a 1 or 2 and then lets the user know which key they typed. It's important to note that even a program as simple as this isn't possible using the native DOS batch file language. The RKEY program must be written to allow DOS to be interactive with a user (see FIG. 13-1).

13-1 Here's RANGE.BAT again!

Name: RANGE.BAT

```
 1: @ECHO OFF
 2: REM An example of RKEY
 3: :START
 4: ECHO Type a 1 or a 2
 5: RKEY
 6: IF ERRORLEVEL 51 GOTO RANGE
 7: IF ERRORLEVEL 50 GOTO TWO
 8: IF ERRORLEVEL 49 GOTO ONE
 9: :RANGE
10: ECHO --That number is out of range
11: GOTO START
12: :ONE
13: ECHO --You typed the number 1!
14: GOTO END
15: :TWO
16: ECHO --You typed the number 2!
17: :END
```

Figure 13-2 is the EBLplus version of a batch file that does essentially the same thing. Line 1 loads EBLplus and makes it permanent. The @ (at) sign is used to suppress the command from being echoed to the screen. Line 2 is the START label. Note that labels in EBLplus begin with a hyphen.

In line 3, the user is asked to input either a 1 or 2 and their input is saved in the variable %0. The two IF statements in lines 4 and 5 compare the input to the numbers 1 and 2. If there is a match, execution branches to the labels ONE or TWO, respectively. If not, line 6 displays the message "That number is out of range," and in line 7 execution branches back to the START label.

Line 8 contains the label ONE and an EBLplus command. EBLplus allows you to place commands after a label (a good idea that DOS should borrow). If the user presses the "1" key, execution will branch to line 8 and then they'll be returned to DOS via the EXIT command in line 9.

If the user presses the "2" key, execution branches to the label at line 10, and the message "You typed the number 2!" is displayed. This program exe-

13-2 This is the EBLplus version of RANGE.BAT

Name: RANGEBL.BAT

```
 1: @BAT /P * EBLplus--make BAT permanent
 2: -START
 3: READ Type a 1 or a 2 %0
 4: IF %0 = 1 THEN GOTO -ONE
 5: IF %0 = 2 THEN GOTO -TWO
 6: TYPE That number is out of range
 7: GOTO -START
 8: -ONE TYPE You typed the number 1!
 9: EXIT
10: -TWO TYPE You typed the number 2!
```

cutes its commands flawlessly, and with a little more logic than DOS batch files.

EBLplus commands and functions

Table 13-1 is a brief list of EBLplus's commands and functions. In addition to these commands, the following math functions can be performed:

+   Addition
—   Subtraction
*   Multiplication
/   Division
\$ Substring (return location of one string within another)
&   Concatenation (connect two strings together)

EBLplus makes quite extensive use of variables. Aside from the environment and replaceable parameter variables (%0 through %9), EBLplus gives you 21 others, six predefined and 15 global variables.

The six predefined variables are as follows:

%Q   "K" if characters are coming from the keyboard, or "S" if they are coming from EBL's keyboard stack.
%R   A return code in hexadecimal (base 16).
%S   The space character.
%V   The default disk drive.
%%   The percent character.
%(The left paren (otherwise, EBL would interpret a left paren as the beginning of an equation).

The 15 global variables are represented by the letters A through O. These variables can be assigned and used by your EBLplus batch files as you see fit.

EBLplus comes with several external function libraries:

BATFUNC1.COM   Common external functions
BATFUNC2.COM   Special external functions
BATMATH3.COM   Floating point functions

Table 13-1

Command	What it does . . .
*	Identifies a line as a comment (like REM).
_	Identifies a label (like :).
BEEP	Beeps the speaker (like ECHO ^G would)
BEGSTACK	Stuffs text (characters) into a keyboard stack, sort of a forced method of redirected input. An "END" statement ends the series of characters that are stuffed into the keyboard stack.
BEGTYPE	Marks the beginning of a series of strings that will be displayed on the screen. An "END" statement ends the series.
CALL	Calls a subroutine within the batch file. CALL can optionally pass parameters to the subroutine.
COLOR	Changes the color of the text on computers equipped with a color monitor.
ELSE	Used with a single or nested IF statements to make decisions.
EXIT	Leaves the batch file and returns to DOS.
GOTO	Branches batch file execution to a specific label.
IF	Used to make decisions based on evaluations. EBL's IF command allows you to compare variables using < (less than), = (equal to— case insensitive), = = (equal to, case sensitive), > (greater than), and, < > (not equal to).
INKEY	Reads a single character from the keyboard
LEAVE	Suspends execution of EBL commands and returns batch file control to DOS. (It doesn't exit to DOS).
READ	Reads input from the user into one or more variables. Both READ and INKEY can have optional prompting strings.
READSCRN	Reads input directly from the screen. Using this command, your program can read text strings displayed by other programs and then act on them accordingly.
RETURN	Returns control from a subroutine back to the line following the previous CALL command.
SHELL	Returns to DOS to execute one command. After a SHELL, batch file control returns to EBL.
SKIP	Jumps forward a number of lines in the batch file. SKIP is like GOTO, but it skips a number of lines rather than branching to a specific label.
STACK	Stuffs characters into a keyboard stack, almost like I/O redirection.
STATEOF	Searches disks and directories to see if a specific file exists.
TYPE	Displays a text string on the screen.

BATALLF.COM	All of the above functions
BMATH87.COM	Co-processor math functions

You add these functions to EBLplus's basic functions by specifying one or a combination of the previously mentioned programs in your AUTOEXEC.BAT file. Or, you can specify each of them individually before trying them out. (Unless the program has been run, its external functions will not be available to EBLplus.)

Table 13-2

BATFUNC1 command	What it does ...
CENTER	Centers a string of characters.
CHDIR	Changes directories or drives.
DATE	Returns the current date.
GETDIR	Returns a string giving the name of the current subdirectory.
KEYPRESSED	Returns a "T" or "F" (true or false) depending on if a key has been pressed.
LEFT	Returns a specific number of characters from the left side of a string.
LOCATE	Positions the cursor on the display.
LOWER	Converts a string of characters to lowercase.
RIGHT	Returns a specific number of characters from the right side of a string.
STRIP	Removes characters from either side of a string.
TIME	Returns the current time.
UPPER	Converts a string of characters to uppercase.
WHATFUNC	Identifies which of EBL's external function packages have been loaded.

Table 13-3

BATFUNC2 command	What it does ...
C2H	Converts characters to hexadecimal values.
D2H	Converts decimal values to hexadecimal values.
H2C	Converts hexadecimal values into character strings.
H2D	Converts hexadecimal values into decimal values.
INT86	Executes an 8086 INT instruction.
PEEK	Reads a byte value from a memory location.
POKE	Puts a byte value at a specific memory location.
REBOOT	Resets the computer.
WHATFUNC	Identifies which of EBL's external function packages have been loaded.

Tables 13-2, 13-3, and 13-4 list the routines available in each of the external function libraries.

Ordering information

EBLplus is available through the Seaware Corporation in Florida. Because of the popularity of EBLplus, however, you can probably download it from a BBS or order it from a shareware software warehouse (it's on PC-SIG's diskette number 124).

Table 13-4

BATMATH3 BATMATH87 command	What it does . . .
ABS	Returns the absolute value of a number.
FLOAT	Returns a floating point result of a mathematical operation.
FRAC	Returns the fraction value of a number.
INT	Returns the integer value of a number.
WHATFUNC	Identifies which of EBL's external function packages have been loaded.

EBLplus is shareware. That means the software is distributed free of charge. If you use it, you're expected to pay for it. An enticement to this fact is that there is no "on-disk manual" that comes with EBLplus. So you really need to pay Seaware the $79 (plus $3 shipping) to get the manual and start using the product. (The manual is well worth it, by the way.)

EBLplus requires an IBM PC, XT, AT, PS/2 or compatible and DOS Version 2.0 or later.

Seaware Corporation
P.O. Box 1656
Delray Beach, FL 33444
(407) 738-1712

Summary

I personally like to work with EBLplus. The reason is that EBLplus is more batch-file-like than other, similar batch file extenders. If I were in a business situation with many employees, I would probably choose Beyond*Bat for that reason.

But keep in mind a basic precept when using any batch file extender: Unless every PC you use has it, its power is limited. Getting used to something like EBLplus is fun, but because not all PCs in the world have a copy, don't get too comfy.

14

Builder

There are batch file extenders and there are batch file enhancers. But none matches the utter slickness of hyperkinetix's Builder—perhaps the ultimate batch file tool. Without giving too much away too early, what Builder does is to take mild mannered batch files and convert them into real monsters: actual COM or EXE program files you can run on any PC.

This chapter is about Builder, the batch file tool that translates meek batch files into humdinger programs. Builder lets you do this without modifying your original batch files in any way. As an addition, Builder also comes with its own batch file extending language that will make your batch files-cum-programs even more powerful. This is amazing stuff.

How it works, and what you get

In a way Builder is yet another batch file enhancer, just like EBLplus or the old Beyond*Bat. It uses DOS's basic eight batch file commands as is, plus all the DOS commands, utilities, the names of programs just as you would in any batch file. In addition to that, Builder has its own language that extends the power of the batch files. Don't let any of this fool you.

Aside from the extended language, Builder is unlike all the other batch file enhancers. Basically, it leaves your batch files alone. None of them need to be changed or altered. Instead, you use a special conversion utility that comes with Builder. It reads in your batch file, subtly changing a few things, and then it creates a separate .BLD file.

Files with the BLD extension are only an intermediate step, however. DOS cannot run them, but Builder can convert them into COM or EXE files. If you're familiar with the way other compiled programming languages work, then note that the BLD files are considered to be *source* files.

The Builder utility converts them into object files, which are then "linked" into COM or EXE files. (The difference between COM or EXE depends upon the final file's size.)

In addition to converting your BAT files into BLD and then COM files, you can create your own BLD files from scratch. These files can be based on original BAT files, or they can incorporate only the special commands and functions found in Builder's own language. Either way, your end result is a COM file that can run on any PC. (hyperkinetix requires no licensing or distribution fee for passing around COM files created by Builder.)

The beauty of all this is you keep what you had originally, but gain something in the process. The folks at hyperkinetix are aware of batch files' shortcomings. But they didn't mess with batch files themselves. Instead, they use batch files as the basis for a new programming language, one that produces "real" program files. Nothing could make your batch files smarter, more elegant, or faster.

With Builder you get two diskettes full of 25 files, 12 of which are example files. The main files are:

BLD.EXE	The command line Builder compiler
BLDTT.LIB	The Builder library file, used by MLINK when creating a COM or EXE file
BUILDER.EXE	The Builder integrated environment and text editor
BUILDER.HLP	Builder's on-line help files
INSTALL.BLD	The source code for the installation routine
INSTALL.COM	Builder's install program (created from INSTALL .BLD)
MANUAL.TXT	Notes, additions, and corrections for Builder's manual
MLINK.EXE	Builder's command line Linker
READTHIS.TXT	Updated information and instructions
SHOW.EXE	A file to display text files

BLD.EXE is the command line version of Builder. You follow BLD with the name of a .BAT or .BLD file. (If it's a .BAT file, Builder will first convert it to a .BLD file; your original batch files are never modified by Builder.) BLD then converts the commands and functions in the BLD file into an object file, which has the same filename but an .OBJ extension.

The program MLINK.EXE is then run (automatically) to convert the .OBJ file into a COM or EXE file. Normally a COM file is created. However, you can opt for the EXE format.

The command line version is a more traditional way to operate Builder. Instead of using it, however, you should consider Builder's integrated environment.

BUILDER.EXE is a combination compiler/editor. You can create your BLD files right there in its full screen text editor, then press the F9 key and they'll be converted into programs—and optionally run—right on the spot. This integrated environment also allows you to import batch files for immediate conversion. And it's a handy editor.

Remember, Builder makes program files. And as such, it behaves a lot like a real programming language. This is why it has steps such as "compile" and "link." The end result here is a program file—not some half-batch half-specialized type of file that can only be run under certain conditions and in certain environments. You're making real programs, which is why Builder is a little bit more intricate than other batch file enhancers.

Builder examples

Builder is more like a real programming language than any other batch file enhancer. It comes complete with its own commands and functions, none of which are that far above the level of a batch file's commands. The programming language is loosely based on DOS's batch file language, some BASIC, and a wee bit of Pascal (as painful as that might be). It incorporates a lot of batch file logic. But that's where the similarity ends.

On a simple level, you can run all of your batch files through Builder and have each of them converted into COM programs. This is really fun, especially for advanced batch files such as the MOVE or CP examples covered earlier in this book. Suddenly, a typical (though useful) batch file becomes a powerful COM program—a real utility.

Because this conversion of batch files runs rather flawlessly, the following example is shown using Builder's own language, in addition to normal DOS and batch file commands.

In FIG. 14-1 you see the source code for a typical Builder file. Remember, this is only a BLD file—source code. It needs to be compiled via BLD and then linked via MLINK to get the final COM program. (Or, if you're using the BUILDER integrated environment, you press a key and all the steps are taken care of for you.)

14-1   Here is a simple Builder file.
Name: HELLO.BLD

```
1: 'This is a demonstration builder program
2:
3: string name
4:
5: say "Enter your name: ";
6: input name
7: echo
8: say "Pleased to meet you, ";name
```

The source code for HELLO.BLD is typical for most Builder programs. You can gather most of what it's doing from your knowledge of batch files so far. The only tricky stuff is the creation of a "string" variable in line 3.

String variables hold text, and we need a place to hold the input for the INPUT command in line 6. The variable "name" is created in line 3 for that purpose. (String variables hold text, whereas "numeric" variables hold values.)

The SAY command in line 5 displays the prompt "Enter your name:" INPUT in line 6 reads the keyboard, assigning the characters entered to the variable name. The ECHO in line 7 (Builder's ECHO—not DOS's) displays a blank line after input is made at the keyboard. This cleans up the display for the next line, 8, which displays "Pleased to meet you," followed by the name entered.

This is an uncomplicated example, but it shows two things: The simplicity of Builder's commands, and how closely the language resembles batch files. Remember, the end result of this is a program file, HELLO .COM. You can run that program on any PC compatible in any country on this planet.

The Builder example in FIG. 14-2 does the same thing as RANGE.BAT, as well as the EBLplus example shown in the previous chapter: a value is input at the keyboard and a message displayed based on the result of that value.

14-2   Here is RANGE.BAT as a Builder language file.

Name: RANGE.BLD

```
 1: REM Here is the Builder version of RANGE.BAT
 2: REM Note that BLD files need no initial ECHO OFF
 3:
 4: :Start
 5:
 6: Say "Type a 1 or a 2: ";
 7: GetKey
 8:
 9: if LastKey == {1} goto One
10: if LastKey == {2} goto Two
11:
12: echo
13: echo That value is out of range!
14: goto Start
15:
16: :Two
17: echo
18: say "You typed number 2"
19: exit
20:
21: :One
22: echo
23: say "You typed number 1"
```

There are a number of ways you could rewrite RANGE.BAT as a Builder file. Easiest of all would be to simply import RANGE.BAT into Builder for a quick-and-dirty conversion. But I tried to create RANGE.BLD with the same flavor as the original without venturing too far into Builder-land. (And there are easier ways to do multiple IF statements in Builder.)

This program makes use of Builder's GetKey and LastKey commands. GetKey reads a key from the keyboard in line 7. The LastKey variable (an internal variable) stores the keystroke's value. It's compared with the keystroke constants {1}, for the 1 key, and {2}, for the 2 key, in lines 9 and 10. Other parts of the program are fairly readable, with ECHO again being used to generate a blank line after input.

But the important thing to realize here is that the end result is not RANGE.BLD. Instead, it's a 5K program file, RANGE.COM. Sure, RANGE .COM is a silly, silly example. But think of the power you could unleash using such a simple language that converts instantly into a program file.

Builder commands

Like most extended batch processors, Builder has a host of commands and functions. In addition to that, Builder also takes advantage of structures and numerous variables. It's almost like a little programming language all by itself (and could be, if there were more math power).

In addition to structures, Builder also incorporates some interesting menu-building commands. Because a lot of batch file programmers write menu systems, Builder's language contains three distinct structure/display commands that build and operate different types of menus for you. Using these commands you can create pull-down menus, bar menus (ala 1-2-3), or pop-up menus anywhere on your display. The menus will even run programs, all as a part of the menu structure.

Table 14-1 contains a list of only a few of Builder's many commands. A complete list comes inside the Builder manual, including examples.

Table 14-1

Name	Description
BEEP	Beeps the speaker
BOX	Draws a box
CALL	Same as batch CALL, but not needed by builder
CASE	Used in the SELECT-END structure
CANCELED	Detects ESC key press vs. no key press
CLOSE	Closes an open file
CLS	Clears the screen, homes the cursor, with optional color change
CURRENTDRIVE	Returns the current drive and a colon
DOSERRORLEVEL	Returns the most recent ERRORLEVEL value
DIREXISTS	Returns a non-zero value if a named subdirectory exists, zero otherwise
DISKFREE	Returns the amount of disk space available
DROPDOWN	Creates a drop down menu/allows you to select items from the menu (could also be considered a control structure)

Table 14-1 Continued.

Name	Description
ECHO	Displays text on the screen
ELSE	Part of an IF-END ELSE-END structure
EOF	Returns zero until the end of a file is reached
EXIT	Quits to DOS with an optional ERRORLEVEL value (return code)
FILE	Creates a file (handle) for use with all the file commands
FILESIZE	Returns a long integer representing the size of a given file
FOR	Same as DOS's FOR, but double quotes are used instead of parenthesis
GETKEY	Reads a key from the keyboard, putting its value into LastKey
GETYN	Waits for a Y or N key press, returning ERRORLEVEL 1 for Y, zero for N
GOTO	Same as DOS's GOTO
GOTOXY	Positions the cursor to a specific X and Y coordinate
IF	The same as DOS's IF, but the strings being compared (with = =) are enclosed in double quotes.
INPUT	Reads a line of text from the keyboard and assigns it to a string
INTEGER	Sets aside space for and creates an integer
INTTOSTR	Converts an integer value into a string of numbers
LASTKEY	Stores the key retrieved by the most recent GetKey command
LENGTH	Returns the length of a string; its size as an integer value
LONGINT	Sets aside space for and creates a long integer
LONGTOSTR	Converts a long integer into a string of numbers
LIGHTBAR	Creates a light bar menu (like in 1-2-3) complete with keystroke search (could also be considered a control structure)
OPEN	Opens a disk file for reading and writing
PAUSE	Same as DOS's PAUSE, but always displays any prompting message listed after PAUSE
POPUP	Creates a pop-up menu at a specific location on the screen (could also be considered a control structure)
PRINTERREADY	Returns a non-zero value if the specified printer port is ready, zero otherwise
READLINE	Reads a line of text from an open file and puts it into a string
REBOOT	Resets the computer
REM	For adding remarks and comments (also the single quote, ', is used)
REWIND	Repositions a file pointer back to the start of a file; used when reading and (re-reading) information from a disk file
ROWCOL	Positions the cursor identical to GOTOXY, but the row value comes first in ROWCOL
RUN	Runs a DOS command as if it were typed at the DOS prompt
SAVEFILE	Saves the contents of an open file
SAY	Displays a text string at an optional X, Y location
SET	Same as DOS's SET, but requires double quotes around the contents strings

Table 14-1 Continued.

Name	Description
SHIFT	Same as DOS's SHIFT
STRING	Sets aside space for and creates a string
STRTONUM	Converts numbers found in a string to an integer or long integer value
TEXT ON	Sets the foreground and background text colors
UNSHIFT	Does the opposite of the SHIFT command, shifting the command lines one notch right instead of left
WHEREX	Returns an integer giving the column in which the cursor is located
WHEREY	Returns an integer giving the row in which the cursor is located
WHILE	Defines the start of a WHILE-END structure. When the integer expression following WHILE is zero, the WHILE-END structure stops repeating
WRITELINE	Writes a line of text to an open file

Ordering information

Unlike EBL, Builder isn't shareware. You can't download it from anywhere and, sad to say, few software stores stock it. You can, however, order it directly from the manufacturer. It retails for just under $150. (Their address is listed below.)

Builder is also discussed extensively in Windcrest's *Enhanced Batch File Programming* book. Not only that, but a demo copy of Builder is available—right in the book itself! While the demo version keeps displaying "demo version" when it runs, buying that book is a great way to get your hands on a hot little piece of software. For batch file mavens, I highly recommend it.

> Builder
> hyperkinetix, inc.
> 666 Baker Street, Suite 405
> Costa Mesa, CA 92626
> (714) 668-9234

Summary

The Builder program operates at two levels: Command line or integrated environment. It converts BAT files into BLD source files without a hitch, or you can add your own Builder-only commands and functions to really make things kick. You then compile and link the result to get your COM file, a program that can be run on any computer that runs DOS.

Builder is perhaps the ultimate way to go beyond batch files. What the folks at hyperkinetix have done is to take batch files from one extreme of the spectrum to the other. You start with a basic BAT file, add some enhancing commands—but nothing beyond the level of most batch file programmers—and then you spit out a program file. Imagine: a real COM file from a BAT file. Ten years ago they would have had you committed.

Part Four

Macros and control languages

This book is about batch file programming, which makes an entire part on macros and control languages seem silly—but, though the title is batch files, the subject is getting the most from your computer. More and more, applications are coming with their own mini-batch processors—call them macros or control languages. Becoming familiar with them is yet another step on mastering the PC. They merge nicely with the batch file concept.

15

All about macros

Here's a term to bandy about at a cocktail party: macro. Try it on a few friends. They'll all nod their head, but don't let them fool you. Few people really know what a macro is, fewer still know what it can do, and only six people know how to write them. There's a lot of power hiding behind that vague computer term; in some cases more power than you can get from batch files.

This chapter is about macros—macros in a general sense. It's not a subject you should skip. Knowing all about DOS and batch files—and all the many interesting utilities—is all well and good, but knowing about macros gives you another edge. In a way, using macros in an application extends your reach. Your control of the computer doesn't end when the batch file launches the application. Instead, using macros you can get inside of the program, control it further, and—generally speaking—macros really make your programs easier to use.

What are macros?

If I were to sum up "macros," I would say that they're handy—they're like a shortcut, a time saver. Before I give you my little song and dance about them, however, let's read what some others have to say about macros.

The following are excerpts from various user manuals on the subject of macros. Some of this is good information, some of it is typical stuff you'd expect to find in a computer manual. (Take all of this lightly, I'll explain everything in detail in just a few paragraphs.):

> "A macro *is a series of keystrokes and special commands (collectively called* macro instructions) *that performs a 1-2-3 task."*
> —The Lotus 1-2-3 "Tutorial" Manual

"Macros expedite your work in a 1-2-3 session. They save time that would otherwise be spent performing simple but repetitive tasks, and they streamline complex procedures."
—The Lotus 1-2-3 Reference Guide

"The Macro feature records keystrokes and plays them back just as they were recorded, much like the redial feature on a telephone."
—The WordPerfect 5.1 Reference

"We really don't need macros. And we don't need cars, either. But few of us would be willing to give up the speed of traveling by car in favor of walking . . . Macros perform at maximum speed without making mistakes. The result? Improved efficiency."
—The AE:Pro (telecommunications) manual

"A macro is a stored series of keystrokes that is activated via the Macro command or by pressing a special key or key combination. Macros make it quick and easy to perform long or repetitious tasks in Magellan."
—The Magellan manual

"The BRIEF macro language gives you the full ability to extend and change the editing environment."
—The BRIEF Macro Language Guide

The introduction to BRIEF's macros is, needless to say, BRIEF. (A popular programmer's editor, BRIEF is big on macros.) The description is still valid—all the above descriptions are valid. But what really is a "macro?"

Macro is short for *macroinstruction*. In English, that means one instruction (or keystroke) in the place of many. Okay, it's an ugly term. If I had my way, we'd all call macros "Helpers," because that's what they are and that's what they do.

In real life a macro would work like this: when the Queen moves her handbag to her right arm, she's bored. Subtle and quick, the one movement is a clue to a much larger set of instructions: "Your highness, they need you back at the palace." One motion sets the whole works into activity, and the Queen is saved from boredom.

Another example would be seeing a beautiful, voluptuous woman walk into the room. You'd elbow your pal and issue the "hubba-hubba" macro. Or you could be a teenager who could replace "I dunno, I mean, no one else is doing anything and Steve and the Gang are already there, but you know what—I don't have any money so we can just sit around and watch people or visit Greg in the shoe store . . ." with the "Let's go to the mall" macro.

Macros have been with PCs almost since day one. They're productivity boosters. And they capitalize on doing what the computer does best: over and over, repetitive, redundancies. The computer can do things a million times over and not complain. If you're using a computer and doing the same thing a million times over, then it's about time you learned a few macros.

Originally macros were used by programmers. There's a lot of redundancy in programming. For example, a programmer may have to write the instructions for "print this on the screen" several dozen times in a program. Rather than do that, they'll create a "PRINTME" or some such macro that contains all of those instructions.

But keep in mind that macros don't shorten computer operations—only the time it takes to type them. When the computer encounters the PRINTME macro, it will *expand* it out into the detailed instructions for printing information on the screen. In this case, the macro is simply a tiny word that represents many. ("That's such an incredibly cool concept," or the "neat-o" macro.)

For the longest time, macros remained in the domain of the computer programmer. After all, they made the programming chore much easier. (Macros were always introduced in programming class the week after you finished your Big Project—when you really could have used macros the most.)

The next time anyone heard of macros were in communications programs. My first, TRS-80 communications program had what they called "function keys." You could assign a series of keystrokes to each function key. Pressing the function key would then play back those keystrokes—like a tape recorder playing back a recording. (This, I still believe, is the true purpose of a function key.)

Macros in other communications programs worked like my TRS-80 function keys, but they operated a bit more like a programming language. They could scan for, or match, certain characters coming down the modem pipe, then automatically send other characters. (The wait-for and send macros.) This way you could construct a macro, or system of macros, to automatically log you on each time you called an on-line computer system.

Later macro developments added such things as decision (IF-THEN) making, file access, and a whole slew of interesting and varied commands. Slowly, macros moved out of the realm of "keyboard stuffers" and into real programming languages. This is about the same point in history when computer users lost interest in macros; they just became too complex for the average person to deal with. Yet, they're there. You paid for them. And they can still help you get your work done, even if you only use them at the "keyboard stuffer" level.

Just about every program sold today comes with some type of macro ability. These range from the simple keyboard playback macros you find in programs like the *Norton Backup*, to the interesting display macros of Lotus' *Magellan*, to the intricate programming language environment of *WordPerfect* 5.1. Just about everything comes with macros, and they can make using software much easier.

About now a question comes up, "Does DOS have macros?" Yes, of course. They're called "batch files."

What can a macro do for me?

A macroinstruction is one that replaces many, which is the concept behind all macros. What they can do for you is make using the computer easier. Contrary to popular myth, macros do not complicate your life.

The limits of a macro depend on the application. Some programs will let you do everything with their macros—even display prompts and make decisions based on input. Other application's macros will only store and playback a series of keystrokes. In either case, macros help you get your work done faster, with less effort.

Macros make life easier mainly through automation. As a simple example, consider a commonly entered series of keystrokes, say your name and address at the end of a letter. You can stuff all those characters—including the carriage returns—into a single macro. So instead of typing all that information, you press ALT – E and it magically appears.

Or consider sticking the date and time into a spreadsheet. Just call up the DATETIME macro and—splat!—there it is. Anything repetitive, any keystrokes you commonly enter, can all be saved into a macro for easy execution. (It's often claimed that macros were invented by programmers who didn't like to type. There's merit to that.)

One notch up from just supplying keystrokes, more powerful macros can be designed. What about all that formatting you sometimes do after you're through editing a long document. You know, you add headers and footers, load style sheets, check pagination and so forth. All that can be accomplished with macros.

Or consider a spreadsheet that monitors several month's worth of information. A specialized print macro could ask the user which months or range of months they'd like to print. Then only those months would be printed. Even more complex macros could display menus and lists of options. (Some macro-nuts have even written trivia quizzes and adventure games using macros.)

All this power is built into most of the major applications. Don't feel obliged, however, to use it all at once. Personally, I write only simple macros because that's all I need (and I'm a simple person). But if I wanted to get fancy, the ability and power is there. (And always consider other users for whom you may be writing macros to simplify their lives.)

Keep in mind that macros are a function of the software—not of DOS. Unlike batch files, there is no common macro interpreter. Sure, certain developers will share macro language types between their products. But everything comes from the application itself, not DOS.

A final reason to use macros is that you paid for them. Since the mid-eighties, the trend for all software is *featuritis*, the creeping elegance and over incorporation of too many features. This started out as a way to make software more useful (and to eat up all that "extra" RAM the PC has). Later, thanks to the snooty magazine software reviewers, a developer couldn't get a product on the shelf without all those features. An easy one to add was macros. But that doesn't subtract from their usefulness or the fact that you paid for them (as well as some other features you may never use).

Types of macros

All macros are different and each macro language is different. There is no common lingo, not like the ANSI or "K & R" C language standards. Instead, macros are each unique to their application. But there are two major types:

- Keystroke stuffers
- Command languages

Nearly all types of macros are keystroke stuffers. You use the macro instead of typing a long sequence of keystrokes at the keyboard. Those keystrokes also include commands to the program, such as SHIFT – F7, BACK SPACE, and other keys that tell the application to perform some task. All the keystrokes are recorded in the macro and played back when you "run" it. Then you watch as the macro types for you.

Command language macros build upon the base the keystroke stuffers establish. Instead of entering just keystrokes into your macro, you could also issue commands. These would be of two types: commands that direct the application to do something (print, save a file, move to some location, etc.) and commands that tell the macro to do something (loop, go to a label, run another macro, etc.).

As an example, Lotus' *Magellan* uses a basic keystroke-stuffer type of macro language that also incorporates all of *Magellan*'s basic commands and functions. Tossed in on top of that are display commands for creating lists of choices and "dialog boxes," and other fancy commands. But there's only a limited capability to make decisions.

The most complete (and hair-raising) macro language I've ever seen is on the *Full Impact* spreadsheet for the "easy-to-use" Macintosh. Their macro language is essentially a mini-C language interpreter, complete with the curly brackets, variables, and structure. You need to be truly insane to master it. (The Mac's *Wingz* spreadsheet macros are rumored to be even more complex.)

All that aside, all types of macros are basically programming languages. It's yet another way to communicate with the computer.

Where do you draw the line? What's the difference between a keystroke stuffer, a macro command language, and a full-on programming language? It's not important. Using the macro is. Even if you only use the macro at the keystroke-stuffer level, you're doing better than ignoring the macro feature altogether.

Creating macros

Making a batch file under DOS is easy: just stick a whole list of DOS commands and batch file directives into a text file, name it something-dot-BAT, and there you are. Creating macros isn't as clean-cut.

There is no macro standard with any PC application. Actually, there are no standards for any PC applications; all of them are different. Only rarely will two programs from the same company share the same commands and function keys. Why then should macros have any consistency?

How you create a macro depends on the application. Usually there's some sort of macro command that gets the whole thing rolling. From that point on, however, there are different ways to create the macro, again depending on the program.

Learning versus programming

There are two general ways to make a macro: the learning method or the programming method. The programming method actually uses both ways, though after "learning" the macro, you usually wade off into some form of macro editor where touch-ups are made. Learning is more common.

A macro is basically a set of recorded keystrokes. To create a macro in the learn method, you tell the program that you're about to make a macro. In essence, you press a key that would be considered the record button on a tape recorder. From that moment on all your keystrokes are saved as the macro.

To end the macro you usually press the same key as when you started recording. Again, this works like a tape recorder; when you're done recording, you press the RECORD button a second time to turn it off. The same holds true with most computer macros.

This is called the "learn" method because you're teaching the computer, telling it "Hey! Pay attention! Memorize these keystrokes. I'm going to want you to play them back for me later."

Additionally, either before or after you enter the keystrokes, you'll save the macro to some filename on disk, or you'll assign it a keystroke of its own. To play back the macro, you then specify that filename or press the proper keystroke. Some programs may even store their macros in a menu or list from which you choose which macro you want to play back.

The drawback to the learn mode is its lack of editing. For example, I'm a fast typist. If I enter my name and address as an "end letter" macro, I may mistype something and have to backspace to correct it. If so, that backspace character winds up as part of the macro. The end result is the same, but to get there, the macro has to make my same original mistakes and then backspace to correct them—just like a tape recorder would pick up a stutter or those "ahs" and "ums" we pepper our spontaneous talk with.

The solution is to use a macro editor to remove the unwanted keystrokes. On a simple level, this is the second way a macro is created. You enter the macro editor, type the commands you want, then you have your macro. That's programming a macro as opposed to creating it in the learn mode.

You can also just start out in the macro editor, entering keystrokes and placing in macro commands where appropriate. But this is a risky undertaking; unless you're very familiar with the program, how will you know if you've entered the right keystrokes? Testing the macro is a good way to find out. Yet, it's still better to create the macro by learning it, then go into the macro programming editor to touch things up or augment.

Steps to creating a macro

In the real world, making a macro is a combination of both the learning and programming methods. It's just easier to switch on the learn mode and type the commands you want. After that, retire to the editor to clean it up and add any programming or extra splash you may feel the macro needs.

Specifically speaking, when you create a macro you'll probably do so using the following steps:

1. Plan the macro
2. Create it
3. Name it
4. Save the macro
5. Do some editing
6. Test the macro
7. Document it

Planning the macro is knowing what you want it to do. You've been sitting there for weeks in *WordPerfect* entering the same text over and over. So you finally break down and decide to create a macro. On the other end of the spectrum, there may be some complex maneuver all office employees are required to undertake in some application. It's up to you to create a simple macro so no one muffs it up. That's planning.

Creating the macro is done by entering the macro command for that application, then teaching it to the computer or entering it directly into the macro editor. To finish creating the macro, you typically enter the same command as you did to start it.

Naming and saving a macro is usually done at the same time. You name a macro before you create it. The macro is then saved once you're done creating it.

Be clever with the names. Most applications will usually let you assign ALT–key macros for the letters A through Z. So make ALT–S the "save" macro and ALT–P the "print" macro. That just makes sense. If they're named macros, then "Save" to save and "Print" to print also comes in handy. Don't baffle the user with complex or nonsense macros. And be wise with the ALT – keys; there are only 26 of them.

Editing the macro is done right after the macro is created. Usually it's to remove some inaccurately entered characters, backspacing over mistakes, or just to add some macro commands to complete the macro.

Testing the macro is simply putting it to work: pressing the macro key, running the macro filename, or choosing it from a list to see if and how the macro works.

Testing is necessary because you may call up the macro in different situations while you're using the application. For example, what if you have a word processor "auto-save" macro that assumes the document has already been saved (with a filename) to disk. If you run auto-save and you haven't yet saved the document, what happens? (Some advanced macro languages have commands and functions that will tell you when a document has been saved, as well as the results of certain operations and other information.)

Documenting the macro doesn't mean you should litter it with a lot of REM statements. Instead, if you're running a complex macro, you might want to display messages on the screen, letting the user know what's going on. Especially if the macro renames or deletes files—display a message and have the user press Y or N before moving on. That's documentation (as well as putting in a few REM statements now and then).

Nesting and chaining

Macros usually have the power to invoke (which is a fancy term for "run") other macros. For example, suppose you have the ALT – I macro which changes underline to italics. But then you want to write a macro that searches the entire document to make such changes. How would you do that?

The answer is to write two macros: the first searches for underlines and, when one is found, the second macro is run. So you enter the "search for underline" code, then when one is found, the macro "presses" the ALT – I key. That runs the second macro.

The technical term for this is *nesting*. You're putting one macro inside of another. Oh sure, you could issue the same keystrokes inside the second macro. But why not just nest the first macro inside the second?

Macros can also run other macros via *chaining*. (Chaining might also be referred to as *linking*. One macro can follow another like links in a chain.) Chaining is the same as nesting, with only a position move. Instead of putting one macro inside another, you place the second macro at the end of the first. So the first macro runs and with its last breath it runs the second macro. That's chaining.

I could just stop here, letting you know that you can nest and chain your macros—which isn't beyond the abilities of most application's macro feature. Instead, consider nesting and chaining as an approach to building more complex macros.

For example, start out with simple macros in your program. The macros only replace some common keystrokes, they're just time savers. But upon that you can build. You can create a complex macro simply by nesting a few of your simple ones together. Then you can make it more complex by chaining in even more modules.

That's really the way a complex macro should start out: as little pieces put together to make something big. If you start out trying to write the King of All the Macros, you'll probably frustrate yourself too quickly.

Using the macro

When a macro is created, you either assign it to a keystroke (usually an ALT–key combination), a filename, or it's placed into a list of other macros. Running the macro is then done by pressing that specific key, entering the name of the macro file, or selecting the macro from a list.

Once you activate the macro, it runs; playing back the keystrokes stuffed into the macro, or running the macro program you've defined. This is the end result that makes macros so attractive. You've now saved time by creating a macro that does many things, all of which can now be done with one simple action.

The only problem with using some macros is getting them to stop. Just like I/O redirection in DOS, where sometimes the redirected input may not supply all the keystrokes and force you to reboot, a macro run amok may be unstoppable. Nearly all macros will stop when you press CTRL–BREAK. Some programs have a Cancel, Clear, Stop, or Undo key that may also halt a berserk macro. This may not be a real big problem, but be aware of it when testing and debugging some of your macros.

Macros and batch files

Finally, there can be a link between macros and batch files. It comes in some applications where you can specify either a default macro or a macro to run via a command line switch.

A default, or start-up, macro is a macro given a specific name or position in a list. When the application first starts, it checks for that name or looks on the list for the default macro. If found, the macro executes.

Default macros are good for initially setting up some applications, changing your colors, setting your position on the screen, moving to the appropriate subdirectory, and so on. (Some applications also allow you to preprogram these features without using a default macro.)

For batch file programming, a better option is the command line switch type of macro. After you specify the program name on the command line, you can usually follow it with some optional switches. For example, when you run your word processing macro, it may look like this:

```
CD \ WP
WP %1
```

The command line parameter %1 is stuck there so that WP.BAT can be fol-lowed with an optional filename just like WP.EXE can, but I recommend you use more than one replaceable parameter with each application you run:

```
CD \ WP
WP %1 %2 %3 %4 %5
```

Some word processors (and other applications) have more than one optional switch. One of these might just be an initial macro switch, allow-ing you to specify with which macro to begin the program. That way you can start the program with:

```
WP CHAP7 /M = FORMAT4
```

This might start a word processor, loading chapter 7 of your Great Ameri-can Novel and running the macro named FORMAT4. Another approach might be to write several word processing start-up batch files, each of which automatically loads some batch file:

Name: WP1.BAT

```
@ECHO OFF
REM This batch file loads the word processor
REM with the default letter formatting macro loaded
C:
CD \ WP
WP %1 /M = FORMAT2
```

The same can be done with batch files to run other programs:

Name: SS3.BAT

```
@ECHO OFF
REM This batch file starts your spreadsheet
REM with the macro file menu, MENU
C:
CD \ SS
SS %1 /MMENU
```

The idea here is integration. You're combining the power and programma-bility of batch files with the power and programmability of macros. As I mentioned in the introduction, you're extending your reach into the pro-gram itself using macros. This is the ultimate way of taking control and customizing your system, as well as the systems for other people who work with you.

Summary

Macros are handy helpers, a single keystroke that replaces dozens of key-strokes and commands in your application. Beyond that macros can take on the load of a full programming language—including decision making, loops, fancy displays, and interaction with the user. All this is a function of the macro ability in your application.

There are two general types of macros: keystroke stuffers and command language macros. Keystroke stuffers simply record all your key-strokes, like the redial feature on a phone. You press the macro key and the keystrokes are then played back. The command language macros extend the power of the keystroke stuffers by giving you decision-making abilities, program structure, and a few more programming language-like abilities.

Creating a macro is done in two ways. Most keystroke replacement macros are created via some macro "learn" function, where you teach the commands to the computer and it memorizes them for later playback. The advanced macro commands are usually added in some form of macro editor.

Finally, macros and batch files can be merged by specifying a macro to run on the command line. If your application lacks this feature, then some programs have a default macro, which can take its place.

16
Macros in popular applications

Nearly all the big applications (save for databases) incorporate some sort of macro feature into their command repertoire. As proof for this, consider all the books on specific applications that cover only macros. There must be something to that—not that macros are so hard they require a book to master the subject, but that macros add a lot of value to the software and they can increase your productivity.

This chapter covers macros in a few popular applications, specifically *WordPerfect*, *Lotus 1-2-3*, and *DESQview*. Other applications that use macros are also mentioned, but *WordPerfect* and *1-2-3* are the major hitters here (and they both show diverse ways of dealing with macros). *DESQview* is also popular, and it has a general macro feature that can be used across a number of applications.

I'm not trying to completely document the macro features of those major applications in these few pages. Instead, consider this as an introduction, something to whet your appetite. If you find the subject interesting and want to pursue it further, check out the applications' manuals or pick up an interesting book on the subject.

Macros in WordPerfect

WordPerfect's macros started out as simple keystroke stuffers. You could assign them to the twenty-six ALT-key combinations (the letters A through Z), or give each macro a unique filename. All keystrokes—including *WordPerfect*'s commands—were stored in each macro, which you could play back at any time. The only major drawback was a lack of a macro editor.

Version 5.0 of *WordPerfect* added a macro editor and several powerful macro commands. This brought the state of *WordPerfect*'s macros up to full programming power. Version 5.1 added more flexibility to the macro editor, plus a few more interesting commands. Today, *WordPerfect*'s macros are some of the most powerful in any application.

Making a macro in WordPerfect

There are two commands in *WordPerfect* that deal with macros:

CTRL – F10	Macro Define (create a macro)
ALT – F10	Macro (run a macro)

CTRL – F10 is the "record button" for *WordPerfect* macros. All keystrokes entered after you press CTRL – F10 are saved into the macro key or file. Then you press CTRL – F10 again to stop recording.

ALT – F10 is used only to run named macros. Any *WordPerfect* macro you assign to an ALT-key combination is run just by typing ALT-plus-that-key. But macros you assign specific names are run with ALT – F10. It doesn't display a list, just a prompt where you enter the macro's name. Press ENTER and that macro is run.

The following steps are used to create a macro in *WordPerfect*:

1. Press Macro Define (CTRL – F10) and enter a name for the macro. *WordPerfect* will prompt you with:

   Define macro:

   Type the name of the macro you want to define, or press an ALT-key combination. Only the letters A through Z can be used with the ALT-key. For a named macro, you must enter any valid filename, up to eight characters but without an extension. (*WordPerfect* saves *all* its macro files to disk in a predefined macro subdirectory, each with an extension of WPM.) Press ENTER.

   In addition to a name, you can also just press ENTER to define the "temporary macro." This is good for quick-and-dirty macros, but it lacks a name and is always replaced the next time you create a temporary macro.

2. Enter a description for the macro. After entering the macro's name, *WordPerfect* prompts:

   Description:

   Here you can enter up to 39 characters to describe the macro. This isn't a required step. In fact, the only time you'll see the description is when you edit the macro (though this might change with future releases of *WordPerfect*).

   After you press ENTER, *WordPerfect* is now ready to record your macro. (Note that the macro is now saved to disk. If you cancel the macro definition, you'll still have a macro file on disk, though it will be empty.)

WordPerfect does not prompt for a description of the temporary macro.

3. Enter the macro's keystrokes. *WordPerfect* is now recording your macro. You'll see the following displayed, flashing in the lower-left corner of the screen:

Macro Def

All keys you type, all commands you enter and options you select— everything is now being recorded as a *WordPerfect* macro. Note that commands you put into your document are entered into the macro as the command itself—not the keystrokes. So if you change the font, only the new font type is recorded in the macro. Any commands you select using the mouse will also be entered in this manner; *WordPerfect* does not record mouse movements as part of a macro, only the commands you select.

4. To finish defining the macro, press Macro Define again (CTRL – F10). After pressing CTRL – F10, the macro will stop recording and be saved to disk. Note that only CTRL – F10 stops recording; ESC or Cancel (F1) don't do the job.

This is the way most macros are defined: the same command that starts the macro also stops it. And it makes sense when you think about it. You can't define a macro within a macro. That would be dumb.

Running the macro

To run a *WordPerfect* macro you press its associated ALT-key combination. ALT – A runs the macro you assigned to ALT – A, ALT – B runs the ALT – B macro, and so on.

If the macro has a name, you must issue the Macro command (ALT – F10) and then type the macro's name. Press ENTER and the macro executes. Or if it's the temporary macro, just press ENTER instead of typing the name.

To run the macro right when *WordPerfect* starts, you must follow WP on the command line with the /M macro switch. For example:

WP /M-MENU

This loads *WordPerfect* and automatically runs the MENU macro.

WP CHAP07 /M-FORMAT1

This runs *WordPerfect*, loads the document CHAP07 for editing, and then runs the FORMAT1 macro.

Editing a WordPerfect macro

Once a macro is entered it can be edited by pressing CTRL – F10 again. You simply enter the macro's name or press the same ALT-key to edit that macro. *WordPerfect* prompts you with:

MACRO.WPM Already Exists: 1 Replace; 2 Edit; 3 Description: 0

Here, *WordPerfect* is letting you know the macro (MACRO.WPM above) already exists. You have three choices:

1 or R   Replace the macro, create a new definition for MACRO.WPM
2 or E   Edit the existing macro; enter the macro editor
3 or D   Display the macro's description, then enter the editor

To edit the macro, type 2, 3, E or D. Pressing 1 or R replaces that macro with a new definition. (Note that you cannot edit the temporary macro.)

If you elect to edit the macro, you'll enter the *WordPerfect* macro editor, as shown in FIG. 16-1.

```
Macro: Action

    File              ITALIX.WPM

    Description       Convert UL to IT
```

```
{ON NOT FOUND}{GO}Step2~~

{Home}{Home}{Home}{Up}

{LABEL}ConvU2I~
    {DISPLAY OFF}{Search}{Underline}{Search}{Block}{Search}{Underline}
    {Underline}{Left}{Backspace}{Search}{Font}2i
{GO}ConvU2I~

{LABEL}Step2~
{Home}{Home}{Home}{Up}{Replace}n{Underline}{Search}{Search}
{Home}{Home}{Up}
```

16-1   Here is the WordPerfect macro editor.

A shortcut method to get into the editor works by first pressing the Home key, then CTRL – F10. Enter the macro's name or press its ALT-key. *WordPerfect* prompts you with the macro's description (which you can, at that point, change), you press ENTER and then you're in the macro editor.

If you need to edit the temporary macro, enter WP{WP} as the macro's name. The macro editor has one large window in which you'll see the contents of your macro. Above the window is the macro's filename and its description, commands and helpful hints are listed below the window.

All text in the window is part of your macro command. Bold text enclosed in curly braces are *WordPerfect* commands, macro commands, or the names of specific keystrokes. Plain text in that window is just plain text that is part of the macro.

To enter or edit the macro, you use the standard *WordPerfect* editing keys. Any text you type becomes part of the macro. (If you're good at *WordPerfect*, you can almost read what the macro is doing.) To insert keys such as Backspace, Home, or the arrow keys, you must press CTRL – V first. Any key pressed after CTRL – V is inserted into the macro editor as a command. If you need to insert a whole slew of commands, type CTRL – F10. Typing CTRL – F10 a second time turns off the insert mode.

For example, to enter the keystrokes "Home-Home-Up arrow" in the macro, you would type the following:

1. CTRL – F10
2. Home
3. Home
4. Up arrow
5. CTRL – F10

In the macro editor you would see these keystrokes shown as follows:

{Home}{Home}{Up}

You can access the macro language command in the editor by pressing CTRL – PGUP. This pops up a little window in the upper right-hand corner of the screen, as seen in FIG. 16-2. The window contains an alphabetic list of all *WordPerfect*'s macro commands. You can scroll through the list with the arrow keys, or type the first letter of an item to scroll right to it. Pressing ENTER inserts that command into your macro.

```
Macro: Action

        File            ITALIX.WPM          {;}comment~
                                            {ASSIGN}var~expr~
                                            {BELL}
        Description     Convert UL to IT    {Block Append}
                                            {Block Copy}

┌─────────────────────────────────────────────────────────┐
│{ON NOT FOUND}{GO}Step2~~                                  │
│                                                           │
│{Home}{Home}{Home}{Up}                                     │
│                                                           │
│{LABEL}ConvU2I~                                            │
│    {DISPLAY OFF}{Search}{Underline}{Search}{Block}{Search}{Underline}│
│    {Underline}{Left}{Backspace}{Search}{Font}2i           │
│{GO}ConvU2I~                                               │
│                                                           │
│{LABEL}Step2~                                              │
│{Home}{Home}{Home}{Up}{Replace}n{Underline}{Search}{Search}│
│{Home}{Home}{Up}                                           │
│                                                           │
│                                                           │
│                                                           │
└─────────────────────────────────────────────────────────┘

                    (Name Search; Arrows; Enter to Select)
```

16-2 The macro commands window is shown here.

When you're done entering or editing your *WordPerfect* macro, you press Exit (F7). That saves the macro and returns you to your document. To cancel any changes made, press the Cancel key (F1). Remember that Exit always saves a macro without prompting you. I get this constantly goofed up; use Cancel if you *don't* want the changes saved.

WordPerfect macro commands

There are dozens of macro commands in the *WordPerfect* macro language. These include commands for making labels, subroutines, structures and loops, and variables. There are even display commands that draw boxes and prompts on the screen. It can get amazingly complex.

The *WordPerfect* macro language is really a programming language. This is a fine example of something extremely useful going beyond the reach of most typical users. Even advanced users won't often bother with something like the *WordPerfect* macro commands. Why? They just don't have the time to memorize them all.

If you're interested in getting complex with *WordPerfect* macros, I recommend a good book on the subject. Windcrest's *WordPerfect 5.1 Macros* is a good one to choose, full of examples and very descriptive. It even comes with a diskette full of macro files already written for you.

Also, WordPerfect Corp. has given you several dozen macros with the program. The keyboard layouts supplied on the distribution diskettes contain lots of interesting macro files for quite a few situations. Even if you don't plan on using them, they're interesting to look at.

Examples

Listed below are some examples of handy *WordPerfect* macros. This isn't a complete list, nor does it go into any detail. Remember, this is a book on batch file programming. But you may find the following macros useful if you're a *WordPerfect* user. (And if you're not, then consider rewriting these macros for your own word processor.)

ALT – S The ALT – S macro is the quick-save macro, saving your document to disk. Note that this assumes that your document has already been named and saved.

To create ALT – S, do the following:

1. Press Macro Define (CTRL – F10) to create the macro
2. Press ALT – S
3. Enter "Quick Save" as the macro's description
4. Press the Save key (F10)
5. Press ENTER
6. Press Y to replace the old document on disk
7. Press CTRL – F10 again to end the macro definition

In the macro editor, the ALT – S macro looks like this:

{Save}{Enter}
y

That's the Save command, ENTER to accept the filename, then Y to over-write the original.

ALT – P This is the quick-print macro, which prints the current document. To create quick print, do the following:

1. Press Macro Define (CTRL – F10) to create the macro
2. Press ALT – P
3. Enter "Quick Print" as the macro's description
4. Press the Print key (SHIFT – F7)
5. Press 1 or F to print the full document in memory
6. Press CTRL – F10 to end the macro definition

In the macro editor, quick print looks like this:

{DISPLAY OFF}{Print}1

The {DISPLAY OFF} command keeps the screen image static while the macro runs. This is added automatically for macros that pop up some menu or scroll the document around. In this case, you won't see the Print menu displayed when the macro issues the {Print} command. Instead, the printer will just hum on up and print the document.

ALT – T ALT – T is my favorite macro—the "transpose" macro. Often you'll be typing along and you'll create one of the world's most popular typos: the transposition. Examples include "teh" instead of "the," "fo" instead of "of," and two-letter combinations in the middle of larger words. The ALT – T macro simply switches those two letters.

To create ALT – T, take the following steps:

1. Press Macro Define (CTRL – F10)
2. Press ALT – T
3. Enter "Transpose" as the macro's description
4. Press the DELete key to delete the first character
5. Press the right-arrow key to move forward a notch
6. Press Cancel (F1) to yank back the deleted character
7. Press 1 to get it back
8. Press CTRL – F10 to end the macro

In the macro editor, ALT – T looks like this:

{DISPLAY OFF}{Del}}{Right}}Cancel{1

To use this macro, place the cursor under the first of the two transposed characters, then press ALT – T.

ALT – B   ALT – B is my "mark block" macro. It selects a paragraph as a block (and it's also used with the ALT – C and ALT – X macros below).

ALT – B is created as follows:

1. Press Macro Define (CTRL – F10)
2. Press ALT – B
3. Enter "Mark Block" as the description
4. Press the Block key (ALT – F4 or F12) to delete start the block
5. Press ENTER to mark up to the end of the current paragraph
6. Press Macro Define to end the macro

In the macro editor, ALT – B looks like this:

```
{DISPLAY OFF}{Block}{Enter}
```

This mark block macro only marks the current paragraph, or only a line of text if there is no paragraph. Because I seem to cut a lot of paragraphs, it comes in handy. Note that "block" is still active when this macro is over, however you can use ALT – C or ALT – X on it to copy or cut that block once you're done marking.

ALT – C   ALT – C is the Copy macro. It takes a marked block and moves it into the "copy buffer." Unlike *WordPerfect* 5.0, however, ALT – C doesn't require you to immediately paste the block by positioning the cursor and pressing ENTER. Instead, you paste the block using ALT – V (below).

To create the ALT – C macro, do the following:

1. Press Macro Define (CTRL – F10)
2. Press ALT – C
3. Enter "Copy Block" as the macro's description
4. Press the Move key (CTRL – F4)
5. Press B for Block
6. Press C for Copy
7. Press Cancel (F1)
8. Press Macro Define to end the macro

In the macro editor, ALT – C looks like this:

```
{DISPLAY OFF}{Move}bc{Cancel}
```

You press Cancel (F1) to get rid of the annoying "Move cursor; press ENTER to retrieve" message. Then to call back the block, use the ALT – V "paste" macro.

ALT – X   My cut block macro is ALT – X. Why ALT – X? Because ALT – C is already taken. And ALT – X fits into the Macintosh scheme of things, where Command-X is cut in every Mac application. Just like ALT – C (and unlike *WordPerfect* 5.0), you don't have to immediately paste the block after it's been cut.

ALT – X is created very similarly to ALT – C:

1. Press Macro Define (CTRL – F10)
2. Press ALT – X
3. Enter "Cut Block" as the description
4. Press the Move key (CTRL – F4)
5. Press B for Block
6. Press M for Move
7. Press Cancel (F1)
8. Press (CTRL – F10) to end the macro

In the macro editor, ALT – X looks like this:

{DISPLAY OFF}{Move}bm{Cancel}

Again, we're marking a block for cutting (which *WordPerfect* calls "moving") and pressing Cancel so we can paste it later with ALT – V.

ALT – V Finally, here is the Paste macro, which pastes a block of text previously cut or copied with ALT – X or ALT – C, respectively.

To create ALT – V, take the following steps:

1. Press Macro Define (CTRL – F10)
2. Press ALT – V
3. Enter "Paste Block" as the macro's description
4. Press the Move key (CTRL – F4)
5. Press R for Retrieve
6. Press B for Block
7. Press Macro Define to end the macro

ALT – V looks like this in the macro editor:

{DISPLAY OFF}{Move}rb

ALT—I I was glad that *WordPerfect* 5 allowed you to enter italics text without some convoluted menu system. (With Version 4.2, I simply rewired my printer driver so italics printed instead of underline.) But I was disappointed that it took three menus to get to the italics on/off switch. So I wrote ALT – I to turn on italics.

To create ALT – I, do the following:

1. Press Macro Define (CTRL – F10)
2. Press ALT – I
3. Enter "Italic On" as the macro's description
4. Press the Font key (CTRL – F8)
5. Press A for Appearance
6. Press | for Italic (Italics)
7. Press Macro Define to end the macro

In the macro editor, ALT–I looks like this:

```
{DISPLAY OFF}{Font}ai
```

Not only does ALT–I turn on italics, but it will also italicize any selected block of text. So this macro is doubly handy.

ITALIX The ITALIX macro (the only named macro in this set) searches your entire document for underline codes and changes them to italics. If you don't like using ALT–I, or you're still in the habit of pressing F8 for underline instead of italics, then this macro is a time saver. Also, this macro is also the only one in the bunch that uses any of *WordPerfect*'s macro language ability.

To create the ITALIX macro, do the following:

1. Press HOME
2. Macro Define (CTRL–F10)
3. Type ITALIX and press ENTER
4. Enter "Convert UL to IT" as the description

After pressing ENTER you'll be in the macro editor. This is required because ITALIX can't be entered from the keyboard alone.

Enter the commands as shown in FIG. 16-3. (These were also shown in FIG. 16-1.)

16-3 These are the commands for the ITALIX macro.
```
{DISPLAY OFF}
{ON NOT FOUND}{GO}Step2~~

{Home}{Home}{Home}{Up}

{LABEL}ConvU2I~
    {Search}{Underline}{Search}{Block}{Search}{Underline}
    {Underline}{Left}{Backspace}{Search}{Font}2i
{GO}ConvU2I~

{LABEL}Step2~
{Home}{Home}{Home}{Up}{Replace}n{Underline}{Search}{Search}
{Home}{Home}{Up}
```

The command {ON NOT FOUND} is entered by pressing CTRL–PGUP. Select {ON NOT FOUND} from the list, press ENTER and it will appear in the text. {GO} is selected the same way. Then type "Step2 ~ ~".

This command tells the macro processor that once a search command generates a "Not Found" message, macro execution is to pick up at the label "Step2".

Following that instruction, we ensure that we're at the top of the document by issuing the HOME, HOME, HOME, up-arrow command. Enter those keystrokes by pressing CTRL–F10, then HOME, HOME, HOME, and up-arrow. Press CTRL–F10 again.

The next section, between the {LABEL} and {GO} commands, is a loop named ConvU2I (for convert underline to italics). It scans the entire document for underline text, blocks that text, then switches on the italics attribute for that block. What this does is to change all underline text to underline-plus-italics. (Because you can't do a 1:1 replace for underline to italics.)

You can enter all commands between the {LABEL} and {GO} commands by pressing CTRL–F10 and their corresponding keys. ({Search} is F2, {Underline} is F8, {Block} is ALT–F4, {Font} is CTRL–F8.) The "2i" should be entered after pressing CTRL–F10 a second time (it's plain text).

The second series of commands, the {Label} Step 2 ~, is where we go back to the top of the document and delete all the underlines. In essence, we've changed the underlines to underline-plus-italics, and now we're going to strip out all those underlines. This is how you switch from underline to italics in *WordPerfect*, and having a macro that does so is most handy.

When you're done editing, press Exit (F7) to return to your document. That macro is saved.

Macros in Lotus 1-2-3

As a writer, my forte lies with word processing. Spreadsheets are something I rarely use. (I just can't be an expert in everything, you know.) So this information on *1-2-3* will be rather brief (especially given that the subject of the book is, after all, batch files). Before getting into it, I seriously recommend a good book on the subject of *1-2-3* macros to all you spreadsheet maniacs. There are plenty out there.

1-2-3 made its reputation on macros. Besides having more power (and graphics!) than the original *VisiCalc*, *1-2-3* offered its users macros. You could do amazing things with *1-2-3*'s macros, making life easier for yourself and everyone else in the office. Better programs came out, but none had those *1-2-3* macros, so they all fell by the wayside.

Today *1-2-3* is still king of the hill, and it has an impressive and powerful macro language. Personally, I think *1-2-3* is more primitive and klutzy than some of the other offerings on the market (which also have their own macros). Yet if you want to mention macros, you can't pass up *1-2-3*.

Making a macro in 1-2-3

1-2-3 has powerful macros, equal to or surpassing the power of *WordPerfect*'s macros. Again, we have a program that comes with its own internal mini-programming language. But you don't have to use all aspects of the macro language to get the most from *1-2-3*.

Another interesting thing about *1-2-3* is that it does its macros a lot differently than *WordPerfect*. The macros are part of the spreadsheet, usually hidden off in one corner, away from the important data. In one way this is odd; it means there's some potentially confusing information on the worksheet which some users might stumble over and accidentally erase. On the other hand, it fits in nicely with the spreadsheet metaphor, keeping all your information handy on one worksheet.

To make a macro in *1-2-3*, you take the following steps:

1. Find a place in the spreadsheet for the macro. Macros in *1-2-3* can be local to the current spreadsheet, or they can be associated with several spreadsheets. In either case, you need to find a location in the spreadsheet where you'll begin writing the macro.

   In a spreadsheet where the macro is local, find a spot away from the real worksheet data. Usually a few lines below the bottom line of the worksheet is fine. (Some users page down to enter the macro, others will tab right a screen.)

   Note that you'll need three columns for the macro (which is what everyone recommends). So don't start writing it in column A, or the far left column on the screen.

2. Compose the macro commands. *1-2-3*'s macro commands are primarily of the keyboard-stuffer type, though there are many additional programming language-like commands. But generally speaking, the macro commands you enter will be keystrokes that are fed back into *1-2-3*. Because of this, all your macro commands must be labels. If the command starts with a / (slash) or @ (at sign), remember to press the apostrophe character (') first.

   The macro commands usually go into the second column of the macro definition, and they all line up in the same column (see FIG. 16-4). Remember to end each line with a tilde character (~), which represents the ENTER key, or the {down} macro command, which simulates pressing the down-arrow key.

   The macro will execute all keystrokes and commands you place into that column, up until the first blank column, a column with numbers in it, or a {Quit} or similar command.

3. Name the macro. There are two types of names you can assign a macro in *1-2-3*: an ALT-key equivalent name (from ALT – A through ALT – Z), or a name of up to 15 characters. ALT-key macros are run by pressing that ALT-key combination. Named macros are selected via the Run (ALT – F4) command.

   To name a macro, place the cell pointer on the first cell of macro instructions. Then press */rnc* for / (menu) Range, Name, Create. This both defines the macro and assigns to it a name/ALT-key combination. To assign an ALT-key to the macro, you enter the backslash character (\) plus a letter A through Z as the name. Non-ALT-key macros simply have a label name up to 15 characters long.

   Press ENTER to accept the name, then press ENTER again to

accept only that single cell as the range. Macro ranges in *1-2-3* need only define the top cell in the instruction column. However, you can name the entire group of commands (in that column) as a range to make moving it around later easier.

4. Document the macro. Macros in *1-2-3* have two types of documentation: the name of the macro, and comments for the column of macro instructions.

   The name of the macro, be it an ALT-key combo or full name, is placed in the first column, at the same row as the first set of macro instructions (see FIG. 16-4). Use the same name as you assigned the macro via the Range command; a backslash for an ALT-key combo, or the name of the macro if you gave it a name. (Remember to type an apostrophe before the backslash.)

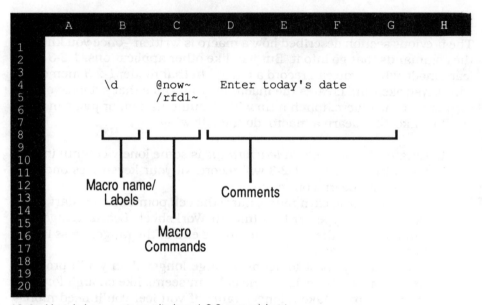

16-4 Here is how a macro sits in a 1-2-3 spreadsheet.

To the right of the macro instructions you should put comments documenting your macro. These are simply labels in a column that describe what's going on.

It's important to note here that your macro instructions usually fit in only one column. You could pack up to 240 characters in a cell, but most *1-2-3* macro maniacs only put a sparse few commands in each cell—like dividing a paragraph up into bite-sized sentences. Since the macro will keep executing down that column, there's no need to worry about breaking it at "just the right spot." And if you keep the commands in a narrow column, it's easier to fit the documentation all on one screen.

This documentation step is more a suggestion (and a tradition) than a requirement. Personally, I just expand what's going on in my documentation.

For example, the macro command may be "/wwc" and my commands are just "Worksheet, Window, Clear."

5. Save the macro. The macro is saved as part of the spreadsheet. It's attached, unlike *WordPerfect* where all the macros are independent, stored in a general MACRO subdirectory.

Also, note that a macro will only work for that particular spreadsheet. (Macros can also be collectively saved in their own spreadsheet, which can then be accessed from other spreadsheets. Refer to the section on the Macro Library Manager for the details.)

Learning a 1-2-3 macro

The previous section described how a macro is written—once you know all the commands that go into it. But just like other applications, *1-2-3* has a learn mode where you can record a macro. In that mode, *1-2-3* memorizes your keystrokes and creates the macro for you. Once that's done, you can further edit the macro, touch it up with documentation, or just run it.

To make *1-2-3* learn a macro, do the following:

1. Create a learn range. A *learn range* is some lonely column in your spreadsheet, where *1-2-3* will record all your keystrokes once you turn on its Learn command.

To create a learn range, move the cell pointer to the start of the range. Then type /wlr for / (menu) Worksheet, Learn, Range. You can now move the cell pointer to the end of the range. Press ENTER to end the range definition.

It's always best to define a range longer than you'll probably need. Four or five cells in one column seems like enough for most short macros. Make a longer range if you feel you'll need more—especially if the macro is to contain a lot of cursor movement. Into that range *1-2-3* will place all your keystrokes. But first you must turn on the Learn command.

2. Record your keystrokes. A learn range is now defined and waiting for keystrokes. To start recording your keystrokes into that range, you issue the Learn command (ALT – F5).

Once ALT – F5 is pressed, the "Learn" status light appears on the bottom of the screen. From that point on, all keystrokes you issue will be saved into the learn range. (You might not see them until you redraw the screen.)

To stop recording, press ALT – F5 again. The "Learn" status light will go off. If you need to touch up the macro, then move over to the learn range and make any editing corrections via the Edit (F2) key. Here you can also enter advanced macro commands.

3. Name the macro. The learn range and Learn command are just there for stuffing keystrokes into some part of the spreadsheet. Essentially what you've done is just created a column of odd-looking labels. You still have to name the range to get it to work like a macro.

   Place the cell pointer on the top row of macro commands, and type /rnc, for / (menu), Range, Name, Create. Enter a name for the macro, with backslash specifying an ALT-key macro, or enter up to 15 characters to give the macro a full name. Press ENTER, then press ENTER again to specify the first cell as the named range.

4. Document and save it. As with the manual macros, remember to document your learn-created macros. Put the macro name in the left column by the top row of the macro commands. Then put any comments to the right of the macro commands. As with the manually created macros, you learn macros become part of the spreadsheet and are only saved when you save the spreadsheet to disk.

Running 1-2-3 macros

There are two ways to run a *1-2-3* macro. The first is to simply press the ALT-key associated with the macro. The second is to use the RUN command, ALT – F3.

After you press Run, you'll see a list of available macros displayed at the top of the screen, as shown in FIG. 16-5. Use the cursor keys to highlight the name of the macro to run, then press ENTER to run it. Pressing F3 (Name) displays a full list of files, as opposed to a row at a time.

Presently, there is no documented way to specify a macro to run when you start *1-2-3* at the command prompt. The *1-2-3* software package does, however, have an automatic, self-start macro that you can specify for each worksheet you load.

The "autoexec macro" is run automatically each time you load a worksheet. It's any macro in that spreadsheet that's given the name "\0" (backslash-zero). But note that your global default setting for Autoexec must be "Yes". (It's always that way unless you turn it off. To check, type /wgd for / (menu), Worksheet, Global Default.)

Stepping through a 1-2-3 macro

Debugging a macro is part of the fun of writing it. Especially when creating macros manually, who knows what they could do? Nothing is more annoying than being sure you've entered all the keystrokes, only to wind up having *1-2-3* spit out dozens of those cute little "blips" at you.

The solution is to step through the macro a keystroke at a time. That

```
E20: [W7]
Select the macro to run:
ADDCOL          CITY           COL_MENU        DELCOL          FIRST
        A           B           C           D       E       F       G
13  \R          {GETLABEL "Round to what place? ",PLACE}
14  R_LOOP      {EDIT}{HOME}@ROUND(
15              {END},{PLACE})~
16              {DOWN}
17              {IF @CELLPOINTER("type")="v"}{BRANCH R_LOOP}
18              {QUIT}
19
20  PLACE       2
21              {RETURN}
22
23
24  \C          {MENUCALL COL_MENU}         Display column-macro men
25              {BRANCH \C}                 Restart column macro
26
27  COL_MENU    Global   Set          Reset      Hide     Unhide  AddCol
28              Set globaSet width of a raReset a ranHide a RedisplaInsert a
29              {GLOBAL} {SET}               {RESET}    {HIDE} {UNHIDE}{ADDCOL}
30
31  GLOBAL      /wgc{?}~                Set global column width to user-spe
32
19-Sep-90  07:42 PM
```

16-5 Here you can see a list of available macros, just above the top of the worksheet.

way you can watch what's going on and stop the macro when you find your boo-boo.

To step through a macro, you must enter the Step command (ALT – F2). The "Step" indicator light will appear on the bottom of your screen. At this time you run, or "invoke," the macro. On the bottom of your screen you'll see each cell of the macro displayed as it's played back. An indicator shows which cell is playing and to the right of it you'll see the cell's contents, the macro commands (see FIG. 16-6).

To continue the macro, press the spacebar or ENTER key. You'll see a highlight move over each of the macro commands, and you'll see the effect of those commands displayed on the screen (if that's what they do). To cancel the macro, press CTRL – BREAK. Then press ALT – F2 again to get out of the Step mode.

Note that the Step mode can remain active—sometimes you may forget it's on. If you press an ALT-key or choose a macro and expect it to zoom off to work—and it doesn't, then the Step mode might be active. Always check. Press ALT – F2 if Step is active to turn it off.

Common mistakes you might find while stepping through macros are misspelled commands ({rigt} instead of {right}), forgetting to put a tilde (~, which stands for ENTER) at the end of a line, or just misanticipating something. Note that you can always stop a macro run amok with CTRL – BREAK.

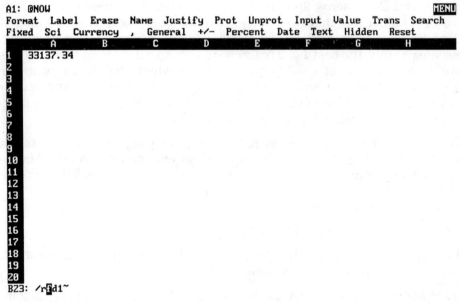

A1: @NOW   **MENU**

Format   Label   Erase   Name   Justify   Prot   Unprot   Input   Value   Trans   Search

Fixed   Sci   Currency   ,   General   +/-   Percent   Date   Text   Hidden   Reset

B23: /r░d1~

16-6   Here a macro is being run a Step at a time.

The macro library manager

Macros in *1-2-3* are all "local," being used only with the worksheet that contains them. The way around this is to put the macros into a library file. By loading that library file into *1-2-3*'s memory, you can then access its macros in any of your spreadsheets.

The macro library manager is a Lotus "Add-in" program. You must load it into memory with the attach command, /aa for / (menu), Add-in, Attach. Then select MACROMGR.ADN. You can optionally assign the macro manager to a function key, ALT–F7 through ALT–F10, or to no key. To put a macro into the library, specify the whole thing as a range and then copy it there using the Save command.

In addition to storing macros in the macro library, you can also use it to store ranges of data that can be accessed by several worksheets. Information such as tax tables, parts lists, or lookup tables can all be put into a central library you can then use for several spreadsheets.

Examples

As I mentioned earlier, I'm no Lotus *1-2-3* expert. The experts have, however, written many books on *1-2-3*, some of which contain useful macro examples for die-hard *1-2-3* users. (Windcrest's *Working with Lotus Macros* is a good example.)

Most *1-2-3* macros find their way into complex spreadsheets. They perform maneuvers that would require many keystrokes with just one, or they present a list of items from which a user can select something. Because of this, the best *1-2-3* macros are very specific. (Most macro books build up some sort of *1-2-3* "application" in which the macro examples function.) But this doesn't mean I'm going to leave you high and dry for some *1-2-3* macro examples. During my personal travels into Spreadsheet-land, I found the following few macros came in handy:

Erase Cells   The Erase Cells macro I use to quickly delete the contents of a single cell or range of cells. (My spreadsheet experience is on the Macintosh where you use the obvious "delete" key to delete a cell. When you're in *1-2-3* and you press the delete key, it blips at you.)

The ALT – E macro looks like this:

```
\e    /re      Erase range of cells, Alt-E
```

The commands are / (menu), Range, Erase. The key equivalent is ALT – E. Believe it or not, I find this particularly handy.

Quick save   Nothing beats a quick save (and a haircut). Back to my Macintosh program: it saves the spreadsheet every five minutes whether I want it to or not. With *1-2-3*, the following macro will quick-save an already-saved document:

The ALT – S macro looks like this:

```
\s    /fs~r     Quick save macro
```

The commands are / (menu), File, Save, ENTER (to accept the name already listed), Replace. If this sounds familiar to the ALT – S, "quick save" *WordPerfect* macro, you're right. I like consistency between applications.

Months   This macro was handy during the old, pre-HAL days of *1-2-3*. (HAL is an add-in that will automatically do what this macro does.) Basically, the fill-in-the-months macro will put the month names Jan through Dec in 12 columns for your spreadsheet.

The MONTHS macro looks like this:

```
\Months   Jan{R}             Enter month, press
          Feb{R}             right arrow key
          Mar{R}
          Apr{R}
          May{R}
          Jun{R}
          Jul{R}
          Aug{R}
          Sep{R}
          Oct{R}
          Nov{R}
          Dec{L}
```

{L}{L}{L}{L}{L}	Backspace back to
{L}{L}{L}{L}{L}	the first cell

To use this macro, position the cell pointer on the first cell of the row you want to contain the months. Press the Run key (ALT–F3) and choose MONTHS to fill in the months.

Note how this macro's name starts with a backslash character. Especially large spreadsheets where you'll have many named ranges, it's a good idea to start all macros with the backslash, so you'll know which are macros and which are just named ranges. (And, no, pressing ALT–M will not run this macro. Only one-letter macros starting with a backslash are ALT-key macros.)

Macros in DESQview

DESQview is a powerful PC control program—an "extended DOS environment." It allows you to run several applications on your PC at once. You can quickly switch between running programs, examine two or more programs at once through various "windows," and you can cut and paste information between them.

DESQview is mentioned here because it has a macro feature, one that applies to all programs that run in its environment. All it really is is a keystroke stuffer—nothing more. But the fact that it works with all programs running under *DESQview* makes it really handy (and consistent).

Before getting dirty, note that it's best to run *DESQview* on a PC with lots of memory, lots of LIM 4.0-compatible EMS "expanded" memory (to be specific). The more the better. And if your PC is of the 386 variety, things work even better.

All about scripts

DESQview calls its macros *scripts*, and the way they're created is with the Learn feature. Learn assigns a series of keystrokes to any key on the keyboard—any key. When you press that key again, *DESQview* plays back the stored keystrokes.

In *DESQview*, scripts are associated with the currently active window, the program that is "on top" or in the foreground when the script is created. Each key you assign a script to is kept in a special area of memory, the *script buffer*. It can then be saved in a script file, which is always automatically loaded every time you start that program window.

If you're not into *DESQview*, the terms here can get confusing. If you are into *DESQview*, then follow along through the next few pages and we'll create a sample script for the "Big DOS" window.

Learning a script

DESQview's Big DOS window is a full-screen, full-memory version of the traditional mono-tasking DOS. The way I run things, I have *WordPerfect* in window 1, *Magellan* in window 2, and Big DOS in window 3. During the course of this book, I wrote the batch files and tested all the programs in window 3—Big DOS. Then to write about them, I switched back to window 1, *WordPerfect*, and jotted down the details.

To learn a script in *DESQview*, you must first be in the same window in which the script will be used. Scripts are attached only to one program at a time, or to the *DESQview* menu system. Their keystrokes can only be played back in that window.

To learn a script, you take the following steps:

1. Press the Learn key, SHIFT–ALT. The actual keystroke is "SHIFT –DESQ," DESQ being the *DESQview* activation key. Unless you've changed this, it should be the ALT-key.

   After pressing the Learn-key, you'll see the Learn menu displayed (see FIG. 16-7). Your available options are:

Start Script	=	Start recording a new script
Display Scripts	D	Display a list of scripts, select one to run
Load Scripts	L	Load a script file from disk

You can press ESC at this time if you want to cancel the script definition.

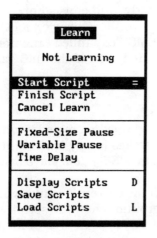

16-7 Here is the Learn feature's main menu.

2. Select Start Script (or =) from the Learn menu. Start Script is highlighted (see FIG. 16-7), so you can press enter to select it. This tells *DESQview* that you're about to put it into record mode. But first it wants to know which key to assign the recording.

   Note that "Start Script" means "start *recording* a script," it doesn't mean you select a script to run. To run a script you simply press the key to which it's been assigned, or you can choose Display Scripts from the menu and select the script from that list.

3. Choose a key to assign the script to. After selecting Start Script, *DESQview* displays a tiny box that asks, "Press the key you want to redefine." Your entire keyboard is open country now. Any key, from the A key to SHIFT – ALT – Omega is open.

Be logical here: don't select a key that will conflict with the program's functions. For example, choosing the F7 key for reassignment in *WordPerfect* would be dumb. Instead, choose something like CTRL – D or some other key that has a nonspecific function. (If you have an extended keyboard, chances are the F11 and F12 keys aren't used much; choose them.)

For Big DOS, I chose the CTRL – D key, so I pressed CTRL – D.

4. Give the script a name and start learning it. After you press a key or key combination, the Start a Script menu is displayed, as in FIG. 16-8. Enter a name for the script, then press ENTER to start recording, or press C to cancel.

16-8 The Start a Script menu is shown here.

```
        Start a Script
             Key: {^D}

Learn Script              ↵
Cancel Learn              C

Script Name DIR Command
```

If you start the script's name with an exclamation point (!), that script becomes the automatic startup script for the window. Each time you open that window in *DESQview*, the script will be loaded and executed. This is quite handy for initial setup of some windows. But note that only one script can have this attribute, and its name should start with an exclamation point.

5. Enter the keystrokes for the script. At this point you're recording the script. *DESQview* assigns all your keystrokes to a script buffer. To make you aware of this, an audible clicking sound is made each time you press a key.

You can insert pauses into the script (which is about as fancy as these macros get). Pauses can wait for certain keystrokes, a number of keystrokes, ENTER, or for a variable amount of time.

To insert a pause, press the Learn key (SHIFT – ALT) during the recording session and choose the type of pause from the Learn menu.

6. Finish the script by pressing Learn again. To stop recording, press Learn (SHIFT – ALT) a final time. The Learn menu is again redis-

played. Right now your options are:

Finish Script	-	Save the recorded keystrokes
Cancel Learn	C	Discard this script

(You can also select a pause here, but if you want to stop recording, select one of the above options.)

Selecting Finish Script stops recording, saving the macro in memory.

Note that the keystrokes you entered, as well as the script's name, are stored internally in a *script buffer*. The script buffer is attached to the current *DESQview* window, and it's loaded each time you open that window. It is not, however, automatically saved. You must do that manually.

7. Save the script buffer. Though it's not officially a step for creating a *DESQview* script, you should save the script buffer, allowing it and all its scripts to be used each time you open that window.

   To save the script buffer, press the Learn key (SHIFT – ALT) and choose Save Scripts or S from the menu. *DESQview* will next display a window allowing you to enter a name for the script. Normally, this is the two letter combination used to open the window, plus "-SCRIP.DVS". For example, the Big DOS script file would be named:

   BD-SCRIP.DVS

   Press ENTER to save the script file.

   Note that you can also select Load Scripts from the Learn menu, to load a previously named and saved script. However, the name BD-SCRIP.DVS (or any such named script file) will automatically be loaded each time you open that window.

Running scripts

To run a script, you simply press the key it's been assigned to. If this doesn't work, then you may have to manually load the script into memory. But normally, just pressing that key will play back the script you want.

Note that you can always select a script from a list. Just press the Learn key, and select Display Scripts, or D. A list of currently recorded scripts is then displayed, and you can pick one using the arrow keys and ENTER, or click on it with the mouse.

To skip a script, you first press the Skip key, the accent grave or back-apostrophe character ( ). That key is a "dead key" in *DESQview*. It's also a prefix key, telling *DESQview* to "ignore all scripts and pass the next key through as is."

Editing a script

Unlike *WordPerfect* or *1-2-3*, a *DESQview* script is stored in an encrypted format in a data file on disk. There is no direct way to get at it and edit its keystrokes. But there are work-arounds.

If you own the *DESQview* companions (Link, Notepad, Datebook, and Calculator), then you can use the Notepad to load up a script file and edit it. As long as you edit the file in the "nondocument" mode, everything works.

If you don't have the *DESQview* Notepad, then you can use the Convert a Script utility that came with *DESQview*.

Odds are pretty good that you haven't installed Convert a Script into your Open Window menu. To do so, go into the Open Window menu (press ALT, then O) and select Add Program (AP). From the list, choose Convert a Script and stick it into your program repertoire.

Convert a Script is a tiny, primitive, and interface-less program that simply reads in a script file and converts it to a text file, or conversely takes a text file and moves it into script format. When you start Convert a Script, it displays the following menu:

```
S) Script to Text File
T) Text to Script File
X) Exit
Selection:
```

Choose which you want, S, T or X. The program will then prompt you for the names of the text and script files, perform the conversion, and exit. For example, to convert my Big DOS script file, I typed S, then entered BD-SCRIP.DVS for the Script File Name, and BIGDOS.TXT for the text file. The program is really easy and simple.

Once the text file is created, you can bring it up for editing in your favorite text editor. In FIG. 16-9, I popped up QEdit and loaded BIG-DOS.TXT.

```
L 1    C 1    IAW    445k    c:\system\dv\bigdos.txt
{Learn {^D} "Dir command"}
dir{Enter}
{Finish}

{Learn {^L} "cls"}
cls{Enter}
{Finish}

{Learn {F12} "!startup"}
{Enter}
hello!
{Finish}

<*** End of File ***>
```

16-9   Here is the Big DOS script file in QEdit.

The macros start with "Learn," their key assignment, and title on the first line. The keystrokes follow, then the last line is {Finish}.

The non-ASCII keystrokes are stored in the familiar curly brace style. A full reference, as well as editing tips, is provided in an appendix in the *DESQview* manual. But note that after any changes, you must reconvert the saved file back to the script format using the Convert a Script program.

Copy and paste

In addition to its script macros, *DESQview* allows you to copy and paste information between its various windows and running applications. (And you thought only *Windows* would let you do that?) The feature is called Mark and Transfer, and it lets you select blocks of text for copying, which can later be pasted into other applications in a variety of ways.

In one sense, this is similar to making a macro; the text you copy with Mark and Transfer is introduced into the second application as *keystrokes*. The copied text doesn't just *splat* into the second application. Instead, it appears to the application (and on the screen) as if you're typing it. And it's really handy.

To copy text, you do the following:

1. Press the DESQ key to bring up the *DESQview* menu. The DESQ key is normally ALT, which you just tap to pop up *DESQview*'s main menu.

2. Select M for Mark. This brings up the Mark menu, which also contains some phone dialing options (as shown in FIG. 16-10). The top four options are primary to copying and pasting text.

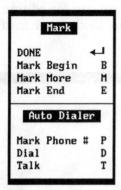

Mark	
DONE	↵
Mark Begin	B
Mark More	M
Mark End	E
Auto Dialer	
Mark Phone #	P
Dial	D
Talk	T

16-10 Here is the Mark menu.

3. Move the cursor to the start of the text. Because you're in the Mark mode, *DESQview* has taken control over your application. You can use the cursor keys, TAB, or the mouse to move the cursor around on the screen. Move it to the start of the text, line of text, or block you want to copy.

4. Press B for Begin. After you press B, the cursor creates an inverse block of text. As you move the cursor about, the box grows larger, engulfing the text you want to copy.

5. Press E to end the selection. After you've rounded up the text you want to copy, press E. That rectangle of text is then copied into *DESQview*'s Mark and Paste buffer. If you want to mark additional text (and put it into the same buffer), select M for More, or use the undocumented A (for Add) command. All the additional text will be stuffed into the same buffer. (And it all stays there until you choose the B command to begin a new block.)

6. Press ENTER when you're done. Or you can press ESC or DESQ (ALT) to return to *DESQview*'s main menu. From there you can move to the window or position on the screen where you want to paste the text.

To paste selected text, you select the Transfer item from *DESQview*'s main menu. To do so, take the following steps:

1. Press the DESQ key to bring up *DESQview*.
2. Select T for Transfer.

You'll see the Transfer menu displayed, as shown in FIG. 16-11. The Transfer menu gives you a number of options for pasting the text back into your document.

16-11 Here is the Transfer menu.

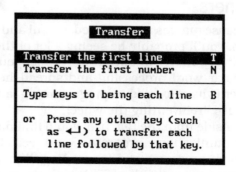

```
              ┌─────────────────────────────────────┐
              │            Transfer                  │
              ├─────────────────────────────────────┤
              │ Transfer the first line         T   │
              │ Transfer the first number       N   │
              ├─────────────────────────────────────┤
              │ Type keys to being each line    B   │
              ├─────────────────────────────────────┤
              │ or  Press any other key (such       │
              │     as ◄┘) to transfer each         │
              │     line followed by that key.      │
              └─────────────────────────────────────┘
```

To paste in the entire block, press ENTER. This follows each line you copied with the ENTER character, putting it into the second application just as you typed it. (Note that trailing spaces in the block are not typed.) If you're pasting into a spreadsheet, you can press the down-arrow key instead of ENTER, that way the information pasted fits into a column of cells.

The T option, ("Transfer the first line") is used to spit out the text one line at a time. *DESQview* will let you type a few keys, then press the DESQ key (ALT) again to see the transfer menu, with the option of pasting in the rest of the text or just another line. (There are windowed prompts displayed on the screen describing what your choices are.)

The N option ("Transfer the first number") is primarily a spreadsheet-user's tool. It weeds through any text you may have copied, and pastes in only the numeric values. After you paste in the number, you can enter other characters and then tap the DES key (ALT) again to paste in any other numbers. Note that only numbers will be pasted when you select this option.

The B option ("Type keys to begin each line") allows you to type a character to be used before text is pasted into the document. For example, if you wanted each line to start with a semicolon, type B then a semicolon.

Note that any other key you press will follow the pasted text into the document. For example, pressing the down-arrow key will cause each line to be pasted and then the "down-arrow key" to be pressed (which is ideal for spreadsheets).

Writing about this feature doesn't show you how well it works. You really need to use it for yourself. Being able to cut and paste between two running programs, a word processor and spreadsheet for example, is an extremely nifty feature to have. (That was probably the main reason for many of the Mark and Transfer feature's options.) Yet, it's a great way to move information between windows in *DESQview*, and it's similar in features to a macro command. The only drawback is that it can't easily be preprogrammed for automatic operation.

Others

Because macros are a desired, useful and fun feature to add to any application, you'll probably be seeing a lot of them in the coming years. Though their popularity might grow in time, you'll most definitely see macros in popular word processing and spreadsheet applications. And, of course, macros have existed in programming language since they thought of the phrase "reinventing the wheel."

Aside from the Big Two, you'll find macros in integrated software, telecommunications programs, and certain specialized utilities such as backup programs and Lotus' *Magellan*. Even DOS has a form of macros referred to as *aliasing*. (This isn't the same as batch file programming.)

Telecommunications programs employ different types of macros than were described in this chapter. Their macros are very interactive, unlike those in any other program. Aside from sending characters out the modem port, a telecommunications program's macros must also examine characters coming in through the modem port. Advanced macros decipher the characters, waiting for a specific combination. They then perform some action based on whether or not those characters were received. It's really handy, but yet another terribly complex aspect of a basically technical piece of software to begin with.

Backup programs use macros to automate the backup process, specifically the daily and weekly type of backups. Office managers will often create backup "sets," each of which is updated on a regular basis. By hooking the backup program's macros into a DOS backup batch file, regular backups proceed on schedule as planned. (Remember that when you write your backup macros.)

Other utility programs have automated macros as well. One of my favorites is Lotus' *Magellan*. It has the handy keystroke stuffer macros. But starting with release 2.0, *Magellan* added some nifty display, message box, and interactive dialog box macros. You can also reassign all of *Magellan*'s commands by using the macros. It's really quite fun (and a heck of a lot easier than some of the other macros described in this chapter).

Aliasing in DOS

DOS is another area where you can find macros—but not in the sense that batch files are macros. These macros should really be referred to as "aliasing," or assigning a longer, detailed command to a short set of keystrokes. (That's still a macro, but in the UNIX operating system it's called aliasing.)

DOS 5 introduced an official aliasing command with DOSKEY. It gives you command line editing keys (in addition to the Function key editing commands), plus a recallable command line "history," and what they call "macros."

DOSKEY is memory-resident. It's initially loaded by typing DOSKEY on the command line (or in your AUTOEXEC.BAT file). Once it's in memory, you add a macro using the following command:

DOSKEY *macro* = *macro_text*

Macro is the name of the macro and all text after the equal sign is assigned to it. In a way, this works like SET does with environment variables (though DOSKEY's macros aren't saved in the environment). After the above command, entering the name *macro* will then play back the macro text.

For example, the following lines in an AUTOEXEC.BAT file would load DOSKEY and setup three DOSKEY macros:

```
DOSKEY
DOSKEY D = DIR /W
DOSKEY H = DOSKEY /HISTORY
DOSKEY M = DOSKEY /MACROS
```

The first line loads DOSKEY, making it resident. The next three lines create three macros: D, H, and M. The D macro is aliased to the DIR command with the /W switch. Typing D at the DOS prompt is now the same as typing DIR /W.

The other two macros, H and M, show off two of DOSKEY's optional switches. The /HISTORY switch displays a history of all previous DOS commands listed at the command prompt. (You select them using the up-arrow key at the DOS prompt; not from the display.) The /MACROS switch lists the currently assigned macros.

As an example of how this works, the following shows what would appear on the screen if you typed only M, which DOSKEY has assigned as a macro:

```
C:\ > M
C:\ > DOSKEY /MACROS
D = DIR /W
H = DOSKEY /HISTORY
M = DOSKEY /MACROS
```

At the next command prompt (after typing the M macro), you see how DOSKEY expands the macro into its full command. After that, a list of the currently loaded macros is displayed on the screen.

The downside to DOSKEY's macros is that they won't work in a batch. Not at all.

For uses of DOS 4 and 3.3, two replacements for the clumsy DOS command line editor are DOSEDIT and CED, the Command Line Editor. DOSEDIT is older and what I use personally (because I like it and I'm stubborn). CED is more powerful and it has a professional-level companion product, PCED, which can be purchased in most software stores.

Both packages give you better DOS command line editing power, a history of recently entered command lines, plus the ability to alias DOS commands. Unlike DOSEDIT (at least in its current incarnation), you can specify a file full of aliases as opposed to popping them in one at a time.

For a single-user system, these utilities are a great way to cut back on your keystrokes. (In an office, it's best if everyone uses the same aliases in the same way.) DOSEDIT has been included on the supplemental programs diskette for you to try. (It's called NDOSEDIT.) I would have liked to include CED, but it was too big and wouldn't fit on the single diskette. And you get DOSKEY with DOS 5.

Summary

Macros are a popular addition to any program. But don't let them blow you away. Think of them on a basic level as a keystroke stuffer: you make the application memorize a series of keystrokes, like a tape recorder. By assigning those keystrokes to some special key combination, you can "play them back" without having to worry about all that typing.

Each program implements macros differently, but all applications usually offer a hefty selection of macro commands, including programming options, loops, file access, display, and macros for interacting with the user.

The best place to learn about these macros is in the application's manual. Sometimes the information is hidden (Lotus lists macro information in three different spots between two manuals). Usually it's complex and confusing. But there are always good books on the subject.

17

Macros and batch programming in Windows

Ever since the Macintosh proved successful and its graphic interface proved popular, the PC has been doomed to imitate it. Doom! Doom! Doom! The most popular incarnation of a graphic interface on the PC is Microsoft's *Windows*, which got a whole lot better and prettier under its 3.0 manifestation.

When IBM and Microsoft point to the PC's future, they point to *Windows*. (And further up the road they point to OS/2, which is kind of like "Super *Windows*.") *Windows* isn't going away, and its popularity among PC users is growing.

Windows is a positive influence on the PC. It makes the computer easier and more fun to use, and it provides a nice integrated environment for your applications. There are two drawbacks to this: Not all software runs nicely under *Windows*. So if you lack any software that absolutely needs *Windows*, why bother with it? And when you use a computer graphically, the need for batch files is totally eliminated. Or is it?

This chapter is about batch files under *Windows*. It could be brief: "With *Windows* you really don't need batch files any more." I could get away with that (since I'm not paid by the word here). But instead, I thought I'd continue the theme of macros and control languages by discussing how they operate under *Windows*. There really is some potential here, even if we are in the left field of batch file programming.

Batch files and Windows?

Yup, batch files under *Windows* is quite a limited subject. *Windows* insulates the user from DOS, and DOS is where you run your batch files. So that leaves us batch file zealots a little hungry for something to do under *Windows*. But let's first consider the possibilities.

Here's my system's batch file with which I start *Windows*:

Name: WIN.BAT

```
 1: @echo off
 2: path = c: \ system \ dos;c: \ system \ util;c: \ system \ batch
 3: set comspec = c: \ system \ dos \ command.com
 4: prompt $p$g
 5: SAY Windows! Blech!
 6: NUMOFF
 7: set temp = F: \ windows \ temp
 8: F:
 9: cd  \ windows
10: win
11: set temp =
```

My system is dual-modal. One mode boots *DESQview*, the other *Windows*. When *Windows* is boot, my system doesn't run an AUTOEXEC .BAT file. Instead, it runs WIN.BAT, which you see above. That explains why this batch file sets the PATH, PROMPT, and COMSPEC environment variables. Line 7 sets the *Windows*' TEMP variable, which tells the program where to store its temporary files.

NUMOFF is a program that turns off my Num Lock key (line 5). *Windows* is kept on my F drive, so we log to F in line 8, change to the *Windows* subdirectory in line 9, and run *Windows* in line 10. When *Windows* is done, line 11 resets the TEMP variable.

That's the way I run *Windows* when I boot. But what about running *Windows* under *DESQview*?

Running *Windows* under *DESQview* (or on a 386 system with *QEMM* or *386MAX* installed) requires that you run it in the real mode (the dumb, 8088-compatible mode). To do so, you specify the /R switch after *Windows*. On my system, that's handled by the following batch file:

Name: WINR.BAT

```
 1: @echo off
 2: say Windows! Blech!
 3: set temp = F: \ windows \ temp
 4: F:
 5: cd  \ windows
 6: win /r
 7: set temp =
```

This is just a mini version of the WIN.BAT program. The AUTOEXEC.BAT-like environment variable settings are gone, and *Windows* is started with the R switch. But other than that, everything is the same.

Running batch file programs

Windows runs two types of programs: *Windows* programs and non-*Windows* (text or DOS) applications. Since a batch file is a program, it falls into the latter category. And just like any COM or EXE file, you can add a batch file into *Windows'* Program Manager and run it.

To add a batch file, you simply place it into the Program Manager. Choose the proper program group and select add from the File menu. Then use the appropriate commands to enter the batch file. Voila, your batch file is now some icon off in the Program Manager window.

To run the batch file, double click it. *Windows* loads DOS and runs your batch file. If it launches an application, then that application will appear in its own DOS window. If the batch file just executes itself, it will run and when done you'll return to *Windows*.

So batch files are possible in *Windows*—but not the real *Windows* solution. (Other types of control languages, covered near the end of this chapter, will offer you more batch file-like power under *Windows*.)

Windows' recorder

Windows has its own, built-in macro capability. You can create macros that record all your keystrokes, mouse movements, or varying combinations and degrees of both, which can be played back in one or all of your *Windows* applications. And just like *DESQview* (or *DESQview* may be just like *Windows* in this case—who knows?), you can cut and paste information between various running programs in *Windows*.

Before getting into it, I must confess that I'm not a big *Windows* fan. It's a great environment if you're running *Windows* applications. For beginners, *Windows* is a lot easier and more comfortable than the intimidating command prompt. But for a command prompt fan such as myself, *Windows* is often frustrating to work with. Keep that in mind if I get nasty over the next few pages.

Using the recorder

The Recorder is a program you'll find in the Program Manager (the main window). It's located in the Accessories group (mini window) and its icon looks like a video camera with two cassettes by it.

The Recorder manages files that contain lists of macros. You can create lists, save them to disk, load in lists made by someone else, merge lists, all sorts of neat stuff. But the Recorder's main job is to create and run macros you define on your own. Before doing that, you need to know what you're recording and where you'll be recording it.

Setting up your applications before using the Recorder is important. The Recorder records keystrokes, mouse movements, or a combination of both—but you need to know for what purpose you'll be recording before you start. This works just like every other macro; know what you do before you start. But with *Windows* you need to put extra emphasis on it. Because you're in an all-encompassing environment, you really need to set things up before you start recording.

For example, if you're recording a macro that puts your name and address at the end of a letter, already in your word processor (or *Windows* Write or the Notepad) *before* you set out to record the macro. Don't fire up the Recorder, then "maximize" the icon, scroll to the text, then type the macro. Because you're recording, all of that action will be saved in the macro. When you play it back, it may error.

There are other caveats for using Recorder, a few of which are listed near the end of this section. Don't get me wrong, it's a handy tool. But set up what you want to record before you fire up the Recorder.

Making a macro

Unlike other macros discussed in the part of the book, *Windows* macros are all learn-mode macros. They're also just keyboard stuffers (and mouse movement stuffers). There is no macro language, nor is there any way to edit a macro once you've recorded it. (If the Recorder proves popular, this may change with future releases of *Windows*.)

To record a macro in *Windows*, take the following steps:

1. Start the Recorder. To make sure everything moves smoothly, even before you setup your application, open the Program Manager and select Recorder from the Accessories group. The Recorder window will open up (as shown in FIG. 17-1).

   There are four menu items in the Recorders window. File loads and saves lists of macros already on disk; Macro deals with recording macros and maintaining macros already recorded; Options sets global options for recording your macros (setup stuff); and Help displays help information about Recorder.

   If macros have already been recorded, you'll see them listed in the window. Each macro is shown in two columns, the first being an assigned keystroke for the macro, the second a description.

   Rather than mess around here now, shrink the Recorder window down to an icon by clicking on the minimize button, or pressing ALT – SPACE, N.

2. Set up the application in which you want to record. This involves everything: Open the proper window, size it, position the cursor, and so on. Once you start recording your macro, everything you do is noted by Record. So perform any setup now.

   Also, make sure what you're going to record is pretty much independent. For example, mouse clicks and drags are all performed relative to the entire screen or the current window. If the

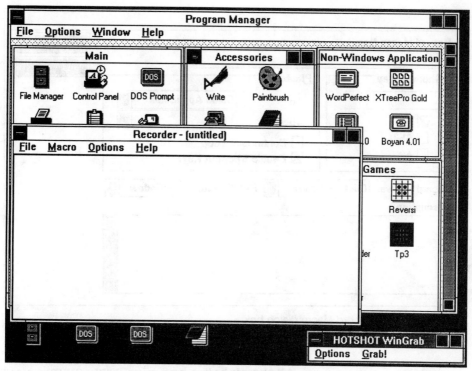

17-1 This is the Recorder's window as shown on the Windows desktop.

screen size changes (say you run the macro on another system with different graphics) or the window is re-sized, the macro may not run properly. Consider that when you record (and maybe use some keystroke equivalents instead of mouse movements).

3. Open the Recorder's icon. It should be minimized on the bottom of the screen. Double click on it, or click once and select *Restore*, or press CTRL–ESC to bring up the Task List and choose Recorder from there. Once the Recorder is open, you'll see the same window as shown in FIG. 17-1.

4. Select Record from the Macro menu. This item starts a new macro. A dialog box is displayed where you set various options for the macro (see FIG. 17-2). This is how you define the type of macro you're recording and set various options.

5. Make your settings in the Record Macro dialog box. Moving from the top of the dialog box down, here's what you'll find:

The *Record Macro Name* input box is where you can enter a name for your macro. Give it a descriptive name so when you see it later in the list you'll know what it does.

The *Shortcut Key* area is where you can assign a key combina-

Record Macro

Record Macro **N**ame:

Shortcut Key

☒ Ctrl
☐ Shift
☐ Alt

Playback

To: `Same Application`
Speed: `Fast`

☐ Continuous Loop
☒ Enable Shortcut Keys

Record **M**ouse: `Clicks + Drags` **R**elative to: `Window`

Description

17-2 Here is the Record Macro dialog box.

tion for the macro. All the alphabet keys plus CTRL, SHIFT, or ALT can be used, plus a variety of keys you'll see in a pop-up menu if you press on the down arrow button. You can really choose any key, but as with most macros, keep them logical and avoid using keys already assigned to some function.

Note that entering a shortcut key is optional. You can run any macro by popping up the Recorder and choosing its name from the list.

The *Playback* area controls how the macro is to be handled once it's run. For example, do you want the macro only to work in one application? If so, choose *Same Application* for the *To* field. Otherwise, select *Any Application* and your macro will work in all *Windows* applications (note that they must be *Windows* applications; Recorder macros will not play back in text/DOS applications run under *Windows*).

The *Speed* item sets the playback speed for the macro, either *Fast* or *Recorded Speed*, which plays things back at the same tempo they were recorded; *Continuous Loop* can be used for self-running (and repeating) demo programs; and *Enable Shortcut Keys* turns on the shortcut key method of running a macro.

Record Mouse tells the macro how to react to the mouse. You can record all mouse movements with *Everything*, only *Clicks and Drags*, or no mouse at all with *Ignore Mouse*. The mouse coordinates are set *Relative to* either the current *Window* or the entire *Screen*.

Finally, there is a large input box where you can enter a *Description* for the macro. (Note that the Preferences item in the Options menu will set the default for many of these items here.)

For a macro such as the one that prints your name and address at the end of a letter, choose a shortcut key (I chose CTRL–E, putting E in the *Shortcut Key* box and clicking *Ctrl*); Select *Any Application* for the playback; and *Ignore Mouse* (it's not used in that macro).

6. After you've made your settings, click the Start button. The Recorder window minimizes and you're back in your application. (This is why it's so important to set things up before starting the Recorder.)

   Note that the Recorder icon is blinking on the bottom of the screen (if you can see it). It blinks as long as you're recording.

7. Do your macro. Enter your keystrokes, move the mouse, do whatever you want. It's all recorded as part of the macro. (Again, Recorder is a keystroke and "mouse-stroke" stuffer.)

8. To finish recording, select the Recorder icon again. Clicking on the flashing Recorder icon brings up the dialog box shown in FIG. 17-3. Select *Save Macro* and click OK to record your macro. Choosing *Resume Recording* continues the macro, *Cancel Recording* stops everything.

17-3 Here is where you tell Recorder to stop recording the macro.

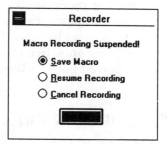

9. All done! You'll now be returned to the Recorder window. You can see your freshly added macro in the list. To use it, you can select it now (double click on it or choose Run from the Macro menu), or return to your application and try the shortcut key.

Things to note

Recorder is *Windows'* angle on macros, just as *DESQview* has its scripts. They're quite handy and always ready, but keep in mind the following points:

- Setup is important. Always set up your program before you record the macros. If you know you're recording, then start up Recorder and minimize it. Then set up your application. Once everything's ready, choose Recorder from the bottom of the screen and go.
- No editing. The macros you create cannot be edited. You can record over them, but once they're entered, they're stored in a special file that you can't get at to edit.
- Use the keyboard instead of the mouse. Always select menu items, commands, or window controls using keyboard equivalents as opposed to the mouse. In some cases, the mouse is the only way to get something done. When possible, though, use the keyboard.
- Consider playback. When you do record mouse movements, consider that the environment you play them back in may not be the same as when the macro was recorded. *Windows* move. Screen size changes with different monitors. There are a lot of elements working against you when you record a macro that relies heavily on the mouse. Also, consider your position in a document or dialog box when you play back a macro. In different modes, these macros can have strange effects.
- Choose shortcut keys wisely. Recorder is pretty liberal in which keys it will let you reassign to macros. Note that there is no "skip" key, allowing a Function, ALT, or CTRL key to return to its original purpose. You would have to clear out the macro list (or delete one macro from the list) to regain control over a specific key.
- Load the macros. These macros you create must be loaded into Recorder before you can use them. (This isn't a caveat, it's just one of those head-hitters: "Oh, duh! I forgot to load the macro files!")
- *Windows* only. Recorder only makes macros that can be recorded and played back in *Windows* applications.

Cutting and pasting

With *Windows* you can cut, copy and paste information between running programs. But before getting off on the subject, note that there is a difference between *Windows* applications and non-*Windows* applications: *Windows* applications are designed to run under and work well with *Windows*. Non-*Windows* applications are everything else: All your old DOS applications and most software that doesn't come from Microsoft.

In a *Windows* application, you can cut or copy text or graphics. *Windows* knows which is which: copying text results in text, copying graphics gives you graphics. (But note that you cannot copy bit-mapped text as text, such as the text you may have in some picture or paint document.)

In non-*Windows* applications, you can select text only as text. You can, however, paste that text into any *Windows* or non-*Windows* application. And it's possible to paste text from a *Windows* application into a non-*Windows* application.

Whew!

It gets confusing. For the next few paragraphs, keep in mind the basic differences between *Windows* and non-*Windows* applications.

Using Windows' edit menu

All *Windows* applications should have some sort of Edit menu. This concept is borrowed from the Macintosh family of computers, which made their original reputation on the ability to cut and paste items from one application to another.

The items (one at a time) are held in a universal clipboard. (This is the Clipboard application found in the Program Manager window, Main group.) Once an item, either text or graphics, has been cut or copied into the clipboard, you can paste it into any other *Windows* application willing to receive it.

What makes all this possible is the universal Edit menu, which nearly all *Windows* applications that create or manipulate data have in their menu bar. The contents and description of the typical *Windows* Edit menu is shown in TABLE 17-1.

Table 17-1

Item	Keystroke	Function
Undo	Alt + Bksp	Undoes some action (specific to the application)
Cut	Shift + Del	Cuts selected item to clipboard (copy & delete)
Copy	Ctrl + Ins	Copies selected item to clipboard
Paste	Shift + Ins	Copies selected item from clipboard into application
Del	Del	Clears selected item

An item (text or graphic) must be *selected* before it can be cut or copied into the clipboard. This is usually accomplished by dragging the mouse over text, or using some tool in a graphic program to select items.

When pasting information into an application, you first position the cursor where you want the text to go, or for graphic applications the image is pasted and selected so you can further manipulate it, moving around to where you want it.

This is really basic *Windows* stuff—truly, "cut and paste." Where things get rough, is when you deal with non-*Windows* applications.

Selecting and marking text

Windows has the ability to copy and paste text in non-*Windows* applications, as well as *Windows*-only applications. But there are differences between the way the two systems work. The most obvious is that your non-*Windows* applications can only cut or copy text to the clipboard, and you can only paste text into them.

Any non-*Windows* application you start in *Windows* is run initially as a full screen text application. You're still in *Windows*, but what you see on the screen is the same as if you were running the program under DOS. You can't really paste any text stored in the clipboard into your document at this point. It's possible, but you must first access the Control-menu box.

The Control-menu box is in the upper-left corner of every graphic window in *Windows*. (It looks like a three-dimensional hyphen.) The problem is you're in a full screen text window running a text application. To make that a graphic window, and access the Control-menu, you can take one of two steps:

1. Press ALT–ENTER to make the full screen text window a graphic window
2. Press ALT–SPACE to directly access the Control-menu

ALT–ENTER takes your text application and shrinks it into a graphic *Windows*-window. But ALT–SPACE is the direct approach, first shrinking your window into a graphics window and then displaying the Control-menu. In either case, once your text application has been converted (or "perverted") to the graphics mode, you can access the editing commands.

There are three groups of items in the Control-menu. These will vary depending on the application and type of PC on which you're running *Windows*:

Window commands:	Restore
	Move
	Size
	Minimize
	Maximize
Program control:	Close
Miscellaneous:	Switch to . . .
	Edit/Paste
	Settings

"Settings" and "Edit" appear only in the 386 enhanced mode. The "Paste" item appears in the other modes.

The "Edit" item has a triangle next to it, pointing to the right. It indicates a sub-menu is attached, one with four menu items:

Mark	Select text using the keyboard
Copy	Copy the selected text to the clipboard

Paste   Paste in text from the clipboard
Scroll   Move around the window (if it's not full size)

Note that there is no Cut item; you can only copy text from a text application. In fact, this copying is only a duplication of the characters on the display (similar to *DESQview*'s Mark and Transfer function, but not as versatile).

There are two ways to select text in a windowed text screen: You can use the Mark command and the keyboard, or use the Select method, which involves the mouse.

Choosing the Mark command switches you into Mark mode. The title of the window will change to "Mark" followed by the window's name. A flashing block cursor then appears in the upper-left corner of the window. You position it using the arrow keys. Then use SHIFT plus the arrow keys to select a block.

The select method of marking text uses the mouse. Just click the mouse pointer in the window and drag out a block of text. Note that the window's title changes to "Select" plus the window's name.

In either mode, *Windows* will blip at you if you press any incorrect keys. Press ENTER to end the selection, ESC to cancel. Pressing ENTER is also the same thing as choosing Copy from the Control-Menu's Edit item. The text you've selected is now in *Windows'* clipboard.

From the clipboard, you can paste the text into any other *Windows'* application (text or graphics), or back into the same application. To paste text into a text application, pull down the Control-menu, select Edit, then Paste. The text will be inserted at the cursor's position.

All this works fine and dandy in the 386 enhanced mode. But in *Windows'* real and standard modes, only the "Paste" item is available in the Control menu. "Paste" will only paste text into your application; text that already exists in the clipboard, and that text can only come from *Windows* applications that have an Edit menu.

Other ways to do Windows macros

Windows is one of those wide open spaces in computerdom. Because it's cheap and popular (well, the software's cheap; upgrading the PC to run *Windows* ain't), *Windows* will be around a while. And thanks to enterprising individuals writing software, there are some interesting *Windows* solutions available. Some of this stuff actually gives you substitutes for batch files under *Windows*.

Two programs worth looking into are *Command Post* and *BatchWorks for Windows*. *Command Post* is one of those "try it for a month and if you like it pay us money" programs. (And they're very adamant about you paying money for it—almost nasty.) *BatchWorks* is a commercial product available from Publishing Technologies.

Command post

I have some friends who are really into *Windows*. One of them is Andy, who is a certifiable *Windows* nut. Whenever I see him, I try to determine who has more *Windows* games. No matter how hard I try, he always gets all the neat stuff before I do. Even Command Post, which he told me gives you all sorts of batch file-like power under *Windows*.

Command Post is like a shell for *Windows* (which is a shell for DOS). It had its heyday for *Windows* Version 2, which really lacked a decent program manager. Command Post gave you the ability to easily launch programs, filling in the open cracks of the older versions of *Windows*.

With *Windows* 3, however, Command Post does more than fill in the cracks—it takes over. Not only does it replace the Program Manager (actually, it just shoves it aside), but it gives you a complete programming language with which you can create your own little *Windows*-like applications. For those who are really into it, this is great! But it's also overwhelming if all you're looking for is a little batch file power.

I'm not that intimate with Command Post, so I can't provide any solid examples. Part of the problem is Command Post's utterly inane installation procedure. Consider FIG. 17-4.

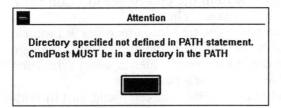

17-4 Here is a friendly installation message from Command Post.

Command Post must be installed from a subdirectory listed on your PATH. If it's not, you must exit *Windows*, modify the path, and re-start *Windows* to install Command Post. (Changes made to the PATH in the DOS *Windows* session will not alter your true path—the one Command Post examines.) Either that, or you copy Command Post to some subdirectory already on the path.

Next, no matter where you select a destination, Command Post will always install itself in its own subdirectory off your root on Drive C. I found this terribly annoying—especially for a program geared toward advanced users. Granted, it's possible to move the directory around, but you have to do that, edit some of your *Windows* *.INI files, and change a bunch of parameters. It was just too big of a hassle for me, especially for software that so ruthlessly reminded me every few seconds that I had to pay the shareware donation.

If you're into *Windows* (which sort of excludes you from the batch file priesthood), then consider Command Post as a way to get back some of the programming power *Windows* doesn't give you. It's shareware, so it can be found almost everywhere. But if you want to order the real version, here's that information:

Command Post
Wilson WindowWare
2701 California Ave. SW, Suite 212
Seattle, WA 98116
(800) 762-8383

PubTech's BatchWorks

I got excited when I saw BatchWorks in the software store. I knew I had to write an update to this book and I knew *Windows* was an important part of the PC's future. So I phoned up Publishing Technologies and spoke to Marshal. I told him the situation, and he agreed to send me BatchWorks in the mail so I could write about it.

Six weeks later I don't have BatchWorks, so I can't tell you a thing about it.

From what it says on the box, however, BatchWorks gives you the ability to create custom dialog boxes and macros for running *Windows*. It looks like a lot of fun. "Batch files in *Windows*," it says.

If you'd like to try out BatchWorks, then find it in a store and buy it. If you want to order it directly from Publishing Technologies (or at least make the attempt), here's that information:

BatchWorks for Windows
Publishing Technologies
7719 Wood Hollow Drive, Suite 260
Austin, TX 78731
(800) PUB-TECH

Summary

Macros is a subject that's just a little outside of the realm of batch files. There's a connection, certainly: You can continue to automate your computing processes by launching a macro when your batch file starts some application. But then we get off into macro land. Walk further and there's cut-and-paste. And *Windows*? *Windows* rules out batch files altogether.

But there are still ways to make using *Windows* more productive. *Windows* can be started with batch files, and you can run batch files under *Windows*. *Windows* also has the Recorder, which allows you to create macros for one or all of your *Windows* applications. Finally, there's cut and paste, which can cut and copy text and graphics between *Windows* applications, and copy and paste text to and from text applications in *Windows*' 386 enhanced mode.

Part Five

Hard disk strategies

Here is where batch files get put to use. Sure, you can use the techniques described in this book to write some really efficient and useful batch files. But how can you put them to work? How can you use the knowledge provided here to give yourself the ideal system?

18
Managing your hard disk

A hard disk is the best thing you can buy for your computer. It gives you fast and virtually unlimited storage. Floppy users: imagine having all your programs and data on one big, quick disk. No more need to juggle diskettes or examine gooey labels for the file you want.

However, one of the problems associated with a hard disk is that its organization is up to you. You can put your files and programs anywhere on the hard disk. If you're smart, you'll organize your system into subdirectories.

If you're even smarter, you'll develop a backup strategy that keeps safety copies of all your files and programs on "emergency" diskettes. But how can you learn that?

The DOS manual offers only weak, watered down suggestions on hard disk organization and management. It assumes you'll learn about it on your own, or, better yet, have a service representative come out to your office and do it for you. Ha! You'd be better off putting all your files in the root directory and using the hard disk in the worst possible manner.

Because there's no official method of hard disk organization, many people turn to books on the subject. I co-wrote one such book and it's available through TAB Books (see the introduction for more information). The way I learned about hard disk management was through trial and error.

I was one of the first users at my old job to have a DOS hard disk system. I fiddled with it for hours, organizing subdirectories, writing batch files. I must have moved, deleted, renamed, and created dozens of subdirectories before I finally came upon my ideal setup, which you'll read about later.

Of course, not everyone is like me—or you for that matter. Different users require different things. If you're installing a hard disk and writing batch files for someone else, you'll need to know what they need and then work to meet that need. That's the subject of this chapter—learning how to organize a hard disk to meet a specific need.

Also, this part of this book doesn't assume to be an end-all to hard disk management. There is a lot to organizing a hard drive and using it effectively. If you still have questions or concerns after reading the next few chapters, I'd advise you to pick up a good book on the subject. (No further hints are needed on which book to get!)

What is hard disk management?

No one reading this book should be without a hard disk. There are two reasons for this.

The first reason is that today's software requires the storage capacity and speed that a hard drive offers. If you're using floppy disk drives alone, then the amount of your time a hard drive will save you is worth the cost.

The second reason is that hard drives are not expensive at all. The first hard drive available for my ancient TRS-80 Model III cost just under $2,000. It held a staggering five megabytes of data. Just last week I bought a 90 megabyte hard drive for under $1,000. That's about ten dollars per megabyte compared with $400 per megabyte in 1983. Also, consider that floppy disk drives cost about $80 each and only store a fraction of what a hard drive does. You just can't beat the price. Buy one.

Once you have a hard disk, you'll need to organize it. The organization is done via subdirectories and whatever other approaches you'd like to take. This is a flexible system. Because there are no mandatory subdirectories you need (unlike UNIX and Xenix, or even OS/2 to some extents), you can put files wherever you want, name the directories whatever you want—it's all up to you.

But, just in case you need some assistance, the following are two key points to hard disk management:

- Organization
- Backing up

Organization is the easy part. Basically, it says to put programs and files in their own subdirectories.

Backing up is the hard part. Some would consider backing up to be the "minor" part, but it is important. Besides DOS, BACKUP should be the only other program that you absolutely use every day. Hard disks may be reliable, but only a fool thinks they're indestructible.

Organization

Organization is easy. I'll start by describing the worst-case scenario of organization: Putting all your files in your hard drive's root directory. This is done by one type of person: him who don't know better [sic].

Users used to floppy drives just put everything on "the disk." But a hard drive is a very big disk. If you put everything on a hard drive, you're really going to confuse yourself. A hard drive can have potentially thousands of files on it, unlike the typical floppy which may average only 30 to 60 files.

I won't go into the problems of having 2,000 files all on one drive, all in the same directory. (Well, I will mention filename conflicts, fragmented and slow directory access, a disk becoming "full" when it still has megabytes of space available, and a generally tacky appearance that will make even novice hard drive users shun you.) DOS offers three useful utilities to keep this from happening:

MKDIR or MD
CHDIR or CD
RMDIR or RD

Using these three internal commands, primarily MKDIR and CHDIR, you can organize your hard drive into subdirectories. That's all the DOS manual says. How you do it is up to you.

Of primary concern is to keep your root directory clean. Somewhere, in the marble pillared halls of hard disk management, there is the following phrase chiseled into an arch:

Keep the root clean

No, this doesn't apply to horticulturists or dentists. Instead, it refers to that goal of hard disk management: organization. The root, or top, directory of a hard disk needs to have only three files in it:

COMMAND.COM
AUTOEXEC.BAT
CONFIG.SYS

Even then, two of these files are optional. COMMAND.COM can be placed in another directory (using the SHELL command in CONFIG.SYS, in which case CONFIG.SYS needs to be in the root). And AUTOEXEC.BAT and CONFIG.SYS can be removed if need be.

Other than those three files, everything else should be a subdirectory entry. Your goal is to create those subdirectories carefully and logically and then place your programs and files into them.

In the following sections, I'll show you several approaches. None of them are right and none of them are wrong. They're just popular ways of tackling the same problem. Also included are various batch file examples to supplement each of the directory structures.

Simple approach

If you're just starting out, you can forget the "example" provided for you in the DOS manual. It's impractical. Instead, you should start with the basics: Create a subdirectory for DOS (see FIG. 18-1). The DOS directory was created by typing:

C> MD DOS

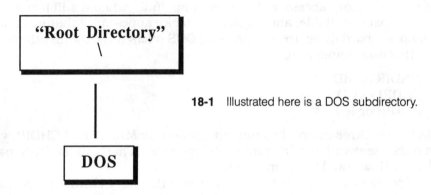

18-1   Illustrated here is a DOS subdirectory.

To see what it looks like, change to your DOS directory:

C> CD DOS

Pull a directory and you will find \DOS void of files:

C> DIR

```
Volume in drive C is BRAND NEW
Volume Serial Number is 000A-0001
Directory of C: \ DOS
        <DIR>   2-17-89   8:56p
        <DIR>   2-17-89   8:56p
   2 File(s) 32491072 bytes free
```

Your next task is to copy all your DOS programs and files from your DOS distribution diskettes into the \DOS directory on your hard drive. Put the DOS diskette in drive A and type:

C> COPY A:*.* C: \ DOS

or, because you're already "in" the DOS directory, you can type:

C> COPY A:*.*

Some of the files copied will be duplicates. For example, you don't need a second copy of COMMAND.COM in your \DOS directory, so delete it:

C> DEL COMMAND.COM

(Make sure you're in the \DOS directory before typing that command!)

You can also delete any other files you may think you'll never need. I'd advise against deleting anything now (other than COMMAND.COM). But later, you can delete some of the files you'll never use to free up some space. (And you'll still have the originals on the distribution diskette in case you need them.)

If your version of DOS came with more than one diskette, insert each succeeding diskette into drive A and copy files from them as well:

C> COPY A:*.*

Organizing directories

After you've put DOS on your hard drive, neatly tucked away into its own subdirectory, you should create subdirectories for each of your applications programs. For the example, I'll assume you have a spreadsheet (SuperCalc), database program (R:BASE), word processor (MultiMate), and a directory for playing games (see FIG. 18-2).

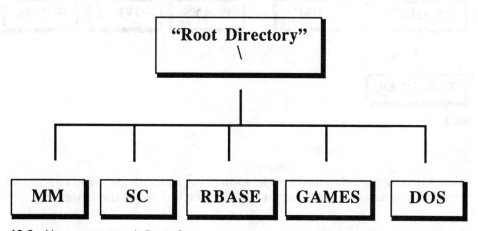

18-2 Here are more subdirectories.

Into each of these subdirectories you'll install the respective programs. Then, as a second layer of organization, place under each subdirectory various data files. For example, the following subdirectories might go under the MM subdirectory:

\ LETTERS
\ MISC
\ WORK
\ POETRY
\ NOVEL

You can have as many subdirectories as you like, one for each category of your writing. Or, rather than have only a second layer of subdirectories, go

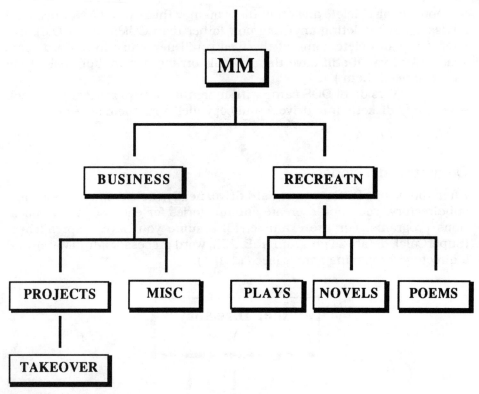

18-3 You can go nuts with organization.

nuts with organization and create something like FIG. 18-3. You can get as detailed and as organized as you like. In fact, the more the better.

Setting the path

All this organization means is that you'll need to supply your system with a fairly useful PATH command—one that can anticipate just about any situation.

If you only had one subdirectory layer of data files under your programs' subdirectories, the following path would work nicely:

```
PATH = C:\DOS;..
```

Remember how ".." equals the parent directory? This would allow one layer of data subdirectories below each of your primary program subdirectories to have access to the program files. Also, DOS should always be on the path, allowing you access to all the important external DOS commands.

If you chose to go with a highly specific and organized subdirectory structure, then the following path may come in handy:

```
PATH = C:\DOS;C:\MM;C:\SC;C:\RBASE;C:\GAMES
```

Okay. Let's get real nuts. Use the SUBST command to "alias" some popular directories:

```
SUBST D: C:\DOS
SUBST M: C:\MM
SUBST S: C:\SC
SUBST R: C:\RBASE
SUBST G: C:\GAMES
```

Now your path can look like this:

```
PATH = D:\;M:\;S:\;R:\;G:\
```

Remember to add the LASTDRIVE command to your CONFIG.SYS file if you use SUBST. Also, if your system already has a drive D, SUBST won't let you alias D: for \DOS; choose another letter.

Detailed approach

The following is a more detailed approach to using subdirectories. It's a hybrid between the above, simple example, and a totally souped system that will be discussed later. This is the exact system I use on my computer at home—and have used successfully for years. It proves quite flexible.

The first step to this approach is to group your files and programs. For most people, this isn't necessary. But if you use more than one word processor, or spreadsheet, or if you write programs, this type of organization will come in handy.

The primary "branch" of the directory tree structure I call SYSTEM. Under the SYSTEM directory are all files associated with my computer SYSTEM, each placed into their own subdirectory: DOS, for the DOS programs; UTIL, for miscellaneous utilities; MACE for the MACE utilities; NORTON, for the Norton Utilities; HERCULES, for the Hercules graphics card utilities; MOUSE, for my mouse programs; TOOLS, for my backup program and other hard disk tools (caching programs and electronic disk drivers); and BORLAND, which contains the *SideKick* and *SuperKey* programs (see FIG. 18-4).

I also use a number of word processors. Each of them is kept in the WP directory (see FIG. 18-5).

In a third main subdirectory, I keep all the other files I use on my system. This includes a spreadsheet, plus a C and Assembly language development system (see FIG. 18-6).

In addition to all those second-level subdirectories, there are third- and fourth-level directories. For example, under the \OTHER\MASM directory are about a half dozen directories for the programs that I've written in assembly language (including an \OTHER\MASM\BATCH directory for the files written for this book).

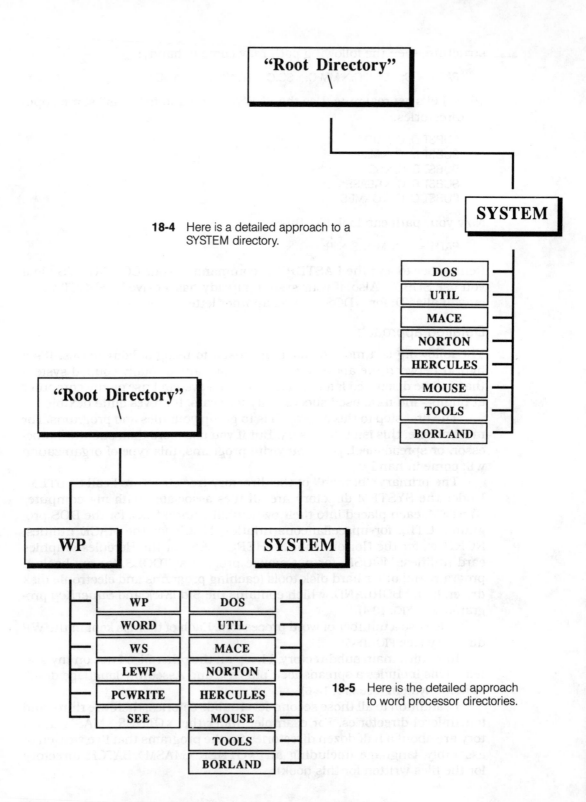

18-4 Here is a detailed approach to a SYSTEM directory.

18-5 Here is the detailed approach to word processor directories.

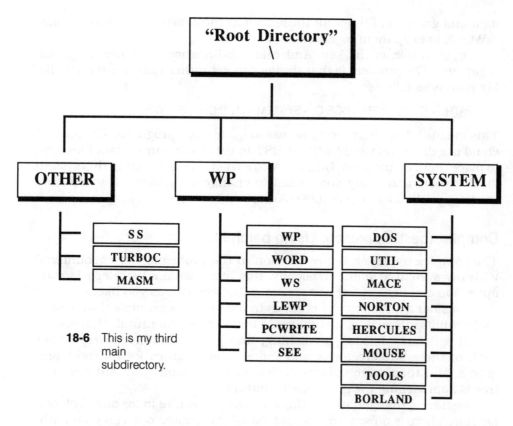

"Root Directory"
\

| OTHER | WP | SYSTEM |

OTHER
- S S
- TURBOC
- MASM

WP
- WP
- WORD
- WS
- LEWP
- PCWRITE
- SEE

SYSTEM
- DOS
- UTIL
- MACE
- NORTON
- HERCULES
- MOUSE
- TOOLS
- BORLAND

18-6 This is my third main subdirectory.

Two other main subdirectories exist off the root directory: \TEMP and \WORK. (Some users might have a \JUNK directory instead of \TEMP.)

\TEMP is my temporary files subdirectory. I put into that subdirectory just about anything and everything. For example, when I get a new program to try out, I install it in \TEMP. If I like the program, I figure out where else on the hard drive to put it, and then make a permanent subdirectory for it.

I also place into \TEMP files that I download from national networks or local electronic bulletin boards. I can then examine them to see if they're worth keeping or not, keeping them all in one place until I know what to do with them.

\WORK contains a varying number of subdirectories depending on which projects I'm working on. Normally, I keep data files in subdirectories under the appropriate program subdirectory. For example, \OTHER\SS\DATA contains all my spreadsheet data, and \WP\WP\LETTERS contains all my correspondence written in WordPerfect. But the contents of \WORK vary and may not necessarily relate to another program in another subdirectory.

For example, if I'm working on a novel or play, I'll put it under \WORK. If I'm working on a large project for the office, using spreadsheet

data and graphics, I'll put all those files in their own subdirectory under
\ WORK to keep them together.

Organization is the key. And this subdirectory structure keeps me
organized. The problem is that things can get rather unruly after a while.
My path is as follows:

PATH = C:\SYSTEM\DOS;C:\SYSTEM\UTIL;C:\WP\WP;..

This means I don't have ready access to quite a few programs. Of course, I
could use drive "aliasing" with SUBST to get at some important files, and
to place them on the path. But, as I said earlier, I've been using this system
for five years and really don't want to change it. However, if you'll keep
reading, you'll see one possible solution:

Complex (best) approach: Using batch files

The complex approach is my solution to the problems I've encountered
with my system at home. Basically, this organizational strategy is wide
open. You can have as few or as many subdirectories as you like.

Consider a directory structure as in the previous example. But, just to
make things interesting, mentally add in database, communications, integrated software, desktop publishing, and games subdirectories. Under
each of these subdirectories add more subdirectories for different programs, and then more subdirectories for data. Soon, your subdirectory
tree is approaching the great oak in stature.

Assuming that you use all those programs, you're in for one heck of a
joy ride. There is no way you should list all those directories on your path.
Consider that each time you type in a command, DOS looks for the program (first .COM, then .EXE, then .BAT) in the current directory, then in
every subdirectory on the path. That's three times the number of path
entries you have. That's a lot.

The solution is in batch files. For each program you may ever need on
disk, you write a batch file—even if it's only a two-line batch file. The batch
file takes care of all the details. But to make it work, you still need to set the
path. But you add the name of a special batch file subdirectory:

PATH = C:\SYSTEM\DOS;U:\;C:\SYSTEM\BATCH;..

\SYSTEM\DOS is left on the path because the DOS programs are very
important and you should have a direct path to them at all times. "U:" is
an alias for a utility program subdirectory. Because you probably use a lot
of utilities on your system, you should also have access to it. (Incidentally,
making liberal use of the SUBST command to alias drive letters is another
way to whittle down a complex subdirectory structure.)

The "..." entry is kept in the path because it will still come in handy
when you "manually" change directories to run programs. But for the
most part, all the programs you run will be executed via batch files in the
\SYSTEM\BATCH subdirectory.

For example, the following batch file runs your spreadsheet:

Name: SS.BAT

```
1: @ECHO OFF
2: REM Run Spreadsheet
3: C:
4: CD \OTHER\SS
5: PATH = C:\SYSTEM\DOS;C:\SYSTEM\UTIL;C:\OTHER\SS
6: SS
7: REM Restore old path
8: PATH = C:\SYSTEM\DOS;U:\;C:\SYSTEM\BATCH;..
```

For every program on your disk, there will exist a batch file. In fact, you only need change a few things to make the SS.BAT file run a word processor:

Name: WORD.BAT

```
1: @ECHO OFF
2: REM Run Microsoft Word
3: C:
4: CD \WP\WORD
5: PATH = C:\SYSTEM\DOS;C:\SYSTEM\UTIL;C:\WP\WORD
6: WORD
7: REM Restore old path
8: PATH = C:\SYSTEM\DOS;U:\;C:\SYSTEM\BATCH;..
```

Because all these batch files are in the batch file subdirectory, you will always have access to any of your programs. If you add software to your system, simply write a new batch file to run that program and put the batch file in \SYSTEM\BATCH (or whatever your batch file subdirectory is called).

Some programs may use batch files to start themselves. For example, the following batch file is used to start the PAINT program that comes with the Microsoft Mouse:

Name: PAINT.BAT

```
1: FRIEZE P1
2: PBrush E 1HER 720 348 0
```

You could put this ready-made batch file into your batch file directory, but change it as follows:

```
1: @ECHO OFF
2: REM Paint Program
3: C:
4: CD \OTHER\PAINT
5: PATH = C:\SYSTEM\DOS;C:\OTHER\PAINT
6: FRIEZE P1
7: PBRUSH E 1HER 720 348 0
8: PATH = C:\SYSTEM\DOS;U:\;C:\SYSTEM\BATCH;..
```

Now the PAINT program is available all over your hard drive.

This method can further be simplified by taking full advantage of SUBST to shorten some popular directories.

The BIN approach

Another approach that borrows from the batch file method covered above is the single \BIN directory. This is actually an idea stolen from UNIX, where most of the important programs and utilities (sometimes several hundred of them) are all stored in a general \BIN subdirectory. MS-DOS converted UNIX hackers love this method.

Basically, you stick everything—everything—into a \BIN subdirectory. You toss utilities, batch files, and DOS commands (the ones you use often; not the entire DOS subdirectory) into the \BIN subdirectory. That means your entire system's path will look like this:

```
PATH = C: \ BIN
```

That's it! Of course, when you run other programs, your batch files can augment the path to something else. Otherwise, all your eggs are in one basket (so to speak).

The only drawback I find to this approach (and the reason I don't use it myself) is that \BIN gets awfully big after a time. Sure, for only a few applications and a smattering of utilities, \BIN is nice and tidy. But on my system, \BIN would have close to 300 files in it. Granted, you can argue it either way: Three subdirectories of 100 files each is almost as bad. But I don't like to scroll through long DIR listings, so I use my own method.

The bottom line is that organization is always up to you. Choose whatever approach works best with the way you work. If you like \BIN, use it. If you want multiple subdirectories, use them. But keep batch files central to the scheme. That's the key to running an organized system on a PC.

Backing up

No one likes to back up, but it really isn't a bother if you do it right. The object is to develop a backup strategy. Now, I'm not going to sit here and wag my finger at you, explaining how important backups are.

There are quite a few "fast" backup programs on the market, offering themselves as better alternatives to the DOS BACKUP program. Because this isn't a complete book on the subject, I'm just going to say to use the BACKUP program that came with DOS. It may not be blindingly fast, but it's free and it works. But first a rule:

Always RESTORE files to a hard drive with the same DOS version that was used for the BACKUP.

Backup has changed over the years. The current version of BACKUP is actually quite smart—and quite incompatible with past releases. If you're going to back up your hard drive because you're reformatting it for a new version of DOS (which isn't necessary, by the way), you will want to BACKUP using the new DOS's BACKUP program. (First, boot the new version of DOS, then run the BACKUP program.)

But, normally, an entire hard disk backup isn't always necessary. Instead, using the strategy mentioned below, you will be able to get by safely with a minimum of time wasted on backups.

1. Back up your entire hard drive at least once a month, twice in an office setting.
2. Back up the files you use every day every day.
3. Back up all modified files once a week or so.

Step two is the most important. At the end of each day you should back up the files you work on. For example, when I'm done using my computer tonight, I will have backed up all the files and subdirectories that have to do with this book (some three megabytes worth).

Step one is only necessary once in a while. For most users, you'll typically work on one project over a period of time. During that time, the majority of files on your hard drive will just sit there, not being used or modified. There's no point in backing up the entire drive in those instances. Backing up your current work is much more important.

The only times you'll want to back up your entire hard drive are:

- Before taking the computer in to be repaired—even if the problem isn't related to the hard drive.
- Before moving the computer.
- Before installing a new piece of hardware.
- Before upgrading to a new version of DOS. (You may want to optionally reformat the drive with the new version of DOS, then RESTORE your files to it.)
- Once a month or more often

Finally, I recommend a weekly backup of all modified files on your system. This is what's known as an *incremental* backup. It takes care of the incidental files you modify, but doesn't catch a daily backup of your work files. Together with the monthly full and daily work backups, this will keep your system well up to date in case of any mishaps.

Using batch files to back up

To ensure that you're doing your proper quota of backing up, use the CALL command to include the batch file in FIG. 18-7 in your SHUTDOWN

18-7 This program helps you back up your hard disk.

Name: BACKUP.BAT

```
 1: @ECHO OFF
 2: REM BACKUP.BAT program: provides various types of backup
 3: REM This program should be on the path so that it's available
 4: REM at all times.  Also, note that the DOS BACKUP.COM program
 5: REM has been renamed to B_U.COM.
 6: REM This program incorporates programs on the supplemental
 7: REM programs diskette.  Like:
 8: :MAIN MENU
 9: CLZ
10: BOX C=20,1;63,18
11: LOCATE 30,3
12: ECHO Hard Disk Backup Options
13: LOCATE 25,6
14: ECHO F1 - Backup the entire hard drive
15: LOCATE 25,8
16: ECHO F2 - Backup only modified files
17: LOCATE 25,10
18: ECHO F3 - Backup only C:\WP\BOOK
19: LOCATE 25,12
20: ECHO F10 - Cancel
21: :GETINPUT
22: LOCATE 30,15
23: READKEY /F Your choice:
24: IF ERRORLEVEL 10 GOTO END
25: IF ERRORLEVEL 3 GOTO ONLY
26: IF ERRORLEVEL 2 GOTO MODIFY
27: IF ERRORLEVEL 1 GOTO ALL
28: GOTO GETINPUT
29: :ONLY
30: CLZ
31: BOX "Backing up C:\WP\BOOK to drive A:"/C
32: B_U C:\NOVELS\BATCH A:
33: GOTO END
34: :MODIFY
35: CLZ
36: BOX "Backing up modified files only"/C
37: B_U C:\*.* A: /S/M
38: GOTO END
39: :ALL
40: CLZ
41: BOX "Backing up entire hard drive"/C
42: B_U C:\*.* A: /S/H
43: :END
44: LOCATE 1,24
```

batch file. If you don't have a SHUTDOWN.BAT file, then just type the name of this batch file every day before you shut the computer down.

You will notice that the name of the DOS BACKUP program has been changed to B_U. This is so you can call this batch file BACKUP.BAT without any conflicts.

BACKUP.BAT makes liberal use of some of the programs on the supplemental programs diskette—among them: CLZ, LOCATE, READKEY and BOX. If you have these programs, be sure that they're on your system's path. (Put them in a UTILITY subdirectory, if you have one.) Primarily, these programs serve to give this backup program a pretty interface, as shown in FIG. 18-8.

```
Hard Disk Backup Options


F1 - Backup the entire hard drive

F2 - Backup only modified files

F3 - Backup only C:\WP\BOOK

F10 - Cancel


Your choice:
```

18-8 Here is BACKUP.BAT's user interface.

The "main menu" is generated between lines 8 and 21. First, the screen is cleared in a fancy way (9) and a box is drawn (10). The menu text will be located inside the box using a combination of LOCATE and ECHO statements.

Input for the batch file is provided by the READKEY statement in line 23. The /F switch tells READKEY to read the function keys as ERRORLEVELs 1 through 10. Lines 24 through 27 evaluate the input and branch to the appropriate subroutine.

Lines 29 through 33 backup files from a specified directory, specifically a directory in which you do most of your recent work. Again, CLZ is used to clear the display (30) and BOX is used to display a message (31). In line 32, the BACKUP command (renamed B_U) is run to do the backup. (If BACKUP.COM weren't renamed, and "BACKUP" were used instead of "B_U," the BACKUP batch program would continually run itself.) Once the backup is completed, batch file execution branches to line 43. Incidentally, the example uses C:\WP\BOOK. For your own backups, you will probably change this.

Lines 34 through 38 back up only those files modified since the last backup. The /S switch of the BACKUP command backs up all subdirectories under the current directory (in this case, that's the entire drive), and /M is used to back up only modified files.

Lines 39 through 43 back up all files on the hard drive—a complete backup. The /F option is new with DOS 3.3. It allows BACKUP to run the FORMAT program in case it encounters an unreadable disk. If you have DOS 3.3, you should always specify the /H command. (Be sure FORMAT is on your system's path when you do so.)

The very last line of this batch file moves the cursor to the bottom left position on the screen (44). This is in case you press F10 to cancel the batch file. If the cursor isn't moved, your system prompt will appear in the middle of the screen (because of READKEY and the LOCATE statement) and look awkward.

Other helpful hints

Hard disk organization and backing up are the major components of managing your hard disk. But there are many more, less important but still significant aspects of hard disk management. Again, this isn't an end-all book on the subject. But you might look into some of the following techniques to complete your "ultimate system."

Menu/shell software

I extremely dislike menu or "shell" software so I'm going to be very brief. Basically, this software is supposed to "help" you use your computer by avoiding DOS. I think that's like someone helping you learn to drive your car by not teaching you the rules of the road. Unfortunately, DOS shells proliferate and quite a few users (gulp) like them.

Menu or shell software allows you to use your system with that one-keystroke effect. Basically, some genius (you, usually) builds the shell program, telling it where all your files are located and which keys will activate those files. Then the shell program takes over, and using some hokey graphics display, will allow you to "easily" manipulate your computer system using that one keystroke.

For beginners and the computer reluctant, these programs are fine. In fact, the next chapter shows you how to write one using batch files and what you've learned about DOS from this book. (How's that for being hypocritical?)

DOSSHELL

Starting with Version 4.0, DOS comes with its own shell program. It's not a bad program, either. (Though I still feel the same way about shell programs in general.)

DOSSHELL features an easy-to-use menu interface. If you have a mouse, it's even more easy to use. Without the mouse, DOSSHELL is awkward to use but still manageable (but you can forget getting at that F11 key if you don't have one).

You can run programs from the shell, or simply use the shell's utilities to manage your system. Advanced capabilities of the shell allow you to customize its operation, allowing new users to take advantage of the shell in as painless a manner as possible.

DOSSHELL for DOS 4 was nonintuitive, but Microsoft improved upon that when they rewrote DOSSHELL for DOS 5. It's now a graceful and elegant program shell, and it's still free with DOS.

Other DOS shells

There are dozens of shell programs on the market. Some are ridiculously low in price, for example *DOS-A-MATIC*. The most popular is *Direct Access*, available from Delta Technology.

Other DOS shells exist in the shareware market, quite a few of which are nothing more than a collection of batch files. (This means you should check them out if you find them, just to see how others work batch files into the shell formula.)

Peter Norton puts out a DOS shell called the *Norton Commander*, which is pretty popular among the techie types. And PC Dynamics' *Menu-Works* is popular in computer stores for demoing software, not to mention its colorful menus and sounds attract people to the screens like moths to a porch light.

Because DOS shells and menus proliferate, partially thanks to DOS's natively ugly nature, there will doubtless be more and more of these shells to pick and choose from in the future. Keep an eye out for them in your local computer store's shareware bin, the user group's library, national on-line networks, as well as the "real" software stores.

Keyboard enhancers

Way back when DOS was young, some enterprising software hackers figured out that you could "hook into" the keyboard interrupt vector inside the machine. While this sounds dangerous and stupid to everyone reading this, some amazing products developed. Of primary concern are keyboard enhancers.

Keyboard enhancers are programs that allow you to record and play back a series of keystrokes—like a tape recorder. Most of them are activated by pressing a certain key combination, say ALT–plus. After typing ALT–plus, the keyboard enhancer program (memory-resident, of course) memorizes all the keys you press, up until the time you press ALT–plus again. Then it asks you to assign those keystrokes to another key. Say you choose F1. Now, every time you press F1, the keyboard enhancer will repeat, or play back, all the keystrokes you recorded. Neat-o.

Using these enhancers, you could make typing long pathnames and answering repetitive questions easy. Or, if you were paying attention in chapter 3, you can use ANSI.SYS to do the same thing (see FIG. 18-9).

This is the same NIFTY.BAT program introduced in chapter 3. The difference is that I've changed the string commands to make them a bit more useful (and apply them to the theme of this chapter).

One of the keyboard enhancers, *SuperKey* from Borland, also allows you to have "pop-up" screens. For example, you can program the ALT–H

18-9 You can use ANSI.SYS to enhance your keyboard.

```
Name: NIFTY.BAT

 1: @ECHO off
 2: ECHO ^[[0;104;"C:";13p;"CD \";13p
 3: ECHO ^[[0;105;"CD \WP\WP";13p
 4: ECHO ^[[0;106;"DIR A:"13p
 5: ECHO ^[[0;107;"DIR *.BAT";13p
 6: ECHO ^[[0;108;"DEL *.BAK";13p
 7: ECHO ^[[0;109;"DEL TEMP*.*";13p
 8: ECHO ^[[0;110;"FORMAT A:";13p
 9: ECHO ^[[0;111;"CD \WORK\BOOK";13p
10: ECHO ^[[0;112;"CD \SYSTEM\TOOLS";13p
11: ECHO ^[[0;113;"SHUTDOWN";13p
```

(for help, get it?) key to have a little help window appear each time it's pressed. You can change the menu being displayed. For example, during the run of one batch file you can echo the message:

    ECHO Press ALT-H for help

Then, using *SuperKey*, you can define the pop-up menu for ALT – H. When the user presses that key, zip!, up comes the menu. People are impressed by this.

If this all sounds a little redundant after reading chapter 15 (the macro chapter), you're right. Keyboard enhancers can be considered "macros for DOS," in a way.

Eek! A mouse

Whether you like them or not, mice are here to stay. In fact, trying to use the OS/2 Presentation Manager without a mouse is a waste of time and an exercise in frustration. If you don't have a mouse now, you will be buying one within three years. Promise.

To make owning a mouse attractive, the mouse makers (aside from Disney) supply their input devices with a bunch of interesting programs "for free." You usually get a painting program, a few games, a sample something-or-other that you're supposed to practice using your mouse with—and they also toss in a Menu program.

The Menu program can come in really handy. Sadly, the documentation for writing your own menus suffers, but you can still use the menus provided. One of them is bound to be used with DOS.

Using a DOS menu with a mouse is fun. Depending on the rodent, the menu may pop up on the screen when you press a mouse button. You'll then be able to choose from a list of popular DOS commands using the mouse. Unfortunately, the mouse interface really doesn't work well with DOS—not at this time at least.

General utility batch files

One last thing you can do to help manage your hard disk is write some useful batch file utilities, like the one in FIG. 18-10. This program first checks for any files in your \JUNK directory. If any files are found, they are deleted. Next, the GLOBAL utility is used to march down your subdirectories, deleting all *.BAK, then KILL*.*, then TEMP*.* files.

18-10 CLEAN.BAT checks and deletes JUNK directory files.

Name: CLEAN.BAT

```
1: @ECHO OFF
2: REM This batch file removes all offending files from the drive
3: REM Even if you don't have a \JUNK directory
4: IF EXIST \JUNK\*.* DEL \JUNK\*.* <YES
5: CD \
6: REM Use the SWEEP utility to remove unwanted files
7: GLOBAL DEL *.BAK
8: GLOBAL DEL KILL*.*
9: GLOBAL DEL TEMP*.*
```

Log batch files

A second type of batch file that comes in handy is a log batch file. This batch file maintains a list of activities, who was using the computer and when they started and stopped. Because IBM computers keep track of the time, all that's needed is a program to "spit out" the current time.

I wrote two programs that assist in creating a computer log for my hard disk management book. They are STIME and ETIME. STIME displays the following:

Start Time = Thursday, February 18, 1988 @ 11:14 am

ETIME displays:

End Time = Thursday, February 18, 1988 @ 11:15 am

Using these two files and I/O redirection you can create a log file letting you know what you've used your computer for, and for how long. For example, FIG. 18-11 is a modification of the SS.BAT program discussed earlier in this chapter.

Line 6 of FIG. 18-11 ECHOes "Work on Spreadsheet", appending it to whatever information is already in the file LOGFILE.DAT in the WORK subdirectory on drive C. STIME is used to append the start time to the file (7). After you're done spreadsheeting [sic], ETIME appends your finish time to the file (8). At the end of the day, LOGFILE may look like FIG. 18-12.

The last two lines were probably added by a SHUTDOWN.BAT file. Simply another ECHO statement was used to add "System Shutdown." And a final ETIME >> C:\WORK\LOGFILE.DAT was used to add the final shutdown time.

18-11 This is a modification of the SS.BAT program.

```
 1: @ECHO OFF
 2: REM Run Spreadsheet
 3: C:
 4: CD \OTHER\SS
 5: PATH = C:\SYSTEM\DOS;C:\SYSTEM\UTIL;C:\OTHER\SS
 6: ECHO Work on Spreadsheet >> C:\WORK\LOGFILE.DAT
 7: STIME >> C:\WORK\LOGFILE.DAT
 8: SS
 9: ETIME >> C:\WORK\LOGFILE.DAT
10: REM Restore old path
11: PATH = C:\SYSTEM\DOS;U:\;C:\SYSTEM\BATCH;..
```

18-12 This is what your log file may look like at the end of the day.

```
Work on Spreadsheet
Start Time = Wednesday, August 3rd, 1988 @ 11:57 pm
End Time = Thursday, August 4th, 1988 @ 7:32 am
Work on Word Processor
Start Time = Thursday, August 4th, 1988 @ 7:34 am
End Time = Thursday, August 4th, 1988 @ 7:49 am
System Shutdown
End Time = Thursday, August 4th, 1988 @ 7:55 am
```

Using a simple log file system such as this, you can print a written record of your computer time and, if you have them, bill your clients accordingly; or, with just a few extra lines in some batch files, have individual user's names ECHOed to a log file. It makes tracking computer usage easier.

Summary

Hard disk management is an interesting area to go into, one that's perfect for batch files. Fundamentally, hard disk management boils down to hard disk organization and backing up.

As far as organization goes, a good way to use files and programs on your hard drive is via batch files kept in a special batch file subdirectory. Each batch file runs your programs, customizing the path and environment.

For backing up, various BACKUP batch files can be written and, using the RKEY function from a previous chapter, or any of the key reading utilities provided on the supplemental programs diskette, you can customize the backup to be as specific or general as you need.

Finally, there are numerous other programs available that will assist in hard disk management, organization and use. There are menu generating and user "shell" programs that can make using your system easy; keyboard enhancers that provide complex macro functions; the computer mouse for users who are afraid of the keyboard [sic]; and other helpful batch files you can write to make your system more manageable.

19
Batch file menus

I know, I know. Anyone who's read the previous chapter will be thinking to themselves, "Golly, he just spent part of the last chapter ripping menu programs to shreds. Now what?"

The truth is that menu and shell programs can make a computer system a lot easier to use. Face it, not everyone is going to enjoy using a computer as much as you do. In fact, there is a faction out there that claims computers have no place being used by people who don't like them. Yet, it will happen. When it does, it's nice to give those people a break by making the system a little more tolerable.

This chapter shows you how you can use batch files to create a comfortable, insulating shell program; a menu system that will make the computer easier to use.

Creating a batch file shell program

A lot of people complain that DOS is too technical. Although this is true, it's also true that the more technical and complex something is, the easier it is to manipulate it into something that isn't. Using your knowledge of DOS, plus the hints provided in this book, you can create a program that will make using DOS a lot easier for the compu-phobes and DOS-terrified among the general populace.

I think you'll find that writing these programs is a lot easier using shell programs. If you like, however, you can always buy those commercial shell programs. The problem is that you already know batch files. With the commercial programs, you'll need to learn the way they do things before you can get off and running. So why take the extra trip?

Three steps to writing a shell program

There are three steps to writing a good shell program. Keep these things in mind and your efforts will be successful:

Step one is never to assume that your user is dumb. This is one thing that immediately turns people off to computers. Never talk down to a user or make them feel inferior. The "this is the on/off switch" approach may work for some simple-minded people, but most of the people who use computers are motivated and productive individuals. They simply may not have the time to learn something as cumbersome as DOS. Give 'em a break and have your shell program treat them as they deserve.

The second step to writing a good menu system is to know what the user wants. No, they don't want to "use the computer." If they do, they should learn DOS. Instead, there may be only one or two operations that someone needs to do on the computer. Find out what your user's tasks are and then write your menu program to accommodate them.

The third step is never to get too cute. Actually, steps one and two are the most important. I added this step because (well, three makes a good number and) some programmers get carried away with shell programs. Fancy displays, moving icons, cutsie little bleeps and zippy noises might make the computer "seem fun to use," but they annoy most people after a while. Think productivity and efficiency and you'll realize that being cute is only used to sell software—not get the job done.

Now that you know these steps you'll need to apply them. For your own practice, it's good to work with a subject you know: Yourself. However, in the real world, you'll probably end up writing a shell program for someone else. (Remember step two: what do they want?) For this book, I'll use the example of Peggy, a former publisher of mine who does basically three things with her computer:

- Writes letters and memos
- Sends TELEX messages
- Works a spreadsheet
- Reviews a database and generates reports

Peggy knows how to use the software responsible for those four jobs very well. (Remember, she's not dumb!) Her problem is with using DOS, which she really doesn't have time to mess with. To make her job a little easier, I'll show you how I would build a batch file menu system customized to her needs.

Designing the system

To implement the shell, you should first structure the user's system to meet their needs, and indirectly, to satisfy your own sense of organization. This involves creating all the required subdirectories and setting up an appropriate file structure. For simplicity's sake, make only one subdirectory for each different program on the computer, plus a subdirectory for DOS. Then, place under those subdirectories data directories where your user will put their files.

(Remember, the user still needs to know about filenames, saving and loading. You should never confuse someone by making them remember subdirectories and backslash combinations. Let the shell's batch files take care of that for you.)

Figure 19-1 shows the directory structure I would set up for Peggy. Each one of the programs she uses is placed into its own subdirectory. Then, under the SYSTEM subdirectory are three additional subdirectories: DOS, BATCH, and UTILITY. Into each of the program subdirectories, dBASE, WP, SS, PCCOM, the respective programs would be installed: the database program, the word processor, the spreadsheet, and a communications program for sending the TELEX messages. Under each of the program subdirectories would be placed a data subdirectory (not shown in FIG. 19-1).

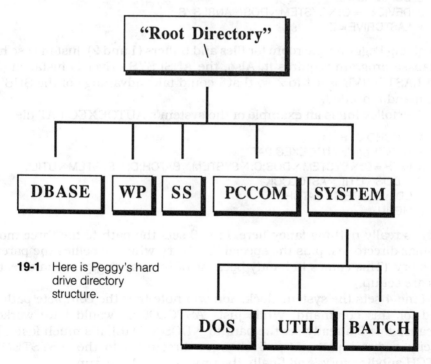

19-1 Here is Peggy's hard drive directory structure.

At this point you might wonder why Peggy would need such a complex \SYSTEM directory. After all, a single subdirectory could contain all DOS files, batch files and utilities and still keep her system simple. There are two reasons:

The first is for organization. Her system will be run by batch files. To make managing them easier, I'm putting them all in one place. Sure, I could have put them in a \BATCH subdirectory off the root, but putting it in \SYSTEM (along with \UTIL) keeps the root directory "clean."

The second reason is for myself—or whoever is the office computer manager. Not only will Peggy be using her computer, but the local office computer guru will as well. If that guru is me, I'll want to set up a system that I am familiar with and that I can get around quickly. So I went with a familiar structure.

CONFIG.SYS and AUTOEXEC.BAT

The following is an example of Peggy's computer's CONFIG.SYS file. If I knew that she was running a particular program that required a specific configuration, I'd make sure that the proper statements were placed in CONFIG.SYS. For demonstration purposes, I'll use the following:

```
1: FILES = 20
2: BUFFERS = 33
3: DEVICE  = C:\SYSTEM\DOS\ANSI.SYS
4: LASTDRIVE = Z
```

I'm giving Peggy ample room for files and buffers (1 and 2), just in case her database program requires it. Also, the ANSI.SYS driver is installed (3), and LASTDRIVE is set to Z so that I could take advantage of the SUBST command if needed.

The following is an example of the system's AUTOEXEC.BAT file:

```
1: @ECHO OFF
2: REM Peggy's AUTOEXEC.BAT
3: PATH = C:\SYSTEM\DOS;C:\SYSTEM\BATCH;C:\SYSTEM\UTIL;..
4: \DOS\UTIL\ASTCLOCK
5: CD \SYSTEM\BATCH
6: MENU
```

There's really nothing fancy here. Line 3 sets the path to the three most popular directories, plus the special ".." entry which specifies the parent directory. (This comes in handy because of the way Peggy's data directories are set up.)

Line 4 sets the system clock. You will note that the complete path is used for this command. While just "ASTCLOCK" would have worked (because line 3 already set the path to \DOS\UTIL), it's much faster to specify a direct path. Line 5 changes directories to the \SYSTEM\ BATCH subdirectory. And finally the program MENU is run.

MENU.BAT

MENU, the final command in AUTOEXEC, is a batch file. It's the "main menu" batch file where Peggy makes her decisions. For example, she

19-2 This is the key program that makes Peggy's computer painless to use.
Name: MENU.BAT

```
1: @ECHO OFF
2: REM Peggy's shell program, main menu
3: REM Make sure we're in the right directory
4: REM for displaying messages
5: C:
6: CD \SYSTEM\BATCH
7: CLS
8: TYPE MENU.MSG
9: PROMPT $e[17;30HChoice:
```

could type "1" here to start word processing. Remember, the point to all this is to make the system easier for Peggy to use.

The program MENU.BAT (see FIG. 19-2) is the key program that makes Peggy's computer painless to use. It does three things:

First, MENU.BAT makes sure that the system is currently logged to drive C and the current directory is \SYSTEM\BATCH (5, 6).

Second the screen clears (7) and a text file is displayed (8). The text file displays Peggy's menu choices. It could have easily been done with ECHO statements, but that method proves slow and awkward looking. It's much better to display the text file. (This batch file assumes the text file to be in the \SYSTEM\BATCH directory, otherwise a full pathname would be used in line 8).

Finally, the tricky part is to incorporate the system prompt as an input device. Line 9 sets the prompt first with an ANSI command, and then with the word "Choice: " (followed by a space character).

The ANSI command is ^[[17;30H. This moves the cursor on to row 17, column 30 on the screen. At that point the word "Choice" is displayed. The net effect is of an integrated menu display (see FIG. 19-3).

```
┌─────────────────────────────────────────┐
│              Main Menu                   │
│                                          │
│   Type the number of the item you want:  │
│                                          │
│          1. Word Processing              │
│                                          │
│          2. Spreadsheet                  │
│                                          │
│          3. Data base                    │
│                                          │
│          4. Send Telex                   │
│                                          │
│   Special Functions:                     │
│                                          │
│          A. Return to DOS                │
│                                          │
│          B. Backup Files                 │
│                                          │
│          C. Turn computer off            │
│                                          │
│             Choice:                      │
└─────────────────────────────────────────┘
```

19-3 Here is Peggy's main MENU.

To the unsuspecting user, "Choice:" simply looks like a place to input a number. It's really the vicious and cryptic DOS prompt in disguise.

At this point, Peggy can press "1", "2", "3" or "4" to get her work done, or press "A", "B" or "C" to do the special functions. Each number or letter must be followed by an ENTER (as is true of all DOS commands). Again, the secret here is that all those one-letter responses are batch files (see FIG. 19-4). The file 1.BAT runs Peggy's word processor. It first changes directories (3) and then the PATH to be more accommodating to the word processor (4).

19-4 This is the batch file for word processing.

```
Name: 1.BAT

 1:  @ECHO OFF
 2:  REM Run the word processor
 3:  CD \WP
 4:  PATH=C:\SYSTEM\DOS;C:\SYSTEM\BATCH;..;C:\WP
 5:  REM Enter the word processor's name:
 6:  WP
 7:  REM All done, go back to the menu
 8:  PATH=C:\SYSTEM\DOS;C:\SYSTEM\BATCH;C:\SYSTEM\UTIL;..
 9:  CD \SYSTEM\BATCH
10:  MENU
```

In line 6, the word processing program is run. Then, after Peggy is done word processing, the old PATH is reset (8), the system changes directories to the batch file subdirectory (9), and finally the MENU program is run again (10), making the circle complete.

The other batch files, 2 through 4, are only simple modifications to 1.BAT (see FIG. 19-5).

The only additions you may need to the types of batch files that run a user's programs are macro files. To make life easier, writing a few custom macros in the applications would (again) greatly simplify computer use. If those macros can be started from the command line when the application is run, then specify them in your batch files.

Batch files 1.BAT through 4.BAT correspond to keystrokes that would start those applications. The letters A, B and C, on the other hand, correspond to system functions.

```
Name: A.BAT

1: @ECHO OFF
2: CLS
3: ECHO You're now in DOS...
4: VER
5: ECHO Type "MENU" at any time to return to the menu program
6: PROMPT $p$g
```

The "A" batch file returns Peggy to DOS (or, more likely, returns the office computer manager to DOS). The most important change is the PROMPT

19-5 These batch files are for spreadsheet, database, and communications applications.

Name: 2.BAT

```
 1: @ECHO OFF
 2: REM Run the spreadsheet
 3: CD \SS
 4: PATH=C:\SYSTEM\DOS;C:\SYSTEM\BATCH;..;C:\SS
 5: REM Enter the spreadsheet's name:
 6: PLAN
 7: REM All done, go back to the menu
 8: PATH=C:\SYSTEM\DOS;C:\SYSTEM\BATCH;C:\SYSTEM\UTIL;..
 9: CD \SYSTEM\BATCH
10: MENU
```

Name: 3.BAT

```
 1: @ECHO OFF
 2: REM Run the data base
 3: CD \DBASE
 4: PATH=C:\SYSTEM\DOS;C:\SYSTEM\BATCH;..;C:\DBASE
 5: REM Enter the data base's name:
 6: DBASE
 7: REM All done, go back to the menu
 8: PATH=C:\SYSTEM\DOS;C:\SYSTEM\BATCH;C:\SYSTEM\UTIL;..
 9: CD \SYSTEM\BATCH
10: MENU
```

Name: 4.BAT

```
 1: @ECHO OFF
 2: REM Send a TELEX
 3: CD \PCCOM
 4: PATH=C:\SYSTEM\DOS;C:\SYSTEM\BATCH;..;C:\PCCOM
 5: REM Enter the communication program's name:
 6: AEMS
 7: REM All done, go back to the menu
 8: PATH=C:\SYSTEM\DOS;C:\SYSTEM\BATCH;C:\SYSTEM\UTIL;..
 9: CD \SYSTEM\BATCH
10: MENU
```

statement in line 6, which restores the system to a typical drive/pathname type of prompt. MENU can still be typed at this point to return Peggy to her menu system. (If the PROMPT is not changed back, it will continue to be the word "Choice" displayed near the center of the screen.)

Name: B.BAT

```
1: @ECHO OFF
2: REM Backup the disk
3: CLS
4: ECHO Make sure you have a pile of diskettes handy.
5: PAUSE
6: BACKUP C:\ *.* A: /S/F
7: ECHO ^G
8: MENU
```

B.BAT is just a quick-and-dirty example of a backup routine. A much better routine was covered in the previous chapter, and could easily be incorporated here by changing it's name to B.BAT. The only thing odd here is the ECHO ^G statement in line 7. This causes the computer's speaker to beep, alerting Peggy that the backup is complete. Then, as is true with all these batch files, control returns to the menu.

Name: C.BAT

```
1: @ECHO OFF
2: REM this is Peggy's shutdown.bat file
3: CLS
4: ECHO Stand by to turn your computer system off
5: REM Put the computer's PARK program here:
6: PARK
```

Again, C.BAT is another quick-and-dirty example of a shutdown batch file. The only thing this one does is to park the hard drive (6) once it's done. Other items could be added to C.BAT if they were required before Peggy turns her system off.

If you do design this type of menu system, about the most important thing to remember is to turn it off when you're done. This implies the simple steps performed in the example A.BAT above. Changing the system prompt using the ANSI commands is really nice for entering information in a "menu." But, for regularly running a system, it's a pain.

Adding complexity

While the above example of a batch file shell does the job, it's really not as smooth as it could have been. I avoided adding too much complexity to it so you could see the basic idea. Still, there are many nice little touches you can add to enhance the performance and appearance of a batch file shell.

You can add different layers to this type of shell as deep as you want. For example, different menu options could display different menus (and change the prompt again). Everything still works the same way, you're just running another menu batch file rather than running a program.

You can also get fancy with the CALL statement, using certain batch files as subroutines. Or you can opt to use the READKEY utility instead of using the PROMPT command for input. READKEY has the advantage of controlling input. However, it has the disadvantage of not giving you immediate access to the system if you need it.

You should try to avoid using groups of ECHO statements wherever possible. Create text files with your information listed in them. If you feel like getting creative, use the color ANSI commands for fancy menu displays.

Finally, as the *coup de grace* of the batch file shell, you can use enhanced batch file languages such as Builder or EBL to write your shell. This is taking one foot out of DOS and planting one foot in a customized shell program. In other words, it might be a better choice to buy a program that already does the job for you if you need that complexity. Yet, it's still another way you can enhance a shell or menu program.

Using PATH

One weak point of the above shell example was how the PATH kept changing. This could be avoided by adding variables in the environment for each possible path, then using SET to change the Path. If you try this, remember to specify enough space in the environment. (See chapter 4.)

The following are environment variables that could be defined by AUTOEXEC:

```
WPPATH = C: \ SYSTEM \ DOS;C: \ SYSTEM \ BATCH;..;C: \ WP
SSPATH = C: \ SYSTEM \ DOS;C: \ SYSTEM \ BATCH;..;C: \ SS
DBPATH = C: \ SYSTEM \ DOS;C: \ SYSTEM \ BATCH;..;C: \ DBASE
COMPATH = C: \ SYSTEM \ DOS;C: \ SYSTEM \ BATCH;..;C: \ PCCOM
SYSPATH = C: \ SYSTEM \ DOS;C: \ SYSTEM \ BATCH;C: \ SYSTEM \ UTIL;..
```

To change the path, the new path can be specified in a batch file as follows:

```
PATH = %WPPATH%
```

That's it! To restore the path, use the following:

```
PATH = %SYSPATH%
```

The batch file interpreter expands the variable names (between the percent signs) when the batch file is run. The net effect will be the same, but with a lot less typing.

Here's an even better trick.

If you'll notice, the first part of the path is always the same. Therefore, it would be easier and take up less space if the following variable were established:

```
SAME = C: \ SYSTEM \ DOS;C: \ SYSTEM \ BATCH;..;
```

This way, setting or changing the path is as easy as:

```
PATH = %SAME%C: \ WP
```

and:

```
PATH = %SAME%C: \ SS
```

and so on.

As you work with your own shells, and see how they run, you'll probably think of more tricks. Just keep in mind step three from earlier in this chapter: Don't get carried away with being too cute!

RESTPATH

As your menu files get more complex you'll want them to perform more and more tricks. Some of them, the PATH command in the previous section as an example, are possible using the tools DOS gives you. Others aren't as easy, which is why I wrote the RESTPATH command.

RESTPATH isn't necessarily for batch file menus. It's for any system that's run via batch files in a \BATCH subdirectory. The problem with running your system this way is that you never know where your batch file started from. For example, assume for some reason that you're on drive I in the "root" directory. (Drive I is a SUBSTituted drive.) You want to run an UPDATE batch file.

What UPDATE does is to copy key files from your hard drive to a diskette in drive A. To do this, UPDATE changes drives and directories to find all the files you want copied. When UPDATE is done, it's in the drive and directory of the last file copied. Yet, you started out on drive I. How could the batch file return you to where you started?

(Think about this one for a time. How could it be done? I stewed over this for about two hours before it finally came to me—okay, okay, I had a jelly donut as well!)

Here's a hint. The CD command is used alone to display the current drive and directory. You can redirect the output of CD to a file:

```
CD >> C:\CDIR
```

This puts the name of the current drive and directory into the file CDIR in the root directory on drive C. CDIR may contain something like the following:

```
I:\WORK\MAKEUP
```

That's the current directory. But how can we get that information back into DOS, allowing us to get back to that drive and directory?

The answer is RESTPATH. RESTPATH is used with the CD command's redirected output to restore you to the same directory from which you started. To move you back to drive I and the \WORK\MAKEUP subdirectory, you'd enter:

```
RESTPATH C:\CDIR
```

The file CDIR contains "I:\WORK\MAKEUP". RESTPATH reads this information, then logs to drive I and the \WORK\MAKEUP directory. So, to bring an end to this question, here is how to restore your drive and directory for all your batch files. At the top of your batch files put the following command:

```
CD > C:\CDIR
```

(Or you can use "TEMP" or put the file in a JUNK directory.)

Then, near the bottom of your batch file, add the following two commands:

```
RESTPATH C:\CDIR
DEL C:\CDIR
```

This restores the path, bringing you back to where you were when you started, and then the CDIR file is neatly removed. Convenience at its best.

You should note, however, that RESTPATH has no output. Instead, it uses ERRORLEVEL values to communicate to your batch file what happened. The ERRORLEVEL values returned by RESTPATH are as follows:

0   Drive/directory properly restored
1   File not found, the file specified after RESTPATH was not found or no file was specified
2   Syntax error, the information in the specified file was probably not a drive/directory listing or not created by CD >

Testing for these errors is rather fruitless. Because RESTPATH will probably be used at the end of a batch file, there's really nothing more you can do as far as restoring the drive and directory is concerned.

A friend pointed out, however, that you could conceivably use REST PATH as a quick replacement for a combination change drive/directory command. So, for example, instead of having the following two lines in a batch file:

```
I|:
CD \ WORK \ MAKEUP
```

You could simply use:

```
RESTPATH C: \ BATCH \ MPATH
```

MPATH would contain "I: \ WORK \ MAKEUP". This way, RESTPATH would be quicker than using the two separate commands.

Summary

Even though I personally detest menu-driven computer systems, it's possible to use the knowledge you've gained from this book to successfully write a batch file menu system. This system can be used by those people who detest DOS but need to get work done anyway.

The way you implement a batch file menu system is by examining the needs of the person who will use it. Once that's done, simply keep the system clean, avoiding junking up the batch file menus with a lot of bells and whistles, and you should have a happy—and productive—computer user on your hands.

Part Six

Batch file cookbook

This part of the book is a reference work—like a cookbook, but more like an encyclopedia. It provides information on each of the DOS and OS/2 batch file directives, plus a few extra DOS and OS/2 commands that are primarily used by batch files.

20
Cookbook introduction

The following is a list of each of the batch file directives in this reference:

% (percent)	COMMAND	IF
: (colon)	ECHO	NOT
= =	ENDLOCAL	PAUSE
@ (at)	ERRORLEVEL	REM
ANSI	EXIST	SET
CALL	EXTPROC	SETLOCAL
CLS	FOR	SHIFT
CMD	GOTO	

Each directive is listed alphabetically, with the single character commands and operators listed in their ASCII order (%, :, =, @). Provided with each directive is a description of what it does, how it relates to DOS, plus an example program and a test run.

You can use this section as a reference when writing your own batch files. Every effort has been made to make sure that this information is up to date and works with each version of DOS. Where exceptions occur they are noted.

Reference

Each batch file directive is listed at the start of each entry. Single character commands are followed by their name in parenthesis, such as % (percent) or = = (double equal signs).

Next to the name of the batch file directive is its type. There are no official types, only the four that I use to describe the various directives:

Command ANSI, CALL, CLS, (just about everything else)
Statement REM, IF,

Variable	ERRORLEVEL, EXIST
Operator	= = (double equal signs), NOT

A *command* batch file directive is a direct order, it does something immediately. For example GOTO branches to the indicated label; CALL executes a second batch file; SET assigns an environment variable. Most batch file directives are commands.

There are only two statements, REM and IF. IF is a statement because it involves a decision based on a comparison. It doesn't really give a direct order. REM isn't a command because it simply identifies a comment; it does nothing by itself.

The only variables, aside from the % (percent) variables, are ERRORLEVEL and EXIST. These two variables are used with the IF statement to hold a program's return code or determine if a file exists.

The operators are = = (double equal signs) and NOT. Both of these are used with the IF statement to compare variables or to negate the result of a test, respectively.

After identifying whether the batch file directive is a command, statement, variable or operator, four items are determined:

- Whether the directive can also be issued directly on the command line
- The DOS versions in which the directive can be used
- The OS/2 modes in which the directive can be used (real or protected)
- The type of command, internal or external

If a batch file directive can be used on the command line, the cookbook will list the following:

Command line: Yes

Otherwise, "No" is listed. There is an explanation of why this is so at the end of the entry.

The "DOS versions" entry indicates when the batch file directive was introduced. Only a few of the directives have been around since DOS Version 1.0. More were introduced with Version 2.0, and one more with Version 3.3:

DOS Versions: 2.0 and up

If the batch file directive is an OS/2 protected-only command, then "N/A" is listed for the DOS version:

DOS versions: N/A

The "OS/2" entry determines whether the batch file directive can be used with OS/2. Nearly all batch file directives can be used in the OS/2 real mode. However, some directives are specific to the protected mode:

OS/2: Protected mode

The "Type" entry indicates whether it's internal or external. Internal commands are part of COMMAND.COM and always remain in memory. External commands are located on disk:

Type: Internal

Following these items is a description of the command and what it does. For example:

@ hides command lines in a batch file, preventing them from being displayed. It's normally used with the initial ECHO OFF command.

This is followed by the format of the command. Optional parameters are listed after (or before) the command in italics:

@ *commands*

Below this is a description of the optional parameters, along with a few examples of how the batch file directive is used.

A program example is provided to show the batch file directive in a simple batch file. If there are any variations of usage, additional program examples are provided, along with "test runs" that describe or illustrate the batch file's output.

A final section titled "IN DOS . . ." is used to describe how the batch file directive behaves different at the DOS command prompt—or if it behaves at all.

At the end of the entry is a list of similar or related commands, plus a reference to a specific chapter in this book (where applicable).

% (percent sign) command

Command line—No
  DOS versions—2.0 and up
        OS/2—Real and Protected modes
        Type—Internal

% (percent sign) is used to identify a variable in a batch file. It has three separate applications: replaceable parameters, environment variables, and for use with the FOR statement.

Replaceable parameters

Format: %*value*

value is a number from zero through nine. It specifies the items typed on the command line in the order that they were typed. %0 is the name of the batch file; %1 is the first item typed after the batch file name; %2 is the second; %3 is the third; and so on. Items are separated by the space character.

Examples

C> TEST THIS IS A TEST

"TEST" is the name of the batch file. "THIS IS A TEST" composes the individual items used by the replaceable parameter variables. In order they are:

%0   TEST
%1   THIS
%2   IS
%3   A
%4   TEST

As the replaceable parameter variables are encountered in the batch file, the batch file interpreter will expand them to their appropriate values. For example:

ECHO %1

will be replaced by:

ECHO THIS

when the batch file runs. Replaceable parameters allow your batch files to work with variables, but only variables entered on the command line.

Program example 1

1: @ECHO OFF
2: ECHO Replaceable parameters are:
3: ECHO One = %1
4: ECHO Two = %2
5: ECHO Three = %3
6: ECHO Four = %4

Test Run 1   The following is typed to start the batch file:

C> TEST FIRST SECOND THIRD FOURTH

Replaceable parameters are:

One   = FIRST
Two   = SECOND
Three = THIRD
Four = FOURTH

If a replaceable parameter variable doesn't exist (one wasn't entered on the command line), then that variable will be equal to the null string, or "".

Environment variables

Format: %*name*%

name is the name of an environment variable assigned with the SET command. It can be any length and include spaces and reserved characters. *name* is expanded by the batch file interpreter to equal the string assigned to it by SET.

Examples

    SET test = Hello, Kirsten

This places the string "TEST = Hello, Kirsten" into the environment table. TEST, the variable name, is capitalized by the SET command. To use the variable TEST, it must be surrounded by single percent signs:

    ECHO %TEST%

The batch file interpreter searches the environment table for TEST. If found, it expands TEST into the appropriate string. In the above example, this would be:

    ECHO Hello, Kirsten

Had the variable TEST not been found, the batch file interpreter would "expand" it to a null string:

    ECHO

In other words, no error would occur.

Program example 2

    1: @ECHO OFF
    2: SET STATUS = IN
    3: IF "%STATUS%" = = "IN" GOTO FOUND
    4: ECHO Not in
    5: GOTO END
    6: FOUND
    7: ECHO Status is %STATUS%
    8: :END

Test run 2

    Status is IN

FOR variables

Format: %*char*
Format: %%*char*

char can be any single character except for >, <, | or, with DOS versions prior to 4.0, *char* cannot be a number. It is used by the FOR command to specify a group of files. If the FOR command is used at the DOS prompt, then only one percent should be specified. When FOR is used in a batch file, two percent signs should be specified.

The batch file interpreter does not expand the FOR variable. (It does, however, "eat" one of the percent signs—which is why two of them need to be specified inside a batch file.) Instead, FOR uses its variable as a placeholder for the commands used with the FOR statement. The variables represent a group of files the commands act upon.

Example

    FOR %A in (*.BAK TEMP*.* JUNK*.* KILL*.*) DO DEL %A

The command "DEL %A" will be repeated for each of the files represented between the parenthesis. The %A is the placeholder for those filenames. In this example, FOR is used to DELete four separate groups of files.

Program example 3

    1: @ECHO OFF
    2: FOR %%F IN (*.DOC README %1) DO TYPE %%F
    3: :END

Test run 3 (The batch file will TYPE to the screen any file in the current directory with a .DOC extension, any file named README, and any file matching the replaceable parameter variable %1.)

In DOS . . .

The character % is only used with the FOR command on the DOS command line. In this instance, only one percent sign needs to be specified with the FOR variable.

DOS does not use the replaceable parameter variables %0 through %1, nor will it expand them or environment variables.

It's also important to note that DOS considers the % character a valid character for a filename. However, the batch file interpreter will not see a single % in a filename (because of how it deals with variables). If you specify a filename in a batch file and that filename has a % in it, you must specify % twice. Therefore:

    ANNUAL%.DAT

should be listed in a batch file as:

    ANNUAL%%.DAT

ALSO SEE . . . FOR, ECHO, SET, SHIFT, = = (double equal signs)

: (colon) command

Command line—Yes
  DOS versions—2.0 and up

OS/2—Real and Protected modes
Type—Internal

The character : (colon is used to identify a label. The label is used by the GOTO statement, however, the : character is not specified by GOTO.

Format: :*label comments*

label is the label identifying the line. It can be from one to eight characters long and can contain any characters except for a period, semicolon, equal sign, or characters not allowed in a filename (see appendix E). If the label is followed by *comments*, then the space character identifies the end of the label and the start of the *comments*.

comments are any optional characters appearing after the label. The batch file interpreter ignores any characters after the eighth character of a label, or after the space character, whichever comes first. You can use this "feature" to include comments with your label. For example:

    :HERE < - This is where I want you to branch

"HERE" is the label. The rest of the line is ignored by the batch file interpreter and is used as a comment.

Example

    :LABEL1

The : is used to identify the label named "LABEL1". If the following command were issued:

    GOTO LABEL1

the batch file interpreter would scan the entire batch file (from start to finish) for the : character followed by "LABEL1". If found, batch file execution will pick up at the following line. If not found, a "Label not found" error will result, and the batch file will immediately stop.

The colon can also be used alone on a line. In this instance, the colon serves only to "pretty up" the listing:

    @ECHO OFF
    :
    ECHO Don't I look nice?
    :

Of course, blank lines are allowed in batch files, as well as using the colon alone.

Program example 1

    1: @ECHO OFF
    2: GOTO LABEL1
    3: REM This line is skipped
    4: :LABEL1

```
5: ECHO I found it!
6: :END
```

Text run 1

I found it!

When the batch file interpreter encounters a line starting with a :, it assumes that line to be a label and ignores it (does not execute the line as a command). Therefore, you can also use the colon character simply as a device for adding comments to a file. But be careful not to confuse those comments with a label elsewhere in the program.

Program example 2

```
1: @ECHO OFF
2: :THIS IS A COMMENT
3: ECHO batch file starting...
4: GOTO THIS
5: REM this line will probably be skipped
6: :THIS
7: ECHO I'm Done!
8: END
```

Test run 2

```
batch file starting...
batch file starting...
batch file starting...
```
(etc.)

GOTO looks for the first matching label from the top of the file through the bottom. Because the colon in line 2 is carelessly used as a comment, execution never branches to the intended label at line 6.

In DOS . . .

The colon is a reserved character in DOS, used to separate a drive letter from a pathname. If you type a colon on a command line in DOS you'll get a "Bad command or filename" error.

ALSO SEE . . . GOTO, REM

= = (double equal signs) operator

Command line—N/A
  DOS versions—2.0 and up
    OS/2—Real and Protected modes
      Type—Internal

The characters = = (double equal signs) form a comparison operator used with the IF command. It's similar to the single equal sign used with IF-THEN statements in BASIC.

Format: *variable* = = *string*

variable and *string* are two string values that are compared by the = = operator. Both can be variables or both can be strings, though typically the first value is either a replaceable parameter variable or an environment variable. If both strings are equal, the IF statement is true (see IF).

Both sides of the double equal signs must have some value. If you forget either one of the values, or if one value is a variable that turns out to be empty, then you'll get a Syntax Error. (See the second example below.)

Examples

    IF %STATUS% = = IN

This command compares the value of the environment variable STATUS with the string IN. If both sides of the equal sign are equal (both strings are the same), then the IF test will be true.

    IF "%1" = = "

This command uses the double equal sign to check to see if the variable %1 is equal to anything at all. If so, the IF test will pass (because "" = = "", %1 is not expanded by the batch file interpreter). However, if %1 is equal to something, the batch file interpreter will expand it and the IF test will fail.

    IF "%NAME%" = = "Shelly Ann"

In this instance the IF test may fail. Unlike BASIC and other programming languages, "Shelly Ann" is considered two separate items by the IF command. Even if NAME does equal "Shelly Ann", the batch file will error because it assumes "Ann" to be a command and not part of the comparison test.

Program example

    1: @ECHO OFF
    2: SET TEST = in
    3: IF "%TEST%" = = "in" ECHO It's %TEST% there!
    4: SET TEST =
    5: :END

Test run

    It's in there!

Format: *variable* CONST = = CONST

When used in the above format, = = tests for the existence of a variable.

variable is either an environment variable or a replaceable parameter. CONST is a string constant, either a single letter or a complete word. If *variable* exists, the IF statement will be false. Otherwise, because the batch file interpreter expands *variable* into nothing (a null string), the statement will be true.

    IF !%1 = = !

If the replaceable parameter isn't set to anything, then the IF statement is true. Otherwise, %1 is equal to something. Note that this strategy will always avoid a possible Syntax Error in case a replaceable parameter has no value.

    Other variations on this format are:

"variable" = = *""*
NUL*variable* = = NUL

In DOS . . .

The IF statement works on the command line. However, environment variables are not expanded by the command line interpreter, therefore an IF test would be rather silly.

ALSO SEE . . . IF,% (percent)

@ (at) command

Command line—No
  DOS versions—3.3 and up
      OS/2—Real and Protected modes
        Type—Internal

The character @ hides command lines in a batch file and prevents them from being displayed. It's normally used with the initial ECHO OFF command.

Format: @ *commands*

commands are batch file or DOS commands. @ is placed before batch file commands so that the commands will not be displayed. @ suppresses the displaying of commands regardless of whether ECHO is on or off.

Example

    @ECHO OFF

This command is usually used as the first line in a batch file. ECHO OFF suppresses the batch file from being listed to the screen as it's run. The @ sign suppresses ECHO OFF from being displayed. The net result is a "silent" batch file.

    Normally @ is only used once with the initial ECHO OFF statement. However, you could use @ for every line in the batch file to stop it from being displayed. See "Program example #2" below.

    You can write an entire batch file and precede each line with an @ sign to suppress the display. However, you should not put an @ sign in front of a label. In fact, the batch file interpreter will not display any line beginning with a colon character whether ECHO is on or off.

Program example 1

> 1: @ECHO OFF
> 2: ECHO The initial @ECHO command
> 3: ECHO did not display on the screen.
> 4: :END

Test run 1

> The initial @ECHO command
> did not display on the screen.

Program example 2

> 1: @ECHO These strings are echoed to the screen,
> 2: @ECHO but because of the @ sign, you do not see
> 3: @ECHO the ECHO command displayed.

Test run 2

> These strings are echoed to the screen,
> but because of the @ sign, you do not see
> the ECHO command displayed.

In DOS . . .

@ does not work on the DOS command line. (Think about it—it would be redundant: The @ command would turn off the display!)

@ is a valid character in a filename. If you want to specify a program or file in your batch program that starts with the @ character, you must use two @ signs. Therefore, to run the program @NOON in your batch file, you'll need to specify:

> @@NOON

ALSO SEE . . . ECHO

ANSI command

Command line—Yes
  DOS versions—N/A
        OS/2—Protected Mode only
        Type—External

ANSI is used to turn the ANSI screen driver on or off.

Format: ANSI *switch*

switch is either on or off. ANSI ON turns the ANSI driver on; ANSI OFF turns it off.

After issuing the ANSI ON command, OS/2 displays the following:

ANSI extended screen and
keyboard control is on.

After issuing ANSI OFF, the following is displayed:

ANSI extended screen and
keyboard control is off.

ANSI ON is usually used in the OS2INIT.CMD batch file. This way, each new protected mode session you start will be able to use ANSI.

Example

ANSI ON

This command turns the ANSI screen driver on. ANSI commands issued in batch files will now control the screen, change screen color, or reassign keys on the keyboard.

ANSI OFF

This command disables the ANSI screen driver. Normally, ANSI is off.

Program example

1: @ECHO OFF
2: ANSI ON
3: ECHO ^[[2J
4: ANSI OFF

Test run

ANSI extended screen and
keyboard control is on.

(The screen will clear.)

ANSI extended screen and
keyboard control is off.

In DOS . . .

DOS and OS/2 Real mode batch files have no control over the ANSI driver. It must be loaded when the computer is first started by installing the ANSI.SYS device driver in the CONFIG.SYS file.

ALSO SEE . . . chapter 5

CALL command

Command line—Yes
   DOS versions—3.3 and up

OS/2—Real and Protected modes
Type—Internal

CALL allows you to call another batch file, then return to the original batch file. It works like the GOSUB command in BASIC.

Format: CALL *filename*

filename is the name of a batch file. CALL will execute all the commands in the batch file and then execution returns to the calling batch file.

Normally, when you use the name of another batch file as a batch file command, the first batch file stops and control passes to the second batch file. However, by using CALL, you can have one batch file run several other batch files. Control always returns to the original batch file program.

Example

    CALL NEXT.BAT

The above command causes the batch file NEXT.BAT to be run. After NEXT.BAT is finished, execution returns to the statement immediately after CALL in the first batch file.

Program examples

Name: CALL1.BAT

    1: @ECHO OFF
    2: ECHO Running second batch file now
    3: CALL CALL2.BAT
    4: ECHO Back in first batch file again.
    5: :END

Name: CALL2.BAT

    1: ECHO Now executing second batch file...
    2: PAUSE
    3: :END

Test run

    Running second batch file now
    Now Executing second batch file...
    Strike any key when ready . . .
    Back in first batch file again

You should note that the second batch will continue with the same ECHO state as the first batch file. Therefore, if ECHO is off in the first batch file, it will continue to be off for each batch file CALLed.

In DOS . . .

CALL does work on the command line, but it's unnecessary; simply type in the name of a batch file you want to run and save yourself five keystrokes.

ALSO SEE . . . COMMAND, GOTO

CLS command

Command line—Yes
  DOS versions—1.0 and up
          OS/2—Real and Protected modes
          Type—Internal

CLS clears the screen and moves the cursor to the "home" position, location 1, 1.

Format: CLS

CLS has no options, though it's output (the ANSI escape sequence to clear the screen) can be redirected to a file.

After the CLS command is issued, either directly from the command prompt or in a batch file, the screen will be cleared and the cursor moved to the home position.

Example

    CLS

After the above command, the screen will be cleared.

CLS is used when you want your batch file to start off on a clear screen. It really comes in handy with older versions of DOS that left the telltale batch file marker "ECHO OFF" lingering on the screen.

Program example

    1: @ECHO OFF
    2: CLS
    3: ECHO Off to a fresh start
    4: :END

Test run   (The screen will clear.)

    Off to a fresh start

You can use the ANSI escape sequences to clear the screen with the ECHO command. The ANSI clear screen sequence is ESC[2J:

    ECHO ^[[2J

This ECHO command will also clear the screen.

In DOS . . .

CLS is more of a DOS command than a batch file-specific one. But it's best put to use in batch files.

ALSO SEE . . . chapter 3

CMD command

Command line—Yes
  DOS versions—None
        OS/2—Real mode only
        Type—External

CMD is used to run a second copy of CMD.EXE, the OS/2 command processor.

Format: CMD *switches commands*

switches can be one of two switches specified after CMD: /C and /K.

/C is used to specify certain *commands* that will be passed to the copy of the command processor. The *commands* can be any OS/2 command or command line, including the name of a batch file. After the *commands* have been executed by the new command processor, control returns to the original command processor.

/K is also used to specify *commands* for the new copy of the command processor. The difference between this switch and /C is that /K keeps the command processor in memory after *commands* have been executed. Control does not return to the original command processor (you must type EXIT to return).

If both *switches* and *commands* are omitted, then a second copy of the command processor is started. The old environment, including any environment variables, the PATH and PROMPT strings, are copied to the new command processor's environment. Typing EXIT returns you to the previous command processor.

Examples

    CMD /K DIR

This command causes a second copy of the command processor to be run. The first command given the processor will be DIR. After the directory is listed, control stays with the second copy of CMD.EXE. To return to the original CMD.EXE, type EXIT.

    CMD /C NEXT.CMD

CMD is used to run a second copy of the command processor. The second copy of CMD.EXE runs the protected mode batch file, NEXT.CMD. Once NEXT.CMD has finished, control returns to the original copy of the command processor.

Program example

    1: @ECHO OFF
    2: ECHO Now running second command processor
    3: ECHO Type EXIT to return here.
    4: CMD /K
    5: ECHO Welcome back!

Test run

Now running second command processor
Type EXIT to return here.
[C:＼OS2]**EXIT**
Welcome back!

Control returns to the middle of the batch file, to the line right after the CMD /K command was issued.

In DOS . . .

The COMMAND.COM program can be run a second time to start up a second copy of the DOS command processor. COMMAND only has the /C switch that works exactly as it does for CMD.EXE above.

ALSO SEE . . . COMMAND, CALL

COMMAND command

Command line—Yes
  DOS versions—2.0 and up
        OS/2—Real mode only
          Type—External

COMMAND starts a secondary command processor. In batch files, COMMAND is used with the /C switch to "call" another batch file.

Format: COMMAND /C *filename*

filename is the name of a batch file. After COMMAND /C is typed, the batch file *filename* is executed. When *filename* is done, control returns to the first batch file, not DOS.

    Normally, when a second batch file is included as a command in a batch file, the first batch file stops and the second one starts. Control is never returned to the first batch file.

    Using COMMAND /C, you can "call" batch files, similar to the GOSUB statement in BASIC. After the second batch file is done, control returns to the first.

Example

COMMAND /C SECOND

The batch file interpreter will look for and load the file SECOND.BAT. After SECOND.BAT has run, control returns to the current batch file.

Program examples

Name: COMM1.BAT

1: @ECHO OFF
2: ECHO Running second batch file now
3: COMMAND /C COMM2.BAT

4: ECHO Back in first batch file again.
5: END

Name: COMM2.BAT

1: @ECHO OFF
2: ECHO Now executing second batch file...
3: PAUSE
4: :END

Test run

Running second batch file now
Now Executing second batch file...
Strike any key when ready . . .
Back in first batch file again

If you get a "Bad command or filename" error when running the first program above, it's probably because COMMAND.COM isn't on your system's path. You can solve this by changing line 3 in COMM1.BAT to:

3: C:\ COMMAND /C COMM2.BAT

Or, to be really nifty about things, you can use the environment variable COMSPEC, which naturally contains the location of your COMMAND .COM file:

3: %COMSPEC% /C COMM2.BAT

COMMAND also has a second switch, /P, similar to the /K switch for CMD.EXE (see CMD). The /P switch will keep COMMAND.COM in memory, but it also causes COMMAND.COM to run any AUTOEXEC.BAT file found in the root directory. You could run a second batch file simply by naming it AUTOEXEC.BAT and putting it in the root directory. But this isn't the purpose Microsoft had in mind for the /P switch. (See the SHELL command in chapters 2 and 5.)

In DOS . . .

COMMAND can be used to "call" a batch file as described above, though it's redundant. Instead, COMMAND is used at the DOS prompt to start another command processor. The complete environment table, including PATH, PROMPT, and COMSPEC, is copied and a new copy of COMMAND .COM is loaded into memory. To leave the new copy of COMMAND.COM, type EXIT.

ALSO SEE . . . CMD, CALL, GOTO, chapter 2

ECHO command

Command line—Yes
  DOS versions—2.0 and up

OS/2—Real and Protected modes
Type—Internal

ECHO turns command echoing on or off. Also, ECHO sends an optional string of characters to the display.

Format: ECHO

When used without any parameters, ECHO merely repeats the current "state" of the ECHO command. For example:

ECHO is off

or

ECHO is on

Format: ECHO *switch*

switch is either ON or OFF. The default is ECHO ON, meaning that all commands in a batch file are displayed as they are executed. Normally, ECHO OFF is used at the start of every batch file to suppress the echoing of commands.

ECHO OFF

This command suppresses the echoing of batch file commands to the screen. The batch file will run silently unless an ECHO ON statement is encountered.

Format: ECHO *string*

string is a string of up to 124 characters that will be echoed to the display, or console device.

Examples

ECHO

This displays either "ECHO is on" or "ECHO is off" depending on the current state of the ECHO command.

ECHO ON

This command turns echo on. Since ECHO is always on each time a batch file starts, you don't normally need to use this command unless you have previously turned ECHO off. Also, you don't need to end a batch file with ECHO ON to "reset."

ECHO OFF

This command turns off the echoing of commands during batch file execution.

ECHO Grandma makes the best cookies

sends "Grandma makes the best cookies" to the console. Because ECHO uses DOS's devices, you can also use I/O redirection with ECHO to send the output elsewhere. For example:

    ECHO Jim is here > > LOGFILE

appends the string "Jim is here" followed by a carriage return and line-feed to the file LOGFILE.

    ECHO ^L > PRN

This command comes in very handy. It sends a Control L character to the printer device, PRN. The effect of this command is to eject a page from the printer.

    ECHO .

This command is used to ECHO a "blank line" to the display. Normally, when ECHO is used by itself, it repeats the status of the ECHO command. However, when followed by a period, ECHO displays only the period. (In older versions of DOS, ECHO followed by some spaces would display only the space. But, with the new and improved versions of DOS, ECHO followed by spaces is the same as ECHO followed by nothing.)

When ECHO is used in a batch file with either an environment variable or a replaceable parameter variable, it ECHOes the contents of that variable. (Actually, what happens is that the batch file interpreter first expands the variable and then ECHO displays that expanded string.)

    ECHO %STATUS%

If the environment variable STATUS is set equal to "IN," then the batch file interpreter expands it as follows:

    ECHO IN

The word "IN" will be displayed.

    ECHO %1 is the first argument

The batch file interpreter will expand %1 to the value of the first replaceable parameter, the first item typed after the name of the batch file on the command line.

Program example 1

    1: @ECHO

Test run 1

    ECHO is on

Program example 2

    1: @ECHO ON
    2: REM THAT LINE REALLY ISN'T NECESSARY

3: ECHO YOU CAN SEE EVERYTHING AS IT RUNS
4: :END

Test run 2

C> @ECHO ON

C> REM THAT LINE REALLY ISN'T NECESSARY

C> ECHO YOU CAN SEE EVERYTHING AS IT RUNS

C> :END

In DOS . . .

Because ECHO generates redirectable output, the main reason for using it on the command line is with I/O redirection. For example, ejecting a page from the printer with ECHO ^L > PRN, appending data to the end of a text file with > >, or creating new, one line text files.

ALSO SEE . . . COMMAND, GOTO, % (percent), @ (at)

ENDLOCAL command

Command line—Yes
  DOS versions—N/A
        OS/2—Protected mode only
        Type—Internal

ENDLOCAL restores the environment settings and changes to the drive and directory that were active when the SETLOCAL command was issued.

Format: ENDLOCAL

ENDLOCAL restores the drive, directory and environment that were saved by a SETLOCAL command. You can use ENDLOCAL as often as you like in your batch files. Each time it's used your original drive, directory and environment will be restored.

    ENDLOCAL need only be specified if you wish to restore your drive, directory and environment before the batch file stops. Otherwise, the OS/2 batch file interpreter restores your drive, directory and environment when the batch file is finished (provided a SETLOCAL command was previously issued).

Example

    ENDLOCAL

After the above command is encountered in a batch file, the drive, path and environment will be restored to exactly what they were when the SETLOCAL command was issued.

Program example

```
1: @ECHO OFF
2: ECHO Here's how we start:
3: CD
4: SET
5: REM Save stuff
6: SETLOCAL
7: ECHO Now let me change some things...
8: A:
9: CD \ OLD
10: PATH = \
11: PROMPT = Help!
12: CD
13: SET
14: ECHO And now, back to normal:
15: ENDLOCAL
16: CD
17: SET
18: :END
```

Test run

```
Here's how we start:
C: \ OS2
COMSPEC = C: \ OS2 \ PBIN \ CMD.EXE
PATH = C: \ ;C: \ OS2 \ BIN;C: \ OS2 \ PBIN
PROMPT = $i[$p]
Now let me change some things...
C: \ OLD
COMSPEC = C: \ OS2 \ PBIN \ CMD.EXE
PATH = \
PROMPT = Help!
And now, back to normal:
C: \ OS2
COMSPEC = C: \ OS2 \ PBIN \ CMD.EXE
PATH = C: \ ;C: \ OS2 \ BIN;C: \ OS2 \ PBIN
PROMPT = $i[$p]
```

In DOS . . .

The only way to retain the contents of the environment table in DOS would be to start a new copy of the command processor. The batch file could then end with an EXIT statement, by which the contents of the environment would be restored.

The RESTPATH program on the supplemental programs diskette can be used to restore an original drive/directory. (See chapter 11 and appendix K.)

ALSO SEE . . . SETLOCAL, SET

ERRORLEVEL variable

Command line—N/A
  DOS versions—2.0 and up
        OS/2—Real and Protected modes
        Type—Internal

ERRORLEVEL is a variable that contains the return code for a previously run program. ERRORLEVEL is used only with the IF statement.

Format: IF ERRORLEVEL *value commands*

value is a comparison value for ERRORLEVEL. It ranges from 0 through 255 and is compared with the return code of a previously run program. If the return code (the value of ERRORLEVEL) is greater than or equal to *value*, then the IF test is true, and the specified *commands* are executed.

The tricky thing about ERRORLEVEL is remembering that it compares values greater than or equal to the return code of the previous program. Also, keep in mind that not every program has a return code. Only a few DOS programs and some utilities take advantage of this feature.

Examples

    IF ERRORLEVEL 13 GOTO LABEL

If the return code of the most recently run program is 13 or greater, batch file execution branches to the label LABEL.

ERRORLEVEL is often used with several IF statements to determine the exact return code of the most recently run program:

    IF ERRORLEVEL 5 GOTO FIVE
    IF ERRORLEVEL 4 GOTO FOUR
    IF ERRORLEVEL 3 GOTO THREE
    IF ERRORLEVEL 2 GOTO TWO
    IF ERRORLEVEL 1 GOTO END
    REM Must be ERRORLEVEL zero here...

Program example

    1: @ECHO OFF
    2: REM It's assumed the program BLECH returns an
    3: REM ERRORLEVEL value of either 1 or 0
    4: BLECH
    5: IF ERRORLEVEL 0 GOTO ZERO
    6: ECHO Errorlevel one returned
    7: GOTO END
    8: :ZERO
    9: ECHO Errorlevel zero returned
    10: :END

Test run

    BLECH!
    Errorlevel one returned

In DOS . . .

The ERRORLEVEL variable always has a value of zero when an IF statement is used on the command line.

ALSO SEE . . . IF, EXIST, NOT

EXIST variable

Command line—N/A
 DOS versions—2.0 and up
  OS/2—Real and Protected modes
  Type—Internal

EXIST is a variable set to either true or false depending on if a specified file exists. EXIST is used only with the IF statement.

Format: IF EXIST *filename commands*

filename can be an individual file's name, or a group of files specified via wildcards. It cannot be the name of a subdirectory. If *filename* exists, then the IF test is true, and the specified *commands* are executed.

Examples

    IF EXIST README TYPE README

If the file named README exists, the command TYPE README will be executed. Otherwise the IF test fails and the next line in the batch file will be executed.

    IF EXIST C:\JUNK*.* GOTO KILLALL

If any files exist in the \JUNK subdirectory on drive C, batch file execution will branch to the label KILLALL.

EXIST can also be used with the NOT conditional. In that case, the IF statement is true only if the specified file or files do not exist.

    IF NOT EXIST *.* ECHO Directory Empty!

Program example

    1: @ECHO OFF
    2: IF EXIST *.BAT GOTO FOUND
    3: ECHO There are not batch files here!
    4: GOTO END
    5: :FOUND
    6: ECHO There are batch files here!
    7: :END

Test run

There are batch files here!

In DOS . . .

EXIST can be used with IF on the command line to test for the existence of a file or group of files.

ALSO SEE . . . IF, ERRORLEVEL, NOT

EXTPROC command

Command line—N/A
  DOS versions—N/A
          OS/2—Protected mode only
          Type—Internal

EXTPROC is used to start a batch file interpreter besides CMD.EXE. Using EXTPROC, you can have a third-party batch file processor execute your batch file commands.

Format: EXTPROC *filename*

filename is the name of a batch file processor.

   EXTPROC must be the first command given in a batch file. Normally CMD.EXE executes OS/2 batch files. However, by using EXTPROC, you can have third-party batch file interpreter do the job. This avoids the memory-resident mess that most DOS batch file enhancing programs must go through.

Example

    @EXTPROC FASTBAT.EXE

This line, the first line in the batch file, specifies the program FASTBAT .EXE as this batch file program's batch file processor. From this line on, FASTBAT will be executing the batch file commands.

Program example Because no secondary batch file processors exist for OS/2 yet, a Program Example and Test Run are not possible. Just remember that EXTPROC must be the first command in the batch file. (Other commands in the batch file may be specific to the external batch file processor.)

In DOS . . .

Third-party batch file extension languages are readily available for speeding up batch file execution, or just provided a richer batch file programming environment. (See Part Three of this book for more information.)

ALSO SEE . . . chapters 12, 13, and 14

FOR command

Command line—Yes
  DOS versions—2.0 and up
        OS/2—Real and Protected modes
        Type—Internal

FOR is used to repeat a command for a given set of filenames.

Format: FOR %*variable* IN (*set*) DO *command*

variable is the name of the FOR variable. It's a single letter or character, but not a number nor the symbols <, >, or |. *variable* is used to represent each of the filenames specified by *set*. In DOS, *variable* is preceded by a single percent sign. In batch files, *variable* is preceded by double percent signs.

   set specifies a group of filenames, either individual files or groups of filenames with wildcards. It can also specify program names, in which case "DO *command*" will run the series of programs enclosed in parentheses.

   command is a DOS command. The DOS command will be performed on the filenames mentioned in *set* via the *variable*. In other words, *variable* is used as a placeholder for each of the filenames in *set*. Don't forget the DO before *command*.

   Using FOR you can repeat a specific DOS command for several groups of files. This avoids having to type the same command a number of times for a number of files.

Examples

    FOR %A IN (*.COM *.EXE *&.BAT) DO DIR %A

%A is the *variable*. It will be used to represent the three groups of files specified in the *set*: *.COM, *.EXE, and *.BAT. For each of those files, the command "DIR %A" will be performed. The final result will be a directory of all .COM, .EXE and .BAT files in the current directory.

   The above command does the same thing as the following:

    DIR *.COM
    DIR *.EXE
    DIR *.BAT

%A takes on each of the filenames in the *set* for the DIR command.

    FOR %F IN (JUNK TEMP KILLME OLD) TO DEL %F

This command will delete all the following files in one fell swoop: JUNK, TEMP, KILLME and OLD.

    FOR %P IN (RUNME DIAGS CLS HELLO) DO %P

Here, FOR is used to run four different programs or DOS commands. DO

%P is used to run each of the commands without you having to type four different command lines, or list four different lines in a batch file.

Program example

```
1: @ECHO OFF
2: FOR %%D IN (*.DOC MANUAL PRINTME.*) DO COPY %%D PRN
3: END
```

Test run   (All files with the .DOC extension, the file named MANUAL, and all files starting with PRINTME will be copied to the printer.)

In DOS . . .

The FOR command can be used at the DOS prompt to cut down on your typing time. Remember to specify a single percent sign at the DOS prompt and only use double percent signs in batch files.

ALSO SEE . . . % (percent)

GOTO command

Command line—N/A
DOS versions—2.0 and up
OS/2—Real and Protected modes
Type—Internal

GOTO is used to branch batch file execution to a specified label.

Format: GOTO *label*

label is a name used to identify the line execution branches to. It can be from one to eight characters long and can contain any characters except for a period, semicolon, equal sign, or characters not allowed in a filename (see appendix E). If the label is longer than eight characters or contains a space, only the first eight characters or any characters up to the space will be considered as the label.

By using GOTO, you can have your batch file skip over sections of code, branch to a specific routine, or execute one part of the code over and over. GOTO works well with the IF statement to act upon a certain condition.

The batch file GOTO works exactly the same as the BASIC language GOTO command. The difference is that a label is used in batch files, rather than a line number.

After the batch file interpreter encounters a GOTO statement, it searches the entire batch file from start through finish for the *label*. If the *label* is not found, the batch file stops immediately with a ''Label not found'' error. Lines containing labels are identified by a leading colon (:) character.

Example

GOTO STEP5

This causes the batch file interpreter to GOTO the line starting with :STEP5.

The batch file interpreter always searches for a label starting from the top of the batch file down. Only the first matching label is used, so duplicate labels will be ignored by GOTO.

Program example 1

```
 1: @ECHO OFF
 2: REM Test the GOTO statement
 3: GOTO LABEL1
 4: :LABEL2
 5: ECHO At label two
 6: GOTO END
 7: :LABEL1
 8: ECHO At label one
 9: GOTO LABEL2
10: :END
11: ECHO Done!
```

Test run 1

```
At label one
At label two
Done!
```

Program example 2

```
1: @ECHO OFF
2: REM A Shifting example
3: :LOOP
4: IF "%1" = = "" GOTO END
5: COPY %1 A:
6: SHIFT
7: GOTO LOOP
8: :END
```

Test run 2   (The program copies a group of files to drive A.)

Test program #2 uses GOTO to form a loop. The GOTO in line 7 continuously executes lines 3 through 6. Line 4 tests for the end of the loop, in which case GOTO is again used to end the batch file.

In DOS . . .

The GOTO statement does not cause an error on the command line nor does it do much of anything else either.

ALSO SEE . . .: (colon), CALL

IF statement

Command line—Yes
DOS versions—2.0 and up
OS/2—Real and Protected modes
Type—Internal

IF is used to test for a condition. If the condition is true, then a DOS command will be executed.

Format: IF *condition command*

condition is an evaluation made by the IF command. There are three sets of *condition*s that IF can evaluate using the following:

= = (double equal signs)
ERRORLEVEL
EXIST

= = (double equal signs) are used to compare two string values. Either string value may be a replaceable parameter or environment variable. If the two strings are equal, then the IF statement is true and the indicated *command* is executed.

ERRORLEVEL is a variable that contains the return code from a previously run program. ERRORLEVEL is followed by a comparison value. If the return code is equal to or greater than that value, the IF statement is true and the indicated *command* is executed.

EXIST is used to test for the existence of a file or group of files (using wildcards). If the indicated files exist, then the IF statement is true and the indicated *command* is executed.

The NOT prefix can be used with any of the above *condition*s to reverse their results. For example, IF NOT EXIST tests to see if a file does not exist, IF NOT *string*= =*string* tests to see if two strings are not equal. In this case, if the results of the IF comparison are NOT true, then the indicated *command* is executed.

command is any DOS or batch file command. It can even be another IF statement. Keep in mind, however, that unlike other versions of the IF command in other programming languages, the batch file IF does not have a corresponding THEN statement. If you use THEN, you'll get an error.

Examples

IF %STATUS% = = IN GOTO MAIN

If the string value of the environment variable STATUS is equal to "IN", then the command GOTO MAIN will be executed. Otherwise, the next statement in the batch file is executed.

IF ERRORLEVEL 1 ECHO Ouch!

If the return code from the most recently run DOS program is equal to one or more, then "Ouch!" will be echoed to the screen.

```
IF EXIST READ.ME TYPE READ.ME
```

If the file named READ.ME is found in the current directory, then it will be TYPEd to the screen.

```
IF NOT "%1" = = "" GOTO CONTINUE
```

When a NOT appears in an IF statement, it helps to read it from the inside out. Therefore, this IF statement checks to see if the first replaceable parameter exists:

```
"%1" = = ""
```

If %1 is equal to anything, the IF test will be false. However, because NOT is specified, the reverse will hold true and the command GOTO CONTINUE will be executed. If %1 is not equal to anything, the IF test will be false (because NOT is used).

IF statements can also be "nested." That is, one IF statement can follow another:

```
IF %FIRST% = = CHERRY IF %SECOND% = = CHERRY IF
%THIRD% = = CHERRY ECHO You just won seven bucks!
```

Program example

```
1: @ECHO OFF
2: REM If test program
3: IF EXIST *.* ECHO There are files here!
4: IF %PROMPT% = = $p$g GOTO YAWN
5: IF %PROMPT% = = $P$G GOTO YAWN
6: ECHO My, what an interesting prompt you have
7: GOTO END
8: :YAWN
9: ECHO You have a boring prompt
10: :END
```

Test run

```
There are files here!
You have a boring prompt
```

In DOS . . .

The IF statement can be used on the command line without any modifications. However, an ERRORLEVEL test in an IF statement will always return a value of zero.

ALSO SEE . . . = = (double equal signs), ERRORLEVEL, EXIST, NOT

NOT operator

Command line—N/A
 DOS versions—2.0 and up
  OS/2—Real and Protected modes
  Type—Internal

NOT is used with the IF statement to reverse the results of the IF statement's test.

Format: IF NOT *condition command*

condition is an evaluation made by the IF statement. It is either a string comparison using = = (double equal signs); a test for a file's existence using EXIST, or a return code test using ERRORLEVEL. NOT precedes the *condition*. If the *condition* evaluates to true, NOT reverses it to false. If *condition* evaluates to false, NOT reverses it to true.

   command is a DOS or batch file command. Normally, if *condition* is true, *command* will be executed. However, when NOT is specified, *command* will only be executed when *condition* is false.

Example

    IF NOT EXIST READ.ME ECHO No READ.ME file was found

This IF statement tests for the existence of a file named READ.ME. If the file does not exist, the IF statement is true and "No READ.ME file was found" will be displayed.

Program example

    1: @ECHO OFF
    2: IF NOT EXIST *.BAT GOTO NONEFOUND
    3: ECHO There are batch files here!
    4: GOTO END
    5: :NONEFOUND
    6: ECHO There are no batch files here!
    7: :END

Test run

    There are batch files here!

In DOS . . .

NOT can be used with the IF statement on the command line just as it's used in batch files.

ALSO SEE . . . IF

PAUSE command

Command line—Yes
 DOS versions—1.0 and up

OS/2—Real and Protected modes
Type—Internal

PAUSE is used to display a message and then wait for the user to press a key on the keyboard.

Format: PAUSE *message*

message is an optional message displayed before the PAUSE command's message. You should be careful when specifying a *message* because it's not displayed to the screen like the ECHO command. Instead, the only way to see the *message* is to keep ECHO ON.

Besides the optional message, PAUSE displays the following:

    Strike a key when ready . . .

It then waits for the user to press a key on the keyboard. Once a key is pressed, the batch file continues.

It's important to note that not every key will cause the PAUSE command to continue. The "a key" description is rather vague to many users. In fact, the following keys will have no effect with the PAUSE command:

Shift keys: Left, Right, ALT, CTRL (control)
Option keys: CAPS LOCK, NUM LOCK, SCROLL LOCK
Dead keys: 5 on the cursor pad, Foreign language dead keys

Example

    PAUSE

After the above command, the following is displayed:

    Strike a key when ready . . .

After the user presses a key, usually the spacebar, the batch program continues.

PAUSE is useful in batch files to give the user a chance to read a message or to make a decision. For example:

    ECHO Press Control-Break to stop or
    PAUSE

The above two commands are often used one after the other to give the user a chance to "Break out" of a batch file. The display will show:

    Press Control-Break to stop or
    Strike a key when ready . . .

If the user strikes any key, the batch file continues. Otherwise, by pressing CTRL – BREAK, the batch file will ask if the user wants to stop, and they can press "Y" to get out.

Program example

    1: @ECHO OFF
    2: PAUSE

3: ECHO And now, with ECHO ON...
4: ECHO ON
5: PAUSE Doesn't this work great?

Test run

Strike a key when ready . . .
(a key is pressed)
And now, with ECHO ON...

C> PAUSE Doesn't this work great?
Strike a key when ready . . .

In DOS . . .

PAUSE can be issued at the command prompt to display the same message as it does in batch files. After pressing a key, control returns to the command prompt.

ALSO SEE . . . ECHO

REM statement

Command line—Yes
  DOS versions—1.0 and up
        OS/2—Real and Protected modes
        Type—Internal

REM allows comments, or REMarks, to be used in batch files.

Format: REM *comments*

comments can be an optional string of characters, usually offering useful information about the batch file or explaining a batch file procedure.

The REM statement is primarily used for placing comments into batch files. REM is not executed as a command and anything following it is ignored by the batch file interpreter.

Examples

REM This is the tricky part

"This is the tricky part" is a comment specified after the REM statement.

REM Reset old path

This remark may appear before the SET command is used to change an environment variable.

REM IF EXIST *.BAK DEL *.BAK

In this example, REM is used to "comment out" a regular command in the batch file. To reactivate the command, the REM statement can be deleted.

Program example

>1: @ECHO OFF
>2: REM ECHO This command will not work
>3: REM ECHO because REM has made it into a comma.
>4: ECHO Ah, so!

Test run

>Ah, so!

In DOS . . .

REM can be used on the command line, in which case anything you type after it will be ignored by the command interpreter.

ALSO SEE . . . : (colon)

SET command

Command line—Yes
  DOS versions—2.0 and up
          OS/2—Real and Protected modes
          Type—Internal

SET allows you to assign system, or environment, variables.

Format: SET *variable* = *string*

variable is the name of an environment variable. It can be any length, though shorter is better, and may contain letters and numbers and spaces (any characters before the equal sign). Uppercase and lowercase letters are converted to uppercase when *variable* is stored in the environment.

string is a string of characters. When *variable* is used in a batch file, it will be replaced by *string*. If *string* is omitted, *variable* is removed from the environment. If *variable* already exists, any specified *string* replaces its previous value.

SET is used to create environment variables. These variables can be used for storing information or temporary string values. PATH and PROMPT are two environment variables, though they are set by the PATH and PROMPT commands. (They could be created with the SET command as well.)

If SET is used without both the *variable* or *string* values it displays a list of the current variables in the environment table and their string values.

Examples

>SET STATUS = ON

Places the string STATUS=ON into your system's environment. When

%STATUS% is used in a batch file, the batch file interpreter will expand it to "ON."

> SET GIRLFRIEND = Lola Palooza

Sets "Lola Palooza" to the variable GIRLFRIEND. Lola Palooza need not be in quotes.

> SET ANSWER = "Goodbye, Mr. Chips"

Sets the entire string, "Goodbye, Mr. Chips" into the environment table—even the quotes. When %ANSWER% is used in a batch file, it will be expanded by the batch file interpreter to "Goodbye, Mr. Chips".,

> SET STATUS =

Removes the variable STATUS from the environment. The equal sign must be specified.

Program example

```
 1: @ECHO OFF
 2: SET TESTING = It works
 3: ECHO A demonstration of SET:
 4: ECHO Here is what the SET command displays by itself:
 5: SET
 6: PAUSE
 7: ECHO And here's a demonstration of SET assigning a variable:
 8: ECHO TESTING = %TESTING%
 9: SET TESTING =
10: :END
```

Test run

```
A demonstration of SET:
Here is what the SET command displays by itself:
PATH =
COMSPEC = C: \ AUTOEXEC.BAT
Strike any key when ready . . .
And here's a demonstration of SET assigning a variable:
TESTING = It works
```

(You will note how the TESTING variable is removed from the environment in line 10 above. This frees the space used by the variable and is good practice when using temporary environment variables.)

In DOS . . .

Typing the SET command on DOS displays a list of assigned variables, as well as the system variables COMSPEC, PATH, PROMPT. Additionally, SET can be used at the command prompt to assign environment variables that can be used in batch files.

Environment variables cannot be echoed on the DOS command line.

For example:

C> ECHO %STATUS%

This command simply displays "%STATUS%" on the following line. On the batch file interpreter expands percent sign variables.

ALSO SEE . . . ECHO, = =, %

SETLOCAL command

Command line—Yes
 DOS versions—None
    OS/2—Protected mode only
    Type—Internal?

SETLOCAL saves the current drive, directory and environment settings.

Format: SETLOCAL

SETLOCAL remembers the drive, directory and environment at the time the SETLOCAL command was issued. After SETLOCAL, you can change your drive, directory, and environment. The original settings can be restored at any time using the ENDLOCAL command.

SETLOCAL can only be used once in a batch file. Any further use of SETLOCAL will be ignored by the OS/2 batch file interpreter.

(For a program example see ENDLOCAL.)

ALSO SEE . . . ENDLOCAL, SET

SHIFT command

Command line—No
 DOS versions—2.0 and up
    OS/2—Real and Protected modes
    Type—Internal

SHIFT shifts the replaceable parameter values, %0 through %9.

Format: SHIFT

SHIFT has no arguments. Instead, after the SHIFT command is issued, the values of each of the replaceable parameters is shifted "down." For example: the value of %1 becomes %0, the value of %2 becomes %1, and so on.

After the SHIFT command, %0 is SHIFTed away. Any parameters after %9 are shifted into %9, one for each use of the SHIFT statement. This way, additional arguments (beyond %9) on the command line can be used as replaceable parameters.

Example

C> LOGIN 10:12 LITTLE HENRY

The replaceable parameters for this command line are:

%0 - LOGIN (the name of the batch file)
%1 - 10:12
%2 - LITTLE
%3 - HENRY

After the SHIFT command is used once, the replaceable parameters will be:

%0 - 10:12
%1 - LITTLE
%2 - HENRY

If SHIFT is used a second time, the replaceable parameters will be:

%0 - LITTLE
%1 - HENRY

Program example

```
1: @ECHO OFF
2: ECHO First parameter is now %1
3: SHIFT
4: ECHO But after the SHIFT command, it's %1
```

Test run

(Assuming the following was typed after the name of the batch file: FIRST, SECOND.)

```
First parameter is now FIRST
But after the SHIFT command, it's SECOND
```

(For an excellent program example, refer to SHIFTARG in chapter 7.)

In DOS . . .

The SHIFT command has no effect at the DOS command prompt. However, it is interesting in that you enter the word SHIFT and press ENTER and nothing happens. Try doing this on an officemate's computer and it will leave them baffled (because they won't be able to find a SHIFT.COM file in any directory)!

ALSO SEE . . . %, = =

A
ASCII

The old ALT-keypad trick

Characters not on the keyboard—specifically, the Extended ASCII codes 128 through 255—can be entered using what's come to be known as the ALT-keypad trick. To enter these characters (any ASCII character, actually), press and hold the ALT key, type the character's decimal ASCII code on the keypad, then release the ALT key. Once the ALT key is released, the character appears.

For example, to enter the "a" character, ASCII 160, do the following:

1. Press and hold the ALT key.
2. Type 1 then 6 then 0 on the keypad.
3. Release the ALT key.

Voila, you have the "a" character!

A-1 ASCII Character set and IBM Extended ASCII codes and characters.

IBM ASCII Character Set

Display Character	Value Decimal	Hexadecimal	Binary

Control Characters:

^@ NUL	0	00h	00000000
^A SOH	1	01h	00000001
^B STX	2	02h	00000010
^C ETX	3	03h	00000011
^D EOT	4	04h	00000100
^E ENQ	5	05h	00000101
^F ACK	6	06h	00000110
^G BEL	7	07h	00000111
^H BS	8	08h	00001000
^I HT	9	09h	00001001
^J LF	10	0Ah	00001010
^K VT	11	0Bh	00001011
^L FF	12	0Ch	00001100
^M CR	13	0Dh	00001101
^N SO	14	0Eh	00001110
^O SI	15	0Fh	00001111
^P DLE	16	10h	00010000
^Q DC1	17	11h	00010001
^R DC2	18	12h	00010010
^S DC3	19	13h	00010011
^T CD4	20	14h	00010100
^U NAK	21	15h	00010101
^V SYN	22	16h	00010110
^W ETB	23	17h	00010111
^X CAN	24	18h	00011000
^Y EM	25	19h	00011001
^Z SUB	26	1Ah	00011010
^[ESC	27	1Bh	00011011
^\ FS	28	1Ch	00011100
^] GS	29	1Dh	00011101
^^ RS	30	1Eh	00011110
^_ US	31	1Fh	00011111

Standard Characters:

	32	20h	00100000
!	33	21h	00100001
"	34	22h	00100010
#	35	23h	00100011
$	36	24h	00100100
%	37	25h	00100101
&	38	26h	00100110
'	39	27h	00100111
(	40	28h	00101000
)	41	29h	00101001
*	42	2Ah	00101010
+	43	2Bh	00101011
,	44	2Ch	00101100
-	45	2Dh	00101101
.	46	2Eh	00101110
/	47	2Fh	00101111
0	48	30h	00110000
1	49	31h	00110001
2	50	32h	00110010
3	51	33h	00110011
4	52	34h	00110100
5	53	35h	00110101
6	54	36h	00110110
7	55	37h	00110111
8	56	38h	00111000
9	57	39h	00111001
:	58	3Ah	00111010
;	59	3Bh	00111011
<	60	3Ch	00111100
=	61	3Dh	00111101

Char	Dec	Hex	Binary
>	62	3Eh	00111110
?	63	3Fh	00111111
@	64	40h	01000000
A	65	41h	01000001
B	66	42h	01000010
C	67	43h	01000011
D	68	44h	01000100
E	69	45h	01000101
F	70	46h	01000110
G	71	47h	01000111
H	72	48h	01001000
I	73	49h	01001001
J	74	4Ah	01001010
K	75	4Bh	01001011
L	76	4Ch	01001100
M	77	4Dh	01001101
N	78	4Eh	01001110
O	79	4Fh	01001111
P	80	50h	01010000
Q	81	51h	01010001
R	82	52h	01010010
S	83	53h	01010011
T	84	54h	01010100
U	85	55h	01010101
V	86	56h	01010110
W	87	57h	01010111
X	88	58h	01011000
Y	89	59h	01011001
Z	90	5Ah	01011010
[	91	5Bh	01011011
\	92	5Ch	01011100
]	93	5Dh	01011101
^	94	5Eh	01011110
_	95	5Fh	01011111
`	96	60h	01100000
a	97	61h	01100001
b	98	62h	01100010
c	99	63h	01100011
d	100	64h	01100100
e	101	65h	01100101
f	102	66h	01100110
g	103	67h	01100111
h	104	68h	01101000
i	105	69h	01101001
j	106	6Ah	01101010
k	107	6Bh	01101011
l	108	6Ch	01101100
m	109	6Dh	01101101
n	110	6Eh	01101110
o	111	6Fh	01101111
p	112	70h	01110000
q	113	71h	01110001
r	114	72h	01110010
s	115	73h	01110011
t	116	74h	01110100
u	117	75h	01110101
v	118	76h	01110110
w	119	77h	01110111
x	120	78h	01111000
y	121	79h	01111001
z	122	7Ah	01111010
{	123	7Bh	01111011
|	124	7Ch	01111100
}	125	7Dh	01111101
~	126	7Eh	01111110
Δ	127	7Fh	01111111

IBM's Extended ASCII Character Set:

Char	Dec	Hex	Binary
Ç	128	80h	10000000
ü	129	81h	10000001
é	130	82h	10000010
â	131	83h	10000011
ä	132	84h	10000100
à	133	85h	10000101
å	134	86h	10000110
ç	135	87h	10000111
ê	136	88h	10001000
ë	137	89h	10001001
è	138	8Ah	10001010
ï	139	8Bh	10001011
î	140	8Ch	10001100
ì	141	8Dh	10001101
Ä	142	8Eh	10001110
Å	143	8Fh	10001111
É	144	90h	10010000
æ	145	91h	10010001
Æ	146	92h	10010010
ô	147	93h	10010011
ö	148	94h	10010100
ò	149	95h	10010101
û	150	96h	10010110
ù	151	97h	10010111
ÿ	152	98h	10011000
Ö	153	99h	10011001
Ü	154	9Ah	10011010
¢	155	9Bh	10011011
£	156	9Ch	10011100
¥	157	9Dh	10011101
₨	158	9Eh	10011110
ƒ	159	9Fh	10011111
á	160	A0h	10100000
í	161	A1h	10100001
ó	162	A2h	10100010
ú	163	A3h	10100011
ñ	164	A4h	10100100
Ñ	165	A5h	10100101
ª	166	A6h	10100110
º	167	A7h	10100111
¿	168	A8h	10101000
⌐	169	A9h	10101001
¬	170	AAh	10101010
½	171	ABh	10101011
¼	172	ACh	10101100
¡	173	ADh	10101101
«	174	AEh	10101110
»	175	AFh	10101111

Table A-1 Continued.

▓	176	B0h	10110000
▓	177	B1h	10110001
▓	178	B2h	10110010
│	179	B3h	10110011
┤	180	B4h	10110100
╡	181	B5h	10110101
╢	182	B6h	10110110
╖	183	B7h	10110111
╕	184	B8h	10111000
╣	185	B9h	10111001
║	186	BAh	10111010
╗	187	BBh	10111011
╝	188	BCh	10111100
╜	189	BDh	10111101
╛	190	BEh	10111110
┐	191	BFh	10111111
└	192	C0h	11000000
┴	193	C1h	11000001
┬	194	C2h	11000010
├	195	C3h	11000011
─	196	C4h	11000100
┼	197	C5h	11000101
╞	198	C6h	11000110
╟	199	C7h	11000111
╚	200	C8h	11001000
╔	201	C9h	11001001
╩	202	CAh	11001010
╦	203	CBh	11001011
╠	204	CCh	11001100
═	205	CDh	11001101
╬	206	CEh	11001110
╧	207	CFh	11001111
╨	208	D0h	11010000
╤	209	D1h	11010001
╥	210	D2h	11010010
╙	211	D3h	11010011
╘	212	D4h	11010100
╒	213	D5h	11010101
╓	214	D6h	11010110
╫	215	D7h	11010111
╪	216	D8h	11011000
┘	217	D9h	11011001
┌	218	DAh	11011010
█	219	DBh	11011011
▄	220	DCh	11011100
▌	221	DDh	11011101
▐	222	DEh	11011110
▀	223	DFh	11011111
∝	224	E0h	11100000
β	225	E1h	11100001
Γ	226	E2h	11100010
π	227	E3h	11100011
Σ	228	E4h	11100100
σ	229	E5h	11100101
μ	230	E6h	11100110
τ	231	E7h	11100111
φ	232	E8h	11101000
θ	233	E9h	11101001
Ω	234	EAh	11101010
δ	235	EBh	11101011
∞	236	ECh	11101100
φ	237	EDh	11101101
∈	238	EEh	11101110
∩	239	EFh	11101111
≡	240	F0h	11110000
±	241	F1h	11110001
≥	242	F2h	11110010
≤	243	F3h	11110011
⌠	244	F4h	11110100
⌡	245	F5h	11110101
÷	246	F6h	11110110
≈	247	F7h	11110111
·	248	F8h	11111000
·	249	F9h	11111001
·	250	FAh	11111010
√	251	FBh	11111011
ⁿ	252	FCh	11111100
²	253	FDh	11111101
∎	254	FEh	11111110
	255	FFh	11111111

B
ANSI.SYS commands

In the following, the italic *n* represents an integer ASCII value. For example, if you want *n* to represent the value 42, replace it with the ASCII characters "42" not the byte value 42. If more than one replaceable integer value appears in a command string, they are numbered *n1*, *n2* and so on.

"ESC" represents the escape character, ASCII 27 (1B hexadecimal, or "^[").

Locate cursor

ESC[*n1*;*n2*H

n1 is a row number and *n2* is a column number. After the above command, the cursor will be positioned at row *n1* and column *n2*. If both parameters are omitted, as in ESC[;H, the cursor is sent to position 1,1— the upper left corner of the screen.

Position cursor

ESC[*n1*;*n2*f

This command operates the same as the previous command, though it's not as common and rarely used.

Move cursor up

ESC[*n*A

Moves the cursor up *n* number of rows. If *n* is omitted, the cursor moves up one row. If the cursor is at the top row, this command is ignored.

Move cursor down

ESC[*n*B

Moves the cursor down *n* number of lines. If *n* is omitted, the cursor moves down one row. If the cursor is at the bottom row, this command is ignored.

Move cursor right

ESC[*n*C

Moves the cursor right *n* number of columns. If *n* is omitted, the cursor moves right one column. If the cursor is at the far right column, this command is ignored.

Move cursor left

ESC[*n*D

Moves the cursor left *n* number of columns. If *n* is omitted, the cursor moves left one column. If the cursor is at the far left column, this command is ignored.

Save cursor position

ESC[s

The current cursor position is saved. To restore it, use the following command.

Restore cursor position

ESC[u

Restores the cursor to its position as saved by the ESC[s command sequence.

Erase display

ESC[2J

This sequence clears the screen and puts the cursor into the upper left corner.

Erase line

ESC[K

The line the cursor is on will be erased from the cursor's position to the end of the line.

Set graphics rendition

ESC[nm

n takes on a number of values, each changing the foreground and background color attributes of the screen:

0   Normal text
1   High-intensity
2   Low-intensity
4   Underline on (monochrome displays only)
5   Blinking on
7   Inverse video on
8   Invisible text
30 Black foreground
31 Red foreground
32 Green foreground
33 Yellow foreground
34 Blue foreground
35 Magenta foreground
36 Cyan foreground
37 White foreground
40 Black background
41 Red background
42 Green background
43 Yellow background
44 Blue background
45 Magenta background
46 Cyan background
47 White background

EXAMPLE: ESC[34m turns on a blue foreground color.

Two or more of the attributes can be selected at once using the following format:

ESC[n1;n2;...n^nm

Different color attributes can be specified by separating each with a semicolon (;). The final attribute is followed by the lowercase "m." For example:

ESC[37;44m

This sets white characters on a blue background.

Set/reset mode

ESC[=nh

The "mode" in this case is the screen mode, the resolution of characters or graphics pixels. *n* carries 7 values, from 0 through 6:

    0   Monochrome text, 40 × 25
    1   Color text, 40 × 25
    2   Monochrome text, 80 × 25
    3   Color text, 80 × 25
    4   Medium resolution graphics (four color), 320 × 200
    5   Same as 4, but with color burst disabled
    6   High resolution graphics (two color), 640 × 200
   14   Color graphics, 640 × 200
   15   Monochrome graphics, 640 × 350
   16   Color graphics, 640 × 350
   17   Color graphics, 640 × 480
   18   Color graphics, 640 × 480
   19   Color graphics, 320 × 200

These commands are useful when creating special large character screens, for example, for children or the handicapped who have trouble reading the regular display.

Character wrap ON

ESC[= 7h

Part of ANSI's VT100 legacy is the ability to "wrap" characters on the screen. That is, if a character is displayed in column 80 (the far right hand column), the next character will be displayed on the next row in the first column. This is character wrap.

If character wrap is disabled, then all characters displayed after the 80th character on a line and before a carriage return character will be displayed in column 80. (See chapter 3 for a demonstration.)

Character wrap on is the default of the ANSI.SYS driver.

Character wrap OFF

ESC[= 7l

This command disables character wrap. Note that the final character in the command string is a lowercase L, not a one.

Keyboard key reassignment

ESC[*n1*;*n2*p

n1 is the ASCII code for a key to redefine. *n2* is the ASCII code that will be produced when *n1* is pressed. For example:

ESC[71,84p

This assigns capital "G" (ASCII 71) as capital "T" (ASCII 84), Whenever a capital G key is typed, DOS will display a T. To reassign the lowercase characters, use the following:

ESC[103;116p

Keyboard string reassignment

ESC[0;*n*;"*string*"p

n is an extended keyboard code. *string* is a string of characters that will be produced every time the specified key is pressed. For example:

ESC[0;113;"DIR"p

This assigns the string "DIR" to the key combination ALT – F10 (see below). To add a carriage return after the DIR command, use:

ESC[0;113;"DIR";13p

(See chapter 3 for a complete example of keyboard reassignment.)
The extended codes for the function keys are as shown in TABLE B-1.

Table B-1

	Normal	**Shifted**	**Control**	**Alt**
F1	0;59	0;84	0;94	0;104
F2	0;60	0;85	0;95	0;105
F3	0;61	0;86	0;96	0;106
F4	0;62	0;87	0;97	0;107
F5	0;63	0;88	0;98	0;108
F6	0;64	0;89	0;99	0;109
F7	0;65	0;90	0;100	0;110
F8	0;66	0;91	0;101	0;111
F9	0;67	0;92	0;102	0;112
F10	0;68	0;93	0;103	0;113

NOTE ON KEY REASSIGNMENT: You can only "unassign" the keys by rebooting your computer—or by running an unassign program. Also, note that because most applications do not use DOS routines to read the keyboard, these reassignments will probably not take effect in any of your programs.

C
Keyboard scan codes

The PC's keyboard is controlled by a special microprocessor right inside the keyboard. When you press on a key, the microprocessor interprets the keystroke and sends a code called a "scan code" for that key to the computer. Put simply, this is a funky way to read the keyboard.

This appendix contains a list of the scan codes generated by your keyboard. All these codes are the same for all IBM-compatible PCs. As can be seen by the charts at the end of this appendix, the scan codes are laid out with really no rhyme or reason (when compared with other keyboards).

Scan codes

1	ESC	17	W	32	D
2	1 !	18	E	33	F
3	2 @	19	R	34	G
4	3 #	20	T	35	H
5	4 $	21	Y	36	J
6	5 %	22	U	37	K
7	6 ^	23	I	38	L
8	7 &	24	O	39	; :
9	8 *	25	P	40	' "
10	9 (	26	[{	41	~
11	0)	27	]}	42	left shift key
12	— _			43	\ |
13	= +	28	ENTER	44	Z
14	BACKSPACE	29	CTRL	45	X
15	TAB	30	A	46	C
16	Q	31	S	47	V

48	B	62	F4	76	5 (keypad only)
49	N	63	F5	77	right arrow 6
50	M	64	F6	78	+ (keypad plus key)
51	, <	65	F7	79	End 1
52	. >	66	F8	80	down arrow 2
53	/ ?	67	F9	81	PGDN 3
54	right shift key	68	F10	82	INSert key
55	PRTSC (print screen)	69	NUMLOCK	83	DELete key
56	ALT key	70	SCROLL LOCK	84	SYS REQ (AT keyboards only)
		71	HOME 7 (keypad numbers only)		
57	spacebar			87	F11
58	CAPS LOCK	72	up arrow 8	86	F12
59	F1	73	PGUP 9		
60	F2	74	— (keypad minus key)		
61	F3	75	left arrow 4		

Keyboard layouts

C-1 PC/XT.

C-2 Convertible PC.

C-3 PC/AT.

C-4 Enhanced PC, "101" keyboard.

D
Prompt commands

The following are command characters, or prompt commands, that can be included with the PROMPT command (to change your system prompt). All commands are preceded by the $, dollar sign. (See TABLE D-1.)

Table D-1

Command	Displays
$$	$, dollar sign character
$b	| character
$d	the date (according to the system clock)
$e	the ESCape character
$g	> character
$h	backspace (erase previous character)
$l	< character
$n	the logged disk drive letter
$p	the logged disk drive and subdirectory
$q	= character
$t	the current time (according to the system clock)
$v	DOS version
$_	Carriage return/line feed (new line)

ANSI.SYS commands are included by using $e, the ESCape character. (For examples of various prompts, refer to chapter 3.) Any other characters, including spaces, listed after the PROMPT command will become part of the system prompt.

The standard system prompt is ng, or the drive letter followed by the > character.

The date and time displayed by $d and $t are according to the country and other system parameters that can be set in the CONFIG.SYS file. See chapter 4.

OS/2 adds the commands in TABLE D-2 to PROMPT.

Table D-2

Command	Displays
$a	The ampersand character, &
$c	Left parenthesis, (
$f	Right parenthesis,)
$i	Undocumented, possibly a hook into an internal routine

E
DOS device names

Shown here are the DOS device names:

AUX	First serial port
CLOCK$	System clock
COM1	First serial port
COM2	Second serial port
COM3	Third serial port
COM4	Fourth serial port
CON	"Console," keyboard or screen
LPT1	First printer
LPT2	Second printer
LPT3	Third printer
NUL	"Nul," or dummy, device
PRN	First printer

Filenames

The format of a filename is as follows:

filename.ext

filename is a string of from 1 to 8 characters (excluding those listed below).

ext is an optional string of from 1 to 3 characters, separated from *filename* by a period.

Characters not allowed as part of a filename:

. " / \ [ ] : | < > + = ; ,

Also not allowed are spaces and any ASCII control code (decimal 31 or less). However, often not mentioned is that high-order, or "extended," ASCII characters are allowed as part of a filename.

Filenames can be preceded by a drive letter, followed by a colon. After the colon can optionally come the file's full pathname.

Pathnames

A pathname is the full name of a file, including all subdirectories. Subdirectories are named just like files and each is separated by a backslash. The only limitation on a pathname is that the entire name (including drive letter, colon, and filename/extension) can be no more than 63 characters long.

F
DOS function keys

When you enter text on the DOS command line, or in EDLIN, you're manipulating a "template." This template contains the same characters as was previously entered (either in DOS or EDLIN). Using special function keys, the template of text can be edited, saving typing time. The editing also takes place in any program that uses DOS Interrupt 21h, Service Ah (10 decimal) to read a line of text from the keyboard.

The following keys can be used to edit a DOS command line or a line of text in EDLIN.

F1 or right arrow   Move right one character in the template.

F2 *char*   Display characters up to character *char*.

F3   Display remaining characters in the template.

F4 *char*   Deletes remaining characters up to the character *char*.

F5   Reset the template, replacing it with the characters entered so far.

F6 or CTRL – Z   Display a ^Z (end of file) character. This character is entered to signal the end of a file—especially when you're creating files from the keyboard using the "COPY-CON" function.

F7   Display a ^@, the null character.

left arrow or BACKSPACE   Move left one character in the template. Note that backspace does not delete any characters in the template.

INSert   Begin inserting characters in the template. Type INSert a second time to reenter the overwrite mode (new characters you type will replace the old characters in the template).

DELete   Remove characters from the template.

ESCape   Cancel editing on the template, replace with original template, move cursor to first character position.

CTRL – V (EDLIN only)   Typing a CTRL – V is a special prefix character. It causes the next character typed to be accepted as an ASCII control code. For example, the ESCape character is normally written as ^[. To enter this character in EDLIN using CTRL – V, type CTRL – V followed by [. To enter a CTRL – C, type CTRL – V followed by a C. (Refer to appendix A for more information on control characters.)

Special function keys

The special function keys perform some miscellaneous duties while you're in DOS. There are ways to make other keys perform the same duties. Refer to appendix B on ANSI.SYS under Keyboard String Reassignment for the gory details.

NUM LOCK   Activates the numeric keypad on some keyboards.

CAPS LOCK   Causes all alphabet characters to be displayed in uppercase (the default is lowercase).

SHIFT – PRTSC   Prints the contents of the screen to the printer. If the printer is turned off, some computers may ignore this command. Other computers will "lock up" and wait for the printer. If you have a printer, turn it on and let the screen dump continue. Otherwise, reset.

CTRL – P or CTRL – PRTSC   Turn on "echo" to Printer mode. All characters DOS sends to the screen (or any other program that uses the DOS print character functions) will also be sent to the printer. To turn this mode off, press CTRL – P, or CTRL – PRTSC, a second time. Again, as with SHIFT – PRTSC, if the printer is turned off, DOS may wait for it or display an error message.

CTRL – S or CTRL – NUM LOCK or PAUSE   Pauses the display. To restart the display, type a second CTRL – S. Unfortunately, typing a second CTRL – NUM LOCK does not restart the display. Just type any other key.

CTRL – C or CTRL – BREAK   Halts DOS from displaying or performing some other activity (copying, backing up, etc.). For some operations, CTRL – C will stop the going's on. Other times, DOS must receive a CTRL – BREAK (the "Break" key is actually SCROLL LOCK). It depends on how the program was written to intercept the DOS interrupt service 23h. Generally speaking, CTRL – BREAK will stop 'em cold 100 percent of the time.

ALT   The ALT key can be used in conjunction with the numeric keypad to produce any ASCII, or Extended ASCII, character. These characters are numbered from 0 through 255. To display any character, hold down the

ALT key and type the character's number on the numeric keypad. For example, to produce ASCII 89 (the letter "Y"), do the following:

1. Press and hold down the ALT key.
2. Type an 8 on the keypad.
3. Type a 9 on the keypad.
4. Release the ALT key.

ASCII 89 will be displayed.

This works for all ASCII and Extended ASCII codes—even within applications programs. The only time this special ALT key character generating doesn't work is when certain memory-resident programs are loaded, for example, *SuperKey*.

G
EDLIN

EDLIN isn't the best text editor on the planet Earth. However, it does have some advantages over all other text editors: it comes free with DOS (so everyone has it), and it's one of the few editors that allows you to easily enter control characters in your text.

Summary of EDLIN's commands

Insert Line:

I	Inserts a new line at the current line. When creating a new file, I inserts line 1.
nI	Inserts a new line number *n*.
.I	Inserts a new line at the current line.
#I	Inserts a new line at the bottom of the file.
+ nI	Inserts a new line *n* lines down from the current line number.
—nI	Inserts a new line *n* lines up from the current line number.

List:

L	Lists the 11 lines before the current line, the current line, and 11 lines after the current line.
xL	Lists 23 lines starting with line *x*.
,yL	Lists the 11 lines before line *y*, line *y*, and the 11 lines after line *y*.
x, yL	Lists the lines from *x* through *y*.
P	"Page" or print from the current line down 23 lines.

,yP	Print from the current line through line *y*.
x,yP	Print from line *x* through line *y*.

Delete:

D	Deletes the current line.
xD	Deletes line *x*.
x,yD	Deletes lines *x* through *y*.
,yD	Deletes all lines from the current line through line *y*.
x,.D	Deletes all lines from *x* through the current line.

Copy:

x,y,zC	Copies the block of lines from *x* through *y* and places them at line number *z*.
x,x,zC	Copies the single line *x* to line number *z*.

Move:

x,y,zM	Moves the block of lines from *x* through *y* and places them at line number *z*.
x,x,zM	Moves line *x* to line number *z*.

Search and replace:

S string	Searches for the characters in *string*.
x,ySstring	Searches for the characters in *string* between lines *x* and *y*.
x,y?Sstring	Searches for the characters in *string* between lines *x* and *y*, stops and asks "OK?" for each occurrence. Pressing "Y" continues the search, "N" cancels.
Rstr1^Zstr2	Replaces all occurrences of *str1* with *str2* in the range of lines from *x* through *y*.
x,y?Rstr1^Zstr2	Replaces all occurrences of *str1* with *str2* in the range of lines from *x* through *y*. When *str1* is found, replace stops and asks "OK?" Pressing "Y" replaces, pressing "N" cancels.

Edit:

n	Selects line *n* for editing.
−n	Selects line *n* lines up for editing.
+n	Selects line *n* lines down for editing.
.	Selects current line for editing.

Disk:

nA	Appends lines from the disk file into memory. (This command only works if the file being edited is too big to fit into memory.)
nT	Transfers text to disk starting with line *n*. If *n* is omitted, the current line is used.

_n_W	Writes a specific number of lines to disk. (Used only for files too large to fit into memory at once.)
End:	
E	Ends edit, saves file, renames original file to *.BAK.
Q	Cancels edit, does not save changes.

H

DEBUG

All commands can be issued as either upper- or lowercase. All numeric values are in hexadecimal, or base 16, format.

A *address*   Enter the mini-assembler and start entering assembly language commands. *address* is optional, if omitted, 100h is used.

C *blk1 r blk2*   Compare the block of memory *blk1* with *blk2* for the range *r*.

D *address r*   Dump, or Display, memory contents at *address* for range *r*. *address* is optional and if omitted the current address is used.

E *address list*   Enter, or Edit, the bytes at *address*. *list* is an optional list of information to place at *address*. *list* can be ASCII data in which case it should be enclosed in quotes.

F *address r list*   Fill the bytes starting at *address* for the range *r* with the values in *list*.

G = *address*   Go, or start executing instructions, at *address*.

H *n1 n2*   Add two values, *n1* and *n2*, then subtract them. The two results are displayed on the following line.

I *port*   Input one byte from the specified *port*.

L *address d s1 s2*   Load into memory at *address* from disk *d* (where 0 is drive A, 1 is B, etc.) the data from sectors *s1* through *s2*. If a program name has been specified with the N command, L alone loads that program into memory.

M *r address*   Moves the bytes in the range *r* to *address*.

N *pathname*	Names the program specified by *pathname*. Using the L or W command will cause that file to be loaded or saved, respectively.
O *port n*	Outputs the byte *n* to the port *port*.
P *address n*	Proceed, or execute the following instruction, such as an INT, CALL or LOOP instruction. *address* specifies the optional location of the instruction and *n* is a repeat count.
Q	Quit.
R *register*	Change the contents of the 8088 register *register*.
S *r list*	Searches for *list* in the range *r*. (*r* specifies two addresses.)
T *address n*	Trace, or execute the single instruction at *address*. *n* is a repeat count.
U *address*	Unassemble the machine code at *address*. *address* may optionally be a range of memory locations, or a specific address followed by a range value.
W *address d s1 s2*	Write the data at *address* to disk *d* (where 0 is drive A, 1 is B, etc.) sectors *s1* through *s2*. If a program name has been specified with the N command, W alone writes that program to disk.
XA *h*	Creates (allocates) a handle (*h*) to a specific number of pages of expanded memory.
XD *h*	De-allocates the handle created with XA.
XM *1,p,h*	Maps the logical expanded memory page *1* to the physical page *p*, using handle *h*.
XS	Displays the expanded memory status.

Note: DEBUG does not perform properly on files with an .EXE or .HEX filename extension. To DEBUG these programs, rename them first to a .BIN or .COM file extension, then use DEBUG.

I
ERRORLEVEL return codes

DOS programs that use ERRORLEVEL

BACKUP

0   Normal exit.
1   No files were backed up (all were already backed up or none existed).
2   File sharing conflicts. Not all files were backed up.
3   CTRL – BREAK was pressed, halting the backup.
4   Error, program stopped.

DISKCOMP

0   Normal exit.
1   The diskettes didn't compare.
2   CTRL – BREAK was pressed, halting the compare.
3   Hardware error (diskette missing, etc.).
4   Initialization error.

DISKCOPY

0   Normal exit.
1   A read/write error occurred during the copy.
2   CTRL – BREAK was pressed, halting the copy.
3   Hardware error.
4   Initialization error.

FORMAT

0   Normal exit.
3   CTRL – BREAK was pressed, halting the format.
4   Error, program stopped.

5 "N" was pressed when the user was asked if they wanted to format their hard drive.

GRAFTABL

0 Normal exit.
1 A previously loaded character table has been replaced by the most recently specified table.
2 No previously loaded character table existed and no new table has been loaded.
3 An improper parameter was specified, nothing done.
4 Incorrect DOS version.

KEYB

0 Normal exit.
1 Bad parameter (usually a syntax error).
2 Keyboard definition file not found or bad.
3 Unable to create table (memory problem).
4 CON device error.
5 Unprepared code page request.
6 Translation table not found.
7 Incorrect DOS version.

REPLACE

0 Normal exit.
2 Source file(s) not found.
3 Source or target path was not found.
5 Read/write access denied. (Change the files with ATTRIB.)
8 Not enough memory to run REPLACE.
11 Bad parameter found or invalid format used.
15 Nonexistent drive specified.
22 Incorrect DOS version.

RESTORE

0 Normal exit.
1 No files found.
2 File sharing conflicts, not all files restored.
3 CTRL–BREAK was pressed, halting the restore.
4 Error termination, program stopped.

SETVER

0 Normal exit.
1 Unknown switch specified.
2 Unknown filename specified.
3 Not enough memory.
4 Improper DOS version number (format).
5 Program entry could not be found.

6   DOS system not found.
7   Invalid drive specified.
8   Too many parameters specified.
9   Parameters missing.
10 Error reading IBMDOS.COM or MSDOS.SYS file.
11 Version table is corrupt.
12 DOS system files do not support version tables.
13 No space left in version table.
14 Error writing IBMDOS.COM or MSDOS.SYS file.

XCOPY

0   Normal exit.
1   No files found to copy.
2   CTRL – BREAK was pressed, halting the copy.
4   Initialization error/not enough memory/syntax error.
5   Write error/disk write protected.

Batch file example

The following batch file can be used to determine if a program has an ERRORLEVEL return code:

Name: ERRCHK.BAT

```
1: @ECHO OFF
2: REM Errorlevel checking program
3: ECHO Errorlevel checker version 1.0
4: IF nothing%1 = =nothing GOTO error
5: ECHO Running program %1...
6: %1 %2 %3 %4 %5 %6 %7 %8 %9
7: IF ERRORLEVEL 2 GOTO TWO
8: IF ERRORLEVEL 1 GOTO ONE
9: IF ERRORLEVEL 0 GOTO ZERO
10: :TWO
11: ECHO Errorlevels higher than "1" detected
12: GOTO END
13: :ONE
14: ECHO Errorlevel of "1" detected
15: GOTO END
16: :ZERO
17: ECHO Errorlevel of zero returned
18: GOTO END
19: :ERROR
20: ECHO Program not specified.
21: :END
```

J
Batch file errors

Aside from DOS errors ("File not found," "Bad command or filename") the following batch-file specific errors might pop up from time to time:

Batch file missing
The batch file you're running can no longer locate itself to load in the next line.

Cannot start COMMAND, exiting
You've used COMMAND /C to "call" other batch files and there are too many files already open.

FOR cannot be nested
You attempted to use a second FOR as the command portion of a FOR command.

Label not found
The batch file interpreter could not locate a label associated with a GOTO statement.

No free file handles
Cannot start COMMAND, exiting
See "Cannot start COMMAND, exiting" above.

Out of environment space
You attempted to alter the environment and there is no more room.

Syntax Error
A command was mistyped, or a double equal sign not used with an IF statement.

Terminate batch job (Y/N)
Either CTRL – C or CTRL – BREAK was pressed to halt the batch file.

K
Floppy disk contents

This book has a supplemental floppy disk. (You can order using a form found in the back.) On the disk you will find all of the batch files listed in this book. Additionally, I've ventured out into public domain and shareware lands and collected what I think are the best batch file software helpers and utilities. I couldn't fit all of them on the diskette, but I did manage to squeeze as many as possible into a 360K formatted floppy.

This appendix contains a listing of the supplemental program diskette's contents and filenames. Additionally, there are instructions here for transferring the diskette's contents to your hard drive. (There was no room left on the diskette for an INSTALL.BAT program. So you must pick and choose what you want with some disk utility, or just copy the whole darn thing over using XCOPY or COPY, as shown below.)

Disk contents

The supplemental programs diskette contains eight subdirectories, each of which describes the type of programs you'll find in it:

\ANSI	ANSI-related programs, device drivers
\BATPROGS	All significant batch files mentioned in this book
\CHRON	Time-related programs and utilities
\DISPLAY	Programs that manipulate the display
\HIDING	File hiding utilities
\Q&A	Interactive batch file programs (queries)
\TESTS	Programs that test conditions
\UTIL	General utilities

Note that there are no "sub-subdirectories" on this diskette.

The following sections list all the files on the diskette, plus a brief description of what each one does. Note that all of the COM and EXE files have accompanying documentation (DOC) files.

In the \ANSI subdirectory you'll find:

ANSIDR30.COM	Ansi-Draw, an ANSI color screen generator
ISANSI.COM	An ANSI test program, to see if an ANSI driver is active
NANSI.SYS	A complete replacement for DOS's ANSI driver
ZANSI.SYS	A faster replacement for DOS's ANSI driver

In the \BATPROGS subdirectory you'll find:

Fifty-five batch files mentioned in this book, plus a few other goodies you might not have been suspecting. (There are too many to list them all here.)

In the \CHRON subdirectory you'll find:

ETIME.COM	A time stamping program, marking the "end time"
NOW.COM	A time stamping program, marking the current time
STIME.COM	A time stamping program, marking the "start time"
TSTAMP.COM	A time stamping program
WAIT.EXE	A wait-for and wait-duration pausing utility

In the \DISPLAY subdirectory you'll find:

BIGTITLE.COM	This program displays big messages
BLANKS.COM	Display a number of blank lines on the screen
BOX.COM	Draws a certain type of box anywhere on the screen
CLZ.COM	Clears the screen in a funky manner
ECOH.COM	An "inverse" ECHO statement
GREET.COM	A program that greets you for the time of day
HOLD.COM	A replacement for DOS's PAUSE
LOCATE.COM	A cursor location utility
REPT.COM	Repeats a given character a specified number of times
SAY.EXE	A mondo-ECHO replacement, complete with cursor location
TUNE.COM	Plays notes on the speaker

Lurking in the \HIDING subdirectory you'll find:

FINDHIDE.COM	Locates hidden files in the current directory
HIDE.COM	Hides a file
UNHIDE.COM	Unhides a file

In the \Q&A subdirectory you'll find:

ANSWER.COM	Stuffs keyboard input into the environment
ASK.COM	Asks a Y/N question, returns ERRORLEVEL value

FAKEY.COM	Stuffs keyboard buffer, BIOS I/O redirection
INP.BAT	Demonstrates the INPUT.COM program
INPUT.COM	Gets input from the keyboard
READKEY.COM	Gets input from the keyboard (includes Fkeys)
REPLY.COM	Gets input from the keyboard
TASK.COM	ASK command with a timeout

In the \ TESTS subdirectory you'll find:

ACCESS.EXE	Determines the accessibility of a drive, directory or file
DPATH.COM	Stores the current drive and directory in the environment
DTEST.EXE	Tests a disk, returns disk size/whether it's formatted
RESTPATH.COM	Restores a path saved with the CD > command
VERNUM.COM	Returns the current DOS version as an ERRORLEVEL

In the \ UTIL subdirectory you'll find:

FF.EXE	A fast file find utility
GLOBAL.EXE	Issue commands in all subdirectories (better than SWEEP)
MORE.COM	A replacement for DOS's MORE command
NDOSEDIT.COM	A command line editor
RENDIR.COM	Renamed subdirectories like REN renames files

Installing the diskette

There is no INSTALL program on the supplemental programs diskette. Also, there are no hidden files, no secret directories, and it's not copy protected. To move the files over to your hard drive or another diskette, just COPY the ones you want.

If you have DOS 3.3 or later, you can copy the entire diskette, subdirectories and all, with the following:

    XCOPY A: \ *.* /S

This moves *all files* in *all subdirectories* from the floppy diskette in drive A to the current subdirectory on your hard drive.

The previous edition of this book came with a "helpfile" system of batch files—a menu program. Due to the size and number of programs included on this diskette, there was no room for HELPFILE.

L
Product information

The following products are mentioned in this book. The manufacturer or distributor's name is included here for those desiring additional information:

BatchWorks for Windows
Publishing Technologies
7719 Wood Hollow Drive, Suite 260
Austin, TX 78731
(800) PUB-TECH

Brief
Solution Systems
541 Main Street, Suite 410
South Weymouth, MA 02910
(800) 821-2492

Builder
hyperkinetix, inc.
666 Baker Street, Suite 405
Costa Mesa, CA 92626
(714) 668-9234

Command Post
Wilson WindowWare
2701 California Ave SW, Suite 212
Seattle, WA 98116
(800) 762-8383

EBL
Seaware Corporation
P.O. Box 1656
Delray Beach, FL 33444
(407) 738-1712

The Norton Editor
The Norton Utilities
Peter Norton Computing, Inc.
10201 Torre Avenue
Cupertino, CA 95014
(800) 441-7234
(800) 626-8847 (CA only)

PC Write
Quicksoft, Inc.
219 1st Ave N #224-B
Seattle, WA 98109-9911
(800) 888-8088

QEdit
SemWare
4343 Shallowford Road, Suite C3
Marietta, GA 30062
(404) 641-9002

SideKick
SuperKey
Borland International
1700 Green Hills Road
Scotts Valley, CA 95066
(800) 331-0877

WordStar
WordStar International, Inc.
201 Alameda del Prado
Novato, CA 94949
(800) 227-5609

Additionally, PC-SIG is an excellent source for hard to find utilities and useful public domain programs. Besides the programs that come on the supplemental programs disk, you should check out the following PC-SIG diskettes:

#78, 627, 1235	PC WRITE, the first of many shareware word processors/text editors
#82	BATCH FILE UTILITIES, various batch file utilities #124 - EXTENDED BATCH LANG., batch file language extender
#124	EXTENDED BATCH LANG., Version 3.05 of EBL
#205	DOS UTILITIES No. 13, some older, yet still useful utilities
#273	BEST UTILITIES, excellent, must-have utilities
#319	DOS UTILITIES No. 16, good selection of DOS utilities
#356, 650	FANSI-CONSOLE, ANSI.SYS replacement (two diskettes)
#373	DOS UTILITIES No. 17, interesting and useful DOS utilities
#765	GALAXY, more than a text editor, it's a full blown word processor but good for batch files
#829	NEW YORK EDIT, a program editor version of the popular New York Word word processor
#874	ZZAP, a diskette modifying utility
#1273	VISUAL DISPLAY EDITOR, VDE, Programmer's love this text editor
#1510	SCREENPAINT, color/graphic screen creator, perfect for menus
#1565	PROBAT I, helps you create interesting batch files
#1902	HACKER, lots of interesting batch file utilities

If you'd like to locate a specific program, give PC-SIG a call. Their tech support people are perhaps the most friendly and helpful you'll ever encounter.

PC-SIG
1030D East Duane Ave.
Sunnyvale, CA 94086
(800) 245-6717

Index

RENDIR (con't.)

replaceable parameters, 206-209,
257
    command-line input, MOVE.BAT,
    208
    display, BATARG.BAT, 207
    environmental variables, 213-215
    FOR variables, 215-216
    SHIFT command,
    SHIFTARG.BAT, 211-213
    test for nothing, 209-211
REPLY.COM, 278-279
REPT.COM, 288
reserved words, DOS, 257-258
RESET.BAT, 299
RESTORE, 100
RESTPATH, 288-289, 409-411
Return/ENTER key, xxi-xxii
RKEY, 301-304
RMDIR (see RD)
root directory, 41, 44-45, 47, 383
ROWCOL utility, NU, 284

S

SA utility, NU, 284
SAY.COM, 289
scan codes, keyboard, 461-463
screen displays
    ANSI.SYS commands, 70-78,
    455-459
    big-character titles,
    BIGTITLE.COM, 277
    character display, ANSI.SYS, 71
    character wrap, 458
    clear screen, ANSI.SYS Erase
    Display command, 71, 456
    clear screen, batch file, 73-74
    color setting, AUTOEXEC.BAT,
    141-142
    color setting, ANSI.SYS Set
    Graphics Rendition command,
    72, 457-458
    color setting, FLAG.BAT, 75-76
    color setting, FLAG.DAT, 76
    cursor position, ANSI.SYS, 71,
    455, 456
    cursor position, ANSI.SYS
    Position Cursor command, 73
    cursor position, LOCATE.BAT, 77
    inverse type, ECOH.COM, 277
    menu display, MENUEX.BAT, 76
    mode setting, MODE, 140-141,
    240-241
SECOND.BAT, 231, 239
sessions, OS/2, 169-170
SET command, 89, 447-449
    environmental variables, 109-111
    set COMSPEC, 94

view environment, 90-93
Set Graphics Rendition, ANSI.SYS
    command, 72, 457-458
SETENV, 114
SETLOCAL, 449
SETVAR.BAT, 294-296
SETVER.EXE, 126
SHARE, 130
SHELL, 28-29, 94-95, 120, 121,
131, 137
    EBLplus, 309
    expanding environment space,
    113
shells/shelling, 28-29, 61-62, 94,
    396-397, 401-402, 408-409
SHIFT, 6, 30, 196, 211-213, 449
SHIFTARG.BAT, 211-213
SHUTDOWN.BAT, 119, 156-161
SideKick, 143, 194
SMARTDRV.SYS, 126
SORT filters, 16-17, 39, 57
sorting
    directories, 15-19
    print-out of sort, 18
    reverse sort, 18
speed of execution, batch files,
    270-272
spreadsheet batch files
    2.BAT, 407
    SS.BAT, 391
SS.BAT, 391, 400
STACKS, 120, 121, 131-132
STARTUP.CMD, 177
status variables, 116, 243
STIME, 279
strings of text, 243
subroutines, 221, 229-230
SUBST, AUTOEXEC.BAT, 142
supplemental floppy disk, 285-290,
    485-487
    ASK.COM, 285-286
    BLANKS.COM, 286
    BOX.COM, 286
    CLZ.COM, 286
    GREET.COM, 286-287
    HOLD.COM, 287
    ISANSI.COM, 287
    LOCATE.COM, 287
    READKEY.COM, 287-288
    REPT.COM, 288
    RESTPATH.COM, 288-289
    SAY.COM, 289
    VERNUM.COM, 289-290
supplier/manufacturers, 489-490
SWITCHES, 120, 121, 132
syntax errors, 267-268
SYS commands, 66

SYS files, 47
SYSINIT routines, 27-29

T

telephone dialing (DIAL.BAT), 21
TEMP variables, 108-109, 112
temporary files, 249-253
test utilities, 280-281
text editors, 11, 191-195
text files, 9
TM utility, NU, 284-285
TREE command, 45-46
TSRs (see memory-resident
    programs)
TSTAMP, 279
TYPE, 8, 36, 199-200

U

UNDO-C.BAT, 114-116
UNIX, 42-43, 106
UPDATE, 410
Upper Memory Blocks (UMBs), 61
user shells (see shells/shelling)
utilities, public domain (see public
    domain utilities)

V

variables, 7, 206-211, 220
    %, 416
    DIRCMD, 112-113
    DOSSHELL, 112-113
    EBLplus, 311
    environmental (see
    environmental variables)
    FOR, 215-216
    global or public, 238
    local, 238
    status, 116, 243
    TEMP, 108-109, 112
VDISK.SYS, 66
VERNUM.COM/VERNUM.BAT,
    289-290
VOpt program, 142

W

WAIT.EXE, 279
wildcards, 50-51
WIN.BAT, 366
WINDOW utility, NU, 284
Windows, 163, 365-377
    AUTOEXEC.BAT, 144
    batch file running, 367
    Command Post macro-creation,
    376-377
    cutting and pasting, 372-375
    DESQview environment,

498 Index

Other Bestsellers of Related Interest

PRACTICAL PARADOX™: Applications And Programming Techniques
—Ken Knecht

Here's the real resource of Paradox s rudimentary artificial intelligence-based techniques. Leading off with step-by-step instructions on the use of Paradox in the direct mode, it provides sample programs as well as helpful screen printouts of key features. 256 pages, 148 illustrations. Book No. 2743, $18.95 paperback only

HIGH-SPEED ANIMATION AND SIMULATION FOR MICROCOMPUTERS
—Lee Adams

Create realistic simulations, high-speed animation, and exciting 3-dimensional computer graphics with BASIC! Using 40 professional-caliber programs, Adams demonstrates advanced animation techniques for all of the IBM® PC family of computers—including PCs, XTs, ATs, and PCjrs. He shows you how to design and direct lifelike animation and simulations or create 3-dimensional animated images. 476 pages, 370 illustrations. Book No. 2859, $21.95 paperback only

EXPERT SYSTEMS: Programming in Turbo C® —Frederick Holtz

This practical guide is geared toward the Turbo C user who wants to learn the basic concepts of AI and expert systems. From simple game-playing to the establishment of fast-access databases to AI programming, this book concentrates on the practical rather than the theoretical aspects of AII. Working examples demonstrate the concepts, with several complete Turbo C programs included that perform practical or instructional functions. 216 pages, 34 illustrations. Book No. 2990, $17.95 paperback only

VENTURA® PUBLISHER: A Creative Approach—Elizabeth McClure

Here is the definitive handbook to desktop publishing with Ventura Publisher! McClure goes beyond the user's manual to show even the experienced user how to extend the powers of Ventura Publisher. With its presentation of DTP concepts and techniques and discussions of available hardware and software options, it offers you a complete, up-to-date source of reference. Numerous examples, samples applications, and illustrations add to its usefulness. 240 pages, 105 illustrations. Book No. 3012, $17.95 paperback only

THE C4 HANDBOOK: CAD, CAM, CAE, CIM—Carl Machover

Increase your productivity and diversity with this collection of articles by international industry experts, detailing what you can expect from the latest advances in computer aided design and manufacturing technology. Machover has created an invaluable guide to identifying equipment requirements, justifying investments, defining and selecting systems, and training staff to use the systems. 448 pages, 166 illustrations. Book No. 3098, $44.50 hardcover only

QUATTRO™ SIMPLIFIED
—John R. Ottensman, Ph.D.

Quattro is a brand-new generation in the evolution of integrated spreadsheets for data analysis, management and display from Borland international. This book provides all the essentials you'll need to get Quattro up and running almost immediately. Each major aspect of the program is detailed with simple, yet realistic, examples and there's plenty of explanation on such new Quattro features as user-modified menus, integration and customization of graphics, and the use of basic macros. 304 pages, 219 illustrations. Book No. 3111, $27.95 hardcover only

COMMUNICATING WITH CROSSTALK® XVI AND CROSSTALK® MARK 4—Mark A. Schaffer

Individuals, small businesses, and Fortune 500 corporations alike have come to rely on Crosstalk to meet their telecommunications needs. This book documents the proven Crosstalk software package. Detailed instructions walk you through installation and operating procedures. Modems, baud rates, ports, and additional hardware considerations are covered. 224 pages, 52 illustrations. Book No. 3120, $16.95 paperback only

ENCYCLOPEDIA OF EXCEL—The Master Reference—Robin Stark and Shelley Satonin

Here is the definitive handbook to Excel for the IBM versions. A comprehensive guide to Excel commands and functions, it includes over 250 alphabetically arranged entries! To ensure quick access to needed facts, *Encyclopedia of Excel* is thoroughly cross-referenced and indexed three ways. In addition to the comprehensive main index, an index of applications directs you to specific examples. 432 pages, 150 illustrations. Book No. 3191, $31.95 hardcover

PROGRAMMING WITH R:BASE FOR DOS—Cary N. Prague,
James E. Hammitt, and Allan P. Thompson

R:BASE for DOS is Microrim's database management software that introduces a new dimension to DBMS technology. Now you can put that technology to work for you. Comprehensive and authoritative, it examines this software's powerful database language. Among its many advantages is the use of simple commands to create database structures and to add, change, and delete data items. 512 pages, 384 illustrations. Book No. 3196, $24.95 paperback only

80386 MACRO ASSEMBLER AND TOOLKIT—Penn Brumm and Don Brumm

Expand your programming horizons with this guide to writing and using assembly language on 80386-based computers with Microsoft Macro Assembler (MASM), 5.1. This collection of useful macros illustrates the concepts presented. There is also a detailed discussion of MASM syntax and grammar, plus coverage of the options and their usage. 608 pages, 284 illustrations. Book No. 3247, $35.95 hardcover only

HANDBOOK OF DATABASE MANAGEMENT AND DISTRIBUTED RELATIONAL DATABASES—Dimitris N. Chorafas

This book provides database users and designers with the tools necessary to make informed decisions and to keep pace with the advancement of database technology. Now you can identify your needs, define the requirements, evaluate your priorities, choose supports, and determine solutions that are effective both in terms of cost and performance. 720 pages, illustrated. Book No. 3253, $49.95 hardcover only

TURBO PASCAL® TRILOGY: A Complete Library for Programmers, Featuring Versions 5.0 and 5.5 —Eric P. Bloom and Jeremy G. Soybel

Covering all releases of Turbo Pascal from Version 2.0 through 5.5, this updated guide and reference is actually three books in one. It includes a primer on Turbo Pascal complete with working examples: a reference guide to all language elements, procedures, and functions available in Turbo Pascal, highlighting the differences among the various versions; and a complete library of over 50 ready-to-use functions and source-code examples. 784 pages, 229 illustrations. Book No. 3310, $29.95 paperback only

EXPLORING PARALLEL PROCESSING—Edward Rietman

Overcome the barriers that hold down your computing speed and start on the processing of the future. Complete with practical examples you can use right away, Rietman's book is a look at all the strategies currently under study for parallel processing. It is liberally illustrated with programs and models in BASIC and C. This book also explains how to use three powerful add-in boards. 288 pages, 190 illustrations. Book No. 3367, $18.95 paperback only

MICROCOMPUTER LANs—2nd Edition
—Michael Hordeski

Pull together a multi-user system from your standalone micros. With this book, you gain an understanding of how networking actually happens. This comprehensive source helps you make the right decisions and cut through the confusion surrounding LAN technology and performance. You'll evaluate your alternatives intelligently, set up networks that allow for growth, restructure or upgrade LAN configurations, and effectively manage network systems. 384 pages, 135 illustrations. Book No. 3424, $39.95 hardcover only

EXCEL MACROS FOR THE IBM® PC
—Shelley Satonin

Here is all the information you need to set up and use macros to change worksheets, print out, create graphs and charts, and manipulate databases in a fraction of the usual time. Satonin uses many simple examples and illustrations to explain the basics of macro writing and includes a complete dictionary of Excel macro functions for easy reference. You'll find recipes for building dozens of advanced macros that you can use as is or customize. 272 pages, 151 illustrations. Book No. 3293, $19.95 paperback only

Prices Subject to Change Without Notice.

Look for These and Other TAB Books at Your Local Bookstore

To Order Call Toll Free 1-800-822-8158
(in PA, AK, and Canada call 717-794-2191)

or write to TAB Books, Blue Ridge Summit, PA 17294-0840.

Title	Product No.	Quantity	Price

☐ Check or money order made payable to TAB Books

Charge my ☐ VISA ☐ MasterCard ☐ American Express

Acct. No. _____ Exp. _____

Signature: _____

Name: _____

Address: _____

City: _____

State: _____ Zip: _____

Subtotal $ _____

Postage and Handling
($3.00 in U.S., $5.00 outside U.S.) $ _____

Add applicable state and local
sales tax $ _____

TOTAL $ _____

TAB Books catalog free with purchase; otherwise send $1.00 in check or money order and receive $1.00 credit on your next purchase.

Orders outside U.S. must pay with international money order in U.S. dollars.

TAB Guarantee: If for any reason you are not satisfied with the book(s) you order, simply return it (them) within 15 days and receive a full refund. **BC**